Practical Contract Law for Paralegals

◆ ◆ ◆

An Activities-Based Approach

EDITORIAL ADVISORS

ASPEN COLLEGE SERIES

Practical Contract Law for Paralegals

◆ ◆ ◆

An Activities-Based Approach

Fourth Edition

Laurel A. Vietzen

Professor Emeritus
Elgin Community College

Published by Wolters Kluwer in New York.

Wolters Kluwer Legal & Regulatory US serves customers worldwide with CCH, Aspen Publishers, and Kluwer Law International products. (www.WKLegaledu.com)

To contact Customer Service, e-mail customer.service@wolterskluwer.com,
call 1-800-234-1660, fax 1-800-901-9075, or mail correspondence to:

Wolters Kluwer
Attn: Order Department
PO Box 990
Frederick, MD 21705

Printed in the United States of America.

5 6 7 8 9 0

ISBN 978-1-4548-7347-1

Library of Congress Cataloging-in-Publication Data Names: Vietzen, Laurel A., author. Title: Practical contract law for paralegals : an activities-based approach / Laurel A. Vietzen, Professor Emeritus Elgin Community College. Description: Fourth edition. | New York : Wolters Kluwer, 2016. Identifiers: LCCN 2016012485 | ISBN 9781454873471 Subjects: LCSH: Contracts — United States. | Legal assistants — United States — Handbooks, manuals, etc. Classification: LCC KF801.Z9 V54 2016 | DDC 346.7302/2 — dc23 LC record available at http://lccn.loc.gov/2016012485

About Wolters Kluwer Legal & Regulatory US

Wolters Kluwer Legal & Regulatory US delivers expert content and solutions in the areas of law, corporate compliance, health compliance, reimbursement, and legal education. Its practical solutions help customers successfully navigate the demands of a changing environment to drive their daily activities, enhance decision quality and inspire confident outcomes.

Serving customers worldwide, its legal and regulatory portfolio includes products under the Aspen Publishers, CCH Incorporated, Kluwer Law International, ftwilliam.com and MediRegs names. They are regarded as exceptional and trusted resources for general legal and practice-specific knowledge, compliance and risk management, dynamic workflow solutions, and expert commentary.

Summary of Contents

List of Contracts and Clauses	xxiii
Preface	xxv
Acknowledgments	xxvii
Note to Students	xxix
Introduction to Law and Preparation for Self-Guided Learning	xxxiii
1. What Is Contract Law?	1
2. Sources of Contract Law: Common Law and Uniform Commercial Code	21
3. Agreement	39
4. Invalid Assent	59
5. Consideration	75
6. Legality	91
7. Capacity	111
8. Statute of Frauds	127
9. Third Parties/Secured Transactions	145
10. Performance: Required or Excused?	169
11. Remedies	187
12. Contract Interpretation	209
13. Working with Contracts	227
Appendix A Sample Client Interview for Assignment	251
Appendix B Sample Land Exchange Agreement	255

Appendix C Self-Tests 259
Appendix D Self-Tests Answer Key 273
Glossary 283
Index 297

Contents

List of Contracts and Clauses xxiii
Preface xxv
Acknowledgments xxvii
Note to Students xxix

Introduction to Law and Preparation for Self-Guided Learning

A. Sources of Legal Authority xxxii
B. Steps in Preparing to Research a Legal Issue xxxiii
C. Formulating a Query xxxv
Assignment Intro-1: CALR Search Queries xxxvi
D. Primary Authority xxxvi
1. Statutes xxxvi
2. Judicial Decisions xxxvii
a. Trial Courts vs. Appellate Courts xxxviii
b. Reading Cases xxxviii
c. Briefing Cases xxxix
Facts xl
Issue and Holding xl
Reasoning xl
E. Practical and Ethical Issues xli
Assignment Intro-2: Prepare a Case Brief xli
Review Questions xlii
Crossword Puzzle xliii

1

What Is Contract Law?

Introduction 2

Assignment 1-1: Paralegals in Contract Law 3

A. What Is a Contract? 3

1. Types of Contract: Express or Implied 4
2. Types of Contract: Unilateral or Bilateral 4

Assignment 1-2: Questions Concerning Exhibit 1-1 5

Exhibit 1-1: Sample Option and Consignment Contracts 5

3. Other Classifications of Contracts 8

Exhibit 1-2: Letters of Credit and Bills of Lading 8

Assignment 1-3: Find Examples of Unilateral and Implied Contracts 9

B. Alternatives to Contract 9

1. Gifts 10
2. Promissory Estoppel 10

Assignment 1-4: Discuss Hypothetical, Find Estoppel Case 11

3. Quasi-Contract 12

Assignment 1-5: Discuss Quasi-Contract, Find a Case 13

C. Practical and Ethical Issues 14

Assignment 1-6: Find Relevant Ethical Rules 14

Career Corner 16

Review Questions 17

Crossword Puzzle 18

Sample Case: Finding and Briefing Cases for Assignments 19

2

Sources of Contract Law: Common Law and Uniform Commercial Code

A. Common Law 22

Assignment 2-1: Find Adoption of Restatement 23

B. Uniform Commercial Code 23

1. Coverage 23

Assignment 2-2: State Adoption of UCC 23

Exhibit 2-1: Coverage of the UCC 25

Assignment 2-3: Find Cases Defining "Goods" 26

2. Departures from Common Law 26

C. Other Statutes 27

D. International Law 28

E. Administrative Law 29

Exhibit 2-2: Agencies and Jobs 30

Assignment 2-4: FTC and State Agencies in Contract Law 31

F. Practical and Ethical Issues 32

G. Dealing with Changes in the Law 32

Review: Research for Drafting, Interpreting, or Litigating a Contract Issue 34

Career Corner 34

Review Questions 35

Crossword Puzzle 36

3

Agreement

A. Offer 40
1. Definite Terms in an Offer 41
2. Essential Terms 41
Assignment 3-1: Find UCC Gap-Filling Provisions and Case 42
3. Communication of an Offer 42
4. Lifespan of an Offer 43
a. Revocation 43
b. UCC Firm Offer 44
Assignment 3-2: Find UCC Firm Offer Rule 44
c. Rejection/Counteroffer 45
Assignment 3-3: Discussion of Hypothetical, Find Counteroffer Case 45
d. Termination by Operation of Law 46
Illegality 46
Passage of Time 46
Death/Insanity 46
B. Acceptance 47
1. Implied Acceptance 47
2. Mailbox Rule 47
3. Mirror Image Rule 49
4. Battle-of-the-Forms Rule 49
Assignment 3-4: Battle-of-the-Forms Questions 50
C. Practical and Ethical Issues 50
Assignment 3-5: Research Ethical Issue 51
D. Preparing for Contract Negotiations 53
Assignment 3-6: Contact Negotiations Practice 54
Career Corner 55
Review Questions 55
Crossword Puzzle 57

4

Invalid Assent

A. Fraud 60
B. Misrepresentation 61
Assignment 4-1: Find Misrepresentation Case 62
C. Mutual Mistake 63
D. Duress 63
E. Undue Influence 64
Exhibit 4-1: Clauses Negating Undue Influence 65
F. Unconscionability 66
Assignment 4-2: Ethical Rules Questions 67
G. Practical and Ethical Issues 68
Exhibit 4-2: Rule 1.16 Declining or Terminating Representation 68
Career Corner 70
Review Questions 70
Crossword Puzzle 72

5

Consideration

A. Consideration: An Overview 76
B. Inequitable Consideration 77
C. Conditional Contracts 79
1. "Each Party Must Get/Give Something," *But the Parties May Not Know, at the Outset, What That "Something" Is* 79
2. Output, Needs, and Exclusive Dealing Contracts 80
D. Bargained-For 80
1. "To Which That Party Was Not Legally Entitled Before the Contract" 80

Assignment 5-1: UCC Research 81
2. Preexisting Obligations 82
E. Modification of Existing Contracts 83
Assignment 5-2: UCC Research, Modification, and Waiver 84
F. Settlement of Disputes 85
Assignment 5-3: Find a Case 85
G. Practical and Ethical Issues 86
Assignment 5-4: Research Ethical Rules 86
Assignment 5-5: Analyzing Case Law: Restrictions on Right to Practice 86
Assignment 5-6: Analyzing Case Law: Consideration and Statutory Law 87
Career Corner 87
Review Questions 88
Crossword Puzzle 89

6

Legality

A. Violations of Statutes 93
1. Licensing 93
2. Usury and Other Lending Laws 93
Exhibit 6-1: Example of a Confession of Judgment, Also Called a "Cognovits" 94
Assignment 6-1: Research State Law Concerning Consumer Loans 94
3. Gambling 94
Assignment 6-2: Pyramid Schemes 95
4. Blue Laws 95
5. Torts 95
6. Public Policy 95
Exhibit 6-2: Unfair Clauses 96

B. Exculpatory Clauses 96

Exhibit 6-3: Example Exculpatory Clause 97

C. Restraint of Trade 98

Assignment 6-3: Discussion of Sample Cases 98

Assignment 6-4: Find a Case/Discussion 100

D. Practical and Ethical Issues 101

Career Corner 102

Review Questions 103

Crossword Puzzle 104

Case for Analysis 106

7

Capacity

A. Minors 112

1. Minors as Agents for Adults 112

Exhibit 7-1: Rights of Minors 113

2. Necessities 114

Exhibit 7-2: Emancipation Law 115

3. Fraud 116

4. Ratification 116

Assignment 7-1: Uniform Transfers to Minors Act Research 117

Assignment 7-2: Find a Statute Concerning Minors, Find a Case, Discuss Sample Cases 117

B. Mental Incompetence 118

1. Determining Mental Incompetence 118

2. Intoxication 120

3. Analyzing Incompetence and Intoxication 120

C. Practical and Ethical Issues 120

Assignment 7-3: Ethical Rules, Clients with Diminished Capacity 121

Assignment 7-4: Resources to Assist Elderly Clients, Impaired Lawyers 122

Career Corner 122
Review Questions 123
Crossword Puzzle 124

8

Statute of Frauds

A. Requirement of Writing 128
Assignment 8-1: Find Statute of Frauds 129
B. Narrow Interpretation of the Requirement 129
C. Written Evidence Other than Written Contract 129
D. Contracts in Cyberspace 130
1. Applicable Law 131
Assignment 8-2: Research Use of Electronic Signatures, Find Click-Wrap Case, Find Statute of Frauds Case 132
2. Consent 133
Exhibit 8-1: Bank Customer Consent to Electronic Disclosures 133
3. Record Retention and Access 134
4. Technology 134
E. The Categories 135
1. Promises in Anticipation of Marriage 135
2. Contracts Not to Be Performed Within a Year 135
Exhibit 8-2: Sample Premarital Agreement 136
3. Contracts Involving Land (Real Property) 137
4. Contracts for Sale of Goods for $500 or More 137
5. Promises to Answer for the Debts of Another 138
Exhibit 8-3: Sample Suretyship Contract 139
Assignment 8-3: Case Analysis 141
F. Practical and Ethical Issues 141

Assignment 8-4: Using the Statute of Frauds as a Defense 141
Career Corner 142
Review Questions 142
Crossword Puzzle 143

9

Third Parties/Secured Transactions

A. Parties 146
Sole Proprietorship 146
Partnership 147
Limited Partnership 147
Corporation 148
Limited Liability Company 148
B. Agency 148
1. Establishing Agency 149
2. Agency Duties 150
Exhibit 9-1: Buyer-Broker Agency Agreement 152
C. Contract Beneficiaries 154
Exhibit 9-2: Sample Mortgage Clause Requiring That Borrower Make Lender a Creditor Beneficiary 155
Assignment 9-1: Research State Law, Power of Attorney, and Third-Party Beneficiaries 156
D. Assignment and Delegation 157
1. Assignment 157
2. Delegation 158
3. Novation 159
Exhibit 9-3: Sample Clause Prohibiting Assignment and Disclaiming Agency 159
4. Joint and Several Liability and Guarantors 160
E. Secured Transactions Under the UCC 161
Assignment 9-2: Research State Law, Assignment, Delegation, Liens, and Secured Transactions 163

F. Practical and Ethical Issues 163

Assignment 9-3: Research Ethical Issues Involving Third Parties 164

Career Corner 164

Review Questions 165

Crossword Puzzle 166

10

Performance: Required or Excused?

A. Discharge Due to Unmet Condition 170

B. Discharge by Agreement 170

Exhibit 10-1: Sample Condition Precedent 171

C. Discharge by Operation of Law 171

Exhibit 10-2: Sample Assignment and Novation Agreement 172

D. Impossibility 174

Assignment 10-1: UCC Research 175

E. Breach as Excusing Performance 176

1. Common Law 176

Exhibit 10-3: Example of a Typical Time-Is-of-the-Essence Provision That Also Includes a Non-Waiver Provision 177

Assignment 10-2: Find Cases Involving Specific Clauses 178

Exhibit 10-4: Example Satisfaction Clause 178

2. Perfect Tender Under the UCC 179

F. Other Performance Issues Under the UCC 180

Assignment 10-3: Research UCC Issues 180

G. Anticipating Breach 180

H. Practical and Ethical Issues 182

Career Corner 182

Review Questions 183

Crossword Puzzle 184

Remedies

A. Alternative Dispute Resolution 188

B. Litigation 190

Exhibit 11-1: Sample Jury Instruction Involving Affirmative Defense of Duress 192

Assignment 11-1: Research Rules for Filing Suit 194

C. Remedies: Theory 194

1. Damages 195

2. Equitable Remedies 199

D. Tort Law Versus Contract Law 200

Exhibit 11-2: Chart of Remedies 201

E. Practical and Ethical Issues 202

Assignment 11-2: Questions on Sample Case 203

Review Questions 205

Crossword Puzzle 206

12

Contract Interpretation

A. Components of a Written Contract 210

1. Identifications 210

Assignment 12-1: Search for Information on Corporations 210

2. Recitals 211

3. Consideration 211

4. Definitions 212

Assignment 12-2: Draft Definitions 212

5. Body 213

6. Signatures and Acknowledgments 214

Assignment 12-3: Notary Public Information 215
B. Parol Evidence Rule 215
Assignment 12-4: Research Parol Evidence Rule 217
C. Rules of Construction 217
Assignment 12-5: UCC Research 219
D. Practical and Ethical Issues 219
Assignment 12-6: Interpret a Case, Proofread Contracts 221
Exhibit 12-1: Sample Construction Contract 222
Career Corner 223
Review Questions 223
Crossword Puzzle 224

13

Working with Contracts

A. Incoming Contracts 228
1. Checklist for Incoming Contracts 228
2. Understanding Particular Provisions 230
a. Financing 230
b. Warranties 231
c. Shipment 232
B. Creating a Contract 232
1. Assessing Client Needs and Negotiating 232
2. Drafting: Forms and Boilerplate 234
a. Characteristics of a Good Contract 234
b. Formbooks and Checklists 236
Assignment 13-1: Drafting Contracts and Working with Forms 237
c. Legalese 238
d. Active Voice and Front-Loading 238
e. Parallel Construction 239

f. Sexism and the Plural Pronoun 239
g. Misplaced Modifiers 239
h. Padding 240
Assignment 13-2: Analyze Sample Client Interview 241
C. Contracts with the Federal Government 243
D. Practical and Ethical Issues 245
Assignment 13-3: Questions on Unauthorized Practice of Law 246
Career Corner 246
Assignment 13-4: Ethics Question 247
Review Questions 247
Crossword Puzzle 248

Appendix A Sample Client Interview for Assignment 251
Appendix B Sample Land Exchange Agreement 255
Appendix C Self-Tests 259
Appendix D Self-Tests Answer Key 273

Glossary 283
Index 297

List of Contracts and Clauses

Option to Purchase Land	5
Consignment	6-7
Software Limited Warranty	31
Premarital Agreement Acknowledgments	65
Plea Agreement	65-66
Formal Recital of Consideration	78-79
Confession of Judgment	94
Exculpatory Clause	97
Indemnification	97
Declaration of Self-sufficient Minor	113
Premarital Agreement	136-137
Surety	139-140
Buyer-Broker Agency	152-154
Property Insurance Clause from Mortgage	155-156
Prohibition on Assignment	159
Sublease Clause	159
Miscellaneous Lease Clause	161
Mortgage Contingency	171
Assignment/Novation	172
Force Majeure	175
Time Is of the Essence	177
Satisfaction Clause	178
Jury Instructions	192-193
Consequential Damages	196

Liquidated Damages 197

Attorney's Fees and Costs 198

Parts of Sample Employment Contract
- Identifications 210
- Recitals 211
- Consideration 211-212
- Defined Terms 212
- Body 213
- Signatures 214

Merger Clause 216

Sample Construction Contract 222

Severability Clause 234

Sample Land Exchange Agreement 255

Preface

Since 1989 I have been a teacher in, and (for more than 20 years) coordinator of, an ABA-approved paralegal program. Before that, I was a transactional lawyer in private practice and worked with many excellent paralegals. My experiences in practice, in surveying countless graduates and employers, and in working to obtain initial approval and reapproval by the ABA have taught me the importance of:

- Teaching students to be independent learners so that they can arrive on the job as self-starters
- Integrating ethics into every topic
- Integrating the use of research and communications skills into every topic
- Ensuring that students have adequate computer skills
- Encouraging students to engage with the material so that they retain what they learn
- Teaching state-specific law and procedures

It is not easy to achieve these goals with a traditional textbook. Many such books tend to speak in generalities. Many paralegal teachers are adjuncts and may not have the time or resources to create challenging, practical, state-specific assignments to supplement the texts. They may want to develop alternatives to the lecture format, or they may be trying to offer the class alternative formats: online, hybrid, or even independent study.

This book is intended to go beyond the limitations of the traditional textbook and lecture format to:

- Engage students by making them responsible for finding local law
- Require students to use computer skills to complete assignments
- Include enough hands-on assignments (and guidance for doing those assignments) to ensure that a course offered in an alternative format will be the equivalent of a traditional class
- Include assignments requiring student-led discussion of cases as an alternative to lecture in a classroom setting or to stimulate interaction in an online setting
- Ensure hands-on experience doing legal research, summarizing cases, and finding their own answers so that students can hit the ground running in a law office

- Make students aware of job opportunities and the skills required for those opportunities
- Be adaptable to schools that schedule in semesters, trimesters, or quarters and to schools that integrate contract law into a course that includes other topics

The sample cases are not cases that were highly controversial or that were landmarks in the development of law. Paralegals must understand legal theory, but they are not responsible for developing strategy or arguing cases. The cases were chosen to provide short, easy-to-read vignettes of the real-life practice of law. Many involve lawyers and paralegals as parties. They are intended to give students insights that will help ease the transition from school to the law office.

Textbook Resources

The companion Web site for *Practical Contract Law for Paralegals: An Activities-Based Approach,* Fourth Edition, at http://www.aspenparalegaled.com/vietzen_contracts offers additional resources for students and instructors, including:

- Study aids to help students master the key concepts for this course. Visit the site to access interactive StudyMate exercises such as flash cards, matching, fill-in-the-blank, and crosswords. These activities are also available for download to an iPod or other handheld device.
- Instructor resources to accompany the text
- Links to helpful Web sites and updates

Blackboard and eCollege course materials are available to supplement this text. This online courseware is designed to streamline the teaching of the course, providing valuable resources from the book in an accessible electronic format.

Instructor resources to accompany this text include a comprehensive Instructor's Manual, Test Bank, and PowerPoint slides. All of these materials are available for download from the companion Web site.

Laurel A. Vietzen

May 2016

Acknowledgments

The author gratefully acknowledges permission from the following sources to use excerpts from their works:

The Illinois State Bar Association, 424 South Second Street, Springfield, IL 62701-1779, 800-252-8908, www.isba.org. ISBA Advisory Opinions on Professional Conduct are prepared as an educational service to members of the ISBA. While the opinions express the ISBA interpretation of the Illinois Rules of Professional Conduct and other relevant materials in response to a specific hypothesized fact situation, they do not have the weight of law and should not be relied upon as a substitute for individual legal advice.

Opinion 218 of the D.C. Bar's Legal Ethics Committee (issued June 18, 1991) (Washington, D.C., The District of Columbia Bar). Copyright 2006 by the District of Columbia Bar. Reprinted by permission of the Publisher.

Ethics Committee of the Colorado Bar Association, http://www.cobar.org, 1900 Grant Street, Suite 900, Denver, Colorado, 80203, 301-860-1115.

The Alaska Court System, 820 W. 4th Ave., Anchorage, AK 99501

Note to Students

Students have historically demonstrated their mastery of course material by taking tests. Tests remain an important part of assessment. In this course, you will probably take several tests so that you and your instructor can determine how well you have achieved the knowledge-based goals outlined at the beginning of each chapter.

Employers want more. The paralegal field demands graduates who can apply that knowledge and perform assignments with little or no on-the-job training. To demonstrate your ability to do the job, you should assemble a portfolio of work. Your portfolio can be burned to a CD, uploaded to a Web site, or assembled into a folder or binder. The contents will depend on the job you are seeking. In interviewing for a job at a small general practice firm, you might submit a portfolio containing a selection of assignments from all of your classes. If you are looking for a job in contract compliance, you will want to include many of the assignments you do in this class.

The chart at the beginning of each chapter is intended to correlate the skills employers want with the assignments you will do. Knowing that employers value these skills should inspire you to do your best work and, when appropriate, follow your instructor's comments and suggestions to create an improved version for your portfolio. Of course, many of the skills, such as reading and briefing a case, require lots of practice. Assignments calling for those skills are, therefore, repeated in almost every chapter. Choose your best effort for your portfolio.

Introduction to Law and Preparation for Self-Guided Learning

This text requires that the student do a substantial amount of independent research to find the law applicable in the student's jurisdiction. This chapter provides an overview or refresher course on the concepts necessary to find and analyze law: sources of primary law, use of secondary sources, formulating a search query, reading and analyzing legal authority, and the consequences of bad research.

Skills-based learning objectives	*How you will demonstrate your ability*
Analyze a legal issue and develop search terms to use to find authority addressing that issue.	Assignment: Brainstorm contract issues and prepare search queries.
Identify ethical issues and find state-specific authority addressing those issues.	Assignment: Find and discuss state ethical rules applicable to a contract situation.
Read and brief a judicial decision.	Assignment: Prepare a case brief.

A. Sources of Legal Authority
B. Steps in Preparing to Research a Legal Issue
C. Formulating a Query
D. Primary Authority
  1. Statutes

2. Judicial Decisions
    a. Trial Courts vs. Appellate Courts
    b. Reading Cases
    c. Briefing Cases

E. Practical and Ethical Issues

A. Sources of Legal Authority

Criminal Law
Prosecuted by a governmental body involving a matter of concern to society as a whole

Civil Law
Pursued by an individual or group of people, a business, or a governmental body acting in a private capacity; result may be damages or court

Municipal Law
Local law (as opposed to federal or state law)

Constitution
One of five sources of legal authority

Legislation
Supreme source of legal authority; also called code or statute; enacted by an elected body (*e.g.*, Congress)

Code
Legislation; also called statute

Statute
Legislation; also called code

Judicial Decisions
Source of legal authority; also called common law or precedent

Common Law
Judicial decisions; also called precedent

Case Law
Judicial decisions

Some students will have taken an introduction to law or a legal research class before using this book. For them, the special features of this book will provide an unusual and very valuable opportunity to practice their research and writing skills. Students who have not taken those classes can learn enough about the basics of research to do well in this class just by reading this chapter. Those students will still have much to learn when they study legal research, but they will become comfortable with simple online research.

Let's start with some basics:

1. Success in law is not about enjoying a good argument; it is about having legal authority to support your arguments.

2. There are two types of law: civil and criminal. A **criminal law** matter is prosecuted by a governmental body, such as the district attorney, and involves a matter of concern to society as a whole, such as burglary or murder. The result may be prison time, probation, even the death penalty, if the defendant is found guilty. A **civil law** matter is pursued by an individual or group of private people, a business entity, or a governmental body acting in a "private" capacity. Breach of contract is an example of a civil matter and, if the defendant is found liable (don't use the word *guilty!*) the result is an award of damages (money) or a court order requiring or prohibiting specific actions.

3. Legal authority comes from five sources. These sources exist in federal and state law, and most exist even in local (**municipal**) **law:**
    a. **Constitution** (even municipalities have a charter or other governing document);
    b. **Legislation** enacted by an elected body such as Congress, a state legislature, a county board, or city council (also called **code** or **statute**);
    c. **Judicial decisions,** also called **common law, case law,** or **precedent;**
    d. **Administrative agency regulations and rulings,** such as the "rules and regs" of the Internal Revenue Service, Federal Trade Commission, your state environmental protection department, or a local planning board. An administrative agency is established to administer a particular law or program (*e.g.*, the National Labor Relations Board was created to administer the National Labor Relations Act); and
    e. **Executive actions,** which are executive orders signed by the President or governor (or even the mayor) and treaties signed by the President and approved by the Senate.

4. Legal problems presented by clients are often unique. Lawyers and paralegals can memorize the basics of an area of law, such as contract law, but often don't know "the answer" to the problem presented. To find that answer they must research those sources of law to find authority to support their theories.

5. When you find authority, you must be able to understand, analyze, and write about it, and also **cite**[1] it so that those who read your work can find your sources.

Precedent
Judicial decisions; also called common law; past decisions used to justify current decisions

Administrative Agency
Source of legal authority; administers a particular law or program

Regulations
Established by administrative agencies

Executive Actions
Source of legal authority; including orders signed by the President or governor

Cite
Verb form of citation (*i.e.*, to cite)

Interoffice Memo
Also called objective memo, analyzes fact situation with citations to sources of law

Objective Memo
Also called interoffice memo, analyzes fact situation with citations to legal authority

Adversarial
Argues a position

Primary Authority
One of the five sources of law

Secondary Authority
Material such as textbooks and articles that help locate (finding tools) and understand primary law; form books, handbooks, encyclopedias, digests, and the like; not actual law

Statutory Interpretation
Interpretation of statute's terms; also called statutory construction

CALR
Computer-assisted legal research system

B. Steps in Preparing to Research a Legal Issue

Before you start to research a legal problem you will ask yourself several questions:

1. **Is this a matter of state law or federal law?** By the time you finish your paralegal education, you will usually be able to answer this question without help. Most law relevant to contracts comes from state case law or state statutes. This book will guide you through the law of your own state.

2. **What is the desired work product and how much time should be spent on the research?** These are important questions on the job and in other classes. Paralegals often prepare **interoffice memos** (also called **objective memos**) that cite authority to analyze the client's situation without arguing a position; paralegals also work on **adversarial** memos and briefs that argue the client's position. This book will give you clear instructions on the work product.

3. **Does this project require primary authority or secondary authority?** When you are researching a question of law, you will generally be looking for **primary authority**—one of the five sources previously listed. **Secondary authority** is not, itself, the law; it includes textbooks and scholarly articles that help you understand primary law as well as form books, procedure manuals, and "practice" handbooks that help you accomplish a specific task. Many times a legal problem involves finding the right form or procedure, rather than finding the actual law. Secondary authority also includes material to help you find primary authority when you are using books; these "finding tools," such as digests and encyclopedias, are not necessary when you look for primary law online.

4. **Which of the five sources of law is likely to govern?** Most contract law comes from code (statutes) and case law; there is some relevant administrative law, as discussed in Chapter 2. When a statute governs, it is often written in broad terms (*e.g.*, "seller shall have a reasonable time . . ."); you will need to find cases that provide insight on how courts interpret terms such as "reasonable" in specific fact situations. **Statutory interpretation (statutory construction)** is a major function of the courts and a major purpose of legal research.

5. **Where will I do this research?** At some point in your paralegal career you will learn to use books for legal research, but in this class you will probably complete your assignments using a subscription computer-assisted legal research (**CALR**) system. Your school may provide you with access to WestLaw, Lexis, or some other system. If you do not have access to a subscription CALR system, you can create an account at http://www.lexisone.com that will allow you to search for judicial decisions from all 50 states and the federal system, going back five years, without paying a fee. You can find statutes on a government-sponsored site, without paying a fee.

6. **How should I describe the problem?** As explained below, you must describe your problem in a few words that can be used in an index or to create a query to use in an online search engine.

[1]To cite authority is to give its citation, the address at which it can be found in law books or online.

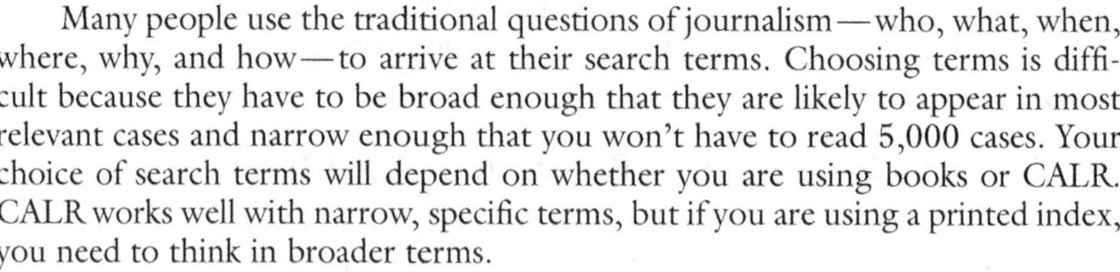

Many people use the traditional questions of journalism—who, what, when, where, why, and how—to arrive at their search terms. Choosing terms is difficult because they have to be broad enough that they are likely to appear in most relevant cases and narrow enough that you won't have to read 5,000 cases. Your choice of search terms will depend on whether you are using books or CALR. CALR works well with narrow, specific terms, but if you are using a printed index, you need to think in broader terms.

Example

If you were researching whether prescribing the drug Allegra has ever resulted in a malpractice case, you would find the term "Allegra" too narrow and unlikely to appear in a print index. However, using the word "Allegra" in a computerized search would probably get you to the most relevant material quickly. On the other hand, the term "prescription" would work well in a printed index, but would probably result in a list with hundreds of cases if used in a computerized search.

Another challenge in brainstorming a problem is the unique language of the law. As you take classes and read cases, this will become second nature to you, but it may seem foreign at first. For example, a problem involving marital property might be classified under "husband and wife" in a legal index; a problem involving a 17-year-old might fall into the category "infants."

Here is a sample of how you might "brainstorm" a problem and develop a list of words and phrases that describe the problem:

Example

Several years ago, Dan Developer knew that he would want to build 50 houses on his vacant property. He wanted to "lock in" the costs, so he approached the local school district and asked whether he could prepay the school impact fees. School impact fees are paid by a developer to help the school district pay the cost of educating students who will enter the local schools because their families have moved into a new development. The district agreed and the parties entered into a contract, under which Dan paid $65,000. Three years later, when Dan applied for permits to begin construction, he was told that the district had enacted a new fee. According to the district, the fee Dan had paid was for school buildings, and the new fee is for equipment and staff. Dan thought he had protected himself against all school fees and asks your firm to research the issue.

Who	School district, developer
What	Impact fees
Where	Subdivision
When	Prepayment
Why	Vested rights*
How	Contract

**An example of a term that may be unfamiliar, "vested rights" refers to rights that have become definite entitlements at a point in time.*

Identifying synonyms and similar terms is an essential part of the process. For example, in the chart, you might insert "builder" next to "developer" and "government agency" next to "school district."

C. Formulating a Query

If you are going to conduct your search using a computer, you will connect several of your search terms to create a query. The **connectors** describe the relationship between your search terms. All of the major CALR services include some common connectors. Some examples of how they work:

Search Query
Terms and connectors or natural language used in CALR search

Connector
Symbol describing relationship between CALR search terms

- You decide to use "developer" and "impact fee" as search terms and enter the query [developer & "impact fee"]. You get a list of hundreds of cases because the "&" connector only requires that each term appear at some spot in the case.
- To narrow the search, use a "proximity" or "near" connector. Most CALR systems have connectors to require that terms be in the same paragraph [/p], the same sentence [/s], or within a specified number of words of each other [search term/# search term]. You might search [developer/25 "impact fee"] to find cases in which the word developer appears within 25 words of "impact fee."
- The term "impact fee" is in quotes because some CALR systems require quotes to identify a phrase; failure to include quotes would cause the system to search for the word developer within 25 words of "impact" or "fee."
- Still have too many results? Add terms: [developer/25 "impact fee"/25 subdivision].
- If you aren't getting enough results, broaden your search to look for [developer or builder/25 "impact fee"]. The "or" connector is often used to search for synonyms.
- Suppose that your search pulls up several cases in which a developer challenged the existence of impact fees, claiming they were unconstitutional. To eliminate these cases, use the "not" connector [%], [developer/25 "impact fee" % unconstitutional].
- Use **root expanders** [!] to pick up variations such as subdivision or subdivide [subdivi!]. To find woman or women you might use a **wildcard** [wom*n]. Most CALR systems automatically search for common variants, such as court, courts, or court's.

Root Expander
Symbol used to pick up word variations in a CALR search

Wildcard
Symbol used to pick up word variations in a CALR search

Variants
Different forms of a root word

If you are not familiar with the connectors and wildcards for your CALR system, you can likely find its use guide when you sign on, usually by using the HELP tab. Many of the CALR providers have online tutorials you can use even before you sign on. Your instructor will show you how to sign on.[2] In addition, Chapter 1 specifically describes the steps taken to research particular problems.

---

[2]The examples are "terms and connectors" searches; it is also possible to search using "natural language" on some systems, by entering a question without connectors. A "field search," with which you search or limit the search by names of parties, judges, or lawyers; by citation; or by dates is also possible, but beyond the scope of this book.

Assignment Intro-1

Brainstorm the following problems and write a CALR search query for each. Remember, you are not trying to find an answer to the problem at this point, but are only practicing formulating queries.

- Jim has leased a building in a strip mall to operate a Francesca's Pizza restaurant. The contract provides that the landlord will not lease space to a "competing business" in the same shopping center, but it does not define that term or give examples. The landlord is planning to lease the space next to Francesca's to a take-out sandwich shop and claims that such a business would not compete with Jim's business. Jim disagrees.
- Dan Developer signed contracts to sell houses in his new subdivision. The contracts provided that each house would have King brand double-pane, vinyl, double-hung windows. Before construction began, King raised its prices substantially. Dan substituted Della brand double-pane, vinyl, double-hung windows and feels that they are substantially the same product. Some of the buyers are claiming that this violated their rights—they want a reduction of the purchase price.
- Dr. Hirsch is a successful psychiatrist (M.D.) and wants to expand her practice by hiring a psychologist (Ph.D.) to do counseling. She is concerned that the psychologist might work for her just long enough to become popular with her patients and then open his own office, and that she could lose patients. She wonders whether a court would enforce a clause, in the employment contract, prohibiting her employee from opening his own counseling business within 50 miles of her office for two years after leaving her employ.

D. Primary Authority

The following is an overview of the primary authority you will find when you use CALR. In later chapters, you will use secondary sources.

1. Statutes

Topic
Generally, statutes are organized by topic, breaking the code into titles, acts, chapters, or sections

Titles
See Topic

Statutes (also called *legislation* or *code*) are enacted by a legislative body (Congress or a state legislature) and are generally organized by **topics,** which are divided into subtopics and sub-subtopics. You should be familiar with the major topics, often called **titles** or chapters, of the statutes for your jurisdiction. Knowing the major topics gives you a starting point for statutory research, even if the most recent amendments may not have been **"codified"** (*i.e.*, put into the topical system). To find your state statutes and look at those topics, start at http://www.ncsl.org/public/leglinks.cfm. Select your state and "statutes" in the boxes.

Codify
To enter a statute into a topical system

Citations to statutes do not use page numbers because the topics can expand or contract. Using references to titles, chapters, acts, sections, or paragraphs eliminates the need to change all references when a law is amended or repealed. For example, Section 17 might be one-half page long or it might grow to eight pages long, but it can still be cited as Section (§) 17. If Section 17 grows to 13 pages, Section 18 will begin on a later page, but it can still be called §18. A citation to a statute generally consists of the name of the law, an abbreviation indicating the source (*e.g.*, U.S.C. indicates that the statute was found in U.S. Code; ILCS indicates Illinois Compiled Statutes), and numbers indicating the title, chapter, act, and/or section.

If you examine an **annotated statute,** the text of the law as enacted by the legislature appears first, followed by references to cases, administrative regulations, law review articles, and other materials that explain and interpret the law. Statutes found on government sites on the Internet are not annotated.

Annotated Statute
Statute with references to articles, cases, and other materials that explain and interpret the law

Reading and comprehending statutes takes a lot of practice. Statutes often include nonspecific language, so that courts have discretion to interpret and apply the law. This is necessary because legislation is intended to govern large groups of people or situations; being too specific would create loopholes. Unlike judicial decisions, which deal with specific situations after they have occurred, statutes often govern conduct in advance. Think about the speed limit that applies in bad weather. It is not a specific number; in most states it is represented by the phrase "safe for conditions" or a similar description. Stating a specific speed would not govern all possible weather situations that could arise in the future on all possible roads. Statutes may also contain long, confusing sentences. A few tips for reading statutes:

1. Look at the index for the whole chapter or act (often located at the beginning of the chapter or act) to get a feel for the law as a whole.
2. Check whether the act has a "definitions" section that defines the terms used in the various sections.
3. Read the sections immediately before and after the section applicable to your research; they may shed light on the statutory scheme.
4. Write out the statute and break long sentences into "outline" form so that you can sort out the "ands" from the "ors."

2. Judicial Decisions

With a few exceptions, print volumes containing judicial decisions (called **reporters**) are not organized by topic and you must use an encyclopedia, digest, or other index to find relevant cases. To avoid this two-step process, CALR is an efficient way of locating judicial decisions. Once you find cases, reading and understanding what you've found requires a solid understanding of court systems.

Reporters
Print volumes that contain judicial decisions

Trial Court
Court in which most cases start, generally concerned with deciding issues of fact

Issues of Fact
Trial courts use testimony and evidence to decide facts (*i.e.*, what happened)

Legal Issues
Determining appropriate consequences of the facts or whether a trial court handled a case properly

Affirm
Appellate or higher court's decision to support or uphold the decision of the lower court

Reverse
Appellate or higher court's decision to invalidate the decision of the lower court

Remand
Appellate or higher court's decision to send the case back to the lower court

Modify
Appellate or higher court's decision to change the decision of the lower court

Dissenting Opinion
Opinion written by a judge who disagrees with the majority; not law but provides interesting facts and opinions about case

Majority Decision
That which governs the outcome of cases; also called decision of the court

Decision of the Court
Majority decision, governs outcome of the case

Concurring Opinion
Written by a judge who agrees with majority decision but for different reasons

Synopsis
Summary of case, often provided in publishers' enhancements

a. Trial Courts vs. Appellate Courts

Most cases enter the legal system in a **trial court.** A trial court is most concerned with **issues of fact.** An issue of fact concerns what happened: Did he shoot the gun? Did she run the red light? Trial courts examine evidence and take testimony to make factual decisions. Factual determinations often resolve the case without any need for legal research. For example, in most situations, if she ran the red light, she is responsible for the collision. Because factual decisions do not make or interpret the law, most states do not report (publish) trial court decisions; therefore, when you find a reported state court case, it is often a case from an appeals court or the highest court in the system. These courts are concerned with **legal issues:** the appropriate consequences of the facts or how the lower court handled the case. Some federal trial decisions are reported.

When you read a decision from an appeals court or the highest court, remember that the court is not hearing a "new" case, but reviewing a decision made by a lower court. The appeals court can **affirm, reverse, remand,** or **modify** (or some combination thereof) the lower court's decision. For example, an appellate court could affirm the trial court's decision that a defendant was responsible for a collision, but find the award of damages unreasonable and reverse and remand on the determination of appropriate damages. If an appellate court determines that a trial court made an error in admitting evidence or making a calculation, the appellate court will generally remand—send the case back the lower court—because it will not accept evidence or make determinations of fact.

Appeals courts use panels of judges. The decision of the majority governs the outcome of the case (whether to affirm, reverse, or remand), but the other (non-majority) judges may write their own opinions. A **dissenting opinion** is written by a judge who disagrees with the **majority decision;** the majority decision is also called the **decision of the court.** A dissenting opinion is not the law, but often provides interesting facts and opinions about the case. A **concurring opinion** is written by a judge who agrees with the majority's decision, but for different reasons.

b. Reading Cases

The physical layout of cases can be confusing. Depending on your source, publishers' enhancements such as a **synopsis** (summary of the case) and **head-notes** (summaries of individual points made in the case) may or may not be included. If headnotes are included, they may include references to supplemental materials and serve as an outline of the case. As you read a case, keep a legal dictionary and a piece of paper close by. You will probably have to look up at least a couple of new legal terms with each case you read. You may also want to draw a timeline on a piece of paper so that you can visualize the events before and during the litigation. Judges usually do not give facts in the order in which they occurred (*i.e.*, chronological order), which can be confusing. Often the first paragraph in the opinion recites **procedural history,** the court decisions that brought the case to its current position (*e.g.,* "Plaintiff-appellant sought review of summary judgment entered by the Circuit Court of Kendall County. The appellate court, second district, reversed. We granted certiorari . . ."). To a beginner, this usually makes no sense until the underlying facts are clear. Skip this paragraph, read the underlying facts and make a **timeline,** and then go back to the procedural history and add it to the timeline (at the end of the underlying facts, of course).

If there are multiple parties, particularly if the judges refer to those parties as "**appellant**" and "**appellee,**" jot down a quick way of identifying the parties (*e.g.,* you might note that appellant = employer; appellee = employee). The appellant is the party bringing the appeal; in other words, this party lost in the lower court. The appellee won in the lower court. Because courts frequently make different rulings on different issues, it is not uncommon for both sides to appeal. For example, the defendant might appeal, arguing that the trial court "**erred**" (made an error) in finding her responsible (**liable**) for a collision. At the same time, the plaintiff might appeal, arguing that the award of $50,000 in damages was insufficient because of the extent of his injuries. Reading an opinion is particularly confusing when the court refers to "plaintiff, cross-appellee," and the like.

One of the most difficult things about reading a judicial decision is that the opinion will contain discussions of several other decisions made by other courts. The primary function of an appeals court is to review the decisions of lower courts with respect to the case under consideration (also called the **case at hand**). An opinion may contain an extensive discussion of what the court below it did and why that was correct or incorrect.

In addition, the appellate-level court may discuss other cases decided in the past (**precedent**) in depth and either **analogize** or **distinguish** those cases—find them similar to or different from, respectively, the case being decided. The court may also discuss the meaning of a statute. It's easy to get lost; it can be helpful to either take notes or physically mark your copy of the case.

When you find a case online, the body of the case may include numbers spaced at intervals to indicate where the page number would change if you were looking at print material. Sometimes you will want to know the exact page number on which a fact or quote appears in a case (**jump cite**). Online citations to precedent may include links, so that you can click on the citation and see the case being discussed.

c. Briefing Cases

The best way to practice reading and truly understanding cases is to write short case summaries, called **briefs.** Although case briefs are not part of the everyday practice of law, they are time-honored teaching tools. Law students must brief several cases for each class they attend daily. You can expect to brief many cases while you are in school.

You will find that each instructor has a preferred format for case briefs. Most instructors will want you to put a heading on the brief, including the name, **citation** (its official "address" within law books), and year of the case. You should also include a section for "facts," a statement of the legal issue(s) on appeal,

Headnotes
Summaries of individual points made in the case, often a publisher's enhancement; may provide references to additional authority

Procedural History
The history of the court decisions that have moved the case to its current position

Timeline
A schedule of the times at which certain events took place

Appellant
Party bringing an appeal; lost in the lower court

Appellee
The party that won in the lower court

Err
To make an error

Liable
Found responsible

Case at Hand
The case under consideration

Analogize
To compare cases and find them similar

Distinguish
To compare cases and find them to be different

Jump Cite
The exact page number on which a fact or quote appears in a case

Brief
Short case summary

Citation
Address at which authority is found in law books or online

the holding, and a summary of the reasoning. Some instructors also want separate sections reciting the procedural history and the contentions (arguments) of the parties. Be sure that you understand which sections your instructor wants included and your instructor's preferences regarding headings, spacing, and so on. A sample of a brief that follows the format described below can be found at the end of Chapter 1.

Facts Because a brief should be brief, one page if possible, it is not usually a good idea to copy the facts as stated by the court. Edit out all insignificant facts. To determine whether a fact is significant, ask yourself: "If this fact were changed, would it change the outcome?" For example, assume the case states that the plaintiff was driving her 2005 Ford Mustang to school, on Maple Street, when the defendant ran a red light and caused a collision. Ask yourself: "Would the result be different if the plaintiff had been driving her 2006 Chevy Aveo to the store on Elm Street when the defendant ran a red light and caused a collision?"

Recite the facts in chronological order, as they happened, and in past tense (because the facts are not continuing to occur). Your instructor may want you to include procedural history in the facts or in a separate section. In either case, the procedural history is important and should be included.

Find an easy way to refer to the parties. Using either plaintiff-defendant or the names of the parties (Smith-Jones) can be confusing, particularly if there are several parties. It is often possible to identify the parties by their roles (*e.g.*, landlord-tenant, husband-wife-child, employer-secretary, or buyer-seller).

Holding
Answer to the legal issue in a judicial decision

Issue and Holding The issue on appeal is never a factual issue such as "whether the light was red." That may have been the issue at trial, but the trial court made a decision. On appeal, something about how the lower court made that decision is in question. Try to identify the ruling or rulings in question and the arguments made by the parties and you will be able to spot the issue.

The **holding** is the answer to the question posed by the issue. It generally includes this court's disposition of the case (affirm, reverse, etc.) and a short summary of the court's conclusion. For example, if the issue is "whether the trial court erred in refusing to permit testimony of a blind witness," the holding might be "Reversed; a witness may not be considered incompetent to testify based on physical disability alone." Do not accidentally state the holding of a lower court.

Reasoning
Summary of the court's explanation of its decision

Reasoning The **reasoning** is a summary of the court's explanation of its decision—the "why" behind the holding. Most instructors prefer that you explain reasoning in your own words. It is almost never sufficient to simply state that the court based its decision on precedent. It is also not helpful to refer to cited cases unless a reader would know what the reference means. Try to explain how the unique facts of this case add to or clarify the law.

Instructors differ on whether dissenting or concurring opinions should be included in a brief. Read these opinions. If they make the facts or the legal arguments more understandable, write a short summary.

E. Practical and Ethical Issues

Contract law presents unique ethical and practical issues for legal professionals. This book includes material on these issues at the end of every chapter. The practice of law is regulated on a state-by-state basis, so ethical rules may be slightly different in different states. You can find your state's Rules of Professional Conduct by using the American Bar Association (ABA) Center for Professional Responsibility at http://www.abanet.org/cpr/links.html. The ABA promulgates "Model Rules," which can be found on the site, but has no enforcement authority, so it is important that you become familiar with the rules enforced in your state.

Assignment Intro-2

Find and print your state's Rules of Professional Conduct, relating to Competence and Candor Toward the Tribunal for use with the discussion questions that follow.

Read the *Moran* bankruptcy case, which can be found online at http://www.leagle.com/decision/1998521231BR290_1472/IN%20RE%20MORAN, and prepare a case brief. The case involves a contract between a lawyer and a client that is ambiguous and not in compliance with ethical rules. It is intended to show the need for good research and show how precedent is used in deciding cases. While most of the cases presented as samples in this book have been heavily edited, this case has only been slightly edited so that you can see how cases look when you find them online.

1. Read the case twice before you write anything.
2. Make a timeline showing the chronology: the accident, the signing of the contingency agreement, the change in the rules, the bankruptcy filing, and so on. You will notice that the court does not present the facts in the order in which they occurred, which can be confusing.
3. Consider the following discussion questions:
   a. Because the original contingency fee agreement made no reference to expenses, it appears that the issue would not have come up if the Morans had not filed a bankruptcy petition. Did the trustee attempt to add a new term to the contract existing between the Morans and Coghlan? Why would that happen? Do you think the trustee was sloppy or deceitful? Should the trustee have been sanctioned?
   b. What is your opinion about why the lawyers did not initially disclose the changes?
   c. Although the decision refers to ethical rules, this is not a disciplinary proceeding under those rules. Do you think that the failure of the attorneys to discover or disclose the change in the rules could be a basis for discipline under your state's ethical rules?

d. Do you think that failure to discover the changes could be considered malpractice if the Coghlan firm had been representing an outside client, rather than itself? Is there any possibility of the Morans suing the firm for malpractice? Did you notice that the Morans were acting without representation by a lawyer in this proceeding?
e. Do you think the sanction was adequate?

Review Questions

1. Identify the three main sources of contract law.
2. Is contract law primarily state or federal law?
3. Acme Builders realizes it underpriced its contract to build Jilly's Bakery and will lose money if it builds at the contract price. Acme intentionally breaches the contract by refusing to begin construction; this will cause substantial delay in Jilly's opening. Is this a civil or criminal matter?
4. While researching a legal question, you are lucky enough to find an article written by a prominent Harvard professor. The article discusses your precise issue in depth. Is the article primary or secondary authority?
5. When you find a statute that addresses your issue, you still might have to look for case law. Why?
6. Identify three types of connectors that can be used in a terms and connectors search and describe the functions of wildcards and root expanders.
7. Page numbers are not used in referring to a particular part of a statute. Why?
8. The relevant statute describes "DUI" as being in control of a "vehicle" while intoxicated. Your client was arrested for riding a horse while intoxicated. Describe strategies you would use to determine whether the horse should be considered a "vehicle."
9. Your DUI client is also claiming that he was not intoxicated while riding the horse, but was suffering a reaction to a prescription drug. What type of issue does this present, and would legal research be appropriate?

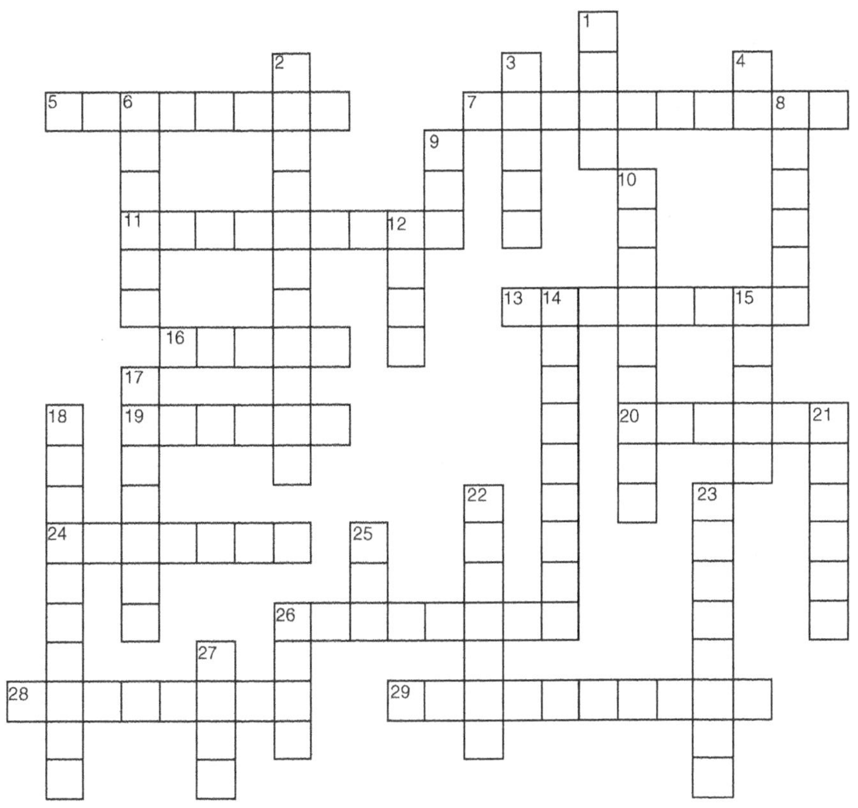

ACROSS

5. ! is the root
7. __________ history; court decisions that led to case's current position
11. party who lost in lower court
13. another term for decision of the court
16. __________ lawsuit generally results in award of money
19. to send a case back to lower court
20. uphold lower court decision
24. another word for legislation
26. for a statute to have been entered into topical system
28. * is the __________, used to find variations such as woman/women
29. __________ opinion; agrees with decision but may state different reasons

DOWN

1. issues of __________ dealt with in trial court
2. type of law made by agencies
3. __________ court decisions are often not published
4. connector useful for finding synonyms
6. quotation marks are used for __________ searching
8. IRS is an administrative
9. % is the __________ connector
10. __________ authority explains or helps locate the law but is not actually law
12. / is the __________ or proximity connector
14. __________ statute has references to cases, articles, etc.
15. statutes are organized by __________
17. __________ law comes from one of five sources
18. __________ opinion, by a judge who disagrees
21. change a decision
22. Loislaw automatically retrieves most __________ forms
23. __________ prosecution can result in prison sentence
25. connector that will find terms in case regardless of proximity
26. another word for legislation
27. initials; Loislaw is this type of research

Practical Contract Law for Paralegals

◆ ◆ ◆

An Activities-Based Approach

1

What Is Contract Law?

This chapter explores the types of contract recognized by law: express, implied, unilateral, bilateral, formal, informal, enforceable, unenforceable, void, and voidable. The role of paralegals in contract law is introduced, along with some of the ethical problems unique to contract law. You will learn to recognize situations that are similar to contracts, but are treated differently: gifts, promissory estoppel, and quasi-contract.

At the end of the chapter is a sample brief of a case concerning issues discussed in this chapter. It includes an explanation of how the case was found, using computer-assisted legal research (CALR) techniques. Students who are not yet confident in their ability to find, read, and summarize cases may want to review the sample before attempting the assignments in this unit.

Skills-based learning objectives	*How you will demonstrate your ability*
Identify a contract as unilateral or bilateral and identify obligations that are implied rather than express.	Assignments: Analyze sample contracts; describe common unilateral and implied contracts.
Identify ethical issues and find state-specific authority addressing those issues.	Assignment: Find and discuss state ethical rules applicable to a contract situation.
Find a judicial decision addressing a particular issue in contract law; analyze and brief the case.	Assignment: Research a contract law issue; prepare a case brief.

A. What Is a Contract?
1. Types of Contract: Express or Implied
2. Types of Contract: Unilateral or Bilateral
3. Other Classifications of Contracts
B. Alternatives to Contract
1. Gifts
2. Promissory Estoppel
3. Quasi-Contract
C. Practical and Ethical Issues

Introduction

Contract
Set of legally enforceable promises

Torts
Law applicable to injuries to people or property

What is contract law? The short answer is that all of law is related to contract law. That is why almost all law schools require that first-year students take a course in contract law. **Contracts** are, themselves, the subject of much litigation; contracts can be used to resolve matters involving crimes (plea agreements), property, **torts** (injuries to people or property), estates and inheritance, divorce and parenting, and businesses. Is it "dry" or boring? Only if psychology is boring; a real grasp of contract law requires a solid understanding of motives, patterns of behavior, communication, negotiation and the balance of power among parties, and probabilities.

Example

Understanding motivation is the key to understanding contract law. Consider: Client is entering a contract with Builder for construction of an office building and wonders how to set the price. A flat price for materials and labor would give Client peace of mind, knowing what the ultimate price will be. Client has limited funds available and wants certainty. But, will Builder be tempted to use the cheapest (perhaps low-quality) materials to maximize profit? Builder is also concerned about the bottom line. If the price of materials goes up as it did, for example, after Hurricane Katrina, he may be working for almost nothing. If the contract is structured so that Client will pay the cost of materials plus XX%, might Builder be motivated to use the most expensive materials? If Client wants to pay the cost of materials plus a set amount for labor, Client is assuming all of the risk with respect to the cost of materials. If Client decides to acquire materials independently, will the price be as good as the price Builder could negotiate? What is the value of Client's time? Can you think of a solution?

Every lawyer must have a good understanding of contract law, and paralegals need to understand the theory and much more. Paralegals play important roles in negotiating, drafting, and implementing contracts and, when a contract is litigated, are often called upon to conduct factual and legal research and assist with trial preparation. To be an effective paralegal, you need to understand contract theory, be familiar with the vocabulary, be able to identify and research legal issues, and have the practical skills for drafting and implementing contracts.

The most important thing you can learn is to work independently. You could try to memorize every word in this book, including every reference to a case or statute, but that would not be of much benefit in the workplace. Many fact situations you encounter on the job will not have been addressed in this book; your state may have unusual contract precedents, or your local courts may have practices not addressed in this book. Most importantly, the law will continue to evolve after this book is finished. This book will give you the language and skills you will need to handle those issues. It's a do-it-yourself approach that should help you retain what you learn well past the final exam. You will be instructed to use the Internet and CALR to research certain issues and find your own answers.

Assignment 1-1

A basic understanding of contract law is essential to working in any area of law, as discussed above, but a higher level of knowledge can take your career to a higher level. Visit http://www.nala.org and answer the following:

1. Briefly describe the paralegal certification program.
2. Find the description of advanced certification for contract management. List the skills identified as necessary for the certification.
3. Find the most recent job analysis report. What percentage of certified paralegals report use of general contract knowledge?

Dealing with a contract in any context involves: determining whether a contract has formed or will form; knowing how to interpret and implement the agreement; and determining the consequences when something goes wrong. This book is organized according to those concerns. The first chapters deal with the elements of formation and are followed by chapters concerning implementation, interpretation, and remedies.

A. What Is a Contract?

When you think of a "contract," do you picture the five pages of mind-numbing, tiny print you signed when you took a car loan? Do you picture yourself going through the cafeteria at work or school with a cup of coffee and toast on your tray, saying nothing, but handing the cashier a five-dollar bill? You should picture both. A contract is a set of legally enforceable promises, entered into by two or more parties, to make their dealings predictable and to allocate risk. The law of contracts will make more sense to you if you remember that people enter into contracts to keep their dealings and risk predictable. Very few people could enter into any relationship, whether buying toast and coffee or building a mansion, without having some way to predict the outcome and risk.

Agreement
"Meeting of the minds"

Manifestation of Mutual Assent
Appearance that an agreement has been reached

Consideration
The give and take that distinguishes a contract from a gift

Capacity
Ability, as determined by age and mental competence, to enter into a contract

Legality
An element of an enforceable contract

Express
Contract with significant terms stated orally or in writing

Implied
Contract formed without express statement of terms, by words and actions

Bilateral
Contract in which both parties make promises

Executory
Contract in which obligations have not been fulfilled

Executed
Contract in which all obligations have been fulfilled contract

Unilateral
Contract formed when one party acts in response to other party's promise

Not all promises are contracts. To be enforceable, a contract must meet certain requirements: **agreement** (also called **manifestation of mutual assent**), **consideration, capacity,** and **legality.** Those requirements are discussed in depth in later chapters. A promise that is not a contract might be enforceable under another theory such as completed gift, quasi-contract, or promissory estoppel; these theories are explained later in this chapter.

1. Types of Contract: Express or Implied

Contracts can be classified in many ways. An **express** contract has its important terms explicitly stated, either orally or in writing. The enforceability of oral contracts is discussed later. A contract can also be **implied** from the words and actions of the parties, even if they never expressed an agreement.

Example

Contract law does not favor the "gotcha" approach to doing business and includes a theory for most situations. Terry, a certified public accountant, has prepared Lee's tax returns every March for the last six years. This year, Terry came back from lunch on March 2 and found an envelope containing all of Lee's receipts and tax forms under the office door. Terry completed Lee's returns and mailed them, along with a bill, to Lee. Can Lee refuse to pay on the grounds that they never entered into an agreement this year? Probably not; a contract was implied.

---

2. Types of Contract: Unilateral or Bilateral

Most contracts are **bilateral,** meaning that both parties made promises. It may be that nothing has been done yet; it may be some time before anything is done, but a contract has formed. Sam orally promises to paint Taylor's building next month; Taylor agrees to pay $3,000, but neither has taken any action beyond making promises. A binding contract exists between them. It is an **executory** contract because there are obligations that have not yet been fulfilled. When Sam paints the building and Taylor pays Sam, it will be a fully **executed** contract.

A **unilateral** contract does not form until one party acts in response to the other's promise. A typical example is an offer of a reward. I may offer $100 for the return of my missing cat, but there is no point in your promising me that you will find the cat. The contract forms when you find the cat.

Examples

Why does this distinction matter? Sometimes it is essential to know exactly when a contract forms.

Bilateral Contract: Sam orally promised to paint Taylor's building next month; Taylor agreed to pay $3,000. Two days later Taylor decided to cancel; it would be more economical to install vinyl siding. Taylor is in breach of contract, and Sam may sue for damages.

Unilateral: On the other hand, assume that Taylor said: "You know that old garage behind my house on Main Street? It needs painting, but I don't want to get involved in any big contract deal. If you have any time next month, get over there and paint it. I've got all the paint and stuff in the basement. When you finish I'll pay you $3,000." Sam just smiled and shrugged but planned to do the job. Two days later, Taylor called Sam and revoked the offer. Taylor has not breached a contract, because no contract had formed. A unilateral contract forms when there is an act in response to a promise, and Sam had not yet acted.

Assignment 1-2

In Exhibit 1-1 you will find samples of a consignment contract and an option contract. Don't worry too much about the component parts of the contract, some of which are labeled. Those are discussed thoroughly in a later chapter. Read the contracts and determine the following:

1. Is the option contract a unilateral or bilateral contract? Think it out: As of the day the option was signed, what does the owner get and what does she give up? On that day, what does the buyer give up and what does she get? Might there actually be two contracts in this situation?
2. Is anything obvious missing from the consignment agreement?
3. Robin's jewelry may be very ugly and overpriced; Betty may be unable to sell a single piece. If she never sells a piece, she never has to pay Robin anything. Does that mean that this is a unilateral contract, which will be accepted only when Merchandise is sold? Think it out: Identify specifically when the contract formed or will form and what each party gave or promised.

EXHIBIT 1-1
Sample Option and Consignment Contracts

OPTION CONTRACT

OPTION AGREEMENT by and between Jan West ("Owner") and Rene Miller ("Buyer").

Identification and defined terms

Buyer hereby pays to the Owner the sum of $10 in consideration for this option, which option payment shall be credited to the purchase price if the option is exercised.

EXHIBIT 1-1
(continued)

Buyer has the option and right to buy the vacant and undeveloped property commonly known as 140 S. Wood Road, more fully described on the survey attached to and made part of this Agreement, within the option period for the full price of $70,000 (Seventy Thousand Dollars).

This option shall remain in effect until August 31, 201X, and thereupon expire unless this option is sooner exercised. To exercise this option, Buyer must notify Owner of same by certified mail within the option period. All notices shall be sent to the owner at 325 River Ave., Dundee, IN.

Time is of the essence in this agreement. Should the Buyer exercise the option, the Owner and the Buyer agree to promptly execute any and all documents necessary to consummate the sale on these terms.

The Buyer may extend this agreement, for a period of six months, by sending certified funds in the amount of $100, by certified mail, to the Owner at the aforementioned address, within the option period.

This option agreement shall be binding upon and inure to the benefit of the parties, their successors, assigns, and personal representatives. Signed this ________ day of May, 201X.

Owner ____________________________ Buyer ____________________________

CONSIGNMENT CONTRACT

Consignee and Consignor are defined terms

Agreement between Elizabeth Jones, owner of Betty's Boutique, "Consignee" and Robin Smith, "Consignor," made August 2, 201X.

WHEREAS:

This section is called recitals

Consignor designs and creates unique jewelry pieces "the Merchandise" and wishes to sell the Merchandise to the public, and

Consignee is the owner of a boutique store at 123 High Street, Geneva, "the Boutique" and wishes to be the exclusive area seller of the Merchandise,

Consignor and Consignee agree as follows:

1. OBLIGATIONS OF CONSIGNOR

a. Consignor shall deliver to the Boutique, on the first Monday morning of each calendar month, a quantity of Merchandise so that the total marked prices of all Consignor's Merchandise on display at the Boutique shall be in the range of $1,000 to $1,200 at all times.

b. Consignor shall attach to each piece of Merchandise a tag on which Consignor has marked the price at which the piece may be sold.

EXHIBIT 1-1
(continued)

2. OBLIGATIONS OF CONSIGNEE

a. Consignee shall at all times display all Merchandise in Consignee's possession in the glass display counter on which the cash register is located.

b. Consignee may display and sell other jewelry, but may not display other jewelry in the same display case as the Merchandise.

c. Whenever Consignee engages in print advertising, such advertising shall contain the statement, "Exclusive Kane County seller of Robin's Eggs jewelry."

d. Consignee shall use best efforts to sell the Merchandise at the marked price and shall not discount the Merchandise. Consignee shall display a sign and enforce a policy that no returns of the Merchandise will be allowed unless the Merchandise is defective. Any Merchandise returned as defective shall be returned to Consignor at the time of the next delivery of Merchandise and shall not be included in the accounting described below. Consignee may sell the Merchandise for cash, check, or credit, but Consignor shall not be responsible for any costs associated with selling on credit or any losses due to fraudulent use of credit or checks.

e. Consignee shall, on the first Monday of each calendar month, prepare an accounting of Merchandise sold during the previous calendar month, and deliver that account statement to Consignor along with a check representing sixty percent (60%) of the total amount paid for Merchandise (exclusive of sales tax) during the previous month.

3. RELATIONSHIP

a. Neither party is an employee of the other; neither has any interest in the business operation of the other except as described in this agreement. Consignee is Consignor's agent solely for the purpose of selling Merchandise.

b. Consignor shall retain title to Merchandise until sold to a customer and shall insure against loss by theft or casualty.

c. This agreement may not be assigned.

d. Consignor shall not sell or allow sale of Merchandise in Kane County except at Boutique.

________________________ ________________________

________________________ ________________________

Signatures Date

Formal
A contract required to be in a particular form

Informal
Contract for which no particular form is required

Void
An agreement with no legal effect

Voidable
One party has power to invalidate contract

Unenforceable
A contract, otherwise valid, that cannot be enforced in court

Limitations Period
Time limit on bringing lawsuit, based on statute of limitations

3. Other Classifications of Contracts

Some contracts must be in a particular form, for example, a **letter of credit.** These are **formal** contracts. All contracts for which no particular form is mandatory are **informal.**

An agreement that has no legal effect is referred to as **void.** If a person enters into a contract to perform an illegal act, for example, the contract is void. Neither party can enforce the contract. On the other hand, a contract's enforceability may be in the hands of one of the parties. For, if an adult and a minor enter into a contract, that contract is **voidable** at the option of the minor. If the minor does not void the contract, it remains in force.

Finally, a contract might be valid, but **unenforceable.** For example, an otherwise valid contract might be unenforceable because the **limitations period** (time limit on bringing a lawsuit) has passed. The parties might choose to honor an unenforceable contract, but they cannot obtain a court order to enforce it.

EXHIBIT 1-2
Letters of Credit and Bills of Lading

Letter of Credit
An irrevocable promise by a buyer's bank to pay the seller when conditions are met

A **letter of credit** is an irrevocable promise by a buyer's bank to pay the seller (generally through the seller's bank) when certain conditions are met. Letters of credit are used, almost exclusively, in international business, to manage unique risks, such as unexpected governmental interference or control of export/import, as well as problems stemming from buyers and sellers dealing in different currencies. The formalities for an international letter of credit are generally dictated by the Uniform Customs and Practices for Documentary Credits established by the International Chamber of Commerce. Letters of credit may also be used in other situations involving a need for an assurance that the buyer can pay, such as auctions. For example, see http://www.arb.ca.gov/cc/capandtrade/auction/forms/example_loc.pdf.

Here is how it works. Suppose that Big Box imports computers manufactured by Shanghai Sal (Sal). Sal banks with the Beijing Business Bank (BBB). Big Box banks at Elgin Federal (EF) in Texas and wants to buy $800,000 worth of computers from Sal. Understandably, Big Box does not want to pay in advance. Sal is willing to ship the computers and give Big Box 60 days to pay if Big Box provides a 90-day letter of credit for the full amount.

1. Big Box goes to EF and requests an $800,000 letter of credit with Sal as beneficiary.
2. EF will issue the letter after Big Box either deposits $800,000 plus fees or is approved for a loan in that amount.
3. EF sends the letter to BBB, which notifies Sal that payment is ready.

EXHIBIT 1-2 (continued)

4. Sal can ship the computers to Big Box with full assurance of payment.
5. On presentation of documents and compliance with terms listed in the letter, EF must transfer the $800,000 to BBB, which will credit Sal's account. If the documents are presented and the terms of the letter are met, the issuing bank is obligated to pay, even if the underlying transaction is not fulfilled (*i.e.*, the computers are never actually received or are defective). The bank is not required to pay if the documents are not presented or the terms are not met, even if the underlying transaction was fulfilled.

The documents and conditions normally include a **bill of lading,** which is documentation of the receipt of goods for shipment, issued by a party in the business of transporting goods; proof of insurance; a certificate showing clearance by customs officials; and a commercial invoice.

Bill of Lading
Documentation of the receipt of goods for shipment, issued by a party in the business of transporting goods

To see a sample letter of credit, go to http://www.fas.usda.gov/excredits/exlc.htm. To see a sample bill of lading, go to http://blanker.org/bill-lading.

Assignment 1-3

- Describe a situation other than an offer of a reward that fits the definition of unilateral contract. Describe a situation, other than the example given in this chapter that fits the definition of an implied contract. You may find it difficult to identify examples, yet you enter into such contracts regularly. It is important that you start to recognize these situations.
- Use CALR to find a case, decided in your state, involving an "implied contract" and a case involving a "unilateral contract" (your instructor will assign your topic). Describe the cases in a few sentences.

B. Alternatives to Contract

Sometimes people develop expectations based on facts that do not establish an enforceable contract. When those expectations are not met, they may try to obtain a remedy in court based on another theory.

Some of these theories are equitable theories. Because causes of action "at law," such as breach of contract, consist of rigid elements, they have often been regarded as too harsh. To mitigate the harshness, common law systems developed alternative equitable theories. These theories also give courts flexibility to fashion remedies that are more "fair" than the traditional "legal" computation of damages. Although an equitable remedy can involve payment of money, its calculation is different. Many jurisdictions traditionally had courts for seeking equitable remedies, called chancery courts, and separate courts of "law," and the courts followed different rules. Some of this inconsistency lingers on, adding to the complexity of the legal system.

Gift
Completed transfer of property without consideration

Donor
Person making a gift

Donee
Person receiving a gift

1. Gifts

As described in Chapter 5, a contract requires consideration (in very simple terms, mutual give and take). When consideration is lacking, the situation may be a gift. A gift becomes irrevocable when:

- a **donor** (person making the gift), with capacity (adult, sound mind, etc.)
- has voluntarily made a transfer
- that has been accepted by the **donee** (person receiving the gift).

A promise to make a gift is not a gift until transfer and acceptance are completed; if it is not supported by consideration, it is not a contract either. Consider: The only reason for identifying a completed gift is to prevent the donor from trying to reclaim the property. A gift that has not yet been transferred is not actually a gift, but only a promise. The only possibility for enforcement of an incomplete gift is promissory estoppel, discussed below.

Example

When looking at the elements of a legal claim, consider it an "all-or-nothing" proposition. When Lou finished his sophomore year at State U with a 4.0 grade point average, Dad was so pleased that he gave Lou a new notebook computer. During his junior year, Lou's grades took a slide. Dad now says that he has the right to reclaim the computer. He is likely wrong—the computer was a completed gift—all of the elements were satisfied. If, on the other hand, Dad had promised a computer and never delivered, Lou is out of luck.

---

2. Promissory Estoppel

Estoppel refers to preventing a person from "going back on his word." The concept applies in various areas of law. Promissory estoppel, an equitable theory that provides an alternative when neither contract nor gift applies, does not apply to all promises.

Alternate Example

At the end of sophomore year Lou told Dad that going to school on a shoestring budget was just too hard. Lou planned to take a year off to save money for "necessities" like a computer. Concerned that Lou would never return to school, Dad wrote a note, promising to give Lou a computer if Lou enrolled in and started classes for junior year. Lou took classes, rather than work, in reliance on Dad's promise, but after the start of the semester, Dad died. Dad's will leaves everything to Lou's stepmother. Lou may be able to make a successful claim against the estate.

Promissory estoppel is a legal theory for enforcing a promise if:

- The defendant knew the plaintiff would rely on the promise;
- The plaintiff did rely on the promise; and
- Enforcement is necessary to avoid injustice.

Promissory Estoppel
Theory under which a promise can be enforced, despite lack of consideration, because of reliance on that promise and knowledge of that reliance

In promissory estoppel cases, no contract ever formed because there was no consideration; the defendant's promise was essentially an incomplete gift. The difference between promissory estoppel and an incomplete gift is reliance on the promise.

Assignment 1-4

Medical Office called Insurance Co. to determine whether Pat Patient had insurance to cover removal of a cyst. A new clerk at the insurance company mistakenly stated that Pat had coverage; in fact, Pat's coverage had expired. Medical performed the procedure and billed Insurance for $1,900. Insurance is refusing to pay and Pat, unemployed for several months, cannot pay. There is no contractual relationship between Medical Office and Insurance. Medical Office has not given Insurance any benefit, payment, or other consideration, that would obligate Insurance to pay Pat's bill, but only acted in reliance.

1. In the previous example, Lou's dad "put it in writing." Does it make any difference that the "promise" in this situation was oral rather than written? Would you have a different opinion of the situation if Insurance had faxed its response? If you are like most people, you may feel, instinctively, that written promises should be enforceable simply because they are written and that oral promises are not enforceable simply because they were not written. Stop thinking like that! The **Statute of Frauds** (discussed later) dictates whether a contract must be in writing. Many oral agreements (including dad's promise, had it been oral, and Insurance Company's promise) are enforceable, but people are (rightfully) concerned with how to prove that the promise was made.

Statute of Frauds
Dictates types of contracts that must be written

2. On the subject of getting past emotional triggers, would your reaction to the examples change if Lou were suing his still-living father or if the Medical Office scenario involved a charity rather than an insurance company? Because estoppel is an **equitable** theory, based on fairness and individual circumstances rather than strict application of legal elements, the parties may matter.

Equitable
Based on fairness and individual circumstances

3. There is no question that the "contract" in this situation is between Pat and Medical Office. Should Insurance be "punished" for Pat's inability to pay, coupled with its employee's mistake?

4. Courts have good reason to protect the definition of a contract and avoid applying the estoppel doctrine freely. Suppose Dad always told Jill that he would pay her college tuition. In reliance, Jill worked only occasionally while in high school and spent all earnings on entertainment. Dad, having been laid off, now tells Jill that she will have to find a way to pay her own tuition. Do you think a court would enforce the promise?

5. Now, check your theories. Use CALR to find a case from a court in your state, in which the court either accepted or rejected a claim of estoppel. Write a summary (**case brief**) to share with the class, focusing on how the court described the "fairness" aspect of the situation. Pay particular attention to the identities of the parties and their relationship, who was at "fault," and any "bad behavior." You can find a sample case brief at the end of the chapter.

Case Brief
Short summary of facts, issues, holding, and reasoning of a judicial decision

3. Quasi-Contract

Quasi-contract
Theory for avoiding unjust enrichment in situations in which a contract did not actually form

Quasi-contract is another theory for avoiding the "gotcha" approach. It is an equitable theory, focused on fairness, rather than the elements of contract law. The "missing element" in quasi-contract is agreement.

Example

An infestation of pine moth has left many dead trees in the neighborhood. Pat, who lives at 123 N. Diane Lane, was told by Trees-R-Us that it would cost $1,800 to remove a dead tree and decided not to have it done. Chris, who lives at 123 S. Diane Lane, entered into a contract with Trees-R-Us for removal of a (smaller) dead tree at a cost of $1,300. Both Pat and Chris have "123" on their mailboxes and no other identification. One morning, Pat woke to the sound of saws in the yard, looked out, and saw Trees-R-Us employees taking down the dead tree. Thrilled at the $1,800 "gift," Pat called in sick and stayed in bed until the workers finished. When the company tries to bill Pat, what will result? The parties never had a contract.

Quasi-contract is a legal theory, based in equity, for compensating a plaintiff if:

- Plaintiff gave some benefit to the defendant;
- Plaintiff expected to be paid;
- Defendant had knowledge of plaintiff's actions and expectations; and
- Defendant would be unjustly enriched if not required to pay.

In the Trees-R-Us situation a contract can be **implied from the facts.** In other situations, the facts reveal nothing about defendant's knowledge. A contract might be **implied by law.** In other words, the law implies that the defendant would have consented in order to avoid unjust enrichment.

Example

Pat falls to the floor, unconscious, while grocery shopping. The store manager calls 911 and Pat is taken to a hospital. When Pat wakes up, the doctors discover that

Pat has been on a starvation diet and had not eaten in almost 24 hours. Pat does not have insurance and does not want to pay the $800 bill for emergency room treatment. Pat would never have agreed to be taken to the hospital or treated had he been conscious, and there is no evidence of behavior on Pat's part from which agreement can be implied, yet Pat may be liable.[1]

It's not "all academic." Institutions that regularly deal with gifts, contracts, and situations that might implicate estoppel or quasi-contract have to be concerned about the distinctions and have to educate their employees to avoid mistakes. Universities, for example, often have guidance online:

http://www.research.uci.edu/sponsored-projects/docs/gift-grant-contract.pdf
http://resadmin.uah.edu/documents/Gifts_Grants_Contracts.pdf
http://ora.research.ucla.edu/RPC/Documents/Gift_vs_grant_staff_Jan_2008.pdf

After examining these sites, how would you characterize a grant? Is it a contract or a gift?

Assignment 1-5

1. Use the Trees-R-Us example to discuss the following questions.
- Should Trees-R-Us receive $1,600 or $1,800? Would some other amount, to compensate for the hourly cost of the workers and equipment, be fair?
- Would it make a difference if Pat's mailbox clearly stated "123 North," along with Pat's last name?
- How can Trees-R-Us establish that Pat knew of the benefit being conferred?
- Should the result change if Pat had been at work when the tree was removed?

Test your theories:

2. Use CALR to find a case from your state that contains the term "quasi-contract" or "unjust enrichment" or "**quantum meruit.**" Write a short summary to share with the class. Focus on how the court determined correct compensation and how the knowledge element was established. The *Cruz* case, briefed at the end of this chapter, is a quasi-contract case. Instructions on how the case was found and a sample case brief are also included.

Quantum Meruit
An equitable theory for determining how to make the plaintiff "whole" where there is no contract dictating the amount to which a party is "legally" entitled; "as much as is deserved" to avoid unjust enrichment. This can involve payment of money, but is not the same as a legal award of damages

[1] *See Cotman v. Wisdom*, 104 S.W. 164 (Ark. 1907).

C. Practical and Ethical Issues

You've just studied two equitable concepts, estoppel and quasi-contract, developed from concepts of "fairness," but working in our legal system is not based in fairness. Our system is an adversarial system; the parties to a legal dispute are not neutral and are not seeking the "fairest" result. A lawyer's obligation, as an advocate, is to zealously assert the client's interests within the bounds of the law. But, in a contract situation, too much advocacy may be contrary to the client's interests. It is generally in the client's best interest that a contract be performed as agreed; arriving at an agreement that is too favorable to one side may motivate the other side to not honor its obligations.

Conflict of Interest
Ethical issue: legal professional's loyalties divided

Another ethical issue in contract law, relating to advocacy, is **conflict of interest.** A lawyer cannot be a zealous advocate if the lawyer has conflicting interests. Conflicts are discussed in ABA Model Rules 1.7-1.11. Using your state's online ethical rules, find and print rules relating to conflicts of interests with current clients, conflicts of interests with past clients, and imputed conflicts of interest.

A lawyer who is uncertain about the application of an ethics rule to a particular situation may seek an opinion from a bar association. The ABA Web site that provided a link to your state's Rules of Professional Conduct also contains links to state ethical opinions. Read Colorado Bar Association opinion 29, which can be found at https://www.cobar.org/index.cfm/ID/22347/CETH/Formal-Ethics-Opinions-/, and the *Spear* case, http://law.justia.com/cases/arizona/supreme-court/1989/sb-88-0009-d-3.html/. The case discusses a lawyer's ethical obligations in entering into a contract with a client and was found by searching for [attorney or lawyer & "conflict of interest" & contract]. Identify the two types of situations that most commonly result in a conflict in a contract matter.

Assignment 1-6

1. Identify the rule of professional conduct that would apply in your state to each of the following situations and discuss potential problems and possible solutions:

- John wants to buy land from his Aunt Lill, in order to build a house. They have agreed to all of the terms and do not want to pay two lawyers. Frank Fuller has been the "family lawyer" for many years and has handled matters for Lill when her parents died (she inherited the land she is now selling to John) and for John when he was involved in an auto accident. John and Lill ask Fuller to prepare all of the documents needed to complete the transaction.

- If Fuller is not willing to act as attorney for both John and Lill, can he act on behalf of one of them? Would it make a difference whether he represents John or Lill?
- Would Fuller be able to represent John if John were buying the land from a church that Fuller attends?
- Fuller has a partner in his law firm, Gail Grady. Could Gail represent either the church or Lill if Fuller were representing John? Could Gail represent John if Fuller were representing the church or Lill?

2. Discuss the following:

- Would the result in *Cruz* be the same if the case did not involve a licensed professional? Suppose that Benny Bigbux asked Sammy Student to help him locate a rare 1959 Mercedes Benz, in mint condition, in time for Benny's annual open house in May. Benny likes to show off his collection of rare cars at this party and agreed to pay Sammy 1% of the ultimate purchase price. Sammy spent hours online and driving to auction houses and finally located the perfect car at the end of April. Unfortunately, Benny and the car's owner are both very eccentric and hot-tempered. They were unable to agree to terms before the open house. Should Sammy be able to recover anything for the time and effort invested in the search?
- If you have reached the conclusion that courts often do consider a party's particular knowledge and sophistication, you are correct. Contracts involving lawyers, who are generally more knowledgeable and sophisticated than their clients, are particularly subject to scrutiny.
- How does the situation described in the Colorado ethical opinion (above) involve two parties with particular knowledge and sophistication? Might the court take a different view if the situation did not involve referrals from a bank?
- What were the unique, aggravating facts in the *Spear* case? Would the court have taken a different view if the property purchased by the client was not sold by the lawyer himself? Is the lawyer's training as a CPA important? Did the back-dating of documents have any particular significance?

3. Because of the nature of a unilateral contract, people sometimes enter contracts without realizing they are doing so, or if they do realize there is a contract, they do not understand its terms. For example, many people sign on to social networking sites without looking at the agreement. Visit http://www.facebook.com and examine the Statement of Rights and Responsibilities.

- How does a user indicate agreement to the terms set forth in the Statement?

- Under what circumstances may Facebook change the terms of this agreement?
- If a user is somehow harmed by Facebook and wants to file suit, is there a restriction on where the suit may be filed?

4. *Forest Park Pictures v. USA Network, Inc.* (2d Cir. 2012[2]) In 2005, Forest Park formulated a concept for a television show called "Housecall," in which a doctor, after being expelled from the medical community for treating patients who could not pay, moved to Malibu, California, and became a concierge doctor to the rich and famous. Forest Park created character biographies, themes, and storylines, which it mailed to Sepiol, who worked for USA Network. The parties had a meeting at which Forest Park "pitched" the show. Initial discussions failed. A little less than four years later, USA Network produced and aired a television show called "Royal Pains," in which a doctor, after being expelled from the medical community for treating patients who could not pay, became a concierge doctor to the rich and famous in the Hamptons. Forest Park sued USA Network for breach of contract. The district court held that the claim was preempted by the Copyright Act, 17 U.S.C. §101, and dismissed. The Second Circuit reversed. Forest Park adequately alleged the breach of a contract that included an implied promise to pay; the claim is based on rights that are not the equivalent of those protected by the Copyright Act and is not preempted.

- The court applied the theory of implied contract, but could this also be considered a quasi-contract situation?
- Did Forest Park simply give USA a gift?
- Might promissory estoppel apply?

Career Corner

Donna S. is Contracts Manager for a medical devices corporation in Seattle, where she evaluates, develops, and negotiates contracts, requests for proposals, and purchase orders. Donna started in the health care industry as a secretary at a time when they used carbon forms for contracts; she did not complete her paralegal education (while working full time) until she was over 40! Donna is quick to credit others for her career growth: "The second operations manager I worked for handed me the company's standard terms and conditions of sale and told me that every week we would review one section (there were 26 at the time). In half a year I would know everything the company considered important in contracting and would be able to discuss it when asked. That led to a promotion. . . . I was fortunate to have several wise managers over the past 20+ years, and several innovative instructors in my paralegal programs who gave me sound advice and encouragement to keep on learning and to become proficient at each position."

[2]http://law.justia.com/cases/federal/appellate-courts/ca2/11-2011/11-2011-2012-06-26.html.

Review Questions

1. What is the difference between promissory estoppel and quasi-contract?
2. Describe an implied contract to which you have recently been a party.
3. Identify three ways in which a conflict of interest may arise and ways in which the law firm might deal with the conflict, based on the Model Rules.
4. Explain how a letter of credit works.
5. Identify the issues presented by the following facts:
   Jay, a newly graduated paralegal, interviewed for a job in the legal department at Acme Co. During the interview, Jay was given an employee handbook. Among other things, the book described vacation benefits; during the first year of employment employees were to have three weeks paid vacation. Jay ultimately had job offers from Acme and from a major law firm. The firm offered slightly better pay than Acme, but Jay wanted the long vacations. Jay never spoke to anyone at Acme about vacation time and did not receive an employment contract when he accepted the job. After working for a few months, Jay asked his supervisor about taking the first week of his vacation time. The supervisor replied that Jay was entitled to only one week in the first year.

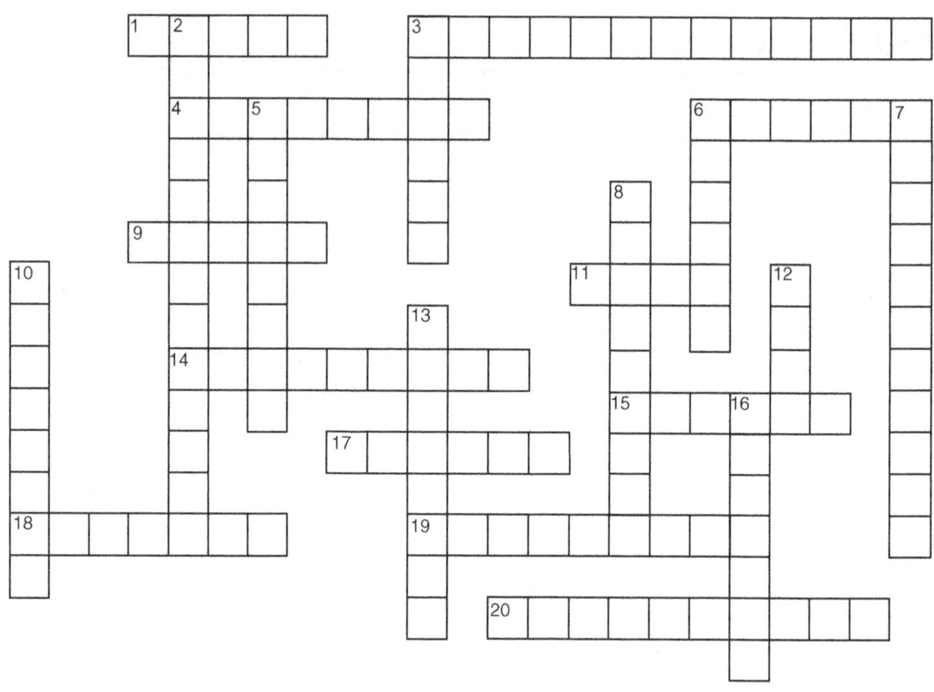

ACROSS

1. ________-contract; based on unjust enrichment
3. the mutual give and take necessary for a contract
4. contract with all duties fulfilled
6. contract that must be in a particular form
9. person who makes a gift
11. of no legal effect
14. contract with duties unfulfilled
15. based on fairness
17. bill of ________; documentation of receipt of goods for shipment
18. contract with terms written or spoken
19. contract formed by mutual promises
20. one party performs an act in response to a promise

DOWN

2. a valid contract might be ________ if the limitations period has passed
3. letter of ________; guarantees payment in international sales
5. promissory ________; promisor knew other would rely
6. statute of ________ determines whether contract must be written
7. ________ period; time for bringing lawsuit
8. both quasi-contract and promissory estoppel require certain ________ on the part of defendant
10. a gift is not complete until there has been a ________ of property
12. area of law dealing with injuries to people or property
13. one party has power to make agreement unenforceable
16. a contract that is not express

Sample Case: Finding and Briefing Cases for Assignments

CALR providers are very similar. If you use your school's subscription to Fastcase, Lexis, or WestLaw, follow instructions for that system. To find the *Cruz* case on the Loislaw system, the terms "quantum meruit" & "quasi contract" were entered in the Illinois case law database.

BRIEF OF *Cruz v. Stapleton*, 251 Ill. App. 3d 83, 622 N.E.2d 1253 (1993)

FACTS: Client sought to buy a house and orally agreed that Broker would assist her. Client gave Broker $500 to facilitate bidding. Client agreed to pay Broker $2000 if he succeeded at securing a contract to buy a house. Two offers failed to result in a purchase. Those offers included statements that Broker's fee would be paid at closing. Client told Broker that she no longer needed his services and requested return of the $500. Broker refused.

PROCEDURAL HISTORY: Client sued Broker for return of the $500 escrow; Broker counterclaimed, seeking $1,264 ($500 escrow plus $763) for his services. The trial court ruled in favor of Client. The appeals court affirmed.

ISSUE/ANSWER: Was Broker entitled to an hourly fee for his work on Client's behalf, under a theory of quasi-contract or quantum meruit?

> Tips:
>
> 1. Put the facts in chronological order and relate them in past tense.
> 2. For brevity, eliminate unnecessary facts. How can you tell whether a fact is necessary? Ask yourself whether changing the fact would change the result.
> 3. Do not make assumptions about the facts.
> 4. To keep track of the parties, create labels, such as "employer/worker" or "driver/passenger."
> 5. Do not include law or reasoning in the facts section.
> 6. You may want to write the procedural history first to remind you of where the case is in THIS court. Don't become confused between what the lower court(s) did and what is being done in this opinion.

No, Broker had no reasonable expectation of payment if he did not succeed in obtaining a contract for a house.

ARGUMENTS/HOLDING: Broker claimed that if he was not entitled to compensation under the oral contract, because that contract called for payment only upon closing of a purchase, he was still entitled to the reasonable value of his services. Broker claimed that Client's termination of the oral contract before he had a reasonable time to find a house made him unable to earn his fee. Rejecting the argument, the court stated that quasi-contract applies when there was no actual contract, but one party had a reasonable expectation of payment. It is not a vehicle for a party who made a bad agreement to ask a court to change that agreement. Broker, a license professional, had no reasonable expectation of being paid for his work if Client did not purchase a house.

2

Sources of Contract Law: Common Law and Uniform Commercial Code

◆ ◆ ◆

This chapter explains the distinction between contracts governed by common law and those governed by the Uniform Commercial Code (UCC). It introduces the contents of the Code as a whole and Article 2, in particular, and explains how and why the Code differs from common law. In addition, you will learn to take a "holistic" approach and be aware that many other sources of law may govern the contracts of the clients you serve.

Skills-based learning objectives	*How you will demonstrate your ability*
Identify the roles of administrative agencies in contract law.	Assignment: Perform online research of state agencies and of agency regulations.
Analyze and use state adoptions of UCC and Restatement.	Assignments: Research state version of UCC; find case adopting Restatement; prepare a case brief.

A. Common Law
B. Uniform Commercial Code
   1. Coverage
   2. Departures from Common Law
C. Other Statutes
D. International Law

E. Administrative Law
F. Practical and Ethical Issues
G. Dealing with Changes in the Law

You are familiar with the five sources of law: the Constitution, the courts, legislative bodies, the executive branch, and administrative agencies. Three of these sources are particularly important in working with contracts: the courts, legislative bodies, and administrative agencies.

These sources are important to your understanding of substantive law and can also dictate your career path. While you might think that "Contract Law" is a narrow specialty in the law, many legal professionals develop expertise in contract law from a particular source. In addition to organizations like the National Contract Management Association, for example, there is a LinkedIn group for UCC-Article 9 Professionals. Members of the American Contract Compliance Association focus on government and employment contracts. The International Association for Contract & Commercial Management offers support for public and private sector organizations and professionals dealing with international contracts. Certifications are available for construction contract managers. For those working with defense and other federal contracts, there are specialized certifications available under the Defense Acquisition Workforce Improvement Act. For further information, visit http://www.fai.gov/drupal/ and http://www.dau.mil/.

A. Common Law

Common Law
Law from judicial decisions; governs contract disputes involving real property, intangible property, and services

Real Estate
Also called real property or realty, consists of land and buildings

Intangible Property
Has no physical existence, such as debt

Intellectual Property
Includes patents, trademarks, copyrights, trade secrets

Services
Actions, not items

Restatement of Contracts
Summary of judicial doctrines on contract law

Contract law evolved in the courts, over the course of hundreds of years. **Common law** (from judicial decisions) and statutes other than the UCC (discussed in the next section) still govern many contract disputes, particularly those involving **real estate** (land and buildings), **intangible property** (not having a physical existence—*e.g.*, the debt your brother owes because he borrowed $500 from you), **intellectual property** (patents, copyrights, trademarks, and trade secrets), and **services** (such as employment contracts and insurance). In some respects common law reflects the assumptions and practices of another age. In addition, the common law evolved differently in different jurisdictions.

In an effort to clarify and simplify the common law, the American Law Institute (ALI; http://www.ali.org) drafted the **Restatement of Contracts** in 1932 and has revised it over the years. A Restatement is essentially a summary of judge-made doctrines that have developed over time; it is persuasive because it is formulated over several years with extensive input from law professors, practicing attorneys, and judges. At its best, the Restatement reflects the consensus of the legal community as to what the law is (and in some areas, what it should become).

Because ALI is a private group, the Restatement is not "the law," but it is well respected. Part of the Restatement becomes the law of a jurisdiction when a court relies on it in making a decision. Courts often do rely on the Restatement because its sections accurately state established law in the jurisdiction, or, on issues of first impression (issues not previously considered by the court), are persuasive to show the trend that other jurisdictions are following.

Assignment 2-1

Have the courts of your state used the Restatement as authority on contract law? Use your computer-assisted legal research (CALR) account to find a case in which a court in your state referred to the Restatement of Contracts.

B. Uniform Commercial Code

1. Coverage

The need for a more modern, uniform body of law gave rise to the **Uniform Commercial Code (UCC).** The UCC was initially developed by a private group that lacked authority to make law, but all 50 states eventually enacted some version of the Code. Because uniformity is most needed when a transaction involves different states, the UCC was drafted to cover transactions that often have roots in different states, including the sale (and, in some states, lease) of moveable items (also called **personal property, chattel,** or **goods**), but it is not limited to interstate transactions. The UCC also covers transactions involving the following:

Uniform Commercial Code (UCC)
A uniform law, enacted as statutory law in all 50 states, in an attempt to harmonize the law of sales and other commercial transactions.

Personal Property
Also called "goods" or "chattel," consists of tangible, moveable items

- **Negotiable instruments** (a signed, unconditional promise or order to pay a certain sum—*e.g.*, checks, notes, certificates of deposit);
- Banking;
- Documents of title;
- Investment securities;
- **Bulk sales** (transfer of a major part of inventory, outside the normal course of business); and
- **Letters of credit** (written documents, usually issued by a bank, promising to honor drafts or other payment instruments issued by its customer or another person).

Assignment 2-2

Visit the Web site for your state legislature and find the online site for your state's code (statutes). A simple way to find the site is to go to http://www.ncsl.org/public/leglinks.cfm and select your state and "statutes." When you get to the page for your state code, bookmark it! Scan the topics until you find your state's version of the UCC. If the list of topics does not contain "Uniform Commercial Code," look at all topics containing the word "commercial."

1. Find the section of the UCC titled "sales," and make a list of the "parts" and major subtopics. You will have to refer to many of these topics in later chapters because they deal with formation and interpretation of contracts and remedies, when something goes wrong. For example, you should find provisions concerning contract formalities and implied warranties.
2. Not all states have enacted all sections of the UCC. Are leases of goods covered by your state's enactment of the Code?

The Articles of the Code are listed on the next page. This book will focus on Article 2, concerning sales of goods, so understanding the term "goods" is essential. Goods include items with a physical existence that are moveable at the time of identification to the contract. A crop of corn growing in the field is not currently moveable, but when it is harvested and set aside to fulfill a purchase contract, it will be moveable—so the crop is covered by the Code. The money used to pay the price of a contract does not come within the definition of "goods," but a collection of coins being sold would come within the definition. Investment securities are not covered by Article 2 but are covered by Article 8. Security interests (liens) on goods, such as a lien to secure financing for the merchandise on the shelves of a store or the financing of an 18-wheel truck, are covered by Article 9.

Out-of-Date?

Some say that the UCC focus on goods reflects the economy of a bygone era, when commerce was driven by tractors and tires. Today's economy is more dependent on information and communication. For that reason, many people believe that the Code should apply to advertising claims and technology products. While recent amendments to Article 2 show movement in that direction, no state has adopted the amendments as of this writing. In addition, some courts apply UCC rules to problems that would not fit within the definition of goods.

Article 2 creates a body of contract law governing a huge number of contracts, but some kinds of contracts implicate other Articles. For example, a contract to have a barn painted is not covered by the UCC; but if the owner writes a check to pay for the service, Article 3, relating to negotiable instruments, governs liability under and handling of the check.

This text focuses on the UCC as it governs contracts for the sale of goods, but there is much more to it. Much of the law governing banking comes from the Code; see http://www.law.syr.edu/Pdfs/0BankingLaw.pdf.

EXHIBIT 2-1
Coverage of the UCC

ARTICLE 1:

Purposes of the law; rules of construction; definitions; general principles (*e.g.*, obligation of good faith)

ARTICLE 2:

Contracts for the sale of goods

ARTICLE 2A:

Leases of goods (not adopted in every state)

ARTICLE 3:

Negotiable instruments

ARTICLE 4:

Bank deposits and collections

ARTICLE 4A:

Funds transfers (banking)

ARTICLE 5:

Letters of credit

ARTICLE 6:

Bulk transfers (repealed in many states)

ARTICLE 7:

Warehouse receipts, bills of lading, and other documents of title (proof of ownership of goods being stored or transported)

ARTICLE 8:

Investment securities (stock and other ownership interests)

ARTICLE 9:

Secured transactions (a security interest is an interest in personal property to secure performance of an obligation; *e.g.*, a loan to buy a car is generally secured by the right to take possession of the car)

For overviews of the UCC, see http://www.law.cornell.edu/ucc/2/overview.html and http://www.law.cornell.edu/ucc/9/overview.html.

Commercial
Between or pertaining to businesses

Consumer
Party to the contract who is not engaged in business but has entered the contract for personal or family reasons

Merchants
Deal in goods of the kind involved in transaction or, by their occupations, hold themselves out as having knowledge or skills relating to the goods or practice

If a contract is mixed (*i.e.,* concerns goods and services), the relevant law depends on the dominant category. For example, payment for installation of custom shelving might be one-third for material and two-thirds for labor. If the contract separates the two—for example, $900 for purchase of materials at LumberLand and $1,800 for carpentry—the UCC may apply to the purchase of materials, while common law applies to the contract for work.

The name "Uniform Commercial Code" is not entirely accurate. Because the UCC has been revised, and different revisions have been adopted by different states at different times, it is not truly "uniform" across the states. Similarly, the Code is not limited to **commercial** transactions (between businesses), but also covers some **consumer** transactions between people not engaged in business. The UCC does contain some provisions applicable only to **merchants,** defined as those who deal in goods of the kind involved in the transaction or who, by their occupations, hold themselves out as having knowledge or skills relating to the goods or practices involved in the transaction, or to whom such knowledge or skills may be attributed.

Assignment 2-3

The meaning of "goods" is sometimes an issue. Use your CALR subscription and search all states for cases (as assigned by your instructor) discussing whether:

- Sale of electricity falls within the definition;
- Sale of computer software falls within the definition.

Summarize the cases.

The UCC was drafted by a private group, with no power to enact laws, and became law only when the individual state legislatures enacted its provisions, so it is important to work with your state's enactment. As with most statutory law, judicial decisions remain an important source of interpretation of the Code. For example, the UCC makes several references to a "reasonable" period of time. What does that mean? Does it mean the same thing when applied to a shipment of lettuce as when applied to a shipment of drinking glasses? To find out, you would have to research cases **decided under the UCC,** involving shipment of produce and cases involving shipment of housewares.

2. Departures from Common Law

The philosophy behind the UCC is to make it easier for people to make contracts that meet their needs, but at the same time to fill in missing provisions, when people fail to cover every possibility. The UCC is intended to promote commerce, reflects modern business practices, and is not as rigid as common law, but the basic framework of contract law remains the same. This book is, therefore, organized according to that basic framework. The differences between the UCC and the common law are discussed in depth in the relevant chapters.

THE UCC

- Encourages fair play
  - Requires that "[e]very contract or duty within this Act imposes an obligation of **good faith** in its performance or enforcement"
  - Imposes greater responsibility on merchants
  - Defines unconscionability as a contract that is fundamentally unfair
  - Upholds certain modifications without new consideration
- Encourages resolution of disputes without resort to litigation
  - Establishes presumptions concerning passing of title (ownership), risk of loss, and transportation
  - Establishes presumptions concerning warranties
  - Establishes rights and obligations concerning performance, breach, and remedies
- Acknowledges the way businesses really operate
  - Allows enforcement of an agreement despite open terms and, in some cases, despite addition of or contradiction of terms
  - Allows formation in any manner that shows agreement
  - Is less rigid with respect to contracts that must be in writing
  - Repeatedly refers to "reasonable" performance, industry practices, and past dealings between the parties

Good Faith
UCC definition: as applied to a merchant, means honesty in fact and the observance of reasonable commercial standards of fair dealing in the trade

C. Other Statutes

Clients in some industries must be made aware of laws, other than contract law, that govern aspects of contracts they enter. While this book cannot cover every statute that has an impact on some types of contracts, you should be aware of the major categories. Note that many of these laws involve disclosure and many are intended to protect consumers, those who enter into a contract for personal or family reasons.

As a working paralegal, you should make it a habit to look for these laws. Surprisingly, clients are often unaware of the many laws affecting their business dealings. Learn to search Web sites of local governing bodies, state legislation, and regulatory agencies to find these laws and you will be a valuable part of the legal team.

- **Real estate transactions** are heavily regulated. For example, federal law includes (among others) the Fair Housing Act, the Interstate Land Full Disclosure Act, the Real Estate Settlement Procedures Act, various environmental laws, and many laws relating to mortgages. Many states have laws requiring disclosures concerning the condition of the property and laws protecting tenants in residential leases. Local law generally includes zoning restrictions and rules regarding the recording of leases, options, and other agreements in the public records of title.

- Contracts involving **lending,** especially consumer loans, may be governed by (among others) the Federal Consumer Credit Protection Act, the Equal Credit Opportunity Act, the Truth in Lending Act, the Fair Credit and Charge Card Disclosure Act, the Fair Credit Billing Act, the Fair Credit Reporting Act, or the Fair Debt Collection Practices Act. Most states also have laws.
- Contracts involving **intellectual property** may implicate state and federal trademark statutes, the federal Patent Act, or copyright laws, as interpreted by common law.
- A contract that may **restrain competition,** for example, by limiting a party's ability to do business with others, may be subject to federal or state antitrust laws.
- Most states have laws concerning the sale of **vehicles;** dealerships are also regulated by the Federal Trade Commission (FTC) (discussed later in this chapter).
- Any business with high **potential for fraud** or an industry history of abusing consumers, such as sale of pre-need funeral packages, or sale of dance lessons or health club memberships, may be subject to special state or local laws.
- Many businesses must be **licensed** by federal, state, or local authorities. For example, it might surprise a client to learn that in some states only a licensed cosmetologist can braid hair for customers.
- Any contract involving a **governmental body or a public official** may be subject to laws concerning bidding, accounting, or conflicts of interests.
- **Employment** contracts may implicate labor and antidiscrimination laws.
- Finally, if a contract involves **countries other than the United States,** the parties must comply with export and/or tariff laws.

D. International Law

Although international law is beyond the scope of this book, you should be aware of the existence of treaties and protocols governing international contracts. Chapter 1 discussed the International Chamber of Commerce publications dealing with letters of credit. In addition, the United States has ratified the United Nations Convention on Contracts for the International Sales of Goods, which is like an international version of the UCC. The United Nations has a Web site on which you can see some of those treaties: http://untreaty.un.org; the World Trade Organization's site is http://www.wto.org.

Contracts within Europe find guidance from the European Union (EU), which has adopted directives aimed at eliminating obstacles to contracting between member countries, particularly with respect to electronic commerce, insurance and banking, intellectual and industrial property, and consumer protection. The

EU does not possess general regulatory power in areas such as contract law but can only intervene in cases that require a solution at EU level. For more information, visit http://ec.europa.eu/internal_market/contractlaw/index_en.htm.

E. Administrative Law

Legislation, including many of the statutes listed above, is often enforced by federal, state, or local administrative agencies. These agencies enact regulations that govern specific aspects of contracts or govern contracts involving a particular type of transaction or a regulated industry.

Example

Consider the administrative agencies that might be involved in the contracts necessary for building and opening a small restaurant, even assuming that the land has already been purchased:

- Contracts for the location and construction of the building might be subject to the requirements of the U.S. Environmental Protection Agency, a state department of environmental protection, the highway department, local zoning and planning commissions, and the local department of building inspection;
- Contracts with employees may require consideration of agency regulations concerning worker safety (OSHA), compensation for workers injured on the job, unemployment compensation, tax and Social Security withholding, wages and hours, even immigration status;
- Contracts with customers may implicate department of health or U.S. Food and Drug Administration regulations;
- Contracts with suppliers may implicate antitrust regulations, regulations concerning truck deliveries. . . .

It is no wonder that many clients regard agencies as the "bureaucracy" that creates the "red tape" that hinders American business. In fact, dealing with agencies can be complicated and frustrating, but there are many good things about administrative agencies:

- Agencies are increasingly user-friendly. It is now possible to access their regulations and forms, complete required filings, and ask questions through Web sites.
- Agencies create and enforce regulations that protect our quality of life.
- Agencies often provide assistance with problems faced by consumers who are not able to retain private lawyers.
- Agencies employ many paralegals. Among federal agencies, the Department of Justice is the largest employer, followed by the Social Security Administration and the Department of the Treasury.
- Expertise in dealing with agencies enables paralegals to find high-level jobs with law firms and corporations.

- Many agencies allow paralegals and other nonlawyers to represent clients in ways that would not be allowed in a court. For example, the Social Security Administration Web site states: "you may appoint any person who is not an attorney to be your representative in dealings with us if the person — (1) is generally known to have a good character and reputation; (2) is capable of giving valuable help to you in connection with your claim; (3) is not disqualified or suspended from acting as a representative in dealings with us; and (4) is not prohibited by any law from acting as a representative." 20 C.F.R. §404.1705(b).

EXHIBIT 2-2
AGENCIES AND JOBS

Almost all federal and state agencies have an employment category called "paralegal," but your education may qualify you for many additional job categories, for example, Contract Specialist, Contract Administrator, or Procurement Analyst. For example, in 2016 the Department of Health and Human Services was advertising to fill this job:

DUTIES

Responsible for all pre-award and post-award functions on contracts, nearly all of which are complex and differ greatly from each other. Acquisitions include cost-reimbursement, cost-sharing, and fixed price type actions.

Responsible for a full range of contracts, including competitive and sole source requirements under special acquisitions regulations governing them.

Review, analyze, and implement acquisition policies and procedures issued by various federal organizations, as well as by the Department of Health and Human Services (DHHS) and the FDA.

Review and evaluate legal administrative and other issuances that impinge on privacy, consultants, and Freedom of Information Act (FOIA) clearance.

Provide technical guidance to junior Contract Specialist on all aspects of pre-award acquisitions and contract administration activities.

QUALIFICATIONS REQUIRED:

[Information concerning federal employment grades omitted.]

B. A 4-year course of study leading to a bachelor's degree, that included or was supplemented by at least 24 semester hours in any combination of the following fields: accounting, business, finance, law, contracts, purchasing, economics, industrial management, marketing, quantitative methods, or organization and management.

Assignment 2-4

1. The FTC is the federal agency most concerned with consumer contracts. Visit http://www.ftc.gov, and navigate through the pages "for business" to "products and services" to find pages explaining the Magnuson-Moss Warranty Act. The Act was intended to improve on the warranty provisions of the UCC. Does the Act apply to oral warranties? Does it require that sellers provide a written warranty? What are the requirements for a full warranty?
2. Navigate through the FTC "legal" tab; list the statutes enforced by the FTC as part of its consumer protection mission.
3. From your state's official homepage, find the list of state agencies, boards, and departments. Identify agencies that govern particular types of businesses. Next, find the page for your state's attorney general (most likely to regulate consumer contracts). Is there a division or department for consumer protection? Identify any consumer protection rules that might be relevant to contracts. Does your state have a "lemon law" applicable to automobile sales? Does it have a three-day right of rescission (cancellation) for certain contracts?
4. Use http://www.usajobs.gov to determine which agencies are currently advertising for contract specialists or contract administrators.

Why regulate specific contract provisions rather than leaving it to the marketplace? After all, every person is free to accept or reject contract terms depending on the particular situation, right? An example of a limited warranty is reproduced below. Would the average buyer read it? Could that buyer understand it? Could the buyer obtain the product without agreeing to this term? Presumably this warranty complied with applicable statutes and regulations; how might this term be different (worse for the buyer) if those statutes and regulations did not exist?

Keep in mind that most contract law, from any of these sources, is backup law. The UCC or common law may dictate whether a set of promises is a contract and may require certain formalities, but the parties are generally free to negotiate the substantive provisions. Much of contract law applies only if the parties have not addressed the topic in their contract.

Do the laws from various sources ever conflict? Yes; for example, some states have specific statutes concerning blood for transfusions. Those laws may conflict with the UCC's general provisions, which include blood within the general category of "goods." Normally the more specific law (the specific "blood" statute) prevails.

Example of a Limited Warranty

This Software is subject to a limited warranty. *Licensor warrants to Licensee that physical medium on which Software is distributed is free from defects in materials and* *workmanship. Under normal use, Software will perform according to its printed documentation. To the best of Licensor's knowledge Licensee's use of this Software according to the printed documentation is not an infringement of any third party's intellectual property rights. This limited warranty lasts for a period of 90 days after delivery. To the extent permitted by law, THE ABOVE-STATED LIMITED WARRANTY REPLACES ALL OTHER WARRANTIES, EXPRESS OR IMPLIED, AND LICENSOR DISCLAIMS ALL IMPLIED WARRANTIES INCLUDING ANY IMPLIED WARRANTY OF TITLE, MERCHANTABILITY, NONINFRINGEMENT, OR OF FITNESS FOR A PARTICULAR PURPOSE. No agent of Licensor is authorized to make any other warranties or to modify this limited warranty. Any action for breach of this limited warranty must be commenced within one year of the expiration of the warranty. Because some jurisdictions do not allow any limit on the length of an implied warranty, the above limitation may not apply to this Licensee. If the law does not allow disclaimer of implied warranties, then any implied warranty is limited to 90 days after delivery of the Software to Licensee. Licensee has specific legal rights pursuant to this warranty and, depending on Licensee's jurisdiction, may have additional rights. In case of a breach of the Limited Warranty, Licensee's exclusive remedy is as follows: Licensee will return all copies of the Software to Licensor, at Licensee's cost, along with proof of purchase. At Licensor's option, Licensor will either send Licensee a replacement copy of the Software, at Licensor's expense, or issue a full refund. Notwithstanding the foregoing, LICENSOR IS NOT LIABLE TO LICENSEE FOR ANY DAMAGES, INCLUDING COMPENSATORY, SPECIAL, INCIDENTAL, EXEMPLARY, PUNITIVE, OR CONSEQUENTIAL DAMAGES, CONNECTED WITH OR RESULTING FROM THIS LICENSE AGREEMENT OR LICENSEE'S USE OF THIS SOFTWARE.*

F. Practical and Ethical Issues

If you work for a law firm, you will regularly encounter or implement the terms of a contract: the contract between the firm and the client. Every state has an agency that regulates lawyers and is, therefore, relevant to that contract. That agency likely is the source of ethical opinions and investigates violations of the Rules of Professional Conduct used in previous chapters.

To find the agency for your state, visit the ABA Web site and locate the State Directory of Disciplinary Agencies. To what extent does the agency involve itself in the attorney-client contract? Does it have a fee arbitration board or a grievance procedure? Does it have a "lawyer search" feature that gives a lawyer's address, disciplinary status, or other information?

G. Dealing with Changes in the Law

CAUTION! THIS BOOK COULD BE WRONG!

Something may have changed while this book was being printed or shipped to your bookstore. As you know, the common law has the potential to change with every case decided. Even statutes are amended regularly. As Professor Larry Garvin wrote in 1999, in the *Florida State University Law Review*, "The Uniform Commercial Code of today is not the Uniform Commercial Code of our youth. . . . Since 1990, most of the Code has been revised or written anew, including those parts now under change. State legislatures have been busy keeping up with the onslaught of revised articles, new articles, and conforming amendments; law professors have come out with many profitable new editions of casebooks; practitioners have attended countless slumbrous CLE sessions in which the new rules were more or less explained. If only through revision, commercial law is a growth industry."

As recently as 2003, the National Conference of Commissioners on Uniform State Laws® (now known as the Uniform Law Commission) and the American Law Institute® approved amendments to Article 2 of the UCC. Individual states have not rushed to adopt the changes and many groups oppose revisions. You may someday work with a client with valid reasons for opposing changes. Let's change the last sentence: To find the current status of your state's version of the Code, visit https://www.law.cornell.edu/uniform/ucc.

How do legal professionals keep up with these changes? As noted by Professor Garvin, they sometimes attend continuing legal education sessions (CLE), but very often they do not have time to attend those sessions. Sometimes governmental agencies amend their forms and information to make practitioners aware of changes. The following language appeared on the Web site for the Illinois Secretary of State:

> The administration of the UCC has an important impact on the economy and upon the rights of the public, in this state & in the United States. The volume of international, interstate & multistate transactions pursuant to the UCC requires that the administration of the UCC be conducted in a manner that promotes both local & multi-jurisdictional commerce by striving for uniformity in policies and procedures among the various states.
>
> Article 9 of the Uniform Commercial Code was amended effective July 1, 2001, as a part of a nationwide effort by the National Conference of Commissioners on Uniform State Laws. The amendments made sweeping changes to the law in Illinois and other states with the purpose of bringing greater certainty to financing transactions. Section 5 of Article 9 charges the Secretary of State's office with the duty of accepting financing statements for filing and maintaining a record keeping system to allow quick and accurate searches by lenders and others.
>
> EFFECTIVE OCTOBER 1, 2001
>
> DUE TO NEW POLICIES IN THE UCC DIVISION ALL FORMS MUST BE TYPEWRITTEN, INCLUDING SEARCHES. THIS MEANS THAT WE WILL START REJECTING ALL HANDWRITTEN INFORMATION, SUCH AS TYPE OF ORGANIZATION, JURISDICTION AND ORGANIZATION ID NUMBER. ALSO PLEASE KEEP IN MIND THAT THE DEBTOR AND SECURED PARTY INFORMATION MUST BE IN ALL CAPS AND 12 POINT TIMES NEW ROMAN FONT.

There is not always an agency to provide notice, however, so a diligent paralegal always checks the current status of the law in the relevant jurisdiction before taking action or making a recommendation. Your ability to check the current status of the law and your inclination to do so will make you a valuable asset to your firm and ensure your success! If your job requires that you keep current, there are a number of sites to check regularly. Find the ContractsProf blog page for UCC legislative updates.

Review: Research for Drafting, Interpreting, or Litigating a Contract Issue

1. Determine whether the contract is governed by the UCC or by common law. The UCC governs any contract that primarily involves the sale of **goods.** Other sections of the UCC govern negotiable instruments, such as checks. Common law governs contracts involving **real property** or **intellectual property** and contracts involving services.
2. Determine the relevant state. If you are dealing with an existing contract, it probably includes a "choice of governing law" provision, in which the parties have agreed that the law of a particular state will govern.[1] If you are helping to negotiate or draft a contract, you may include such a provision. If you are dealing with a contract that has ties to two or more states and that does not include a choice of law, you may have to research choice of law precedents.
3. Familiarize yourself with the relevant provisions of the UCC, as adopted by the relevant state, or the relevant common law of that state.
4. Determine whether the subject of the contract (*e.g.*, consumer financing) or the business involved in the contract (*e.g.*, a lender) is regulated by a state or federal administrative agency that may have rules governing contracts.

Career Corner

Neal Huffman has made a career as an expert in contract law. After serving in the U.S. Army, Neal studied at the ABA-approved Denver Paralegal Institute. He later earned a Master's Degree in Technology Management and has certifications in leadership and communications, as well as the National Contract Management Association Certificate as a Commercial Contracts Manager (CCCM). He is a CORE Registered Paralegal (CRP) through the National Federation of Paralegal Associations. As a believer in giving back to his community, Neal has taught for an ABA-approved paralegal program and is active in several volunteer organizations. After several years of working as a contract manager and senior contract manager, Neal founded his own firm, specializing in business, contracts, and commercial transactions for attorneys, corporate counsel, and commercial businesses. Asked about the future for paralegals in contract work, Neal said: "Contracts management is an exciting—and evolving—career. In many ways, it has not kept pace with technology and thus

[1] A "choice of law" provision requiring application of the law of a jurisdiction with no relationship to the contract or parties may be unconstitutional or violate public policy.

there is vast opportunity, and growth, at the intersection of contracts and contracting tools which will provide significant and dynamic career opportunities for new entrants and future leaders."

Review Questions

1. Which of the following contracts would be covered by Article 2 of the UCC? Explain your reasoning.
   a. A California corporation is buying the Willis Tower (Chicago).
   b. Ian Investor is selling 10,000 shares of stock in McDonald's Corp.
   c. American Pharoah, winner of the 2015 Kentucky Derby, is being sold to a horse breeder in Michigan.
   d. Farmer Brown, planning to quit farming and develop the land, sells his entire crop of apples, to be harvested in three months, as well as the trees themselves, to be cut and processed into mulch immediately after harvest.
   e. Jamie takes a job on an assembly line, manufacturing automobiles, and signs an employment contract.
   f. Farmer Brown hires an exterminator to apply pesticides to his 50-acre farm.
   g. You go to your bank and borrow $1,500 to pay off a high-interest credit card that you used to buy books and clothes last semester. The bank does not require collateral
   h. Harry's, a popular tourist spot that has a maze, cider, and other autumn attractions, buys a whole crop of pumpkins in June, while they are still growing.
   i. A contractor agrees to remodel a bathroom for $10,000, which includes about $3,000 for new fixtures
   j. You agree to take a job, in a neighboring state, for a salary of $45,000 per year
   k. When Lynn sold her house, the buyer insisted on a new furnace. Lynn buys a new furnace, which will be installed before the new owner moves in.
2. What is the Restatement?
3. Why is the UCC not really uniform?
4. In what ways does the UCC acknowledge the informal ways in which modern businesses often operate?
5. In what ways does the UCC encourage fair play?
6. In what ways does the UCC discourage litigation?
7. Identify types of contracts still covered by common law.
8. Other than sale of goods, name the major activities/transactions covered by the UCC.
9. Name the state and federal agencies most concerned with regulating consumer contracts.
10. Identify particular types of contracts likely to be subject to particular statutes or regulations.

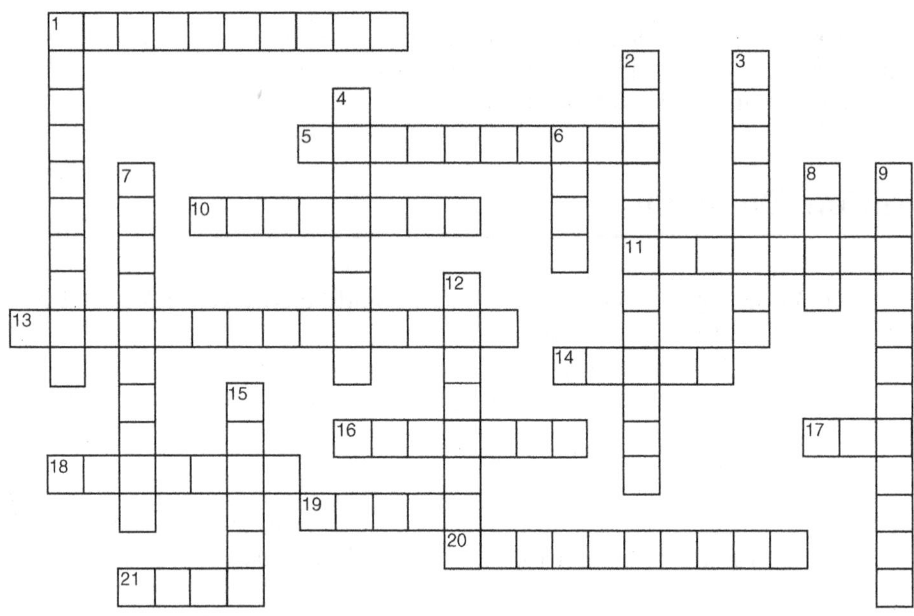

ACROSS

1. property without a physical existence
5. __________ instrument, an unconditional, signed promise or order to pay a certain sum
10. UCC often refers to __________ practices
11. one who is in the business of selling the goods
13. cases are still relevant to __________ of UCC terms
14. UCC imposes a duty of good
16. UCC includes an article dealing with __________ transactions, in which goods serve as security for payment
17. initials; federal agency responsible for consumer protection
18. another term for personal property
19. __________ of goods is covered by UCC in some states
20. a term frequently used in UCC to describe time, etc.
21. __________ dealings between parties; often relevant under UCC

DOWN

1. UCC includes an article dealing with stock and other __________ securities
2. UCC contains __________ regarding risk of loss, transportation, etc.
3. UCC does not cover contracts for
4. __________ property = goods
6. __________ sale of large amount of inventory, not in the regular course of business

7. transactions between businesses
8. __________ property transactions are not covered by UCC
9. __________ property: patents, trademarks
12. a transaction for personal or family use
15. letter of __________; bank promises to honor checks of customer

3

◆ ◆ ◆

Agreement

◆ ◆ ◆

The most common question in contract law is whether the parties reached an agreement and, if so, when it was reached. This chapter focuses on the critical distinction between negotiation and agreement and on the factors relevant to that distinction.

Skills-based learning objectives	*How you will demonstrate your ability*
Identify potential pitfalls during contract negotiation and formation.	Assignment: Analyze cases in which parties' actions were ambiguous.
Locate and analyze provisions in state UCC and judicial interpretations of those provisions.	Assignment: Find specific sections in state adoption of UCC and cases interpreting those sections.

A. Offer
   1. Definite Terms in an Offer
   2. Essential Terms
   3. Communication of an Offer
   4. Lifespan of an Offer
      a. Revocation
      b. UCC Firm Offer
      c. Rejection/Counteroffer
      d. Termination by Operation of Law
B. Acceptance
   1. Implied Acceptance
   2. Mailbox Rule

3. Mirror Image Rule
4. Battle-of-the-Forms Rule
C. Practical and Ethical Issues
D. Preparing for Contract Negotiations

What, exactly, is a contract and when does it form? That is the question posed by a situation described in the *Chicago Tribune* on August 14, 2014. In 2013, Steven Salaita was offered a tenured position at the University of Illinois, at an $85,000 annual salary. Salaita signed the offer letter. Several months later, but before Salaita began teaching at U of I, Salaita posted tweets criticizing Israel in its conflict with Hamas, including some that contained vulgar language. The University informed Salaita by e-mail that he would not have the job. The University stated that his appointment was subject to approval by its board of trustees, and that the appointment would not be submitted to the board because approval was unlikely. Would your analysis of this situation change if Salaita had resigned from another job, sold his house, and moved to Illinois in anticipation of the job?

A contract begins with an agreement. Legal scholars sometimes refer to a "meeting of the minds," but in practice an agreement is the "manifestation" (indication) of mutual assent by the parties. The "manifestation" is important because we cannot read each other's minds and must rely on an **objective standard:** what reasonably appears to be true, based on the surrounding circumstances. Those circumstances include the previous relationship of the parties, the context (in a bar vs. in a business meeting), the words used by the parties, and what motivated the "offer."

Objective Standard
Used to determine whether parties had "meeting of the minds," looks to what a reasonable person would believe, based on circumstances

---

Example

The objective standard is another way in which contract law eschews the "gotcha." Lynn knows that her coworker, Mary, loves an antique bracelet that Lynn often wears. Mary has, in the past, offered to buy the bracelet. While waiting for Mary to return from lunch, Lynn is talking to Donna, another coworker. Lynn tells Donna that Mary is very gullible and that she intends to play a joke on Mary, by falsely promising to sell her the bracelet. Mary walks in and Lynn says: "I am kind of tired of this bracelet, and I'd sell it to you for $300 if you could give me cash by the end of the day." (Is this unilateral or bilateral?) Mary happens to have $300 cash in her purse and pulls it out. While it is true that Lynn can "prove" that she was joking, her actions and words objectively indicated intent to enter a contract. On the other hand, if Lynn had said, "I'd sell it to you for a dollar," would an objective, reasonable observer believe that it was a joke?

But wait! What if, before Mary can respond at all, Lynn says: "Oh Mary, I'm only joking! You are so naïve." It might make a difference because every agreement has two parts: an offer and an acceptance.

Offer
An indication of current willingness to enter into a contract, communicated by the person making the offer

Offeror
Party making an offer

Offeree
Party receiving an offer

A. Offer

An **offer** is an indication of current willingness to enter into a contract, communicated by the person making the offer (the **offeror**) to an **offeree.** To indicate a current willingness to enter into a contract, an offer must be sufficiently definite in its terms. Why do we care whether the terms are definite enough to constitute an offer? If they are not definite enough, there is no response by the offeree that will create a contract. Of course we care whether a contract formed. Without a contract, it was "just talk" and there is no basis for going to court.

1. Definite Terms in an Offer

If, in the above example, Lynn said to Mary, "I'll sell you this bracelet someday, when I am tired of it," could Mary respond, "I'll buy it," and create a binding contract? No, she could not; Lynn's "offer" leaves too many details (*e.g.*, price, timing) unresolved. The parties may not think of every detail and, in some cases, a court will fill in a missing detail with a requirement of "reasonableness," but generally the agreement itself, or the surrounding circumstances, must indicate the subject of the contract (my bracelet versus "a piece of my jewelry"); the **consideration** (price); the parties (not just "I am going to sell my bracelet"); and the time. These factors do not necessarily have to be written or spoken, but they must be ascertainable; a court will not create a contract for people who have failed to do so. On the other hand, courts don't appreciate trickery. If, after weeks of talking about the antique ivory bracelet, Lynn said, "I'll sell you my bracelet tomorrow; bring in $300," and the next day brought in a different bracelet, a court would not likely allow her to claim there was no contract.

Consideration
Something promised, given, refrained-from, or done that has the effect of making an agreement a legally enforceable contract

Do modern businesses always operate with this level of specificity? Consider the following example:

Example

Jerry arrives to open Jer's restaurant for breakfast and discovers that during the night, the container of coffee spilled on the floor. Horrified at the prospect of breakfast customers with no coffee, Jerry calls the supplier. Luckily, the supervisor is in. Jerry says, "Lee, I'm in deep trouble here. Can you get me some coffee by 7:00?" Lee responds, "You're in luck. I have a truck going in that direction, and I'll have him stop before 7:00 and drop off coffee."

Do they have a contract? Jerry thinks so and is counting on it. If there were no contract, Jerry would either run to the store or call another supplier. Lee thinks so too, otherwise she wouldn't send the delivery—she expects to be paid. But, under the common law, would the offer be too indefinite? While Jerry was specific about time, place, and subject matter, there was no discussion of price, quantity, or method of payment.

2. Essential Terms

Common law does not govern this situation, however, because this is a transaction between **merchants** for the sale of goods. The UCC defines a merchant as any person who regularly deals in the kind of goods covered by the contract or who, by occupation, holds himself out as having knowledge or skills peculiar to dealing with the goods in question. The UCC includes specific rules for dealing with **open terms.** In many ways these provisions are intuitive. The UCC is intended to honor the intentions of the parties. If they intended to have a contract, the UCC looks at what they likely intended (i.e., what is reasonable) to fill in the gaps. The parties usually intend to continue to operate the way they have operated in the past (course of dealing) or according to what is standard in their industry.

Open Terms
Also called "gap-filling" provisions; under the UCC a contract may form despite failure to specify certain terms

In the example above, having determined that the parties did intend to make a contract, consider what it would be "reasonable" for the parties to "intend":

- How much coffee will Lee bring? How much does Jerry usually buy? What is the standard size container delivered to restaurants?
- What kind of coffee? Again, what does Jerry usually order?
- What is the price? What price is Lee charging her other customers on the same day? What is the usual delivery charge?
- When will Jerry pay and under what terms? How does Jerry usually pay?

Assignment 3-1

1. Return to the Web site you bookmarked in Chapter 2, and examine your state's version of the UCC:
   - ◆ Find a section, perhaps titled "Formation in General," that allows for open terms. Under what circumstances can a contract exist despite open terms?
   - ◆ Find and list provisions relating to specific open terms, such as price. What seems to be most important in resolving open terms in general? Particularly look for provisions relating to "course of performance."
2. Use computer-assisted legal research (CALR) to find a case, decided in your state, in which the court dealt with resolving an open term under the UCC. Summarize the case for class discussion, focusing on the factors the court looked at in "filling the gap."

3. Communication of an Offer

The offeror must communicate the offer to the offeree. If Pat Paralegal tells Lou Lawyer that he is willing to do freelance work for $40 per hour, and Lou tells Alex Attorney that Pat is available for $40 per hour, Pat has not made an offer to Alex. If you overhear me, angry at my laptop computer, muttering, "I'd sell this *!*!*! thing for 50 cents," I have not made an offer at all.

On the other hand, there can be multiple offerees. General advertising is usually not considered an offer because it is not sufficiently definite, but an ad with specifics could be construed as an offer. Some scholars think of this as a "legal fiction" to protect businesses from mistakes in ads.

Examples

Lou runs an ad in the local paper: "Leaving the state, must sell by Saturday, 1-yr-old 27" Sony plasma TV model X-187, $200 to first cash buyer." J.R. is the first to arrive with cash and says he wants the television, but Lou has disliked J.R. since grade school. Lou says he has changed his mind. J.R. can likely take Lou to small claims court and win.

BigBuy runs an ad in the Sunday paper: "27" Sony plasmas—$19." It's a typo! It should have said $199. J.R. walks into BigBuy, ready to buy and, ultimately, sues in small claims court. In this situation, BigBuy likely wins. The court will say that the ad was an invitation to make offers, not an offer, because it did not contain sufficient detail: how many, terms of payment, and so on.

---

4. Lifespan of an Offer

Once an offer is accepted, a contract forms. A lawsuit may follow if a party refuses to honor that contract (as with J.R. and Lou in the previous example), so it is essential to know whether there was an offer to be accepted. Although an offer with adequate detail may have been communicated, various factors may "kill" that offer before it is accepted.

a. Revocation

The most common way that an offer ceases to exist is by revocation. At common law, an offer that is not, in itself, a contract, can be revoked at any time before acceptance (unless promissory estoppel applies).

Example

The difference between an unaccepted offer and a contract can have a huge impact on the parties. On a Friday afternoon, two weeks before spring break, Pat Professor mentions to one of her students, Sam, that she would like to have her garage painted over spring break. She has all of the materials ready and is willing to pay $1,000. Sam does not immediately accept, wanting to check on family plans before making a commitment. Pat says that Sam can consider the offer over the weekend and give an answer on Monday. Sam decides to accept and, on Monday morning, arrives at Pat's office early. Before Sam can speak, Pat says that she has changed her mind and is going to have vinyl siding installed. Sam is extremely upset, having imagined spending the money, and wants to go to small claims court. Sam will lose. Pat's statement that Sam could take until Monday to decide was an unenforceable gift; Pat got nothing in return (consideration).

Option
An offer, supported by consideration, may not be revoked at will

With the addition of consideration, an offer can be made into a separate contract, called an **option** contract.

Example

The parties can protect themselves. Dale Developer is considering a piece of property for construction of an apartment building. The location is ideal; the price is right. Unfortunately, the property is zoned for single-family housing only. Dale is sure that rezoning is possible, but will take several months. If Dale waits and pursues the zoning issue before purchasing the property, another developer may buy it, even if the owner has promised to hold it for Dale. On the other hand, Dale cannot risk completing the purchase immediately and then being unable to obtain rezoning. Dale could enter into an option contract by paying the owner, perhaps $500, to "hold" the property for six months at the current price. Dale may, or may not, ultimately purchase the property; a decision to actually purchase the property would create a second contract, but the option is a contract in its own right.

---

b. UCC Firm Offer

Firm Offer
UCC rule; no consideration required to hold offer open between merchants

Does the Pat/Sam example seem wrong to you? If so, you are not alone. Again, the UCC is more in line with modern expectations the common law. Under the "**firm offer**" rule, a signed offer, between merchants, to keep an offer open, is binding for a stated time, or, if no time is stated, for a "reasonable" time, not to exceed three months.

Let's put Pat and Sam in a UCC context. Pat has a paint store and is considering offering a new line of products, Sam's stencils. Pat calls Sam and asks about cost. Sam quotes $6,000 for 20 each of the 250 stencils in the Modern Home collection. Pat says he will get back to Sam after he determines whether he has room for the display. An hour later, Sam's chief financial officer comes in and says that the Modern Home collection has become a hot item, having been featured on HGTV, so they should raise the price to $6,800, effective immediately.

Assignment 3-2

- Find the firm offer rule in your state's version of the UCC, and get the section number.
- If Pat faxed Sam a purchase order, two hours after they talked, would Pat have to pay the new price? What other facts would be helpful to making the determination?

If the offer proposed a unilateral contract (promise/act), the ability to revoke is limited, once the offeree has begun substantial performance. For example, if Pat said, "Paint my garage over spring break and I will pay you $1,000," and Sam had begun painting, Pat may not revoke the offer before Sam has had a reasonable chance to complete performance. Similarly, in an **auction without reserve,** the seller has agreed to sell to the highest bidder and not to revoke the offer to sell, even if bids are disappointingly low.

Auction Without Reserve
A seller agrees to sell to the highest bidder and cannot revoke the offer to sell, even if bids are disappointingly low

Auctions have never been more popular. In everything from online auctions to auctions of hard-to-sell houses, buyers are looking for great deals. But sellers don't always want to give great deals. Whether a seller is making an offer or just inviting offers when an item is put up for bid depends on whether the auction is with reserve or without reserve.

c. Rejection/Counteroffer

An offer can also "die" as the result of actions by the offeree. If an offeree rejects an offer, the **rejection** terminates that offer and any subsequent attempt to accept is an offer. For example, Pat Professor asks Sam to paint her garage for $1,000; Sam says, "No, I can't do it. I'm going to Cancun." About an hour later, Sam gets a call and learns that the plans for Cancun have fallen through. Sam goes to Pat's office and says, "I've decided to paint your garage." This is an offer and Pat is free to accept or reject. This makes sense if you consider that Pat may have hired someone else during the hour that has passed.

Rejection
Offeree terminates offer

A **counteroffer** is less clear cut. Suppose that Sam says, "I can't do the job for $1,000; I'd need at least $1,500." Pat just shrugs and walks away. An hour later, Sam returns and says, "Okay, you win. $1,000." Sam is now making an offer, and Pat is free to accept or reject. Sam's counteroffer "killed" Pat's original offer. Again, Pat may have hired someone else during the hour. On the other hand, parties can negotiate without terminating an offer. Sam might say, "How 'bout $1,200?" and, when Pat starts to walk away, yell, "Okay, $1,000!" without having terminated the offer. Whether the exchange constitutes a counteroffer or just negotiation depends on all of the surrounding circumstances, including the amount of time that has passed and the language used.

Counteroffer
Offeree responds to offer with an offer

Assignment 3-3

Some experts say that in the modern business world, contracts are not often formed by discrete offer and acceptance, but "result from a gradual flow of information between the parties followed by a series of compromises and tentative agreements on major points which are finally refined into contract terms." The reality of this ongoing process sometimes makes it hard to distinguish a counteroffer from a negotiation. The parties may have invested substantial time and resources to the negotiation process and may feel that they have an "investment" in keeping the process alive. The parties may even sign a "letter of intent" or an "agreement in principle" in which they indicate an intention to form a contract. In such cases, a party might challenge the assertion that a communication constituted a counteroffer or may assert that the parties have an agreement or a duty to continue negotiations.

1. The 2012 case *Golden Ocean Group Ltd. v. Salgaocar Mining Industries* caused much discussion among those in the international contracts community. An English court found that a contract formed from a series of "disjointed" e-mails. Do an Internet search, find the case, and write a short summary, explaining why you think the parties believed they had formed a contract or why you think they were still in negotiations.
2. Using CALR, find and summarize, for class discussion, a case from your jurisdiction, in which the court dealt with one of the following issues (as assigned by your instructor):
   - Whether an offer was rejected or terminated by a proposal from the other party (focus on how the court characterizes the disputed communication, as a "proposal," a "counteroffer," or a "negotiation"); or
   - Whether the power to accept an offer terminated because of the passage of time (focus on how the subject matter of the contract governed what was "reasonable").

Operation of Law
Events, including death, insanity, destruction of subject matter, and illegality, may terminate an offer

d. Termination by Operation of Law

Illegality An offer can also be terminated by intervening illegality: Pete offers to enter into a contract with Stan for construction of a shed. Pete requests an answer by Monday. Before Stan can begin work, the city amends its zoning ordinance to prohibit outbuildings, such as sheds, in the area. Stan cannot "pull a fast one" by accepting the offer and requiring Pete to pay for a building that cannot be built.

Passage of Time The passage of time can terminate an offer. The time may be stated or may be implied. In the previous example, if Stan had not responded by Monday but had come in on Wednesday and told Pete, "I've decided that I will build your shed over spring break," Stan is making an offer that Pete is free to accept or reject. The original offer ended on Monday. If no time is stated, the law implies a reasonable time. What is reasonable? That is up to a court, which is why every offer should state a time at which it expires.

Even a stated time may be unclear: At noon on Saturday, Billie Buyer signs an offer to purchase a house, including a statement that "Seller may accept this offer within two days, after which this offer shall be void." Suppose that Seller attempts to accept at 1:00 p.m. on Monday, but Buyer has now found another house and likes it better. Is the offer still good?

Death/Insanity The death or insanity of the offeror or the destruction of the subject matter will also terminate an offer. If Pete died or if the land was ruined by mudslide over the weekend, while Stan was still considering the offer, the offer would automatically terminate.

B. Acceptance

If there is a "live" offer to accept, how can it be accepted? Remember, in a bilateral contract situation, the acceptance is by promise; acceptance of a unilateral contract is by act. Some offers dictate a means of **acceptance.** For example, the offer might state: "To accept these terms, return a signed copy to Contractor's office no later than Friday, October 23. . . ." In other cases, the offer does not include specifics about acceptance and, by default, a number of rules apply. Some of these rules may seem unreasonable or impractical, so an offeror should control the situation by communicating an offer that is not ambiguous.

Acceptance
Compliance or agreement by one party with the terms and of another's offer so that a contract forms

1. Implied Acceptance

Normally "pure" silence does not operate as acceptance.

Examples

Read the fine print; you may not be as "silent" as you think. A package containing five movie CDs arrived in your mail today, with a note indicating you should send them back within ten days if you do not want them. You have had no previous contact with the company, but the note states that if you do not return them, you will have agreed to buy the CDs and must pay immediately. Your "silence," in the form of not responding, does not create a contract. On the other hand, if you order five CDs for $1 without reading the fine print, you might find that you have specifically (not impliedly) agreed that you will either return or pay for the CDs mailed to your home every month for the next year.

Acceptance can be implied based on behavior, partial performance, or past dealings.

Behavior, or lack thereof, can establish acceptance, especially when the parties have a continuing relationship. At the end of July, Community College mails all of its part-time instructors offers to teach. Toni Torteacher, a six-year veteran teacher, receives an offer to teach a paralegal class that meets on Thursday nights, beginning on August 24. Toni forgets to sign and return the contract and the college administration does not notice. Toni arrives on August 24 and teaches the class. Acceptance is implied.

The auctioneer yells: "Do I hear 75?" Peggy stretches her arm far above her head, numbered paddle in hand, and the auctioneer yells: "Sold to Bidder 17 at $75."

2. Mailbox Rule

At common law an acceptance is considered effective when "properly dispatched," even if it is not actually received until much later (or perhaps not

Mailbox Rule
Common law rule, acceptance occurs when dispatched by appropriate means

received at all). The **mailbox rule** made sense in times when business communication was done in person or by regular mail, but can result in bizarre situations today.

Example

Barry visits Sela's open house and wants to buy but says, "I can't sign an offer until I talk to my dad because he is helping me with the down payment; he won't be available until late this evening." Sela suggests that Barry return the next day, but Barry is leaving on a business trip in the morning. Afraid that Barry's enthusiasm will die down if too much time passes, Sela writes up terms (price, possession date, property included, etc.), signs it, and hands it to Barry. She tells Barry, "Talk to your dad tonight. Then you can sign this, drop it in the mail, and we'll be all set." Barry is so excited about the house that he drives straight to his dad's office, rather than waiting for evening. After talking it over with his dad, Barry signs the contract, sticks it in an envelope addressed to Sela, and walks with his dad to a mailbox. (NOTE: Barry's dad has witnessed the mailing to prevent paralegal students all over the country from howling, "How will he prove he mailed it then?!?!?!")

About 20 minutes after Barry leaves, one last straggler visits Sela's open house and offers $10,000 more than Barry is willing or able to pay. Sela immediately signs a contract and calls Barry to revoke her offer. Unfortunately, a revocation (like an offer or a rejection) is only effective when communicated. By the time Sela reaches Barry, he has already mailed his acceptance. There is no longer an offer to revoke; there is a binding contract and the probability of a lawsuit. Sela could have prevented this situation by simply writing into her offer "acceptance effective only when received," "acceptance must be by personal delivery," or something similar. Unfortunately, clients often do not understand the need to control their contracts to prevent default law from creating an agreement they would not have wanted.

Whether an acceptance was "properly dispatched" depends on whether the means of acceptance was authorized. Some courts enforce the rule strictly and would find a faxed acceptance unauthorized if the contract called for mailed acceptance. Other courts consider, among other factors, whether an alternative method of communication was timely and whether the method used was the functional equivalent of the method described. If the offer does not specify a means of acceptance, it is assumed that the means by which the offer was communicated is appropriate for acceptance. Proper dispatch also required that the letter be correctly addressed and stamped.

The UCC states that unless otherwise unambiguously indicated by the language or circumstances, an offer "shall be construed as inviting acceptance in any manner and by any medium reasonable in the circumstances." The provision even gives the seller an option to either promise shipment or actually ship goods, in response to an offer to buy goods for prompt or current shipment. While these provisions allow for flexibility, they also create opportunities for disagreement.

In today's world people rarely communicate offer and acceptance by mail, but the mailbox rule can still create problems. A sender may be able to prove that a faxed or e-mailed acceptance was reasonable under the circumstances and was sent on a particular date, even though it was received much later or not received at all.

3. Mirror Image Rule

Mirror Image Rule
Acceptance must be identical to offer

The common law also has the **mirror image rule** for acceptance. Suppose that Sela had written the agreement to call for closing and possession on May 15. Barry's dad wants to attend closing and knows he will be out of town on that date. Barry crosses that date out and inserts May 16 and then mails the acceptance. Sela hadn't seemed to care much about the closing date during their discussion, and in fact she did not care. The change, however, converts what was intended as an acceptance into a counteroffer. The acceptance is no longer the **mirror image** of the offer, and Sela is off the hook.

Does this seem harsh? Does it reflect how modern businesses operate? Consider this situation:

Example

Lou handles purchasing for Taylor's small manufacturing business. On Monday morning, Taylor comes into the office, visibly upset. The company's biggest customer, Ryan, is expecting delivery of 1,000 frames on Friday for an important show. Taylor just discovered that the crate of fasteners needed to finish the frames was infiltrated by mice and moisture. The fasteners are rusty and cannot be used. Taylor thinks that the Ryan order cannot be finished on time and that the company will lose its biggest customer. Lou thinks quickly and says, "If I can get a crate of fasteners here by Wednesday, could you get some folks to work overtime and get it done?" "Brilliant!" screams Taylor. "Do that and you are in for a terrific bonus." Lou pulls out a yellow form, titled "Purchase Order," in use since the Stone Age and never read by anyone since it was written by a lawyer many years ago. Lou fills in all of the important details—the model number of the fasteners, the quantity, the price, the delivery requirements and payment terms—and faxes it to the supplier. Lou never reads the small print on the bottom of the form, and neither does Pat, who takes the purchase order off of the fax machine at the supplier's office. After checking inventory, Pat pulls out a pink form, titled "Confirmation," in use since dinosaurs walked and also never read, and fills in the model number, quantity, price, delivery, and payment terms requested by the purchase order. Pat faxes the confirmation to Lou. Both parties think they have a contract. Counting on delivery, Taylor schedules overtime. Counting on having sold those fasteners, Pat tells another customer that the item is out of stock. But at common law, they would not have had a contract. The small print on the purchase order included a statement that "Supplier shall retain risk of loss with respect to the product until the product has been received within purchaser's building." On the other hand, the small print on the confirmation states: "Supplier shall deliver the product to the loading dock at purchaser's place of business and shall have no further liability for loss after such delivery."

---

4. Battle-of-the-Forms Rule

Battle-of-the-Forms Rule
UCC rule, overrides mirror image rule when merchants use forms

Taylor and Ryan, however, are both merchants, so their contract for a sale of goods is governed by the UCC, which includes the **battle-of-the-forms rule.** Under the rule, the differences between an offer and acceptance do not necessarily mean that no contact has formed. In an effort to implement the intent of the parties, the rule looks to the language contained in the offer and acceptance, the conduct of the parties and whether the differences are caused by the addition of new terms or by contradictory terms.

The "battle of the forms" rule recognizes that business contracts often have us drowning in a sea of paperwork. Because of the rule, parties involved in contract negotiations (or paralegals working for those parties) must carefully monitor any changes or additions to offers and raise appropriate objections immediately.

Assignment 3-4

Find the provision, in your state's enactment of the UCC, dealing with additional terms in acceptance or confirmation:

- ◆ In the battle-of-the-forms example, Supplier's acceptance contained a term "different" from that included in Taylor's offer; can the parties have a contract? What facts, not given in the fact scenario, might determine whether there is a contract?
- ◆ How does the UCC treatment of "additional terms" differ from its treatment of "different" terms?
- ◆ Suppose that the fasteners are delivered to the loading dock, but before they are taken inside, a sudden storm destroys the box and most of the contents are damaged. Will either the provision in the purchase order or the provision in the confirmation dictate liability?
- ◆ If neither the purchase offer nor the acceptance dictates liability, how might that be resolved? (This involves some "sleuthing" through the Code.)

C. Practical and Ethical Issues

Lawyers are often involved in negotiation (offer, counteroffer, and acceptance), particularly in settlement of cases, and face certain ethical questions regularly. The questions often revolve around the extent to which the lawyer can employ "benign" deception, bluffing, or trickery and the answers are not always clear.

The ABA Model Rules of Professional Conduct, Rule 4.1, states that in "the course of representing a client a lawyer shall not knowingly make a false statement of material fact or law to a third person," including the opposing party in a negotiation. Does the rule require that the lawyer correct an opponent's misunderstanding of the facts or law? The answer, as with many issues, is, "it depends." The comments to Rule 4.1 state:

> A lawyer is required to be truthful when dealing with others on a client's behalf, but generally has no affirmative duty to inform an opposing party of relevant facts. A misrepresentation can occur if the lawyer incorporates or affirms a statement of another person that the lawyer knows is false. Misrepresentations can also occur by partially true but misleading statements or omissions that are the equivalent of affirmative false statements. For dishonest conduct that does not amount to a false statement or for misrepresentations by a lawyer other than in the course of representing a client, see Rule 8.4.

Another important consideration is confidentiality. Rule 1.6 states, "A lawyer shall not reveal information relating to representation of a client unless the client consents after consultation." The rule generally "trumps" a lawyer's duty of truthfulness in statements to others, but Rule 4.1(b) provides an exception if disclosure is necessary to avoid assisting the client in a criminal or fraudulent act. For example, the client may prohibit a lawyer from revealing the highest acceptable settlement, but the lawyer cannot affirmatively lie about insurance coverage.

A lawyer can also face tort liability for misrepresentations during negotiation. A lawyer was found liable to an opposing party who settled a claim for a lower amount in reliance on a false representation about the insurance coverage available. *Fire Ins. Exch. v. Bell*, 643 N.E.2d 310 (Ind. 1994).

Other issues that can arise in negotiation:

- What if the client wants to improve his negotiating position by threatening to have the other party prosecuted for a crime?
- What should a lawyer do if the lawyer becomes aware that the client is attempting to commit fraud?
- Insurance companies are often accused of quickly offering unfairly small settlements to people injured in accidents, before they have the chance to contact lawyers; what is the ethical position of a lawyer working for such a company?
- A prosecutor may wish to try to cut a deal with one of several codefendants in order to build a case against the others; may she negotiate plea agreements with those defendants outside the presence of defense attorneys?

Assignment 3-5

Read and summarize the Seventh Circuit case *Citadel Group, Ltd. v. Washington Regional Medical Center*, decided August 15, 2012. http://law.justia.com/cases/federal/appellate-courts/ca7/11-3124/11-3124-2012-08-15.html. Use your bookmarked website for your state's ethical rules.

- ◆ This is an excellent example of a "contract by inches." The parties agreed to a little at a time, leaving the question of how much they had agreed to by the time the relationship broke down. Why? Would the parties have been better off in a "bright line" situation: no contract at all until all terms were agreed-upon? Would a bright-line contract even be possible in a situation like this?
- ◆ Do you agree with the outcome? Would your opinion be different if, instead of seeking lost profits, Citadel had actually lost money?

Use your bookmarked citation for your state's ethical rules.

- ◆ Is there an ethical opinion (under Rule 4.1) concerning deception by silence or by failure to correct the other party's misunderstanding?
- ◆ Find the sections applicable to each of the three "other issues" above.

Example: Offer and Acceptance in the Digital Age

Smoking Everywhere sells e-cigarettes and contracted with CX Digital Media, to help with online marketing of a free e-cigarette promotion. CX Digital would place the ad with its affiliates to generate Web traffic. Smoking Everywhere would pay CX Digital around $45 for every completed sale that came via a customer clicking on an ad placed with one of those affiliates, up to 200 sales per day. After recoding some pages, CX Digital believed it could drive more traffic and increase sales. This exchange, part of a longer IM chat, occurred between "pedramcx" (Soltani) from CX Digital and "nicktouris" from Smoking Everywhere:

> pedramcx (2:49:45 PM): A few of our big guys are really excited about the new page and they're ready to run it
> pedramcx (2:50:08 PM): We can do 2,000 orders/day by Friday if I have your blessing
> pedramcx (2:50:39 PM): You also have to find some way to get the Sub IDs working
> pedramcx (2:52:13 PM): those 2,000 leads are going to be generated by our best affiliate and he's legit
> nicktouris is available (3:42:42 PM): I am away from my computer right now.
> pedramcx (4:07:57 PM): And I want the AOR [agent of record] when we make your offer #1 on the network
> nicktouris (4:43:09 PM): NO LIMIT
> pedramcx (4:43:21 PM): awesome!

CX went from sending around 60-something sales a day to an average of more than 1,200 sales per day and sent Smoking Everywhere an invoice for two months in 2009 that totaled more than $1.3 million. Smoking Everywhere refused to pay. Did the IM conversation modify the existing contract? The district court held that it did:

Touris's response acted as a rejection and counteroffer that Soltani accepted by replying "awesome!" To constitute acceptance, a response must be on terms identical to those of the offer and must be unconditional. A reply that purports to accept an offer but is conditional on assent to additional or different terms is not an acceptance but is a counteroffer. The words and conduct of the response are to be interpreted in light of all the circumstances.

Touris's response of "NO LIMIT" varied from the two specific terms offered and was a counteroffer. Soltani proposed CX provide 2,000 sales per day and that CX be the AOR, a term of art meaning the exclusive provider of affiliate advertising on the advertising campaign. Touris made a simple counteroffer that there be no limit on the number of sales per day that CX affiliates may generate and did not mention the AOR term. Soltani enthusiastically accepted the counteroffer by writing, "awesome!" and by beginning to perform immediately by increasing sales volume. Touris testified he could have been responding to something other than the offer of 2,000 sales per day; but he acknowledged that he had engaged in contract negotiations about "changing the number of leads, changing URLs, deposits, that type of thing," mainly on the phone. Neither party suggested any plausible alternative interpretation for why Touris wrote "NO LIMIT."

Do you see any other plausible arguments that could have been raised?

CX Digital Media, Inc. v. Smoking Everywhere, Inc. (S.D. Fla. 2011), http://dockets.justia.com/docket/florida/flsdce/0:2009cv62020/349462/.

D. Preparing for Contract Negotiations

What usually happens between an initial offer and an ultimate acceptance? Negotiations happen. Like most of the practice of law, successful contract negotiations are more likely to be the result of good preparation than of the negotiator's personality. Successful negotiations do not break down into ultimatums or other aggressive behavior. Remember: if parties are negotiating, it is because they want to reach an agreement and they want that agreement to work. They don't want to have to start over with another party or to end up in litigation.

Begin your preparation with the end of the process: preparing to draft the contract. In later chapters you will learn to consult forms and to brainstorm to make sure that any contract you work on addresses every possible issue. To avoid dragging out negotiations or having to reopen negotiations after the parties think they have a deal—which generates frustration and negative feelings—the negotiator must have a list of every item that will require agreement. Having this list in advance also enables the negotiator to "frame the issues" in a way intended to achieve agreement. For example, if timing is important, the negotiator might want to discuss "incentives for meeting the deadlines" rather than "penalties for late performance."

In consultation with the client, prioritize those items. For example, while some clients want the best possible price, others might be more concerned about time of performance. Don't limit yourself to "what" the client wants, ask "why." If the negotiator understands the client's goals and fears, he may be able to come up with creative solutions when a deadlock appears certain. For example, a client may not want to pay above a certain salary for fear of setting a precedent. If the prospective employee thinks that salary is too low, she might be willing to consider alternatives, such as additional vacation time or payment of professional dues, in lieu of a higher salary. Discuss how the priorities weigh against each other. For example, would the client be willing to pay a higher price for an earlier completion date?

Compartmentalize the negotiation items so that the negotiator does not appear to be taking an "all or nothing" approach and can strategically plan the order in which subjects will be introduced, and, if necessary, make concessions that won't hurt the client. When the parties can agree on a particular section (such as timing of performance), they can feel that they are making progress even if important matters have not yet been resolved.

With respect to those important points, do the research. Make sure the negotiator is provided with information about industry standards, current market prices, and particular difficulties that may justify exceptions. This enables the negotiator to appear fair. If any of the important information is technical in nature, discuss with the negotiator whether it would be valuable to have an expert present for that part of the negotiation. For example, a construction company that wants a high price for building a cantilevered building addition might want to have an engineer or an architect present to explain the technical difficulties and risks.

Consider the other party's goals, the other party's likely priorities, and what will happen to the other party if no agreement is reached. If the parties have negotiated in the past, get information about those sessions and the end result. If possible, obtain copies of contracts your client has entered in the past and that the other party has entered in the past. Find out what worked and what did not work.

You may also be able to research the others involved in the negotiations. If a business is involved, what is its history; what are its strengths and weaknesses? Learn what you can about the negotiators' personalities, their existing business relationships, and their levels of authority at the bargaining table. Make sure that your client's negotiator understands her authority and what additional steps may be required after a verbal agreement (*e.g.*, approval by a board of directors).

Assignment 3-6

Jane and Barb are cousins, preparing to buy a one-bedroom condo at the beach for vacation use. They are very close and have agreed that each will pay one-half of the cost of the condo. Although they do not anticipate any disagreements, they have decided that each should consult an attorney and that they should sign an ownership agreement. Both are in their 60s and they are concerned about what would happen if either would die or become disabled. Barb is a widow, with three adult children and two grandchildren under age five. She is a retired doctor. She is very wealthy and likes high-end things. Jane never married and is a retired teacher. She has fewer financial resources than Barb and wants to be cautious about spending. They have already consulted a decorator, who prepared a plan for furnishing the condo. Barb loves it and wants to accept the proposal, even if she has to pay more. Jane simply cannot pay half of the cost. Prepare a checklist and interview a classmate (in the role of either Jane or Barb) in preparation for negotiations. Your instructor will assign partners to negotiate the necessary terms for a future contract. Keep your work product for a future assignment.

Career Corner

Chanelle B. is Senior Compliance Analyst for a major health care corporation in Maryland. Before working for five years in compliance, she worked as a paralegal and spent more than a year in the FTC Paralegal Honors Program, described in Chapter 4G. Chanelle has a Bachelor's Degree in Paralegal Studies and an M.S. in Forensic Studies. She is a member of the Project Management Institute and is active with many charitable organizations.

Asked what she would like to say to people interested in working with contracts, Chanelle said, "The paralegal field has a great amount of diversity, providing many avenues for professional development. The skills obtained in this particular field can be applied to so many others. Continue to seek new opportunities to further educate yourself and develop new skills. Approach each challenge as a new learning experience. Always maintain integrity in your work and you'll be rewarded."

Review Questions

1. How does a court determine whether there has been a manifestation of mutual assent?
2. Identify all of the ways in which an offer can be terminated before acceptance.
3. Identify the presumptions created by the mirror image rule, the mailbox rule, and even the battle-of-the-forms rule. After examining those presumptions, do you think that they give an advantage to the offeror or offeree? Do you think that courts consider that advantage when called upon to interpret an ambiguous contract?
4. The battle-of-the-forms rule was created to facilitate creation of contracts, but businesses often don't like it. Why not? What do you think businesses commonly include in contracts to avoid the rule?
5. Discuss the issues raised by the following situation:

   Sal Student placed a phone order for new computer software for a drafting class by giving a credit card number and address over the phone. When the box arrived by mail, it contained a "box top user license," stating that: "Opening this box indicates acceptance of these terms. If you do not accept the terms, you must return this box unopened within the next 30 days and your payment will be refunded." The license went on to disclaim all warranties, but Sal never read it. Sal tore open the box and spent the next two weeks trying to get the software to work. It never worked and the company refused to replace it or give a refund.

   - Is software covered by Section 2-207?
   - Does it make a difference that Sal is a consumer, not a merchant?

- Does it make a difference that the initial communication was oral and that the written communication was "accepted" by the act of opening the box?
- Is this situation extremely unfair? "Unconscionability" is discussed in Chapter 4.

6. Discuss the legal issues raised by the following situation:

   Your firm's client, Lee, owner of Lee's Landscaping (LL), has a problem. On April 2, LL gave its standard form contract to a potential client, Rene, for signature. The contract stated a price of $25,000 for the work specified by Rene. It was not signed by LL, but stated that Rene should sign the contract and return it to LL and that "this contract will be deemed accepted by LL when LL either returns the signed contract to homeowner or begins work." LL had intended the clause to provide flexibility. Its work is very dependent on weather and LL wants to be able to take advantage of good weather, even if it has not yet signed a contract and returned it to the homeowner.

   Rene returned the signed document on April 4. The contract extends credit to Rene, so LL immediately ordered a credit report. Unfortunately, it was the busiest time of the year, and LL did not review and approve the report until April 10. On April 13, the area had its first dry day in two weeks. LL sent two trucks and four workers to Rene's property. When they arrived, Rene told the workers to leave. Another company had agreed to do the same work for less money.

   - Is the situation likely covered by UCC or common law?
   - Are there any missing facts about what happened between April 4 and April 13 that might influence your opinion?
   - How would you characterize LL's actions on the morning of April 13?
   - Would your opinions change if the nature of the contract changed, so that LL were a catering service that asserted that it would accept either by signing the customer's signed offer or by delivering food on the day of the party?

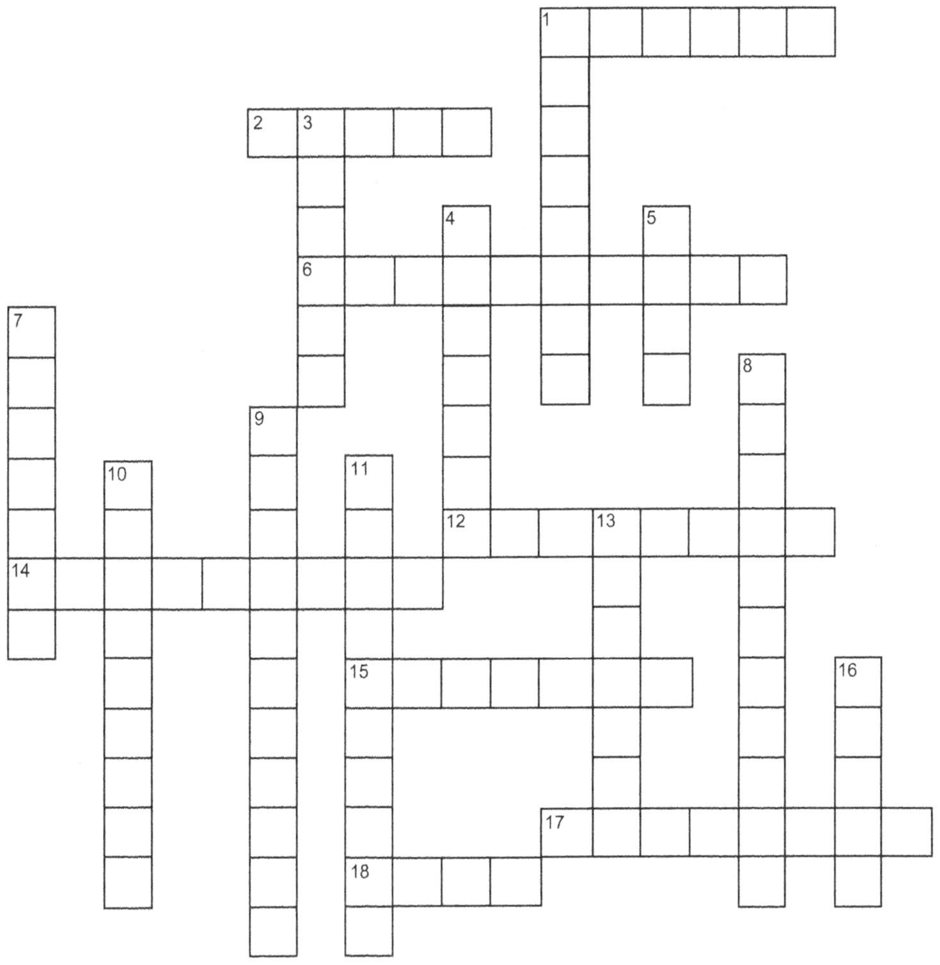

ACROSS

1. ________image rule; common law requirement that acceptance be identical to offer
2. battle-of-the- ________rule of the UCC; negates mirror image rule
6. subsequent ________may terminate offer
12. promissory ________might prevent revocation before acceptance
14. standard used to determine whether an offer was made
15. ________offer can terminate offer
17. at common law, an offer had to have ________terms
18. UCC provides for ________terms

DOWN

1. a person who regularly deals in the goods
3. a person pays to have an offer held open
4. auction without ________; seller may not refuse to sell to highest bidder
5. UCC provides for merchants ________ offer to remain open for a reasonable time
7. common law rule under which acceptance is effective when sent
8. generally does not constitute an offer
9. ________ of property may terminate offer
10. this action by offeree terminates offer
11. before acceptance, this action by offeror terminates offer
13. person to whom offer is made
16. ________ of offeror may terminate offer

4

◆ ◆ ◆

Invalid Assent

◆ ◆ ◆

This chapter explores wrongful conduct, mistakes, and overreaching in the formation of contracts and the remedies available. There is a strong tie-in between this material and issues of capacity, discussed in Chapter 7, and some students may wish to look ahead to that material.

Skills-based learning objectives	*How you will demonstrate your ability*
Analyze state mandatory disclosure laws applicable to specific contracts.	Assignment: Locate and discuss state mandatory disclosure laws.
Analyze and discuss issues relating to fraud, unconscionability, ADR clauses, and ethics violations in attorney-client contracts.	Assignments: Find state ethics rules addressing the issues; analyze a case concerning those rules.

A. **Fraud**
B. **Misrepresentation**
C. **Mutual Mistake**
D. **Duress**
E. **Undue Influence**
F. **Unconscionability**
G. **Practical and Ethical Issues**

Shoplifting is a major problem to retailers. Many retailers have contracted with CEC (http://www.correctiveeducation.com/home/whatiscec#What-is-CEC), a company that provides "restorative justice" for profit. CEC provides "life skills" courses to shoplifters caught by the retailers; shoplifters must pay the company $500 for a six-hour course and sign a confession. If they refuse to do so, they face criminal prosecution. Do the parties (CEC and the shoplifters) really have a meeting of the minds when a shoplifter agrees to these terms?

Sometimes offer plus acceptance does not add up to a contract. The apparent agreement may be invalid because of duress, fraud, mistake, or misrepresentation. Some of these defenses to contract formation, most notably fraud and some instances of duress and misrepresentation, can also be the basis of tort claims. This is significant because it means that the injured party may recover **punitive damages,** which are not normally awarded in contract cases.

Punitive Damages
Damages unrelated to loss, intended to punish

Punitive damages, discussed in Chapter 11, are not tied to actual loss, but are intended to punish bad behavior.

Claims of fraud and misrepresentation may also arise where the parties did not actually enter a contract with each other. Recall the mention of *Fire Insurance Exchange v. Bell,* 643 N.E.2d 310 (Ind. 1994), at the end of Chapter 3. The lawyer who made a false statement about insurance coverage during settlement negotiations was found liable for fraudulent misrepresentation. The lawyer did not enter into any contract with the injured party, who accepted a low settlement in reliance on the false statement, but was, nonetheless, liable to that party.

A. Fraud

Fraud
False statement of material fact, made with intent to deceive, on which another reasonably relies, to his detriment

Fraud in the Execution
Fraud that relates to the nature of the agreement

Fraud in the Inducement
Fraud that relates to the party's motivation in entering the contract

Puffing
"Sales talk"

Silence as Fraud
A party has a duty to disclose and knowingly conceals the truth

Fraud is a false statement of material fact, made with intent to deceive, and justifiably relied upon by an innocent party, to his or her detriment. **Fraud in the execution** relates to the nature of the agreement. For example, Slimy Son-in-Law visits very sick Dad in the hospital and hands Dad a piece of paper, saying, "Sign here, Dad, this is your menu for tomorrow." In fact, it's a contract that allows Son-in-Law to buy Dad's lakefront home for half its real value. **Fraud in the inducement** relates to why the parties entered the contract. For example, I might agree to buy your car for $10,000 because I think it has only 20,000 miles on it; in fact, the odometer was not operating for more than a year and the real mileage is about 35,000. Nonetheless, I did know I was buying a car.

A statement of material fact is something that a reasonable person would care about in deciding whether to enter the contract. A reasonable person would care about the age of the roof, but would she care about the age of the towel bars? Sales-talk statements, such as "This is the best-handling car you will ever drive," are not generally considered statements of fact and are sometimes called **puffing.**

Can silence constitute fraud? Yes, if a party has a duty to disclose or is knowingly concealing the truth. Increasingly, sellers of homes and cars are required by statute or regulation to make disclosures about matters such as defects, mileage, and so on. The common law has required disclosure in situations where one party knows the other is operating under a false belief and cannot discover the truth. For example, Seller wants to sell a house with a basement subject to bad flooding. Seller waits until August, historically a very dry month in her area, scrubs the basement until all odors are gone, installs paneling and carpeting, and creates a nice-looking living area. Buyer never thinks to ask about flooding.

Example

Who would have guessed? Your state may have unique rules concerning obligation disclosure:

> **RCW 64.06.022**
> **Disclosure of possible proximity to farm.**
>
> A seller of real property shall make available to the buyer the following statement: "This notice is to inform you that the real property you are considering for purchase may lie in close proximity to a farm. The operation of a farm involves usual and customary agricultural practices, which are protected under RCW 7.48.305, the Washington right to farm act."

Intent to Deceive
Knowledge of falsity

Intent to deceive is proven by knowledge of falsity. Suppose that Buyer purchases a house in January. Unable to test the air conditioning, Buyer relies on Seller's statement that the system is "fine." Buyer discovers, in July, that the system doesn't work and will have to be replaced at great expense. Assuming that Seller did know that the system was not working, how might Buyer prove that knowledge?

Justifiable Reliance
Reliance on assertion is reasonable

Justifiable reliance means that the parties to a contract are generally required to reasonably look out for themselves. Suppose that Buyer purchases a small print shop from his buddy from the chamber of commerce. Seller has assured Buyer that the business is "great," and that he has "really enjoyed it," so Buyer doesn't bother to check the books. In fact, the business lost money for the last two years. Were Seller's statements "material fact" or just opinion or puffing? Even if a court were to look at such statements as being factual, it would likely conclude that Buyer could not reasonably rely on such statements in making a major purchase.

B. Misrepresentation

Misrepresentation
False statement made without intent to deceive, upon which a party justifiably relies to his detriment

Misrepresentation is a false statement made without intent to deceive, upon which a party justifiably relies to his detriment. How can a person make a false statement without intending to deceive? A person might speak without sufficient knowledge (carelessness) or in the sincere (but mistaken) belief that the assertion is true.

Two important considerations in misrepresentation are whether the statement was "fact" and whether the injured party was justified in relying on the speaker. The two considerations are often intertwined and require careful consideration of the circumstances. Does the listener have reason to believe that the speaker knows actual facts? For example, Mrs. O'Leary's assertion that the vacant lot behind the house she is selling "is going to be a beautiful country club" is likely an opinion on which the buyer has no right to rely. On the other hand, a subdivision developer's statement to all buyers that his vacant property, behind the houses they are buying, will be developed as a country club has different implications. Even assuming that development of a country club became impossible for reasons beyond the control of the speaker, a buyer would be more likely to rely on statements by the developer and more likely to regard the statements as fact, rather than opinion.

Many states require a "special relationship" between the parties, such that the injured party was entitled to rely on the statement. Consider this example: Acme, a company that designs and manufactures small parts, uses its own unique software to design the specifications of those parts and to run the machinery that actually manufactures the parts. In obtaining bids for a new computer system, Acme asked each seller whether its product would run the software. Each seller responded that it would. Unfortunately, Acme did not have the contract reviewed by a lawyer and did not get that promise included in the contract. There was no way to test the claim until the new computers were installed and networked to the manufacturing equipment. The computers, once installed, will perform all other functions (word processing, e-mail, etc.) but will not run the drafting software so that it will communicate with the manufacturing equipment. The seller honestly believed that the computers would run the software, but after months of effort, cannot get the system to function to Acme's satisfaction. Acme regards the system, for which it paid almost $1 million, as worthless; if the seller removes the computers and returns payments made by Acme, the loss may bankrupt the seller's company. Do computer vendors have a special relationship with their customers such that customers are entitled to rely on such assertions? What if the misrepresentation were an assertion, by an architect, that a tenth-story balcony would safely hold 1,500 pounds? The "special relationship" may be based on professional expertise.

Assignment 4-1

1. Does your state require a mileage disclosure when a car is sold? Use the Internet to find the answer. If you do not find an answer in the online statutes, you may have to check with state agencies, such as the office of the attorney general or the office of the secretary of state.
2. Many states require the seller to provide specific disclosures when selling a house. The disclosures can range from a form indicating physical deficiencies to a notice of whether the property has been the scene of a crime, was ever used for a meth lab, was the site of paranormal activity or a suicide, and has been insured. Use the Internet to determine which disclosures are required in your state. Discuss: Why are these disclosures mandatory, and are they fair to the people required to make them?
3. Fraud follows economic trends. In recent years, mortgage-rescue fraud, also called foreclosure-rescue fraud, has been a major problem for unsophisticated homeowners. Use the Internet to determine how this fraud is perpetrated, and determine whether your state has any laws specifically intended to deal with the problem.
4. Use computer-assisted legal research (CALR) to find and summarize, for class discussion, a case from your state involving misrepresentation

by an applicant for insurance. Your search, in your state case law database might be [misrepresent! /p applica! /p insurance]; the use of the expander [!] will allow you to find variations, such as "the applicant misrepresented her use of tobacco," or "the application included a misrepresentation concerning use of tobacco." Did the court allow the insurance company to deny coverage based on the false statement? What was the most important factor in the court's decision?

C. Mutual Mistake

Mistake is a difficult concept. If a party were able to avoid liability under a contract simply because of "buyer's remorse" or fear of financial consequences, contracts would have no real meaning. After all, a contract is all about allocating risk. The concept of mistake is, therefore, generally limited to a **mutual mistake** about the **"basic assumptions" of fact,** in cases where the parties have not specifically allocated risk with respect to assumptions. For example, Seller and Buyer both believe that the farm property is 160 acres. A survey discloses that it is 140 acres. Buyer may avoid the contract. This concerns a basic factual assumption and both parties were mistaken.

Mutual Mistake
All parties are mistaken about a basic assumption

Basic Assumption of Fact
An assumption essential to the value of a transaction

A mistake in judgment or concerning consequences, however, is generally not a basis for avoiding a contract. For example, a buyer may pay too much for a house because he didn't research the market; an injury victim may settle a claim without realizing how difficult life will be with limited arm mobility. A mistake about the law—for example, the tax consequences of a contract—is also generally insufficient to get out of a contract. Many contracts, by implication, allocate risk (and, therefore, responsibility) with respect to those assumptions. For example, a contractor agrees to replace a kitchen floor for a set price, without including any provision for unexpected difficulty. If the work is ultimately more than the contractor expected, he may have to accept the loss.

A **unilateral mistake,** where only one party is mistaken about a basic assumption, could rise to the level of fraud, if the other party has made a false statement or is concealing the truth. In addition, unilateral mistake of fact and mistake of law are grounds for avoiding a contract in some states, if there was a confidential or fiduciary relationship between the parties.

Unilateral Mistake
Where only one party is mistaken about a basic assumption

As you might expect, the Uniform Commercial Code (UCC) takes a more liberal approach and includes a concept called **commercial impracticability.** A party may be excused from contract obligations if an unforeseen circumstance makes performance impracticable. This is discussed further in Chapter 10, on contract performance.

Commercial Impracticability
A party may be excused from contract obligations if an unforeseen circumstance makes performance impracticable

D. Duress

Duress
A wrongful threat, intended to induce action by the other party

A contract may be invalid if it was entered into involuntarily, because of a "wrongful" threat. A threat does not have to be illegal to be wrongful. Physical force, or the threat of physical force, while rare, renders an agreement void. If an agreement is entered into because of economic threats or coercion, the contract may be voidable if the threat was improper. Keep in mind, however, that not all "threats" are improper and that people do have motivations for entering contracts. The fact that a person would rather have avoided the choice does not invalidate the contract.

Example

Pat's dog did substantial damage to neighbor Lou's garden. Pat has repeatedly promised to "make it right," but has not taken any action. Exasperated, Lou tells Pat, "If you don't sign this contract and promise to pay for the landscaper I've hired, I am going straight down to the courthouse and I am going to file a small claims complaint against you." Pat signs the contract and later decides not to pay. The contract is probably valid. A lawsuit is the mechanism that society has established for settling disputes such as this; Lou was simply offering the option of settlement before filing.

On the other hand, assume that on the day the damage was done, before Pat had any opportunity to repair the damage, Lou threatened to poison the dog. Pat signed a contract, agreeing to pay for expensive landscaping services, only out of fear. Pat might be able to claim duress.

Criminal Plea Agreement
An agreement in which a prosecutor and a defendant arrange to settle a criminal case against the defendant

Defendants, having accepted a plea agreement, sometimes claim duress (a plea agreement is a contract under which the defendant enters a plea in a criminal case in return for a reduction in the charges or penalty). A **criminal plea agreement** is unique in that it has two parts—the admission of guilt and the sentencing agreement—and it must be approved by a judge. If the judge rejects the sentencing agreement, withdrawal of the plea generally does not require any showing of duress. For an explanation of withdrawal of a plea when the judge has not rejected the sentencing agreement, see *United States v. Hyde,* 520 U.S. 670 (1997).

Undue Influence
A dominant party takes advantage of that position in entering a contract with party under domination

Fiduciary Relationship
One party is obligated to act in the best interest of the other party

E. Undue Influence

A special relationship can give one person **undue influence** over another; if the dominant party takes advantage of that position in entering a contract, the agreement may be voidable. Often, undue influence involves a **fiduciary relationship,** a relationship in which one party is obliged to act in the best interest of the other party.

Example

The doctor-patient relationship is a classic fiduciary relationship. Dr. Lou treats Pat Patient's severe diabetes; Pat believes that no other doctor could keep the condition under control. One day, Dr. Lou asks Pat to invest in a "pyramid scheme" in which Lou is deeply involved. A pyramid scheme involves paying money to those "up the chain" and counting on getting money as new people are brought into the scheme.

Pat truly does not want to invest $1,000 in this plan, but does so out of fear that Lou will not continue the doctor-patient relationship.

Pat may have another basis for invalidating the contract: illegality, discussed in Chapter 6.

Can a contract involving individuals in a special relationship be valid? Yes, if the agreement involves fair consideration, the dominant party made full disclosure, and the party in the "weaker" position must have had independent advice.

EXHIBIT 4-1
Clauses Negating Undue Influence

When parties on unequal power or in a special relationship enter into a contract, the agreement often recites that the "weaker" party has been informed of his rights and has been adequately represented. Such recitals might be found in a premarital contract, a contract between lawyer and client, or a plea bargain agreement like the one below, found on the Web site of the Department of Justice at http://www.justice.gov/atr/public/guidelines/indl_plea_agree.htm.

From a Premarital Agreement:

ACKNOWLEDGMENTS. Each party acknowledges that he or she has had an adequate opportunity to read and study this Agreement, to consider it, to consult with attorneys individually selected by each party, without any form of coercion, duress or pressure. Each party acknowledges that he or she has examined the Agreement before signing it, and has been advised by independent legal counsel concerning the rights, liabilities and implications of this document.

From a Plea Agreement:

The defendant represents to the Court that the defendant is satisfied that his attorneys have rendered effective assistance. The defendant understands that by entering into this agreement, the defendant surrenders certain rights as provided in this agreement. The defendant understands that the rights of criminal defendants include the following:

a. If the defendant persisted in a plea of not guilty to the charges, the defendant would have the right to a speedy jury trial with the assistance of counsel. The trial may be conducted by a judge sitting without a jury if the defendant, the United States, and the judge all agree.

b. If a jury trial is conducted, the jury would be composed of twelve laypersons selected at random. The defendant and the defendant's attorney would assist in selecting the jurors by removing prospective jurors for cause where actual bias or other disqualification is shown, or by removing prospective jurors without cause by exercising peremptory challenges. The jury would have to agree unanimously before it could return a verdict of either guilty or not guilty. The jury

EXHIBIT 4-1
(continued)

would be instructed that the defendant is presumed innocent, that it could not convict the defendant unless, after hearing all the evidence, it was persuaded of the defendant's guilt beyond a reasonable doubt, and that it was to consider each charge separately.

c. If a trial is held by the judge without a jury, the judge would find the facts and, after hearing all the evidence and considering each count separately, determine whether or not the evidence established the defendant's guilt beyond a reasonable doubt.

d. At a trial, the United States would be required to present its witnesses and other evidence against the defendant. The defendant would be able to confront those witnesses and the defendant's attorney would be able to cross-examine them. In turn, the defendant could present witnesses and other evidence in defendant's own behalf. If the witnesses for the defendant would not appear voluntarily, the defendant could require their attendance through the subpoena power of the Court.

e. At a trial, the defendant could rely on a privilege against self-incrimination to decline to testify, and no inference of guilt could be drawn from the refusal of the defendant to testify. If the defendant desired to do so, the defendant could testify in the defendant's own behalf.

F. Unconscionability

Unconscionable Contract
A contract that is so unreasonable that it is "shocking"

A contract that is so unreasonable that it is "shocking" is referred to as **unconscionable.** Unconscionability can be procedural (*e.g.*, requirements "buried" in the contract) or substantive (*e.g.*, terms that are grossly unfair but not hidden). The UCC provides that a court may refuse to enforce all or part of an unconscionable contract. Unconscionability often relates to inequitable consideration (*e.g.*, paying a grossly inflated price), or to contract provisions so unfair that they are considered to violate public policy; those specific situations are further discussed in later chapters. However, other aspects of a contract can also be unreasonable.

Commercial Contract
A contract between businesses

Bargaining Power
Ability to influence

Adhesion Contract
A take-it-or-leave-it contract in which one party has all of the bargaining power

Courts rarely apply the doctrine of unconscionability to **commercial contracts** (between businesses) or to contracts involving sophisticated parties because the doctrine assumes unequal **bargaining power,** that one of the parties had no ability to reject the terms. A take-it-or-leave-it contract, in which one party had all of the bargaining power, is sometimes called an **adhesion contract.**

In a typical unconscionability scenario, an unsophisticated consumer is presented with a "standard" printed contract to lease an apartment, buy insurance, buy a car, or take a loan. The consumer rarely attempts to read the contract and would likely be unable to understand its terms. The consumer (correctly) assumes that the terms are nonnegotiable in any case. The "fine print" might disclaim warranties, take away the consumer's right to go to court, or describe the consumer's obligation as far beyond what the consumer understands.

A claim of unconscionability raises many issues: Does an unsophisticated consumer really have "freedom of contract" when an entire industry uses essentially the same printed form? Are there legitimate reasons for using printed forms that actually benefit consumers by keeping prices lower? When a court applies unconscionability, is it taking away the incentive to read contracts or act as an educated consumer?

Many recent cases have dealt with unconscionability in arbitration provisions (discussed in depth in Chapter 4). For example, in *Brewer v. Missouri Title Loans,* 2012 WL 716878 (Mo.), a woman borrowed $2,215, secured by the title to her car, at an APR of 300%. The contract, whose terms no consumer had ever successfully renegotiated, provided for resolution of any claim against the company through binding individual arbitration, waiving the possibility of class action arbitration. Because of provisions concerning attorney's fees—the borrower could not recover fees or punitive damages from the company, but the company could recover fees from the borrower—an individual borrower would not likely be able to find an attorney willing to take her case. The company, however, reserved the right to go to court to repossess the car, or to use self-help. The borrower made two payments of more than $1,000, which reduced her loan principal by 6 cents. She filed suit alleging violations of numerous statutes, including the state merchandising practices act. The case was appealed solely on the class arbitration issue. The state supreme court found that a class arbitration waiver in its contract was unconscionable and held that the remedy was to strike the entire arbitration agreement. The U.S. Supreme Court vacated that opinion and remanded. On remand, the Court found that the class arbitration waiver did not, alone, make the arbitration clause unconscionable; but applying traditional Missouri contract law and looking at the agreement as a whole, the court found that Brewer demonstrated unconscionability in the formation of the agreement, appropriately remedied by revoking the arbitration clause.

Assignment 4-2

1. Read *Alderman & Alderman v. Millbrook Homeowners* (2001), https://casetext.com/case/alderman-alderman-v-millbrook-owners-no-cv-00-0802857-s-aug. Identify the factors that are important to a valid (not unconscionable) contract between attorney and client.
2. Find your state's ethical rule concerning termination of the attorney-client relationship. Can a lawyer terminate the relationship if the client is unable to pay the fee (*e.g.,* unexpectedly lost his job)? Does the rule refer to making threats of termination?
3. A current "hot" unconscionability issue concerns contracts in which a consumer agrees to arbitration and gives up the right to go to court in the event of a dispute concerning the contract. Read DC Bar ethics opinion

218, Retainer Agreement Providing for Mandatory Arbitration of Fee Disputes Not Unethical, https://www.dcbar.org/bar-resources/legal-ethics/opinions/opinion218.cfm, which discusses the issue in the context of a contract between a lawyer and a client.

a. The DC Bar had previously indicated that a mandatory arbitration provision in an attorney-client agreement was invalid unless the client was represented by a separate attorney. In this opinion, the Bar indicates that the arbitration provision is valid. What is different?
b. The Bar seems to take the position that arbitration is beneficial in the situation discussed in the opinion. Why?

4. Do the Rules of Professional Conduct or the ethical opinions in your state address the issue of arbitration in a contract between attorney and client? If not, use CALR to find and summarize a case from your state in which the court addresses the issue.

G. Practical and Ethical Issues

What relationship better fits the definition of a fiduciary relationship than attorney-client? But does the existence of that relationship automatically mean that the client was subject to duress or undue influence or that an expensive fee agreement was unconscionable? Obviously not every lawyer-client contract is tainted. In the *Moran* case, assigned in the Introduction chapter, you read a case dealing with an attorney who did business with a client in a way that was unethical.

Read *Alderman & Alderman v. Millbrook Homeowners* (2001) https://casetext.com/case/alderman-alderman-v-millbrook-owners-no-cv-00-0802857-s-aug, in which the court rejects an assertion that the relationship was tainted, and the ethical opinion at the end of this chapter. In the *Alderman* case the client alleged duress and unconscionability as defenses against enforcement of a contract, based on threats to terminate representation. The case was not a disciplinary proceeding, but the court referred to the relevant ethical rule. In Colorado, the rule concerning terminating the attorney-client relationship is Rule 1.16, reproduced in Exhibit 4-2 with permission of the Colorado Bar Association, http://www.cobar.org.

EXHIBIT 4-2
Rule 1.16 Declining or Terminating Representation

(a) Except as stated in paragraph (c), a lawyer shall not represent a client or, where representation has commenced, shall withdraw from the representation of a client if:
  (1) the representation will result in violation of the rules of professional conduct or other law;

EXHIBIT 4-2
(continued)

(2) the lawyer's physical or mental condition materially impairs the lawyer's ability to represent the client; or
(3) the lawyer is discharged.

(b) A lawyer may not request permission to withdraw in matters pending before a tribunal and may not withdraw in other matters unless such request or such withdrawal is because:
(1) the client:
(A) insists upon presenting a claim or defense that is not warranted under existing law and cannot be supported by good faith argument for an extension, modification, or reversal of existing law.
(B) personally seeks to pursue an illegal course of conduct.
(C) insists that the lawyer pursue a course of conduct that is illegal or that is prohibited by these rules.
(D) by other conduct renders it unreasonably difficult for the lawyer to carry out the lawyer's employment effectively.
(E) insists, in a matter not pending before a tribunal, that the lawyer engage in conduct that is contrary to the judgment and advice of the lawyer but not prohibited by these rules; or
(F) deliberately disregards an agreement or obligation to the lawyer as to expenses or fees; or
(2) the lawyer's inability to work with co-counsel indicates that the best interest of the client likely will be served by withdrawal; or
(3) the lawyer's client knowingly and freely assents to termination of the lawyer's employment; or
(4) the lawyer believes in good faith in a proceeding pending before a tribunal that the tribunal will find the existence of other good cause for withdrawal.

(a) When ordered to do so by a tribunal, a lawyer shall continue representation notwithstanding good cause for terminating the representation.

(b) Upon termination of representation, a lawyer shall take steps to the extent reasonably practicable to protect a client's interests, such as giving reasonable notice to the client, allowing time for employment of other counsel, surrendering papers and property to which the client is entitled and refunding any advance payment of fee that has not been earned. The lawyer may retain papers relating to the client to the extent permitted by law.

Career Corner

Rhiannon T. is a contract administrator for a medical equipment corporation. Rhiannon got her first taste of the legal field while interning at a major Chicago firm. She subsequently earned her B.A. and a paralegal certificate from an ABA-approved program. In the interim Rhiannon worked as a national account coordinator for an elevator company and in a medical office as a patient liaison. She is a true believer in learning from a variety of experiences and, as a foster mother of five, she is a busy lady!

When asked what she likes best about her job, she said: "I love the fact that even though I am reviewing contracts, I'm still able to help people. The contracts I am drafting and reviewing are in place to prevent injuries to patients and caregivers. While my role is to protect our company from a business perspective, the contracts I am writing are to make sure people don't get hurt. It gives me great satisfaction knowing I am a part of that process."

Helping others is a major source of career satisfaction. Would you like to help people who have been defrauded in contract situations? How can you get your foot in the door for a job like that? Consider, from https://www.ftc.gov/about-ftc/careers-ftc/work-ftc/honors-paralegal-program:

Review Questions

1. What is the significance of the fact that fraud can invalidate a contract and can also be the basis of a tort lawsuit?
2. What are the elements required to prove fraud? Can breach of contract itself ever constitute fraud? For example, Acme agrees to deliver items to Baker on a specified date. Acme does not deliver the items on that date and notifies Baker that it will not deliver the items. What fact(s) would Baker have to prove to succeed with a fraud claim?
3. Which members of society are most vulnerable to undue influence? Identify several relationships that might be considered fiduciary relationships.
4. Is an objective standard to determine unconscionability or duress possible? How can we distinguish between duress and "bad luck" that motivates entering a contract? Does a party who benefits from an unconscionable contract think it's shockingly unfair? Might that party refuse to deal with people under other terms? How far should courts go to protecting people who enter bad contracts?

5. Almost all of Dr. Carter's patients are covered by an HMO through the two major employers in town. Dr. Carter really does not want to be under contract with the HMO; she thinks it takes away too much of her discretion in caring for patients. On the other hand, her patients will have to find new doctors if she does not contract with the HMO. From the HMO's perspective, its restrictions on referrals and other actions are necessary. Without the restrictions, it would have to raise its premiums above what most employers/patients would be willing or able to pay. Is Dr. Carter signing the HMO contract under duress? Are the HMO restrictions unconscionable? Is Dr. Carter an unsophisticated party without equal bargaining power?
6. When Kim filed for divorce, she really believed she would get sole custody of her child, Joey, because she had been a stay-at-home mother for five years while her husband worked long hours and frequently traveled on business. Things have not gone as expected. Kim has had to start working outside the home and is finding it difficult to balance work and parenthood. The court-ordered temporary support is lower than she expected, and she is behind on paying bills. Worst of all, Kim's husband is planning to reveal to the judge that Kim had an addiction to prescription painkillers a few years ago, and once, while Kim was passed out, Joey (then two years old) wandered out of the house and was brought home by the police. Tired of the whole situation and depressed, Kim signs a settlement agreement under which she will share custody of Joey with her husband on an equal basis. Duress?
7. Discuss the legal implications of the following: Laurie, a beautician at Justin's, has a large client base. She is very talented and hopes to open her own shop when she saves enough money. For now, she is a content employee, paying off a student loan and charge account balances. One day, with no warning, Justin hands Laurie a contract. It recites her current terms of employment, with one difference. The contract contains a statement that Laurie agrees not to open her own beauty shop or work for a competing shop within a 50-mile radius for a period of two years after leaving Justin's for any reason. Laurie does not want to sign the agreement. Justin says that Laurie must sign it right now or else she will be fired and have to leave immediately without access to her client records.

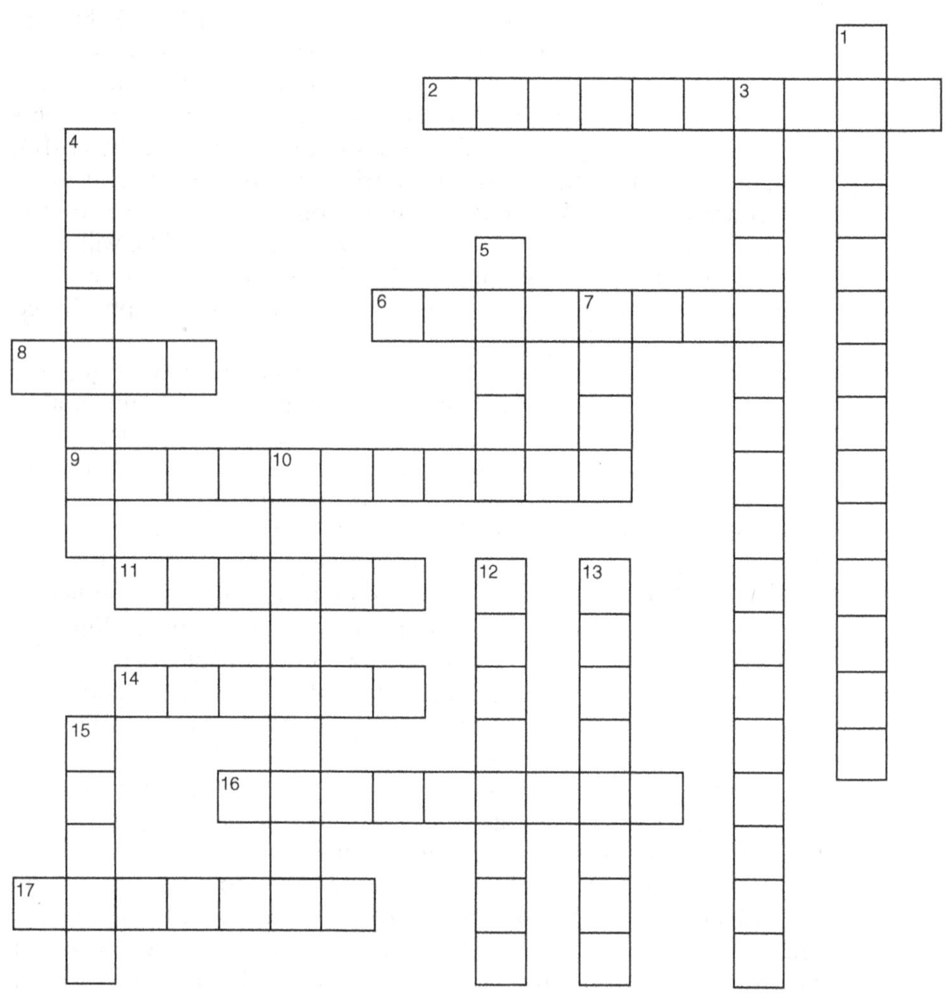

ACROSS

2. fraud in the ________ goes to party's motivation in entering contract
6. fraud may entitle injured party to ________ damages
8. "the roof is nine years old" is a statement of material
9. "silent" fraud
11. person enters contract involuntarily, under threat
14. ________ mistake; a basis to invalidate contract
16. a relationship in which one party is obligated to look out for the best interests of the other
17. sales talk

DOWN

1. shockingly unfair
3. false statement without intent to deceive
4. both fraud and misrepresentation require proof of justifiable
5. a contract may be invalid because of ________ influence; one party essentially controls the other
7. fraud is a basis for invalidating a contract and can also be the basis of a ________ lawsuit
10. fraud in the ________; telling buyer she is signing a loan application when she is actually signing a purchase contract
12. threats of ________ force render agreement void
13. a false statement about a fact that is not important does not concern ________ fact
15. involves intent to deceive

5

◆ ◆ ◆

Consideration

◆ ◆ ◆

This chapter explores one of the most complicated concepts in law: the distinction between a promise that is enforceable as a contract and an unenforceable "gift" promise. That distinction is consideration, the mutual benefit and detriment that characterize a contract.

Skills-based learning objectives	*How you will demonstrate your ability*
Analyze state adoption of UCC relating to consideration.	Assignment: Find specific sections in state adoption of UCC to answer questions.
Analyze consideration issues using case law.	Assignment: Research consideration issue; prepare a case brief.

A. Consideration: An Overview
B. Inequitable Consideration
C. Conditional Contracts
   1. "Each Party Must Get/Give Something" *But the Parties May Not Know, at the Outset, What That "Something" Is*
   2. Output, Needs, and Exclusive Dealing Contracts
D. Bargained-For
   1. "To Which That Party Was Not Legally Entitled Before the Contract"
   2. Preexisting Obligations
E. Modification of Existing Contracts
F. Settlement of Disputes
G. Practical and Ethical Issues

Previous chapters may have given you the impression that contract law is a series of guidelines, rather than a set of rigid rules that can be easily memorized. That is an accurate assessment, but consideration is even more difficult to "pin down," particularly when the circumstances indicate a strong moral obligation to honor a promise.

A. Consideration: An Overview

Consideration
Something promised, given, refrained from, or done, that has the effect of making an agreement a legally enforceable contract

Consideration is the give and take that separates a contract from a gift; love and affection for the **donee**[1] are insufficient to transform a promised gift into a contract. If consideration is not present and has not been excused by law a promise is not enforceable. While the common law once included a concept that contracts "under seal" (sometimes called formal contracts) could be binding without consideration, many states and the Uniform Commercial Code (UCC) have abolished the theory. This may be the root of the common misconception that a promise made in writing is automatically valid.

Example

Blood may be thicker than water, but it is no substitute for consideration.

Stephen Son wrote a note with his blood after pricking his finger with a pin. The document, as translated, read, "Sir, please forgive me. Because of my deeds you have suffered financially. I will repay you to the best of my ability." On the same day, Son also wrote in ink, "I hereby swear [promise] that I will pay back, to the best of my ability, the estimated amount of 170 million [w]ons to [Kim]." The appeals court upheld the trial court's determination that the blood agreement lacked consideration because it "was not a result of a bargained-for-exchange, but rather a gratuitous promise by [Son] who took personally that [Kim], his good friend, had a failure in his investments that [Son] had initially brought him into." The court reasoned the agreement lacked consideration because Son "was not required to and did not guarantee these investments and loans." The court refused to enforce a gratuitous promise even when it was reduced to blood.

Information from an unpublished 2009 decision by the California Court of Appeals.

Have you ever wondered why contests sponsored by sellers often state "no purchase necessary" or allow participants to enter using a "reasonable facsimile" rather than the form found on the product? By allowing participants to enter without the obligation to buy, seller/sponsors hope to avoid contract obligations.

Consideration is sometimes excused by law in cases involving promissory estoppel (discussed in previous chapters), promises to make charitable donations, promises to pay debts that are not legally enforceable (*e.g.*, because of bankruptcy or the statute of limitations), and some promises under which one person "guarantees" performance by another (such as cosigning a loan).

---

[1]The donee is the recipient of a gift; the donor is the giver.

A practical way to look at the consideration requirement is that:

Each party to a contract must get something
We don't weigh the "something," and we don't always know what it will be at the outset.
to which that party was not legally entitled before entering the contract
Legal scholars say that consideration must be "bargained-for."
and each party must give up something to which that party was legally entitled before the contract.

With a bilateral contract that giving and getting is evidenced by promises; with a unilateral contract one party makes a promise and the other gives up something and becomes entitled to something upon performing the requested act. This definition works because it avoids confusion about what can serve as consideration. Let's take it apart:

"Each party must get/give something," ***but we don't weigh that "something."***

We cannot guess at a person's motivation in entering a contract. I might be willing to pay $500 for a ring that belonged to my grandmother, even though, objectively, it is worth only $50. The question is not whether the parties got a fair deal, but whether they got "something." That "something" does not have to benefit the party entering the contract, in the usual sense of that word.

Example

The consideration I receive does not have to benefit me, in a nonlegal sense. I really wish my brother would stop smoking and offer him $5,000 if he can quit for one year. He agrees to do it. In a practical sense, my brother is getting all the benefit if he can keep his promise. I did, however, get something to which I was not legally entitled before the agreement: his promise to stop smoking. What I am giving up is obvious: $5,000. My brother is giving up his legal right to smoke and getting my promise of $5,000. Note that my brother does have a legal right to smoke; if he were to promise to stop street racing he would not be giving up anything to which he is legally entitled.

B. Inequitable Consideration

On the other hand, consideration cannot be **illusory** (just an illusion). The parties must incur some real obligation. If I ask an artist to paint a portrait of my children and tell him that I will pay him $400, "if I like it," have I really incurred any obligation? My "liking" the painting is **subjective** and a court would not likely be able to judge whether the condition has been met.

Illusory
An illusion; stated consideration does not really obligate the party

Subjective
Imposed or influenced by individual position or bias

In other situations, a court can impose a duty of "reasonable" behavior on an agreement that has the appearance of being illusory. For example, I might ask a teen-aged neighbor to mow my lawn this summer and tell him that I will

Objective Standard
Not influenced by personal opinion or bias

pay $40 per mowing if he does a "good job." A court might be able to impose an **objective standard** on "good job," and might or might not be willing to do so, but nobody wants to go to court. The example illustrates the importance of avoiding ambiguity. Courts are most likely to impose an objective standard on commercial contracts. Remember the UCC imposes a duty of good faith. With commercial contracts it is often easier for a court to determine whether a party is acting in good faith respect to a satisfaction clause because there may be industry standards.

Generally a condition calling for approval by a party outside the contract is viewed as objective and, therefore, enforceable. For example, I might require that the painting of my living room walls be done to the satisfaction of my decorator. The court may assume that the decorator will employ objective professional standards and that real obligation has been incurred.

The examples given above involve common law contracts. As you might imagine, the UCC takes a moderate approach. This is illustrated by the "firm offer" rule, discussed in Chapter 3, under which an offer can be made irrevocable for a period of time, without consideration. The gap-filling provisions, for dealing with unstated quantity, delivery, time, and even price terms, can save contracts that might be considered illusory at common law. The obligation of good faith, applicable to "every contract or duty" covered by the Code, also saves contracts that might appear to be illusory on first glance.

Sham
Stated consideration did not really occur

Even with the more moderate approach of the UCC, the consideration requirement is not "just a formality." Consideration cannot be a "**sham.**"

Example

Cal Collector and Dana Dealer sign an option contract, under which Dana agrees to hold an antique car for sale to Cal, at a specified price, for six weeks, while Cal attempts to find financial backing for an auto museum he wants to open. The contract states that Cal has paid $100 for the option, but Cal did not actually give Dana the money and has no intention of doing so.

Courts differ on when consideration crosses the line from being minimal to being a sham. What if the option contract stated consideration of one dollar and Cal actually gave Dana one dollar?

Nominal
Minimal

In some cases, the actual consideration might be unquestionably adequate (*e.g.*, $400,000 for a three-bedroom house), but the parties might recite **nominal** consideration in the contract (*e.g.*, "for $10 and other good and valuable consideration . . .").

Example

Recital
A formal statement

"**Recital**" of consideration:

This type of formal assertion of consideration, written in archaic language, used to be found in most contracts.

NOW THEREFORE, in consideration of the premises and the mutual covenants set forth herein and for other good and valuable consideration, the receipt and sufficiency of which are hereby acknowledged, the parties hereto covenant and agree as follows:

Is it necessary? No, the actual obligations and promises set forth in the contract should establish the real existence (or lack) of consideration. Given the mixed results in cases exploring sham consideration, an attorney would be negligent to allow a client to depend on such a clause as a substitute for real consideration to support an agreement. Might it actually be harmful? Possibly; if such incomprehensible language is one of the first things the client sees in trying to read a contract, might the client decide not to try to read the rest of the document? If the client does not read the contract, how likely is compliance?

If consideration is "shockingly" unequal, a court may invalidate the contract as **unconscionable.** This is especially true if the contract is an adhesion contract, in which one party has no bargaining power. As noted in Chapter 4, situations in which one party has all of the power and the other is unsophisticated, economically disadvantaged, or in extreme need could also implicate duress or undue influence.

There is a modern trend to protect those least able to protect themselves. Courts often review agreements for attorney's fees; most states have legislation limiting interest rates on consumer loans and providing protections for other types of agreements (*e.g.*, "payday loans"). This is discussed further in Chapter 6, on legality.

C. Conditional Contracts

1. "Each Party Must Get/Give Something," *But the Parties May Not Know, at the Outset, What That "Something" Is*

The requirement that one party gets and the other party gives "something" does not mean that the parties have to know exactly what that "something" will be at the time when they enter the agreement. Many contracts are conditional. A **condition precedent** is something that must happen before the contemplated transaction occurs. A **condition subsequent** is an event that might "undo" the contract.

Condition precedent
Event that must occur before the contemplated transaction is completed

Condition subsequent
Event that may "undo" an executed contract

Examples

A condition may protect a party when some uncertainty exists concerning his ability or desire to perform the contract. Bob wants to buy Sal's house but is not sure he can get a mortgage. He writes an offer, including language that he will buy the house for $300,000, "if, within four weeks of acceptance of this offer, I can obtain a mortgage in the amount of $250,000 at an interest rate not higher than 9%." We don't know whether Bob will ultimately buy the house, but we know he is going to do "something." At the very least, he must apply for a mortgage, complete the necessary paperwork, and so on. He has incurred some obligation. If Bob applies for a mortgage but is denied, the contract becomes a fully executed (completed) contract without the sale of the house. On the other hand, if Bob gets buyer's remorse and does not apply for a mortgage, thinking that he has no obligation, he will learn that he is in breach of contract. The contract is valid and creates some obligation, regardless of whether Bob is ultimately able to buy the house.

Laurel wants a great dress for her high school reunion and goes to an expensive, designer shop. The shop, which deals in one-of-a-kind items, does not normally accept returns. Laurel is, therefore, conflicted about buying a $900 dress without asking her husband's opinion of how it looks. The salesperson agrees that Laurel can put the dress on her charge account, take it home, and, if her husband does not like it, return it for a full refund. She writes the agreement (a **condition subsequent**) on the receipt. We don't know whether Laurel will keep and pay for the dress, but she has incurred some obligation. At the very least, she has to return the dress in good condition.

2. Output, Needs, and Exclusive Dealing Contracts

Output Contract
Contract under which buyer agrees to purchase all that seller produces; court may impose requirement of reasonable performance

Needs Contract
Contract under which buyer agrees to purchase all of buyer's needs from seller (see exclusive dealing); court may impose requirement of reasonable performance

Exclusive Dealing Contract
Contract under which parties agree to deal only with each other with respect to particular needs

Of course, the UCC takes a moderate approach (by now, you may see a pattern). The Code includes provisions relating to **"output," "needs,"** and **"exclusive dealing"** contracts that further illustrate that the parties need not know what "something" is at the outset and that a court can impose a requirement of "reasonable" performance.

Examples

Parties entering a contract do not always know, at the outset, what they will need or be able to provide. Colonial Café enters into a contract with Janna's Bakery, under which Colonial will buy all of its baked goods from Janna's for one year and Janna will give Colonial a 10% discount off usual prices. This is a **"needs"** contract. Do we know how much Colonial will buy? No; the whole town could go on the Atkins diet, drying up the market for baked goods. But we do know this: If Colonial buys any baked goods, it will buy them from Janna's and if Janna's sells baked goods to Colonial, it will give a discount. Each party has incurred "some" obligation. This could also be characterized as an **exclusive dealing contract,** because Colonial will only deal with Janna's for its baked goods. These agreements can have antitrust implications, as discussed in Chapter 6, on legality.

Leah, the owner of Unique Boutique, spots a clever little purse made out of a cigar box and finds out that its owner, Elise, made it. Elise makes the purses as a hobby and is happy to agree to sell Leah her entire **"output"** (all of the purses she makes) at $25 per purse for the next six months. She generally makes 2 to 3 purses per week. The law implies "good faith," so that Elise cannot, without being in breach, start drinking lots of coffee, staying up all night, and producing 20 purses per week, nor can she spend the next six months zoned out in front of the television, making 1 purse per month.

D. Bargained-For

1. "To Which That Party Was Not Legally Entitled Before the Contract"

Bargained-for
Each party is induced to enter contract by consideration offered by other party

Legal scholars say that consideration must be **"bargained-for,"** which is another way of saying that each party gets something that he was not entitled to

Assignment 5-1

Using your state's version of the UCC:

1. Identify the sections dealing with unconscionability, and
2. Identify sections dealing with output/needs contracts.
3. Does your state still recognize **contracts under seal** (also called **formal contracts**)?

Contracts Under Seal
Formal contracts

"before the contract" and that each party is induced to "give" by what he will "get." A contract cannot normally be "inflicted" on a party by the delivery of consideration that party did not seek.

Legal scholars often say, "Past consideration is no consideration." Returning to the example at the beginning of this chapter, suppose that I learned that my brother had finally responded to my nagging and stopped smoking and I told him that I was so proud of him that I planned to give him $5,000. The promise is unenforceable because the giving and getting were not in response to each other.

Even judges sometimes struggle with the notion that past consideration is no consideration, particularly when there seems to be a moral obligation. Consider this famous case: A lumber mill worker (Webb) was dropping a huge block from an upper level when the president of the company (McGowin) suddenly appeared below. To avoid crushing the other man, Webb went over the edge with the block, to change its path. Webb suffered crippling injuries. McGowin promised Webb payments and actually made the payments for the rest of his life, but when McGowin died, the executors of his estate stopped paying, claiming the promise was not supported by consideration. Ultimately, the estate was required to make the payments.

You can find *Webb v. McGowin*, an Alabama case, using computer-assisted legal research (CALR), but before you look it up, can you guess the distinction between the case and the situation in which I promised my brother $5,000 because he stopped smoking? Some "moral obligation" agreements, lacking consideration, can be upheld under the doctrine of promissory estoppel. Why not McGowin's promise? Promissory estoppel is based in reliance; Webb did not act in reliance on McGowin's promise. Although commentators have various theories, the case may simply reflect sympathy for a horribly injured party with no other recourse.

In fact, the law has carved out an exception for common "rescue" situations. Suppose that a patient arrives at a hospital by ambulance, unconscious and not accompanied by a relative or friend. Are the doctors who worked to save her life not entitled to compensation? Courts treat the situation as more a problem of offer and acceptance than of consideration and say that a contract can be implied by law. This was previously explained within the discussion of quasi-contract in Chapter 1.

2. Preexisting Obligations

Another important question is whether the parties got something new, something to which they were not already entitled. For example, Jo is having trouble in class. The professor says, "Come in during my office hours and I will tutor you for $30 per hour." Jo will likely not have to pay because the professor was under a preexisting obligation to help students during office hours. In a sense, Jo has already paid for that by paying tuition. Similarly, police officers are often prohibited from collecting rewards for finding missing people or property; they are already paid and legally obligated to find missing people and property. What if the obligation is owed to a party outside the contract? For example, if my brother had already promised to stop smoking, for which our father will pay $1,000, is my subsequent promise unenforceable? The answer differs from state to state.

In looking at whether the parties got something new, keep in mind that one of the main functions of a contract is to allocate risk.

Example

We enter contracts to secure a position. Hal Homeowner is renovating an old house and wants the slate entry floor replaced with ceramic tile. He picks the tile. The salesperson, Sal, comes to the house to measure and talk about installation. Sal says that the job will be fairly easy; they can remove the old floor and install the new one for an hourly rate of $40. Sal says the job will take 18 to 22 hours. Hal says that he needs a firm price so that he can determine exactly what he can afford with respect to other repairs. Sal shrugs, saying, "Suit yourself. You could probably get this done cheaper hourly." The two sign a contract that calls for removal of the slate and installation of the new tile for $1,000. When Sal's employee arrives to do the work, he discovers that the slate was improperly installed. The removal ends up taking 25 hours; the installation takes another 6 hours. Sal feels he is entitled to more than $1,000, but the contract allocated the risk of difficulty to the company. Hal did not get anything he was not already entitled to; Sal had a **preexisting obligation** and was obligated to do the work regardless of the difficulty. In this situation, the contract allocated the risk and the result is "fair" because Hal had no idea what would be required; Sal is in the business and in a better position to evaluate the situation.

Cost-plus Contract
A way of sharing risk

Allowances
Contract total price includes "estimates" for components; if actual price of components differs from allowances, total contract price changes

Incentive Consideration
Consideration changes to motivate faster or better performance

In an effort to avoid the preexisting obligation rule and to create a contract in which risk is shared, some business people will only work at an hourly rate or will give an estimate, rather than a firm price. Other possibilities for risk avoidance or risk sharing include **"cost-plus"** contracts (I will build the garage for the cost of materials plus an additional 20%) and contracts involving **components** (Builder gives a price of $400,000 for construction of a house, which includes a fixed price for some things and **allowances** for other components—*e.g.*, Buyer has a $3,000 "allowance" for light fixtures; if Buyer chooses more expensive fixtures, Buyer will have to pay the additional cost). A contract might also be performance-based or include **incentives** (*e.g.*, Owner will pay Contractor $100,000 for labor if the structure is complete by May 1 and will pay an extra $10,000 if the structure is complete by April 15). In a later chapter, you will learn to examine contract language carefully and evaluate whether risk is being assigned to one party or the other.

E. Modification of Existing Contracts

Would this make a difference? When the job was half finished, Sal went to Hal and said, "Look, we just cannot finish this job at this price. I need you to sign a new deal." Worried that Sal would leave the job unfinished, Hal signed a contract agreeing to pay $1,400. Can Sal collect $1,400? In most states, the answer is no; that would amount to blackmail. The two had preexisting legal duties to each other: Sal to do the job and Hal to pay. Signing a new piece of paper adds nothing. Under the traditional view, there is no consideration for the new contract.

If you look at situations in your own life, you may have a better understanding of this. Suppose that you bought your first new car a few months ago for $19,000. The dealer now calls you and says, "We've just closed out our books for last year, and we took a bad loss. We are reevaluating all of our prices, and we need about $800 more from you."

The UCC does not require consideration to support modification of an existing contract for the sale of goods, if the modification is made in good faith and in response to circumstances that would not have been reasonably foreseeable. Some states have followed this more liberal approach. Even in those states, however, a modification signed under economic duress, such as a threat to walk off the job, would likely be considered invalid.

But, consider this. Sal said, "We can't finish the job at this price, and I need you to sign a new deal, but I don't want an unhappy customer. I know you wanted new baseboard, so I am going to throw that into the deal so that you will know we want you to be happy." The two then sign an agreement under which Hal will pay $1,500 and the work will include installation of new baseboard, which would normally add about $100 to the price. Now, Hal is getting something new: the baseboard. Remember, the law does not weigh consideration. It may not be fair, but Hal has now essentially agreed to pay $500 for baseboard.

An agreement to accept a payment or performance in exchange for a different payment or performance, required under a contract, is known as an **accord and satisfaction.** The accord is the agreement to accept something different and the satisfaction is the actual performance. Sal and Hal reached an accord, the new agreement ($1,500), and the satisfaction (installation of the baseboard) discharges the original agreement.

Accord and Satisfaction
Agreement to accept and give payment or performance, different from that originally required by contract

Consideration is not always money, an object, or a service. It can be the grant or release of a legal right.

Example

Jerry cleans offices evenings and goes to school during the day. One of Jerry's clients, Caveat Realtors, hasn't paid its cleaning bill in several months and now owes $800. Jerry finally tells Caveat that there will be no more cleaning and that the bill is going to be "turned over to a lawyer." The next day, Jerry receives a check from Caveat, in the amount of $500. Jerry really needs the money and decides to deposit it and go after the additional $300 later. On the back of the check, however, where Jerry would endorse it for deposit, Caveat has printed, "Payment in full for all cleaning, 3/1/XX–5/1/XX." Does Jerry give up all right to the additional $300 by signing the check?

Before you answer, consider this: My electric bill for this month is $220. I'd like to relieve myself of some of this outrageous expense by writing a check for $100 and, on the back, writing, "Payment in full. . . . "Many modern businesses handle a high volume of checks and cannot inspect each individually.

Look at the situation in terms of the definition of consideration. Jerry and Caveat had a contract: weekly cleaning in exchange for $100 per week. Each gave and got something. The language on the back of the check is an attempt to **rescind** and create a new contract under which Caveat gets something (three weeks of free cleaning). What does Jerry get in return? Jerry was already entitled to the $500.

Rescind
To terminate a contract before all of its terms are completely performed

In the view of most courts, just putting it in writing does not create an enforceable contract, but the states are not in total agreement about modification of contracts. Some states have developed various exceptions to allow the parties to modify a contract without new consideration if the modification appears to be fair or if the parties have acted on the modification. If Jerry were your firm's client, your supervising attorney might ask you to research your state's position before advising Jerry to cash the check.

Assignment 5-2

The Jerry/Caveat situation is not covered by the UCC. If it were a contract for the sale of goods, the answer might be easier to find. In your state's version of the UCC, identify provisions relating to modification, **rescission,** and **waiver.**

Rescission
Mutual agreement to cancel

Waiver
Intentional relinquishment of right, claim, or privilege

- Does the provision require that a modification be written?
- Is a **waiver** retractable? For example, Factory has a contract with Supplier, under which Supplier delivers a crate of bolts to the Factory loading dock each Monday. For several weeks Supplier was without a full-time delivery driver and delivered the bolts on Tuesdays. Factory accepted the Tuesday deliveries without complaint and, therefore, waived its right to insist on Monday delivery, but would now like to have Monday deliveries resume. Can Factory now insist on Monday delivery or was the agreement modified by the behavior of the parties?

Could Jerry avoid the dilemma by crossing out the "payment in full" language or writing "under protest," "without prejudice," or "all rights reserved" above his signature? You may already know the answer to this. It is not an issue of consideration; it is an issue of acceptance/counteroffer.

F. Settlement of Disputes

Is it possible that Caveat is giving something in exchange? If the $800 debt is a **liquidated debt,** the answer is probably no. A liquidated debt is a debt that is not in dispute. Suppose, however, that the reason Caveat had not paid was dissatisfaction with Jerry. Caveat has a valid claim that Jerry did not do the entire job several times, spilled furniture oil on a valuable rug, and broke some pottery. Caveat was planning to replace Jerry and, possibly, to file suit in small claims court. The debt is **unliquidated** if the amount is in dispute and the settlement of an unliquidated debt can constitute consideration. Jerry would be giving up the claim to $300; Caveat would be giving up its claims with respect to damage and inadequate service. People involved in disputes concerning accidents have to be particularly careful about accepting checks before they know the extent of their damages.

Liquidated Debt
Debt that is not in dispute

Unliquidated Debt
Debt, the amount of which is in dispute; settlement of an unliquidated debt can constitute consideration

It is also possible that in some situations, the agreement to accept an amount less than the full debt could constitute a completed gift. A promise to make a gift is not enforceable, but once a gift is completed, it may not be withdrawn. So, for example, if Son owed Dad $800 and Dad said, "Give me a check for $500, write 'payment in full' on the back, and we'll consider it done," some courts may consider it a completed gift.

In some states the "liquidated debt" rule has evolved, along with the concept of waiver. For example, in some jurisdictions, a landlord's agreement to accept $700 per month instead of $900, as stated in the lease, followed by actual acceptance of the lesser amount, could constitute an enforceable waiver of the unpaid amount. When a client presents an issue, it is always worth researching the possibility of exceptions unique to your state.

Assignment 5-3

Use CALR to find and summarize a case from your state or a neighboring state. Remember to use expanders to find variations such as "unconscionable" or "unconscionability" and "rented" or "rental." Find cases involving:

- Unconscionability in a rental agreement (housing or rental of personal property)
- Whether new consideration is required to support changes to an existing contract
- Parties intentionally stating nominal consideration in a contract when it would be just as easy to state actual consideration. Research cases involving recitation of nominal consideration in real estate transfers and/or cases in which a party is "leasing" property for a stated term and has the right to purchase the property at the end of the term for a nominal price. What motivations underlie these transactions?

G. Practical and Ethical Issues

You have learned that courts do not generally involve themselves in the adequacy or fairness of consideration. Unfortunately, however, courts are sometimes called on to review the fairness of legal fees (the consideration in a contract between an attorney and client), particularly in "fee reversal" cases, in which the "losing" party must pay the "winner's" attorney fees. In addition, fees are subject to an ethical rule.

Assignment 5-4

Examine your state Rule of Professional Conduct relating to fees. In the ABA Model Rules, it is Rule 1.5.

- Is a contingency fee arrangement prohibited for certain cases?
- Does the Rule require that certain fee agreements be written?
- What factors go into the determination of whether a fee is "reasonable"?
- What business practices can a law firm implement to help keep fees reasonable? How can paralegals help?
- Attorney A's aunt was in a major accident, but A does not handle personal injury cases and, therefore, refers his aunt to Firm B. Firm B is able to negotiate a settlement of $600,000 for A's aunt and earns a fee of $200,000. Under what circumstances may A take a referral fee?

Assignment 5-5

Now find and examine your state Rule of Professional Conduct relating to restrictions on the right to practice. The Rule (Rule 5.6 in the ABA Model Rules) is key to understanding *Hurd v. Wildman Harrold Allen & Dixon* (Ill. App. Ct. 1999), which can be found online. Read the case, which involves allegations of duress, unconscionability, and preexisting duty in a contract between lawyers. The Hurd case illustrates an attempt to make such arguments, the unwillingness of a court to accept those arguments, and some ethical issues concerning contracts between lawyers.

- What facts did the court find most important in rejecting Hurd's claims?
- Why did the agreement in the Hurd case limit the extra payment to involuntary separation?
- Why would a law firm try to discourage lawyers from leaving?
- How might this concern motivate a firm to hire paralegals, rather than new lawyers, in some cases?

Have recent economic trends muddied the waters of consideration? Perhaps. Benefits offered by companies in the "roarin' 90s" could send the company into bankruptcy in the recession of the mid-2000s. While companies can avoid their contractual obligations by seeking bankruptcy (as discussed in Chapter 10), they may look for less-drastic ways of reducing the costs imposed by contracts. The assignment that follows will show you how courts use statutory law, other than the UCC, in connection with the requirement of consideration.

Assignment 5-6

First, find and read the rules for the United Airlines Mileage Plus program. Next, read *Lagen v. United Continental Holdings, Inc.* (7th Cir. 2014). An online search of the names of the parties will lead you to the full opinion. While this case focuses on Million-Mile Flyers, consider the Mileage Plus program as a whole. Discuss:

- Did you read the rules of any frequent flyer program to which you belong? Do you think most people read the rules? Do you think people act in reliance on earning those benefits?
- Does the ability of one party to unilaterally change the terms mean that the consideration was illusory and, perhaps, no contract formed? Is this really an ongoing gift? Why do you think there is no discussion of promissory estoppel?
- Do you think the result would be the same if the defendant were not the airline industry, covered by the Airline Deregulation Act? What about common law fraud? Was the advertising truly just a unilateral offer? Had the customers already accepted?

Now consider the 2014 Supreme Court decision, *M&G Polymers USA, LLC v. Tackett.* To what extent did the court rely on federal labor laws and ERISA, the federal pension law? While the contract language was certainly ambiguous, do you think that the lower court (Sixth Circuit) reached its decision based on its own economic concerns?

Career Corner

Channet Jusino, secretary for the New York City Paralegal Association (NYCPA), is a senior paralegal in the Office of the General Counsel for the New York Blood Center. She is responsible for contract administration and management, litigation support, processing of medical/employee information subpoenas, training on contract databases, organizing documentation for audits, preparation of meetings of the board of trustees, and more. Channet supports two attorneys.

After graduating from Seton Hall University with an undergraduate degree in political science and English, Channet received an M.A. in Legal Studies with a concentration in legal management-information and technology, governance compliance-regulations and intellectual property from Montclair State University, in New Jersey. She graduated with a 3.95 GPA, as a member of the Alpha Epsilon Lambda and Phi Kappa Phi honor societies.

Channet loves her work because it gives her a chance to be a part of organizations whose mission involves helping others, whether by promoting the donation of blood or helping other paralegals advance. Channet knows that the paralegal profession helps people by making the practice of law more efficient and more accessible to ordinary people. She emphasizes the importance of paralegal professional groups, such as NYCPA and urges new paralegals to not only join, but to become active in those associations. Her top tip concerning contracts: Read it word by word and then read it again!

Review Questions

1. In what circumstances might an agreement be enforced without consideration?
2. What is illusory consideration and how does the UCC deal with situations that might, at common law, be viewed as illusory because they call for performance to the "satisfaction" of one of the parties?
3. What is a condition precedent? What is a condition subsequent? In each of these situations, we say that there was a valid contract even though the performance originally contemplated does not ultimately occur: Why?
4. Give an example of an accord and satisfaction.
5. Under what circumstances does the UCC allow enforceability of modification of an existing contract without consideration?
6. What is a liquidated debt?
7. What are the special requirements for a contingent fee arrangement under ABA Model Rule 1.5? What kinds of cases may not be handled on a contingency fee basis?
8. In discussing the factors that determine the reasonableness of a fee, the Rule refers to "the likelihood, if apparent to the client, that the acceptance of the particular employment will preclude other employment by the lawyer"; how might acceptance of a case preclude other employment?
9. Identify the issues raised by the following:

   Jay got a new Acme charge card because Acme advertised a low interest rate on unpaid balances. Jay transferred his balance from another credit card to the Acme card. After six months, Acme increased the rate and sent out a mailing that stated that, by continuing to use the card, the customer agreed to the rather significant change. Jay thought the mailing was just more junk mail and never read it. He continued to use the Acme card, paid the minimum payment for a couple of months, and after three months, finally noticed the change. The difference in the interest rate will cost Jay a substantial amount of money.

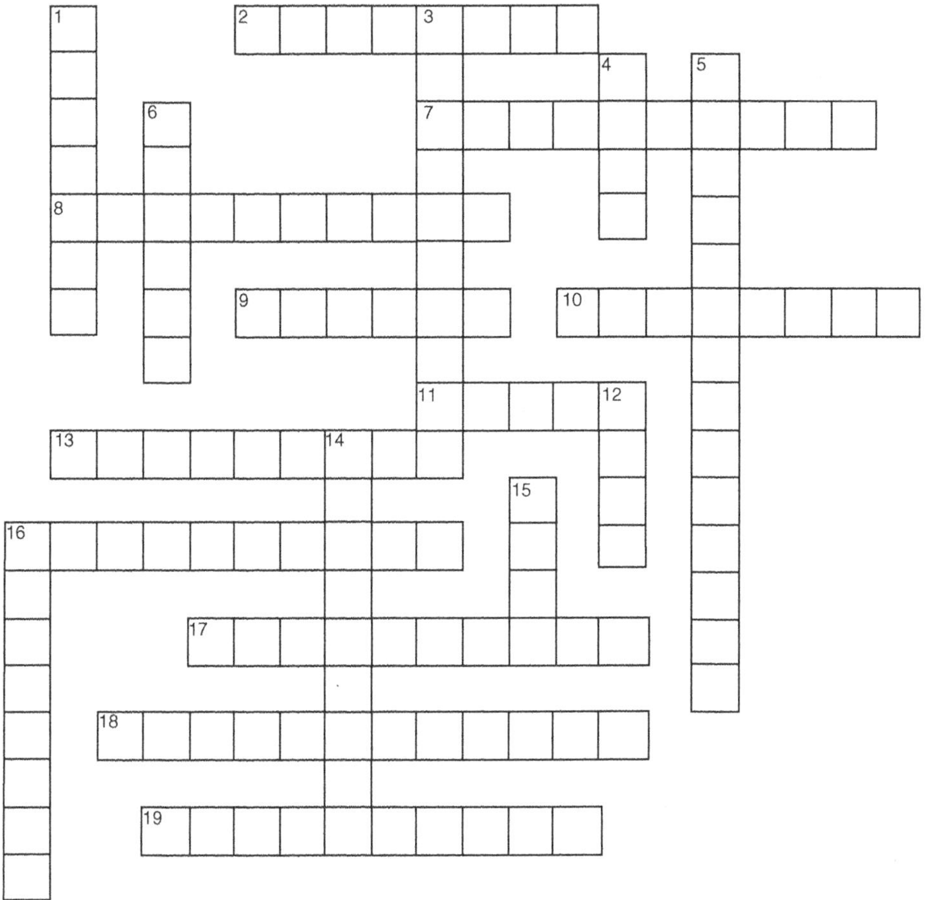

ACROSS

2. stated consideration does not really obligate party
7. _______ power; the ability of a party to negotiate
8. consideration changes to motivate faster or better performance
9. contract to buy company's entire production
10. police officers often cannot collect rewards because they have a pre _______ duty
11. contract—*e.g.*, we will buy all of our dairy products from Acme
13. condition _______ identifies an event that must occur before performance goes forward
16. contract might include _______—*e.g.*, buyer has $3,000 for light fixtures
17. _______ debt not in dispute
18. UCC allows _______ of existing contracts without consideration
19. contracts between businesses

DOWN

1. to terminate the contract
3. condition ________ can undo the contract
4. " ________ consideration is no consideration"
5. consideration so unfair it is shocking
6. ________ and satisfaction
12. stated consideration did not really occur
14. ________ dealing contract can have antitrust implications
15. ________-plus; a way of sharing risk
16. a take-it-or-leave-it contract

6

◆ ◆ ◆

Legality

◆ ◆ ◆

This chapter explores the traditional grounds for finding a contract clause to be illegal, as well as the developing concept of "public policy," protection of consumers, and common provisions that may be unenforceable. The topic overlaps with issues of invalid assent, discussed in Chapter 4, so students may want to review those concepts.

Skills-based learning objectives	*How you will demonstrate your ability*
Identify specific contracts that are prohibited by or require a license under state law.	Assignments: Research state regulation of specific contracts.
Analyze public policy issues in contract enforcement.	Assignment: Use CALR to find a case involving a legality issue; prepare a case brief.

A. Violations of Statutes
  1. Licensing
  2. Usury and Other Lending Laws
  3. Gambling
  4. Blue Laws
  5. Torts
  6. Public Policy
B. Exculpatory Clauses
C. Restraint of Trade
D. Practical and Ethical Issues

Severable
Remainder of agreement can be enforced without unenforceable provision contained in the agreement

Blue-penciling
Court edits parts of a contract

In Pari Delicto
The parties are equally at fault

An agreement that calls for violation of a statute, commission of a tort, or actions that are contrary to public policy is unenforceable. The illegality of one part of an agreement does not always mean that the entire agreement is unenforceable. In some cases a court may find that the rest of the agreement can be enforced without the illegal provision; the illegal provision is **severable.** When a court "edits out" parts of a contract, it is sometimes called **blue-penciling.** In addition, courts have discretion to avoid harming an innocent party, if necessary. The term **in pari delicto** means that parties are equally at fault.

Examples

In a lawsuit concerning construction of a residence, the judge learns that the builder was operating without a license, in violation of a licensing statute. The judge subsequently learns that the homeowners were also in violation of the law; they obtained financing assistance from the city by claiming to be first-time homeowners who intend to live in the house. In fact, they own and live in another house and plan to rent the new house as an income property. The judge may determine the relative "fault" of the parties in determining whether to enforce the entire contract, parts of the contract, or none of the contract.

Attorney Goldstein hired Patterson as a paralegal and agreed to pay Patterson a salary plus a bonus calculated as 10% of Goldstein's attorney's fees from cases on which Patterson worked. Patterson did not know that the arrangement implicated the Florida Bar's Rules of Professional Conduct. Goldstein refused to pay the full bonus and Patterson sought $87,300.00 in unpaid wages. Goldstein argued that the agreement was not enforceable because it was "unethical and thus void as against public policy." The trial court entered summary judgment in favor of Goldstein. The parties did not dispute that the arrangement violated the Rules, which state:

> [B]onuses may be paid to nonlawyer employees for work performed, and may be based on their extraordinary efforts on a particular case or over a specified time period. Bonus payments shall not be based on cases or clients brought to the lawyer or law firm by the actions of the nonlawyer. A lawyer shall not provide a bonus payment that is calculated as a percentage of legal fees received by the lawyer or law firm. . . .

R. Regulating Fla. Bar 4-5.4(a)(4).

The appeals court reversed, stating that to hold this agreement void would permit an unscrupulous attorney to repudiate an agreement after reaping the benefit of the bargain. The doctrine that a contract offensive to public policy is unenforceable is based on the principle that "'[w]here the parties . . . are in pari delicto the law will leave them where it finds them; relief will be refused in the courts because of public interest.'" The corollary is "where the parties are not in pari delicto, the innocent party may recover." Patterson, who is not a member of the Bar, (1) is not regulated by the Rules and (2) did not know that Goldstein was breaking the Rules. *Patterson v. A Law Office of Lauri J. Goldstein, PA*, 980 So. 2d 1234 (Fla. Dist. Ct. App. 2008).

A. Violations of Statutes

For obvious reasons, agreements involving serious criminal conduct, such as buying illegal drugs or hiring a "hit man," are not enforceable. Other agreements that violate statutes in a less flamboyant way might include, for example, rental of property with a promise to exclude minorities. If the violation is **malum per se,** meaning inherently "bad," the agreement is likely unenforceable. Other statutory violations are not inherently bad and are less serious (**malum prohibitum**). The results can vary. The *Baby M* sample case at the end of this chapter includes extensive discussion of statutory violations as well as the more general violations of public policy.

Malum Per Se
Inherently bad

Malum Prohibitum
Not inherently bad; less serious

1. Licensing

If a licensing law is intended to protect the public, agreements in violation of the law are unenforceable. For example, Attorney Bell was disbarred last year. Bell's neighbor, Adams, was unaware of the disbarment and asked Bell to prepare a complicated will and trust agreement. Bell did the work and submitted a bill for $1,000. Adams will not have to pay. The agreement was illegal.

On the other hand, a license requirement may be only a way of raising money. For example, River City requires that all door-to-door sales people go to city hall and pay $10 for a peddlers' license. Unaware of the requirement, Betsy-the-Brownie-Scout goes to Attorney Bell's house to sell Girl Scout cookies. Bell, in a wicked mood because of the disbarment, orders $300 worth of the low-cal cookies that nobody wants. When Betsy delivers the cookies and tries to collect, Bell claims that the agreement was illegal because of the lack of a license. No wonder Bell was disbarred! The contract is likely enforceable.

2. Usury and Other Lending Laws

A **usurious** contract is one that charges an illegal rate of interest on a loan. States have different laws concerning the rate of interest that may be charged on various types of loans. **Consumer loans,** which do not involve businesses, and loans that do not involve regulated banks are most often regulated. Visit the "Lectric Law Library" to find the rate for your state, visit http://www.lectlaw.com/files/ban02.htm.

Usurious Contract
Charges an illegal rate of interest on a loan

Consumer Loan
Loan for personal or family purposes

The interest rate on so-called "payday" or "title" loans is a current hot topic. A related matter is the disclosures made in lending. For an explanation of payday loans and to learn whether they are legal in your state, visit the Consumer Federation of America's Web site, http://www.paydayloaninfo.org/. For an explanation of the Truth in Lending Act, visit https://www.ftc.gov/enforcement/statutes?title=&&page=3.

Some states and the FTC also regulate other aspects of lending contracts. For example, the FTC Credit Practices Rule[1] prohibits "confession of judgment" clauses like the one below. Read the sample clause, which is written in a way that

[1]https://www.law.cornell.edu/cfr/text/16/444.2.

would be incomprehensible to most borrowers. Were you able to determine that, by signing, the borrower was giving up normal legal rights, such as the right to be notified that a lawsuit has been filed and the right to appear in court and raise defenses to the lawsuit? Did you realize that the borrower is agreeing to have judgment entered against him immediately and to be represented by any attorney chosen by the lender?

The consequences of violation of statutes relating to lending can be very different. In some cases, the lender might not be allowed to collect any interest (the court regards the illegal interest rate as severable); in others, the lender might not be allowed to recover even the principal amount (the court finds the illegal provision not severable and the entire agreement unenforceable).

EXHIBIT 6-1
Example of a Confession of Judgment, Also Called a "Cognovits"

Confession of Judgment
A clause that permits immediate entry of judgment without notice or an opportunity to present defenses

To secure payment hereof, the undersigned jointly and severally irrevocably authorize any attorney of any court of record to appear for any one or more of them in such court in term or vacation, after default in payment hereof and confess a judgment without process in favor of the creditor hereof for such amount as may then appear unpaid hereon, to release all errors which may intervene in any such proceedings, and to consent to immediate execution upon such judgment, hereby ratifying every act of such attorney hereunder.

Assignment 6-1

Using your state statutes, find out:

- Does your state require a license for making consumer loans?
- Does your state regulate payday loans?

3. Gambling

Most states now permit some forms of wagering, for example at casinos or racetracks or through a lottery, but may prohibit various agreements relating to gambling. For example, states differ on whether gambling on credit is allowed. In a sense, taking insurance is a form of gambling and many states prohibit taking insurance on another person if you do not have a legitimate financial interest in that person (an **insurable interest**).

Assignment 6-2

A **pyramid scheme** can be a form of gambling. Visit the FTC Web site at http://www.consumer.ftc.gov/blog/telltale-signs-pyramid-scheme, and write a one-paragraph definition of "pyramid scheme."

Pyramid Scheme
Multilevel arrangement in which money is made by recruiting new people

4. Blue Laws

A **blue law,** also called a **Sunday statute,** prohibits certain transactions on Sundays. These laws are less common now, but still exist. For example, a law prohibiting the sale of liquor on Sunday morning is common. Your state may have its own unique Sunday laws; for example, Illinois prohibits auto dealerships from operating on Sundays.

Blue Law
Prohibits certain transactions on Sundays; also called a Sunday statute

Sunday Statute
Prohibits certain transactions on Sundays; also called a blue law

5. Torts

A **tort** is a civil wrong (not a criminal prosecution) that is sometimes based in statute and sometimes based in common law. If an agreement calls for commission of a tort, even if there is no statutory violation, it is likely unenforceable. For example, JB, a successful painter, agrees to make derogatory, false remarks about other brands of paint, such as "it runs," or "that brand takes three coats to cover anything" in return for special pricing on Bozo Paints. The state has no statute dealing with **slander** (false statements that hurt the reputation of another), but the agreement is probably illegal.

In early 2012 New Orleans Saints' coach Sean Payton was suspended for having a "bounty" program, under which he paid players for injuring members of other teams. Think about the contract implications: Unilateral or bilateral? Illegal? If it were not illegal, would accidental injuries be covered?

Slander
False statements that hurt the reputation of another

Contrary to Public Policy
Not good for society

6. Public Policy

Even if no specific statute prohibits the terms of the agreement, a court can refuse to enforce the agreement if it is **contrary to public policy,** meaning that it is not good for society. Courts have discretion to determine public policy by looking at statutes, even if they are not directly applicable, and common law. Governmental entities are, in some states, prohibited from including certain types of clauses in their contracts because those clauses may be against public policy. For an example, see http://www.legal.uncc.edu/prohibitedclauses.html. A sample

Insurable Interest
Legitimate financial interest in a person

case at the end of this chapter, *In the Matter of Baby M,* provides an excellent example of a court analyzing a public policy issue. Certain types of contracts commonly involve consideration of public policy.

EXHIBIT 6-2
Unfair Clauses

Many people think that U.S. law does not adequately protect consumers against unfair clauses and that unfair clauses should be considered illegal or contrary to public policy.

In 1993 the Council of the European Communities adopted a Directive on Unfair Terms in Consumer Contracts, requiring that member states pass laws to protect consumers. In 2002 French courts requested that AOL remove clauses from its subscriber contracts that they called "abusive" or even "illegal." Other Internet service providers may face similar orders, based on clauses that allow the companies to unilaterally modify the contract; clauses that imply acceptance by the subscriber of changes to pricing, billing, and general conditions; and clauses that absolve the company from liability for interruptions or errors in the service.

The European Union (learn more at http://europa.eu/pol/cons/index_en.htm) is taking action to inform and protect consumers. Should the United States be doing more? Some states do more than others. For example, Florida has declared that exculpatory clauses (described below) are unenforceable in residential leases (Fla. Stat. §83.47).

B. Exculpatory Clauses

Exculpatory Clause
Provision that attempts to excuse a party from liability for that party's torts

Tortious
Constituting a tort

An **exculpatory clause** is an agreement provision that attempts to excuse a party from liability for that party's own **tortious** (constituting a tort) actions. If the clause attempts to excuse liability for intentional or reckless conduct, it is generally unenforceable.

Example

Jo, an aspiring model, enters into a contract with Bill, a photographer and publicist. The contract, which Jo did not read, included a statement that Bill would have no liability for any torts committed against Jo. Bill subsequently uses pictures of Jo on a Web site advertising pornography, or perhaps Bill becomes angry during a photo shoot and slaps Jo, breaking her nose. In either case, Bill's actions constitute an intentional tort. If Jo sues Bill, it is likely that a court will not enforce the exculpatory clause because Bill's actions were intentional.

If the exculpatory clause involves negligent torts, the court will look at a number of factors to determine whether it is enforceable. Those factors include:

- Was the clause conspicuous and clear? A disclaimer on the back side of a valet parking receipt, not seen until after the valet drives away with the car, is less effective than a sign at the entrance to a parking garage proclaiming, "We are not responsible for any damage. . . ."
- What is the relationship between the parties and the relative "need" of the parties? In an **arm's-length transaction** the parties have equal power to negotiate terms. That is not often true between employer and employee, doctor and patient, customer and electric company, and a landlord and tenant.
- To what degree can the parties protect themselves? Was the hazard obvious? Was it within control of one of the parties?

In considering exculpatory clauses, keep in mind that a contract only binds its parties. If Stevie takes a job as a driver for Acme Co. and signs an agreement stating that "Acme Co. shall not be liable for the consequences of my negligent driving," the agreement only covers the relationship between Stevie and Acme. Pedestrians and other drivers are not part of that agreement and may sue Acme. The contract clause may then operate as a **hold harmless** or **indemnification** clause, under which one party agrees to compensate the other for losses arising from the contract.

Arm's-length Transaction
Relationship where parties have equal power to negotiate terms

Hold Harmless Clause
One party agrees to compensate the other for losses arising from the contract; also called indemnification clause

Indemnification Clause
One party agrees to compensate the other for losses arising from the contract; also called hold harmless clause

EXHIBIT 6-3
Example Exculpatory Clause

Do you think a typical vacationer renting a boat would read or understand the following?

Renter ________, his/her family, relatives, heirs, and legal representatives do hereby, waive, discharge and covenant not to sue Voyagaire Houseboats . . . for any loss or damage, or any claim or damage or any injury to any person or persons or property, or any death of any person or persons whether caused by negligence or defect, while such rental equipment is in my possession and/or under my use. . . .[2]

The following is an example indemnification in a contract between an insurance provider and a dentist.

Dentist agrees to indemnify, defend, and hold harmless Iota Insurance, Inc., its directors, officers, employees, and agents for any and all claims, liabilities, damages, losses, costs, fees, and expenses arising from or in any way related to any dental or other service performed by Dentist and any employees, associates, contractors, or agents of Dentist.

---

[2]The Minnesota Supreme Court held that this language violated public policy in its 2005 decision *Yang v. Voyagaire Houseboats, Inc.*, 701 N.W.2d 783.

C. Restraint of Trade

Covenant Not to Compete
Provision under which party agrees to refrain from engaging in specified business activities ("noncompete")

The basic policy of the United States favors free trade; and contract provision that inhibits free trade is subject to scrutiny in court. The most common form of provision that might restrain trade (a party's ability to engage in business) is a **covenant not to compete.** Noncompetes, as they are called, are not enforceable independently; they can only be enforced as part of a larger, legitimate agreement.

When a noncompete clause appears in a contract for the **sale of a business,** it is generally enforceable, if it is reasonable in terms of time limit, geographic limitations, and scope of activity covered. What is reasonable depends on the nature of the business and what is necessary to protect the buyer's legitimate interests. In the sale of a business, both parties are normally represented by lawyers and can negotiate terms that both can live with.

Example

Paul's Family Restaurant is a really popular place in Springfield. Dell buys the restaurant for $800,000 because it is so popular. How will Dell feel if, a week after the transaction is closed, the seller puts up a sign on vacant land across the street: "Coming in 6 months . . . the NEW Paul's, featuring your old friends, Chef Stella & Host Dan." If Dell had been smart, the sales contract would have included a restriction: "Seller agrees that Seller will not operate, work in, or represent any restaurant within five miles of the premises for a period of two years." Such a restriction would be reasonable. On the other hand, would it be reasonable to include a restriction for ten years, or one that covered the entire United States, or one that limited the sellers from participating in *any* business? Probably not.

The parties are not so equal when entering an **employment contract.** Employers do have valid reasons to restrict future employment: concerns that customers will move with the employee; concerns that the employee with take secret information to the new employer; and concerns about the cost of training new people. On the other hand, the employee's freedom to change jobs and ability to make a living are also very important. Courts are, therefore, particularly careful in analyzing restrictions on employees. Not only must such a restriction be reasonable in terms of time and geography, it must be related to the employer's legitimate interest. A restriction might be a general promise not to engage in competition with the employer or might be more specific and prohibit the use of certain information acquired as an employee, solicitation of the employer's customers, or "poaching" of other employees.

Assignment 6-3

Based on the *Baby M* case at the end of this chapter and *Cohen v. Lord, Day & Lord* (N.Y. 1989), http://www.leagle.com/decision/198917075NY2d95_1161/COHEN%20v.%20LORD,%20DAY%20&%20LORD, discuss:

1. To what extent did the personal characteristics of the "*Baby M*" parties impact the decision and public perception? What if the surrogate had been a well-educated woman who had originally entered the contract in order to raise funds for experimental treatment of her husband's cancer? What if, instead of leaving with the baby, she had immediately sought judicial review? What if the biological father had a criminal record and an unstable marriage?
2. Do you think the court was considering implications for the future as well as the past histories of the parties? If surrogacy contracts were always enforceable, might wealthy women rent the wombs of poorer women to avoid weight gain, stretch marks, and medical risks of pregnancy?
3. Could the contract at issue in the *Cohen* case be considered punitive? Why? Do you think this influenced the court?
4. Did the law firm have legitimate interests that were injured by Cohen's departure? Could the firm have protected itself by any other means?

Courts will also consider the interests of people outside the contract and may refuse to enforce a covenant if, for example, it would mean that patients would have to travel 100 miles to continue to see the doctor they have been seeing. What is reasonable will, again, depend on the nature of the business and the interest the employer is trying to protect. In addition, courts may consider the impact of the restriction on those outside the contract: patients and clients. The *Cohen* case cited above contains an analysis of a covenant's impact on a lawyer's clients.

Example

It is in the best interests of employers to make restrictive covenants reasonable so that they will be upheld. Lynn, a newly graduated interior designer, is offered a contract to work for Jones Brothers, a Milwaukee-area furniture chain. The job will involve meeting with corporate clients to design and choose furniture for corporate offices. A clause providing: "If employee leaves Jones for any reason, including firing or layoff, employee may not work for any furniture or design business in the state of Wisconsin (including employee's own business) for five years" is likely unreasonable. It might leave Lynn unable to find appropriate employment, and it likely goes beyond the employer's needs. A more reasonable restriction might read: "If employee leaves Jones for any reason, including firing or layoff, employee may not contact any clients of Jones for a period of two years, if employee had contact with the client while employed by Jones."

Another possible restriction is an **exclusive dealing agreement.** For example, Bari's Café agrees to buy its baked goods only from Herb's Bakery in exchange for a 10% discount; Bari's will deal with Herb's exclusively in buying baked goods. An exclusive dealing agreement may, in some situations, violate antitrust laws and should be analyzed carefully.

Assignment 6-4

a. Your instructor will tell you which problems to do, so that your class gets reports on each of these issues. Summarize a case and report to the class, focusing on how a court in your state resolved the situation. In structuring your query, remember to use expanders and to brainstorm for synonyms (*e.g.*, "restrictive covenant," "noncompet!" "promise or covenant or clause /s compet!") Use your CALR subscription or Loislaw to find a case involving:

- A restrictive covenant in an employment contract (what did the court find reasonable/unreasonable)
- A restrictive covenant in the sale of a business (what did the court find reasonable/unreasonable)
- A contract in contemplation of cohabitation by unmarried individuals of opposite sexes
- An exculpatory clause in a rental agreement

b. As assigned by your instructor, find and summarize a case involving one of the following. Focus on how the court avoided harm to an "innocent" party, if it regarded one party as more at fault.

- A party trying to collect for medical or legal services rendered in violation of a licensing law (luckily these are rare cases, you may have to search multiple states)
- A debt with a usurious rate of interest
- A violation of laws regulating lenders (lender licensing, truth in lending)
- A contract to insure the life of another, where the beneficiary did not have an insurable interest
- A gambling debt or agreement or a pyramid scheme
- A lawyer facing civil liability (a malpractice or negligence action) or disciplinary action because of involvement with a contract that included provisions that were illegal or contrary to public policy. You may have to search all 50 states on CALR or Loislaw and look at your ethics opinions site to find this one!

c. Using CALR or a search engine, find and summarize the 2012 Supreme Court of New Jersey case, *Mazdabrook Commons Homeowners' Ass'n v. Khan*. Now find and summarize *Benjamin Crossing Homeowners' Ass'n, Inc. v. Heide*, Court of Appeals of Indiana, http://www.in.gov/judiciary/opinions/pdf/02071201ewn.pdf. These cases demonstrate the importance of researching the law rather than assuming that you can rely on what you learned in school! Courts are generally reluctant to invalidate the terms of an agreement, such as the rules governing a homeowners' association. Why do you think the New Jersey decision differed from the general rule?

d. Discussion:

Tenant leased a warehouse and office space in a business park for a term of five years, but vacated after about half the term. The landlord was unable to find a new tenant and sued under a lease clause that stated: "In the event of termination of this Lease by reason of a violation of its terms by the Lessee, Lessor shall be entitled to prove claim for and obtain judgment against Lessee for the balance of the rent agreed to be paid for the term herein provided, plus all expenses of Lessor in regaining possession of the premises and the reletting thereof, including attorneys' fees and court costs, crediting against such claim, however, any amount obtained by reason of any such reletting." This is called an **acceleration clause.** What does it mean in plain English? Do you think the court should enforce the clause as written? Can you think of a fair solution? Acceleration clauses cause payments to become immediately due upon the happening of stated event.

D. Practical and Ethical Issues

The material in this chapter touches on several "hot" issues in the practice of law:

- Lawyers are prohibited from imposing restrictive covenants on each other. A covenant that might be valid in another employment agreement is likely invalid if it restricts a lawyer because it would, in fact, restrict clients in their choice of lawyers. After reading *Cohen v. Lord, Day & Lord* (N.Y. 1989), http://www.leagle.com/decision/198917075NY2d95_1161/COHEN%20v.%20LORD,%20DAY%20&%20LORD, contrast with the firm's agreement in the *Hurd* case at the end of Chapter 5, on consideration. Do the cases represent two different ways to achieve the same goal? Find the applicable Model Rule or the rule in your state.
- Lawyers are licensed on a state-by-state basis, so that a lawyer may be violating a licensing requirement in, for example:
  - Attending a real estate closing for a long-term client buying a vacation home in a neighboring state
  - Responding to a question e-mailed from another state by a visitor to the firm's Web site
  - Working at the corporate law department in Chicago and giving advice to corporate employees across the country
  - Working in a neighboring state after her law office was destroyed by a hurricane

ABA Model Rule 5.5 addresses multijurisdictional practice and the ABA Commission on Multijurisdictional Practice has a number of proposals to address these and other issues. For information on whether your state has adopted any of the proposals, visit http://www.abanet.org/cpr/mjp-home.html.

- Lawyers must protect client confidences, subject to exceptions relating to a client's criminal activity. Find your state's Rule of Professional Responsibility

(ABA Model Rule 1.6) and identify the situations in which a lawyer is permitted to reveal information relating to representation of a client.

- Does your state's rule require a lawyer to reveal information about a client under court order?
- Is a lawyer required to reveal information about a client if that client has committed a very serious crime?
- Is the ethical rule any different in situations involving fraud on a tribunal (perjury)?

Career Corner

Donna M. is the manager of contract administration at Sears Holdings Corporation, where she has previously held the positions of senior paralegal for vendor management; senior paralegal for contract manager for dealer stores; and paralegal. During her stint as contract manager for dealer stores, Donna managed all legal documentation for more than 760 independent dealers, including contracts, termination/nonrenewal letters, background and asset research and analysis, and audit reports. She worked with others on compliance, close-down, transition, and disaster recovery situations. Before joining Sears, Donna worked as a law firm administrative assistant and earned her paralegal certificate. Donna is an excellent example of upward mobility in the paralegal field.

Donna is particularly proud of one project she worked on for her employer. She coordinated, monitored, reviewed, and documented the filing of 900 UCC-1 and UCC-3 financing statements in all 50 states and Puerto Rico, and sent notification letters to external interested parties. Donna also managed outside vendor relationships and negotiated project costs. What did she learn from the project? Donna says:

> First and foremost, the Uniform Commercial Code ("UCC") is not "uniform." The only "uniform" thing about the UCC is its definition. WiseGeek.com defines the UCC as "a set of statutes governing the conduct of business, sales, warranties, negotiable instruments, loans secured by personal property, and other commercial matters, which has been adopted with minor variations by all states except Louisiana." Nine Articles make up the UCC, with each Article containing provisions related to specific areas of commercial law. There are a myriad of issues related to the searching, creation and filing UCC Financing Statements dependent upon the type of transaction and the location of the goods or transaction. Because of the non-uniformity of the UCC, I believe that this is one practice area where paralegals can easily become subject matter experts. Any paralegal who takes the time to learn the transaction and state specific requirements surrounding searching, creating, filing, amending, continuing, and terminating UCC Financing Statements will quickly become more valuable to the attorney they support, no matter if that attorney practices law in a corporate or law firm environment. When you can move from being just another "legal assistant" to that of the "go-to person," your value to the client or corporation can go up exponentially. And, isn't that why we chose the paralegal path in the first place?

Review Questions

1. What factors determine the enforceability of a restrictive covenant?
2. What factors determine the enforceability of an exculpatory clause?
3. What is an indemnification?
4. What can a court do if only part of an agreement is illegal or against public policy?
5. When might failure to have a required license *not* be a basis for invalidating a contract?
6. Given ABA Model Rule 1.6 and the rules discussed in previous chapters, what should a lawyer do in the following circumstances:
   a. Lawyer becomes aware that client, practicing as a chiropractor, is not a validly licensed chiropractor.
   b. Client is involved in a heated custody battle and it looks like client will win. Last week client's two-year-old child was found wandering several blocks from other spouse's home, alone. Lawyer now learns that client actually took the child from other spouse's fenced backyard, took the child to a spot several blocks away, and, from a nearby public phone, placed the "anonymous" call alerting the police.
   c. Would it make a difference if lawyer learned about the situation described above before it happened?
   d. Would it make a difference if the lawyer learned about the above situation several years after it occurred?
   e. Client wants to include an obviously unreasonable restrictive covenant in an employment contract, to prohibit employees from working for any competitor for six years.
   f. Lawyer learns that the contract client has been using for years contains a false statement about client's credentials.

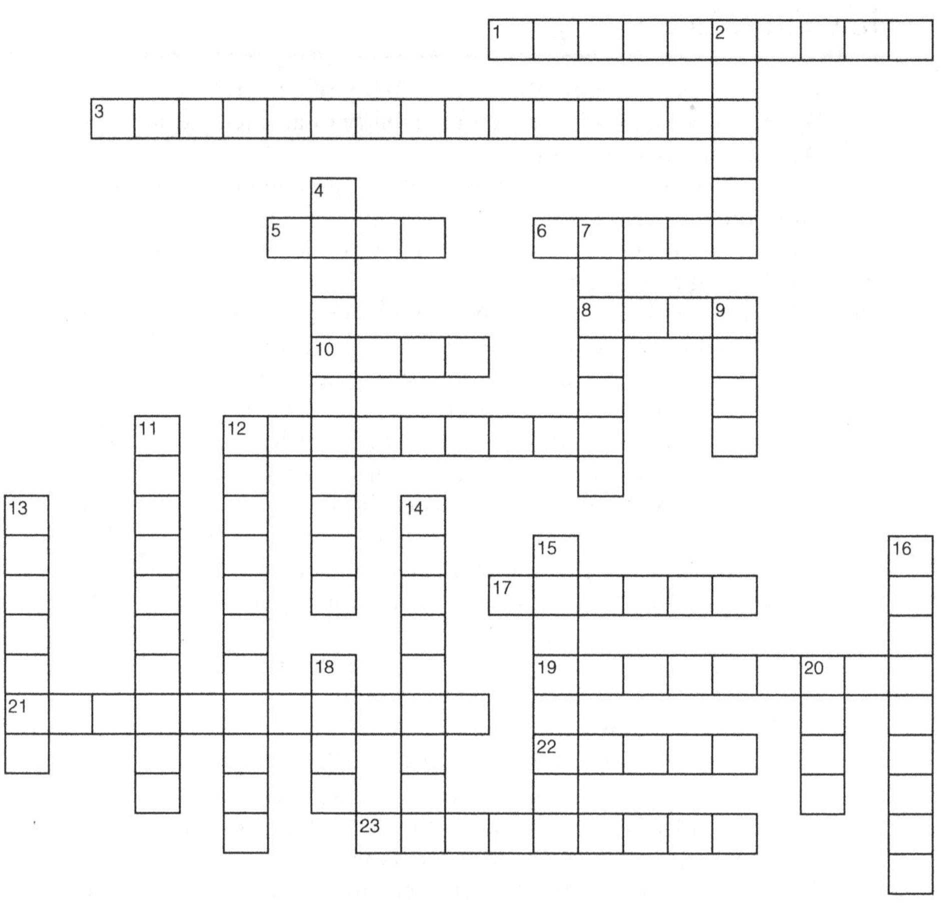

ACROSS

1. _______ of judgment allows immediate entry of judgment without notice or hearing
3. one party agrees to compensate the other for losses
5. _______ harmless; one party agrees to compensate other for losses
6. charging interest at an illegal rate
8. _______-length transaction; the parties had equal power to negotiate
10. in _______ delicto, parties equally at fault
12. _______-dealing arrangement; one party will deal with no others
17. even though no statute makes the conduct illegal, a court can refuse to enforce a contract on grounds of public
19. legal parts of agreement can be enforced without illegal part, which is _______
21. type of conduct least likely to be protected by an exculpatory clause
22. _______ per se; inherently bad
23. to be enforceable, a noncompete covenant must be reasonable in time and

DOWN

2. blue law prohibits transactions on
4. an exculpatory clause must be ________ and clear to be enforceable
7. false statements that hurt the reputation of another
9. a covenant not to compete is most likely to be enforced in ________ of a business
11. courts carefully scrutinize noncompetes in ________ contracts
12. a clause that attempts to excuse a party from liability
13. ________ scheme; a multilevel arrangement in which money is made by recruiting new people
14. ________ interest; a financial interest in person's life
15. ________ loan; borrower is person, not business
16. If a ________ law is intended to protect the public, agreements in violation of that law are likely unenforceable
18. a civil wrong
20. ________-penciling; a court edits a contract

CASE FOR ANALYSIS

IN THE MATTER OF BABY M, A PSEUDONYM FOR AN ACTUAL PERSON SUPREME COURT OF NEW JERSEY

109 N.J. 396, 537 A.2d 1227
February 3, 1988, Decided

[Ed. note: This case has been heavily edited.]

[T]he Court is asked to determine the validity of a contract to provide a new way of bringing children into a family. For a fee of $10,000, a woman agrees to be artificially inseminated with the semen of another woman's husband; she is to conceive a child and after its birth surrender it to the natural father and his wife. The . . . natural mother will thereafter be forever separated from her child. The wife is to adopt the child, and she and the natural father are to be regarded as its parents. [T]his is called a "surrogacy contract," the natural mother called the "surrogate mother."

William Stern and Mary Beth Whitehead entered into a surrogacy contract. It recited that Stern's wife was infertile, that they wanted a child, . . . that through artificial insemination using Stern's sperm, Whitehead would become pregnant, carry the child, deliver it to Stern, and . . . terminate her rights so that Mrs. Stern could adopt. Mrs. Stern's status as a nonparty to the agreement presumably was to avoid the baby-selling statute. *N.J.S.A.* 9:3-54.

Stern agreed to pay Whitehead $10,000 after the child's birth, on delivery to him . . . to pay $7,500 to the Infertility Center. The Center . . . arranged the contract by bringing the parties together, explaining the process, furnishing the contractual form, and providing legal counsel.

The history of the parties' involvement suggests good faith. William and Elizabeth Stern were married in 1974, both were Ph.D. candidates. Due to financial considerations and Mrs. Stern's pursuit of a medical degree, they decided to defer starting a family until 1981. Mrs. Stern learned that she might have multiple sclerosis and that the disease in some cases renders pregnancy a health risk. Her anxiety appears to have exceeded actual risk, which current medical authorities assess as minimal. Nonetheless, fearing that pregnancy might precipitate blindness, paraplegia, or other debilitation, the Sterns decided to forego having their own children. Most of [Stern's] family had been destroyed in the Holocaust. . . . [H]e wanted to continue his bloodline. . . . [The couple] considered adoption, but were discouraged by the substantial delay apparently involved and by potential problems from their age and differing religious backgrounds.

Whitehead's response apparently resulted from her sympathy with others who could have no children; she also wanted the $10,000 to help her family. . . . Whitehead became pregnant. The pregnancy was uneventful and on March 27, 1986, Baby M was born.

Not wishing anyone to be aware of the arrangement, Mr. and Mrs. Whitehead appeared as the parents. Her birth certificate indicated her name to be Sara Whitehead and her father to be Richard Whitehead. Sterns visited the hospital unobtrusively to see the newborn.

Whitehead realized, almost from the birth, that she could not part with this child. She had felt a bond during pregnancy. Some indication of attachment was conveyed at the hospital. She apparently broke into tears and indicated that she did not know if she could give up the child. She talked about how the baby looked like her other daughter. . . . [S]he turned [the] child over to Sterns at the Whiteheads' home. . . .

Whitehead's despair frightened Sterns. She told them that she could not live without her baby, that she must have her, only for one week. Sterns, concerned that Whitehead might commit suicide, believing that Whitehead would keep her word, turned the child over to her. [F]our months later, the child was returned to the Sterns, having been forcibly removed from [a] home in Florida owned by Whitehead's parents. . . . She was brought to New Jersey. The prior order awarding custody to Sterns was reaffirmed. Pending judgment, Whitehead was awarded limited visitation.

Sterns' complaint, in addition to seeking custody, sought enforcement of the contract. Pursuant to the contract, it asked that the child be permanently placed in their custody, that Whitehead's parental rights be terminated, and that Mrs. Stern be allowed to adopt the child.

The trial took thirty-two days. . . . [E]xpressing that the contract was valid, the trial court devoted its opinion to the baby's best interests. . . . [I]nconsistency is apparent. The contract calls for sole custody in Sterns, and termination of Whitehead's rights, regardless of evaluation of best interests. [T]he court awarded custody to Stern based on evidence and analysis as if no contract existed. Its rationalization was that while the contract was valid, specific performance would not be granted unless in the best interests of the child. The issues were as if Stern and Whitehead had had the child out of wedlock and disagreed about custody. The court's awareness of the irrelevance of the contract is suggested by its remark that beyond the question of best interests, "[a]ll other concerns raised by counsel constitute commentary."

The trial court concluded that statutes concerning adoption, termination of parental rights, and payment of money in adoptions, do not apply. It reasoned that because the Legislature did not have surrogacy contracts in mind, those laws were irrelevant . . . that surrogacy contracts are valid and that Stern's rights under the contract were constitutionally protected. . . . Whitehead appealed.

INVALIDITY AND UNENFORCEABILITY OF SURROGACY CONTRACT

Our conclusion has two bases: direct conflict with existing statutes and conflict with public policies, as expressed in statutory and decisional law.

One of the contract's purposes, adoption through private placement, though permitted in New Jersey "is very much disfavored." Its use of money—and we have no doubt that money is paid to obtain an adoption and not for the personal services of Whitehead—is illegal and perhaps criminal. *N.J.S.A.* 9:3-54. [T]here is coercion: the mother's irrevocable agreement, prior to birth, to surrender the child . . . is unenforceable in private placement adoption. Even where the adoption is through an approved agency, formal agreement occurs only *after* birth after the mother has been offered counseling. *N.J.A.C.* 10:121A-5.4(c). Integral to these invalid provisions is the agreement, equally invalid, of the mother not to contest proceedings to terminate her parental rights, as well as her contractual concession, that the child's best interests would be served by awarding custody to the father and his wife—all of this before she has conceived, and, in some cases, before she has the slightest idea of what the natural father and adoptive mother are like.

The foregoing provisions directly conflict with New Jersey statutes, offend[ing] long-established State policies. . . . [T]he entire contract is unenforceable. Stern knew he was paying for adoption of a child; Whitehead knew she was accepting money so that a child might be adopted; Infertility Center knew that it was paid for assisting in the adoption. The actions of all three worked to frustrate the goals of the statute. It strains credulity to claim that these arrangements amount to something other than a private placement adoption for money.

The prohibition of our statute is strong. Violation constitutes a high misdemeanor, *N.J.S.A.* 9:3-54c. The evils inherent in baby-bartering are loathsome. The child is sold without regard for whether the purchasers will be suitable parents. The natural mother does not receive counseling to assist her in making a decision that may affect her for a lifetime. . . . [M]onetary incentive may, depending on circumstances, make her decision less voluntary. . . . [A]doptive parents may not be fully informed of the natural parents' medical history. . . .

[T]ermination of Whitehead's parental rights fails to comply with the stringent requirements. Our law provides for such termination only where there has been a voluntary surrender to an approved agency or to the Division of Youth and Family Services accompanied by a formal document acknowledging termination of parental rights, *N.J.S.A.* 9:2-16, -17; *N.J.S.A.* 9:3-41; *N.J.S.A.* 30:4C-23, or where there has been a showing of parental abandonment or unfitness. A termination may ordinarily take one of three forms: an action by an approved agency, an action by DYFS, or an action in connection with a private placement adoption. The standards for termination are substantially the same, except that whereas a written surrender is effective when made to an approved agency or to DYFS, there is no provision for it in the private placement context. *See N.J.S.A.* 9:2-14; *N.J.S.A.*30:4C-23. . . . [W]here there has been no surrender to an approved agency or DYFS, termination of parental rights will not be granted absent a strong showing of abandonment or neglect. While the statutes make procedural allowances when stepparents are involved, the substantive requirement for terminating natural parents' rights is not relaxed one iota. *N.J.S.A.* 9:3-48c(1). . . . [A] "best interests" determination is never sufficient to terminate parental rights; the statutory criteria must be proved.

In this case a termination of parental rights was obtained not by proving statutory prerequisites but by claiming the benefit of contractual provisions. . . . Since the termination was invalid, adoption by Mrs. Stern could not properly be granted. . . . There is no exception provided by law, and it is not clear that there could be any "order or judgment" validating a surrender of custody as a basis for adoption when that surrender was not in conformance with the statute.

Contractual surrender of parental rights is not provided for in our statutes. In the Parentage Act, *N.J.S.A.* 9:17-38 to -59, there is a provision invalidating any agreement "between an alleged or presumed father and the mother of the child" to bar an action brought for the purpose of determining paternity "[r]egardless of [the contract's] terms." *N.J.S.A.* 9:17-45. Even a settlement agreement concerning parentage reached in a judicially-mandated conference is not valid unless approved by the court. There is no doubt that a contractual provision purporting to constitute irrevocable agreement to surrender a child for adoption is invalid.

B. Public Policy Considerations

The contract's invalidity, resulting from conflict with the above statutory provisions, is further underlined when measured against New Jersey public policy. The basic premise, that natural parents can decide in advance which one is to have custody, bears no relationship to the law that the child's best interests shall determine custody. . . . The fact that the court remedied that aspect of the contract through the "best interests" phase does not make the contract any less offensive to the public policy of this State.

The surrogacy contract guarantees permanent separation of the child from one of its natural parents. Our policy, however, has long been that to the extent possible, children should remain with and be brought up by both of their natural parents. The surrogacy contract violates the policy of this State that the rights of natural parents are equal.

The only legal advice Whitehead received was provided in connection with the contract that she previously entered into with another couple. . . . Whitehead was examined and psychologically evaluated, but . . . [i]t is apparent that the profit motive got the better of the Infertility Center. [T]he evaluation . . . was not put to any use, for the psychologist warned that Whitehead demonstrated traits that might make surrender of the child difficult and that there should be further inquiry. To inquire further, however, might have jeopardized the Center's fee.

Worst of all, however, is the contract's total disregard of the best interests of the child. There is not the slightest suggestion that any inquiry will be made at any time to determine the fitness of the Sterns as custodial parents, of Mrs. Stern as an adoptive parent, their superiority to Mrs. Whitehead, or the effect on the child of not living with her natural mother.

This is the sale of a child, or at least the sale of a mother's right to her child, the only mitigating factor being that one of the purchasers is the father. . . . [A]ll parties concede that it is unlikely that surrogacy will survive without money. That conclusion contrasts with adoption; for obvious reasons, there remains a steady supply, albeit insufficient, despite the prohibitions against payment. The adoption itself, relieving the natural mother of the financial burden of supporting an infant, is in some sense the equivalent of payment.

Second, the use of money in adoptions does not *produce* the problem—conception occurs, and usually the birth, before illicit funds are offered. With surrogacy, the "problem," consisting of the purchase of a woman's procreative capacity, at the risk of her life, originates with the offer of money. Third, with the law prohibiting the use of money in adoptions, the financial pressure of unwanted pregnancy do not lead the mother to the highest paying, ill-suited, adoptive parents. She is just as well-off surrendering the child to an approved agency. In surrogacy, the highest bidders will become the adoptive parents regardless of suitability, so long as payment is permitted. . . . [I]t is clear that it is unlikely that surrogate mothers will be as numerous among those women in the top twenty percent income bracket as among those in the bottom twenty percent.

Putting aside the issue of how compelling her need for money may have been, and how significant her understanding of the consequences . . . consent is irrelevant. There are, in civilized society, some things that money cannot buy. In America, merely because conduct purchased by money was "voluntary" did not mean that it was beyond regulation and prohibition. . . . Employers can no longer buy labor at the lowest price, even though that labor is "voluntary," . . . or buy women's labor for less than paid to men for the same job, . . . or purchase the agreement of children to perform oppressive labor, . . . or purchase the agreement of workers to subject themselves to unsafe or unhealthful working conditions. . . . There are values more important than granting to wealth whatever it can buy, be it labor, love, or life. Whether this principle recommends prohibition of surrogacy, which sometimes results in great satisfaction to all of the parties, is not for us to say. We note here only that, under existing law, the fact that Mrs. Whitehead "agreed" to the arrangement is not dispositive.

Nothing in this record justifies a finding to terminate Whitehead's parental rights under statutory standard. . . . [T]here was no intentional abandonment or very substantial neglect of parental duties without reasonable expectation of reversal in the future[;] the court never found Whitehead an unfit mother and stated that Whitehead had been a good mother to her other children. The decision to terminate Whitehead's parental rights precluded determination on visitation. Our reversal requires delineation of Whitehead's rights to visitation. . . . [T]his factually sensitive issue, never addressed below, should not be determined by this Court.

CONCLUSION

If the Legislature decides to address surrogacy, this case will highlight many potential harms. . . . The problem can be addressed only when society decides what its values and objectives are in this troubling, yet promising, area. . . . The judgment is affirmed in part, reversed in part, and remanded for further proceedings consistent with this opinion.

7

Capacity

This chapter explores the special protections given to minors and incompetent parties when they attempt to enter into contracts. The material also touches on current issues relating to, and protection available outside the judicial system for, vulnerable members of society.

Skills-based learning objectives	*How you will demonstrate your ability*
Analyze statutes and cases relating to contract capacity.	Assignments: Find and cite statutes and cases relating to specific capacity issues; brief cases.
Find and discuss ethical rules concerning clients with diminished capacity.	Assignments: Find and discuss ethical rules relating to specific capacity issues.

A. Minors
- **1. Minors as Agents for Adults**
- **2. Necessities**
- **3. Fraud**
- **4. Ratification**

B. Mental Incompetence
- **1. Determining Mental Incompetence**
- **2. Intoxication**

C. Practical and Ethical Issues

Avoid
Make a contract void; see also disaffirm

Some people are given special protection from contract mistakes in the form of the right to **avoid** (make void[1]) the contract. Those individuals included minors, the mentally incompetent, and some people under the influence of intoxicating substances. The law presumes competence and the burden of proving incompetence is on the party claiming the right to avoid the contract.

A. Minors

Minor
A person who has not reached adult status, typically the day before his/her eighteenth birthday

Majority
The age of adult status (typically 18)

Infant
A minor

Administrator
Responsible for settling a person's financial affairs after death; also called executor

Guardian
Individual with legal responsibility for the minor

A **minor** is defined by statute in most states as a person who has not reached the day before his or her eighteenth birthday (the age of **majority**) At common law, minors were called **infants** and "infancy" lasted until age 21. You may still find the term "infants" in use in many legal research materials. A minor (or the minor's **guardian** or **administrator**) generally has the power to avoid a contract, while the adult does not have the same power.

Example

Minors and adults do not have equal rights in a contract. While her husband, Bob, was out of town, Ann held a garage sale and sold an antique crystal vase to Jill for $200. Jill gave Ann $100 cash (all she had with her) and signed a promise to return with the other $100 later. Jill, who is actually 17, appeared to be in her early 20s and Ann never questioned her age. Jill took the vase home, where it fell off a shelf, shattering. Jill can avoid the contract and not have to pay the remaining $100. In a few states, Jill may even be able to get her $100 back. On the other hand, if Bob came home and told Ann that he loved that vase and is very angry that it is gone, Ann cannot avoid the contract and require Jill to return the vase.

Your immediate reaction might be that this is unfair and that it could cause businesses a lot of trouble. In fact, most minors do enter into contracts and it rarely causes businesses trouble. Not only are most minors unaware of their legal right to avoid, they would have difficulty enforcing that right. In addition, there are a number of exceptions to the protection.

---

1. Minors as Agents for Adults

Agent
One who is authorized to act for or in place of another; representative

If a minor acts as an **agent,** for the benefit of and under the direction of an adult, the adult is the real party to the contract. This is what happens when a mom sends her teenager to the store to pick up milk and bread or even to buy school clothes. (Agency is more fully explained in Chapter 9.) A power of attorney is the document that creates the agency relationship. Assignment 9-1 identifies resources for creating a power of attorney that meets the requirements of your state. The mere presence of an adult during the transaction does not, however, establish agency.

---

[1]The distinction between a void contract, which is not enforceable and has no legal recognition, and a voidable contract, which is valid unless the party with the power to avoid (the minor or incompetent) chooses to disaffirm, is discussed in Chapter 2.

EXHIBIT 7-1
Rights of Minors

States have created various exceptions to the rights of minors to disaffirm contracts. For example:

VERIFICATION OF SELF-SUFFICIENT MINOR STATUS
(15 through 17 years of age—California Civil Code 34.6)

For the purpose of obtaining diagnosis or treatment at the Campus Health Center, or by any physician or dentist associated with the clinic, the undersigned certifies that all of the following facts are true:

1) I am living separate and apart from my parents or legal guardian.

____
Place of Residence of minor (Number and Street)

____
City, State and Zip Code

____
Place of Residence of Parent or Guardian

2) I am managing my own financial affairs regardless of source of income (so long as it is not derived from a source declared to be a crime by law).

____
Name and Address of Bank

____
Name and Address of Employer

____
Other Source of Financial Support —Explain

3) I understand that I will be financially responsible for the charges incurred for my medical or dental treatment and care, and that I may not disaffirm this consent because I am a minor. I am __________ years of age, having been born on the __________day of Month __________, Year __________.

Dated: __________ Signed:

Witness: __________

Imagine that Mom puts $25,000 in Son's account and sends the very mature-looking 17-year-old to buy an expensive car from an unsuspecting older man. The plan is to drive the car for about ten months, avoid the contract, and get the money back. Will it work? Probably not; the seller will likely make the effort to research where Son got the money and be able to prove that Son was actually acting for Mom.

2. Necessities

Necessities
Things indispensable to life; reasonably needed for subsistence, health, comfort, and education, considering the person's age, station in life, and medical condition

Emancipation
Minor is no longer under care/control of an adult

There are laws limiting the power of avoidance with respect to certain contracts, such as student loans, some banking contracts, military enlistment, and obligations that would be enforceable without a contract (such as to pay tort damages or support a child). In addition, a minor can have liability under contracts for **necessities** (also called necessaries). This is similar to the quasi-contract theory discussed in a previous chapter; the minor responsible for the reasonable value (remember the term "quantum meruit") of the goods or services received. What constitutes a necessity depends on the circumstances of the minor, particularly whether an adult is providing necessities. In some (but not all) states, **emancipation** (minor is no longer under care/control of an adult), marriage, or enlistment in the armed forces may either give the minor capacity or make the minor liable for more necessities. To see an interesting discussion of whether housing constitutes a necessity for a minor, read *H & S Homes LLC v. McDonald* (Ala. 2001), http://law.justia.com/cases/alabama/supreme-court/2001/1001736-2.html.

You may wonder about child stars, like the Olsen twins who began their television careers before they were a year old. Some states have special laws to deal with the situation.

Example

Judicial approval of certain contracts for services of infants; effect of approval; guardianship of savings. 1. A contract made by an infant or made by a parent or guardian of an infant, or a contract proposed to be so made, under which (a) the infant is to perform or render services as an actor, actress, dancer, musician, vocalist or other performing artist, or as a participant or player in professional sports, or (b) a person is employed to render services to the infant in connection with such services of the infant or in connection with contracts therefor, may be approved by the supreme court or the surrogate's court as provided in this section where the infant is a resident of this state or the services of the infant are to be performed or rendered in this state. If the contract is so approved the infant may not, either during his minority or upon reaching his majority, disaffirm the contract on the ground of infancy or assert that the parent or guardian lacked authority to make the contract. A contract modified, amended or assigned after its approval under this section shall be deemed a new contract.

New York Arts and Cultural Affairs Law §35.03 et seq. California has a similar law, which became the subject of attention in 2015, when Bindi Irwin, 17, the daughter of the late celebrity-conservationist, Steve Irwin, needed judicial approval of her contract with the television show, *Dancing With the Stars.*

If a minor does avoid a contract, does an adult party have any rights? Restitution, requiring the minor to make compensation, is a complex issue. Most courts are more forgiving with minors as defendants (*e.g.,* in the example below, landlord suing Ed for lost rental income after Ed stops paying rent) and more

EXHIBIT 7-2
Emancipation Law

What is the effect of emancipation in your state? The Vermont law:

12 V.S.A. §7156. Effect of emancipation

§7156. Effect of emancipation

(a) The order of emancipation shall recognize the minor as an adult for all purposes that result from reaching the age of majority, including:

(1) entering into a binding contract;

(2) litigation and settlement of controversies including the ability to sue and be sued;

(3) buying or selling real property;

(4) establishing a residence except that an emancipation order may not be used for the purpose of obtaining residency and in-state tuition or benefits at the University of Vermont or the Vermont state colleges;

(5) being prosecuted as an adult under the criminal laws of the state;

(6) terminating parental support and control of the minor and their rights to the minor's income;

(7) terminating parental tort liability for minor;

(8) indicating the minor's emancipated status on driver's license or identification card issued by the state.

(b) The order of emancipation shall not affect the status of the minor in the applicability of any provision of law which requires specific age requirements under the state or federal constitution or any state or federal law including laws that prohibit the sale, purchase or consumption of intoxicating liquor to or by a person under 21 years of age.

---

harsh with minors as plaintiffs (*e.g.*, Ed suing the landlord for a refund). Many courts require return of the consideration, if the minor still has it, but do not require restitution. While all jurisdictions allow use of minority as a shield to protect the minor from the consequences of bad judgment, only a few allow its use as a "sword" for profit. For example, minor buys a car and stops making payments, minor may have to return the car; if, however, car has been destroyed in an accident, adult may be out of luck. In general, a minor cannot avoid the contract to improve his position. So, for example, a minor could not buy a car from S for $3,000, then sell the car to B for $3,000, then avoid the contract with S and demand the return of his $3,000 without making restitution.

Example

It may appear that the law rewards "bad" behavior by minors. Ed, a handsome 17-year-old bad boy, signs a 12-month lease to rent a cheap, studio apartment for $400 per month. His friends help pay the rent and they use the apartment for drinking, smoking, womanizing, and gambling, until his mom finds out that they are not going to the library every night. Can Ed avoid the lease? Yes, in most states Ed can avoid the lease and have no further liability. In a few states, Ed may get a refund of some money he has already paid in rent because those states treat a minor's contracts as invalid from the beginning. Other states would allow Ed to avoid the lease, but might require him to make **restitution**—to restore the adult's financial position because the consideration itself (use of the apartment for several months) cannot be returned. On the other hand . . .

Restitution
Return of, restoration of, or compensation for

Fred, a hard-working 17-year-old, leaves home because of constant violence and neglect by his alcoholic, unemployed parent. Fred, who works 30 hours each week for a major retailer, looks like a man in his 20s. He signs a 12-month lease to pay $400 per month for a cheap studio apartment. After a few months, Fred is given an opportunity to go into a management training program sponsored by his employer, but he must relocate. Can Fred avoid the lease? The answer depends on the state: In many states, he cannot avoid the lease. Even if he can avoid the lease, it is highly unlikely that the landlord would have to return any part of the $2,400 in rent that Fred has already paid in any state. Fred is liable for the value he received because, otherwise, minors in his position might be totally unable to secure necessities like housing.

3. Fraud

Fraud
False statement regarding a material fact, intended to deceive an individual who reasonably relies on the statement

Would it make a difference if Ed had engaged in **fraud** (a false statement regarding a significant fact, intended to deceive an individual who then relies on the statement) by stating his age as 22 or, perhaps, showing false identification? In most states a minor can disaffirm despite misrepresentation or fraud; the states differ on the minor's obligation to make restitution in such situations. This is particularly complicated by the fact that a minor *is* liable for torts. Fraud is an intentional tort, as well as a defense to contract enforcement. Most courts will not allow a tort lawsuit for fraud if it would amount to allowing the adult to enforce the contract.

Disaffirm
Make a contract void; see Avoid

4. Ratification

Ratify
To acknowledge or validate a contract after its execution

Express Ratification
To state or write intent to honor a contract or, if the contract has been executed, to acknowledge the contract

Implied Ratification
Intent to honor contract or acknowledgment of contract can be inferred from behavior or words

Would this make a difference? Shortly after moving in, Fred sent the landlord a notarized letter, stating that "although I am a minor, I intend to be fully bound to this lease. I will not **disaffirm** (avoid) the lease." No difference; a minor has no power to **ratify** (confirm) before reaching the age of majority. After majority, ratification can be **express** (the minor states or writes an intent to honor the contract or, if the contract has been fully performed, acknowledges the contract) or can be **implied.** Implied ratification can take the form of continuing to use the property or service received under the contract for a time after reaching majority or it can arise from the minor's failure to disaffirm the contract within a reasonable time after majority. Interestingly, in some states, ratification does not take place simply because the minor has continued to uphold his part of the contract, for example, by making payments. The *H & S Homes* case, cited above and in Assignment 7-2, includes an argument that the minor ratified an agreement by waiting a significant period of time before disaffirming.

What happens if property continues to change hands after transfer by a minor? That depends on the type of property. The Uniform Commercial Code (UCC) provides that an innocent party takes goods free of the minor's power of disaffirmance; but in many jurisdictions a minor can reclaim real property, even from an innocent party.

Assignment 7-1

Has your state enacted the Uniform Transfers to Minors Act? It may be part of a group of laws relating to trusts and fiduciaries. The Act allows transfer of property to a custodian without having a guardian formally appointed. The custodian can manage the property and make payments on behalf of the minor. Transfer under the Act satisfies IRS requirements for qualifying a gift for exclusion from estate tax. The Act is an extension of the Uniform Gifts to Minors Act.

- What is the citation to the Act?
- Does the statute include a form to be used for transfers?
- Does the statute include a section exempting those who deal with the custodian from liability?

Another complicated issue concerns a parent's ability to enter into a contract for a minor. Because parents are generally required to provide for their children, there is no question of the parent's liability on contracts for goods and services to benefit a child. On the other hand, what if a parent signs a release from liability and a child is subsequently injured? In many states the field trip release forms signed by parents are ineffective! Courts seem to look to public policy to determine the validity of such a release. You may recall that such a contract, releasing a party from liability, is called an exculpatory agreement. Consider this: If a release also contained a clause under which the parent agreed to indemnify the school/club/park district, and the release was found to be invalid, might the indemnification be upheld? What would be the consequences of such a ruling? Why might it happen and what would be the public policy considerations?

Assignment 7-2

A. In your online state statutes, find the citation for one of the following:
   - A statute concerning student loans to minors;
   - A statute concerning the contractual rights of emancipated minors; or
   - A statute concerning the contractual rights of married minors.

B. Using computer-assisted legal research (CALR), find, summarize, and report to the class, a case:
- ◆ Involving a minor's misrepresentation of age in entering a contract;
- ◆ Involving a contract with an intoxicated person (alcohol or drugs);
- ◆ Involving a person alleging mental incompetence to avoid a contract;
- ◆ Involving a release signed on behalf of a minor;
- ◆ Involving what constitutes a necessity; or
- ◆ Involving a minor's obligation to make restitution after disaffirmance.

Try to find a case from your state, but you may have to search all states. These cases are surprisingly rare.

C. Read *Young v. Weaver* (Ala. Civ. App. 2003), http://caselaw.findlaw.com/al-court-of-civil-appeals/1179933.html, and *H & S Homes LLC v. McDonald* (Ala. 2001), http://law.justia.com/cases/alabama/supreme-court/2001/1001736-2.html, and discuss:

- ◆ Do you think these cases are unfair to the adults involved? Is there a difference between John McDonald's situation and Kim Young's situation?
- ◆ Do you think it should make a difference that these minors lived with the contracts they signed for several months?

B. Mental Incompetence

1. Determining Mental Incompetence

Cognitive Test
Mental incompetence determined by inability to understand the nature and consequences of a transaction

Volitional Test
Mental incompetence shown by inability to act reasonably with respect to a transaction

Mental incompetence is not synonymous with old age or physical disability. Mental incompetence is the inability to understand the nature and consequences of the transaction (the **cognitive** test) or inability to act reasonably with respect to the transaction (the **volitional** test). When a court employs the volitional test, it generally also asks whether the other party was aware of the person's mental condition and whether the contract was one a reasonable person would have made. Mental incompetence can arise from senility, mental illness, delirium, or mental retardation. The contracts of an individual who was incompetent at the time when the contract was entered are generally voidable; incompetence occurring after the contract is formed does not render the contract voidable.

Competence is not synonymous with good judgment. In a case involving a contract made during the manic phase of bipolar disorder, the court stated:

> The manic phase of the illness under discussion is not, however, a weakness of mind rendering a person incompetent to contract within the meaning of Civil Code sections 38 and 39. These sections exclude the manic-depressive psychosis by their very language since they make specific reference to the person's "understanding." This language, as interpreted by the decisions, establishes the "understanding" or cognitive test as the prevailing standard of legal competency. As already pointed out, the cognitive test deals with the mental capacity to understand the nature and purpose and effect of the transaction and not with the motivation for entering into it. The

> manic phase of the manic-depressive psychosis does not impair such understanding, but only relates to the motivation. Notwithstanding the long-standing psychiatric recognition of such psychosis the Legislature has not, in its wisdom, seen fit to broaden section 39 so as to include within its ambit the motivational standard of incompetency.[2]

Some states differentiate between **adjudicated** and **non-adjudicated** incompetents. It is difficult to obtain a court determination (adjudication) of incompetence and, in those proceedings, a guardian is appointed to protect the incompetent individual.

With respect to non-adjudicated incompetents and in states that do not make the distinction, courts generally look at whether the contract involved a necessity and the incompetent's state of mind at the time of entering the contract. Non-adjudicated incompetents (and incompetents in states that do not make the distinction) are generally required to make restitution when they avoid a contract, if the other party had no reason to know of the incompetence. Like minors, incompetents are liable for the reasonable value of necessities and are capable of ratifying contracts when they are competent.

In states that do make the distinction, the contracts of the adjudicated incompetent may be **void**—that is, with no legal effect from the beginning.

Adjudicated Incompetent
Court has declared person incompetent

Non-adjudicated Incompetent
Incompetence has not been determined by court; all contracts must be formed through a court-appointed guardian

Void
With no legal effect from the outset

Example

An adjudicated incompetent often has no liability for contracts. Jenn, an adjudicated incompetent 24-year-old with the mental capacity of a 4-year-old, escapes from the house with her mother's purse. She goes into an art store and pays $300 cash for a glass vase, which she drops on the sidewalk immediately on leaving the store. In states that make the distinction, Jenn's guardian can obtain a full refund; Jenn has no obligation to the store. This is not unfair, if you consider that incompetence rising to the level necessary to obtain an adjudication would be obvious to most people.

You might wonder how an incompetent individual has the financial ability to enter into a contract. According to the National Association on Mental Illness: "Social Security Disability Insurance (SSDI) provides monthly income to almost nine million individuals; as of 2013, 35.2% of recipients qualify for disability based on a mental health condition. The Social Security Administration (SSA) uses its own definitions of disability and its own diagnostic criteria for determining whether an individual has a certain disability." SSDI benefits are also available for individuals unable to work because of addiction to intoxicating substances. If the SSDI recipient is legally incompetent (a minor or an adjudicated incompetent), SSA will appoint a representative payee to receive and manage the payments. The representative payee has obligations but is not the equivalent of a guardian.[3] SSA may appoint a representative payee for a non-adjudicated incompetent recipient, but many mentally ill individuals handle their own funds.

---

[2] *Smalley v. Baker*, 262 Cal. App. 2d 824 (1968).

[3] https://www.ssa.gov/payee/faqbene.htm.

2. Intoxication

Intoxicated
Under the influence of alcohol or drugs

Intoxicated individuals, under the influence of alcohol or drugs at the time of making a contract, are often classified with the mentally incompetent. While the law does not generally protect voluntary drunks from the consequences of their actions, it does not allow others to take advantage of intoxication. Courts look at the cause (bad reaction to prescription medication versus illegal drugs or drinking to excess) and degree (often judged under the same standard as mental incompetence) of intoxication and the other party's awareness of the intoxication. In addition, courts look at whether the intoxicated person ratified the contract by failing to disaffirm promptly on becoming sober.

A person (the principal) who fears becoming incompetent (*e.g.*, the elderly, those diagnosed with degenerative diseases) will sometimes sign a power of attorney, to appoint another person to act as an agent. Agency is discussed in depth in Chapter 9. A durable power of attorney is an appointment of an agent that remains valid despite the principal's loss of mental capacity.

3. Analyzing Incompetence and Intoxication

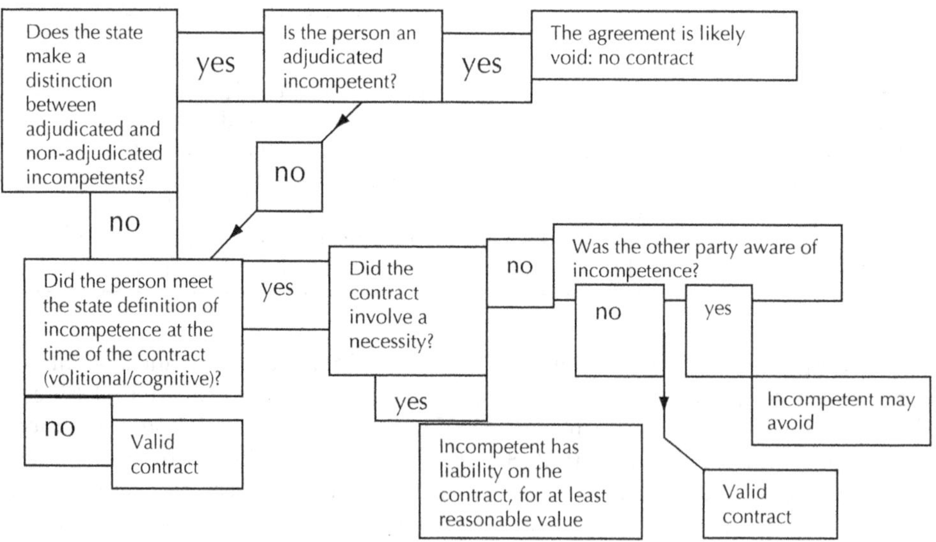

C. Practical and Ethical Issues

As our society ages, contracts that take advantage of senior citizens are becoming a major problem. The elderly are often competent, but very vulnerable. Some of the problems involve "scams" that are fraudulent; for example, a scam artist drives a truck with a sign identifying it as belonging to a home inspector from house to house, knocking on doors and telling residents that their chimneys may be blocked in a way that presents a danger of asphyxiation. Scam artist offers to fix the problem immediately for $100. After getting the money, scam artist does nothing more than climb onto the roof and stick a broom into the chimney. Other problems arise from predatory practices; for example, Terry Telemarketer knows that Ella Elderly lives alone and is very lonely. Terry calls Ella several times a week, knowing that Ella can be talked into buying anything, even though she cannot afford to spend the money.

Sadly, there is often little that can be done after these practices are discovered. Scam artists disappear quickly; a non-fraudulent contract, entered into by a competent senior citizen, is likely valid, even if it was the result of targeting seniors. Governmental bodies are increasingly taking action to educate senior citizens and their families about these practices in advance and to investigate complaints. For example, the FBI has a page on senior citizens as victims of fraud, https://www.fbi.gov/scams-safety/fraud/seniors.

Assignment 7-3

Another issue is dealing with clients who lack capacity. The relevant ABA Model Rule is Rule 1.14. Find the rule for your state and answer the following:

- Does the attorney-client relationship automatically terminate when the lawyer determines that the client has diminished capacity?
- Is a lawyer required to seek appointment of a guardian or conservator immediately upon determining that the client has diminished capacity?
- What is a guardian ad litem; what is a conservator?
- Is the confidentiality requirement different with respect to clients with diminished capacity? When can a lawyer reveal information about a client with diminished capacity?

Many states also have resources. For example, Illinois has a Department on Aging, with a special program to train bank personnel to detect, prevent, and report financial exploitation: http://www.state.il.us/aging/1abuselegal/abuse_financial.htm#bsafe. The Illinois Attorney General also has information about predatory practices and filing consumer complaints: http://www.ag.state.il.us/consumers/index.html.

While the ethical rules relating to confidentiality, conflicts of interest, and dealing with a client under disability, also apply to minors as clients, a lawyer has to be especially careful to understand his or her role with respect to a minor. If the lawyer is court-appointed, the court may be asked to clarify. Some states make the distinction between a **guardian ad litem** (appointed to look out for the best interests of the child during the course of litigation) and an **attorney for the child,** whose role is to advocate the child's position. The best interests of the child do not always coincide with the client's wishes. For example, a teenager involved

Guardian Ad Litem
Court-appointed person to advocate best interests of a child or incompetent during litigation

Attorney for the Child
Attorney whose role is to advocate the child's position

in a custody dispute might want to live with the parent who imposes no curfew and is very lax with discipline.

For examples of state standards for guardians ad litem, visit http://www.guardianadlitem.org.

Assignment 7-4

- Find online resources available to help senior citizens and their families in your state.
- Substance abuse is a serious problem among lawyers. Most states now have **LAPs** (lawyers assistance programs) to provide confidential help to impaired lawyers. Find the Web site describing your state's program.

LAPs
Lawyers assistance programs

Career Corner

I recently corresponded with Mali Dahl, a California contracts-analyst paralegal who told me about her career. Her summary: "'I Finally Know the Answer!' I work as a paralegal (most of the time!) in the legal department of a nonprofit corporation. I say most of the time because I am still transitioning from doing a little bit of everything to being a true paralegal. I support nine attorneys on an ad hoc basis. This summer, I am mentoring three students.

Because the department is small, I get to do a lot of different things including hunting for old contracts—far more difficult than you might imagine, when you consider that we have multiple offices, have migrated from various computer programs and systems, and have experienced employee turnover. I am the 'go-to person' for new people who need help, handle tax exemption transactions, work on statutory filings for authority to do business statutory filings, and much more. I've worked with membership agreements, export control screening, and government contracts. I have drafted license agreements and nondisclosure agreements; even with forms and boilerplate available from past transactions, every transaction has some unique nuance that requires tweaking the terms. I love that I am always being challenged in this job and I like to think I am honing my project management, leadership, general professional and, of course, paralegal skills.

I graduated with honors with my AS in Paralegal Studies in the summer of 2010. I loved my classes and wish that I could take more! Almost immediately, my company received a subpoena and I had the opportunity to assist the general counsel on the response. I discovered, to my amazement, that I absolutely love doing production! I work with our technical folks, administrative staff, outside counsel, our vendors, and my supervising attorney as needed to gather everything. The task requires all of the skills and knowledge I've acquired in doing the six jobs I've held within the company over the last 12 years.

Being at a nonprofit has its drawbacks, especially that money is always tight. No LexisNexis or Westlaw here! The salary may be lower than in private firms, but the company paid for me to become a paralegal and gave me the answer to the age-old question: 'What do you want to be when you grow up?' After decades of being in customer service in different industries and wearing many other hats, I know my answer to that question: a paralegal! Having fun at work, always learning something new and getting paid to do it—how could anything be better than that?"

Review Questions

1. What is the difference between an adjudicated and a non-adjudicated incompetent?
2. What is a necessity and why does it matter?
3. Under what circumstances can a minor enter into a contract enforceable by the other party?
4. Does it (should it) make a difference whether a minor is using minority as a weapon (*e.g.*, to sue an adult for the return of property) or as a shield (*e.g.*, to defend self when being sued by an adult)?
5. What is the difference between a guardian ad litem and an attorney for a child or incompetent? What are the special ethical rules applicable to dealing with an incompetent?
6. Discuss this situation. High school seniors in an Honors English class are required to submit their papers through turnitin.com, which reviews the papers for plagiarism. The site keeps the papers that have been submitted and may, in the future, release them to instructors if similar papers are submitted. The students do not like this but agree to the terms in order to meet the requirements of the class. When the class ends, they file suit to avoid the agreement and have their papers removed. Many were minors when they entered the agreement. Consider: Have the minors had full benefit of the contract; did those who reached adulthood shortly after entering the contract wait too long? Is this a possible duress situation? Could the students seek damages?

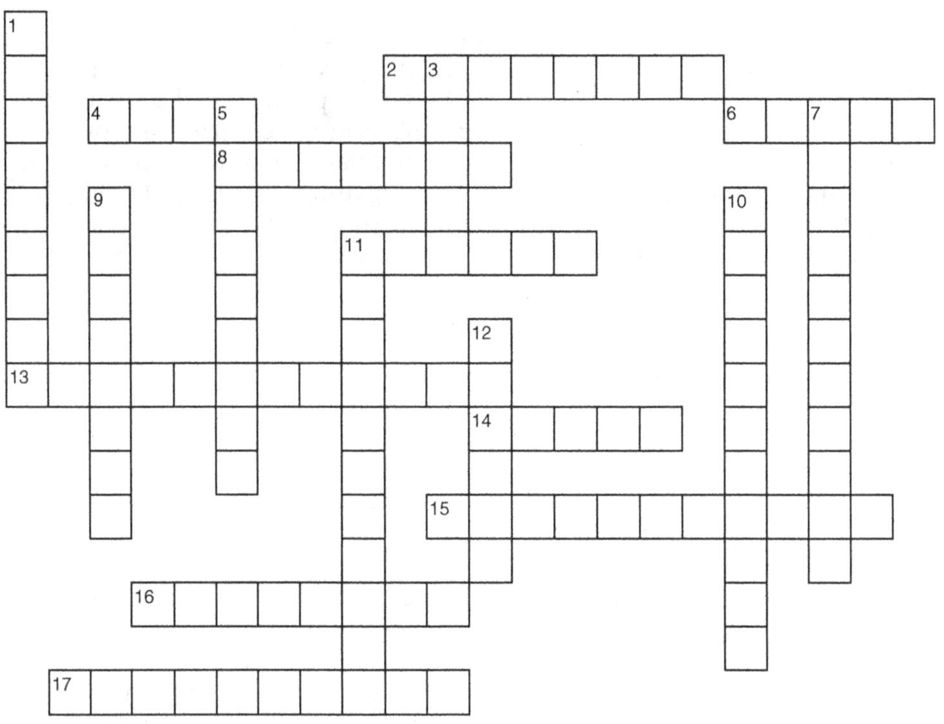

ACROSS

2. reaching the age of ________, a person becomes a legal adult
4. the contract of an adjudicated incompetent may be
6. in most states, a person under age 18 is a
8. ratification can be express or
11. to make a contract good after-the-fact
13. being freed from parental control
14. a false statement on which another is intended to rely
15. although the law does not favor this condition, others may not take advantage
16. legally responsible for a minor or an incompetent
17. a ________ test determines whether a person was able to act reasonably

DOWN

1. a ________ test determines whether the person was able to understand the nature and consequences of acts
3. one who acts on behalf of another
5. a minor may ________ a contract
7. minors and incompetents have some liability for
9. a minor's contract is ________ at the minor's option
10. an ________ incompetent has been declared, by a court, to lack capacity
11. courts differ on whether minors must make ________ to compensate adults for their losses
12. a legal term for a minor

8

◆ ◆ ◆

Statute of Frauds

◆ ◆ ◆

This chapter explores those contracts that must be in writing to be enforceable and provides samples of agreements within those categories. Students will also learn how the law is adapting to deal with the reality that most documents created in the twenty-first century will never be printed on paper.

Skills-based learning objectives	*How you will demonstrate your ability*
Analyze statutes requiring a writing and cases interpreting those statutes.	Assignments: Find, cite, and brief statutes and cases relating to enforcement of contracts not in writing.
Analyze the requirements of electronic signature laws and issues relating to "click-wrap" contracts.	Assignment: Find and discuss electronic signature laws.

A. Requirement of Writing
B. Narrow Interpretation of the Requirement
C. Written Evidence Other than Written Contract
D. Contracts in Cyberspace
    1. Applicable Law
    2. Consent
    3. Record Retention and Access
    4. Technology
E. The Categories
    1. Promises in Anticipation of Marriage
    2. Contracts Not to Be Performed Within a Year
    3. Contracts Involving Land (Real Property)

4. **Contracts for Sale of Goods for $500 or More**
5. **Promises to Answer for the Debts of Another**

F. **Practical and Ethical Issues**

A. Requirement of Writing

As you know, most contracts are not written, but a few are not enforceable without a **writing.** Some types of contracts are more likely to be entered into based on emotion, rather than clear thinking, or are particularly susceptible to fraud, perjury, and failure of memory. The original Act for the Prevention of Fraud and Perjuries was enacted in England in 1677 to deal with those concerns by requiring written evidence of the agreement. Every state has adopted some form of what is now called the Statute of Frauds. Law students often use a mnemonic device (MYLEGS) to remember the major categories of contracts "within" the Statute in most states:

Anticipation of	Marriage	
Cannot be performed within one	Year	
	Land	real estate contracts
Promises by an executor to pay	Estate's debts	
Sales of	Goods over $500[1]	added by the UCC
	Suretyship[2]	

Negotiable Instruments
A promise or order to pay, such as a check; can be passed along like cash

Security Interests
Interest in personal property to secure performance of an obligation; evidence of indebtedness

Many states have added categories, such as contracts promising to make a will with specified gifts, promises to lend money, ratification of contracts entered while a minor, assignments for the benefit of creditors, contracts authorizing an agent to buy or sell real estate, and contracts to pay commission to real estate agents (remember the promissory estoppel sample case, *Cruz*, from Chapter 1). The Uniform Commercial Code (UCC) also requires a writing for certain leases of goods, **negotiable instruments, security interests,** and other sales contracts for more than $5,000 (§1-206) that might not fall within the definition of "goods" (such as sale of royalty rights).

Of course, just remembering "MYLEGS" or the words the letters represent is overly simplistic. Before we get into the details of what those letters mean, let's look at some general principles.

[1]2003 Amendments to UCC Article 2 would raise the amount to $5,000; check to see whether your state has adopted the change.

[2]Both promises by an executor to pay estate debts and suretyship are, in essence, promises to pay the debts of another.

Assignment 8-1

Using either your state Web site or CALR, find the categories covered by the statute of frauds for your state. To formulate your search, consider this: The Statute of Frauds is a limitation on civil lawsuits. A civil lawsuit, based on a contract of a type covered by the statute, may not be pursued unless there is a writing, so the Statute limits the rights and remedies available in court.

B. Narrow Interpretation of the Requirement

In some cases, the Statute of Frauds is the legal "technicality" people love to hate: competent parties have made a legal agreement, supported by consideration, not tainted by fraud or any other problem, and there is plenty of evidence to prove that agreement, but the agreement is not enforceable because it is not in writing. Because of such cases, exceptions and "tricky" ways of reading the requirement have evolved in the courts. So, if you think that the definitions of the categories represented by MYLEGS are overly complicated, you are correct! Courts like to find ways to take agreements out of the categories covered by the Statute.

Most courts hold that if the Statute of Frauds is not raised as an affirmative defense,[3] it is **waived,** meaning that the argument has been abandoned. The Statute may also be waived if the party who is not seeking enforcement admits in court or in court documents that an agreement existed. The Statute may not be raised after the contract has been fully performed and, in some cases may not be raised after one party has performed. Although not all courts would agree, some courts have held that conduct consistent with the existence of a contract will excuse the need for a writing. Also keep in mind that if the otherwise valid contract is unenforceable because of the Statute of Frauds, some states allow recovery in quasi-contract or promissory estoppel.

Waived
Claims have been abandoned

C. Written Evidence Other than Written Contract

Written evidence need only amount to an acknowledgment of agreement by the **party "to be charged,"** meaning the party trying to get out of the contract. The written evidence does not have to be a formal contract and does not even have to be an **integrated** statement of the agreement.

Party to Be Charged
Party attempting to avoid contract liability

A memo or notes (including a collection of notes), in any form, can be sufficient, depending on the facts. The writing may be generated by a computer, or it may be scrawled on a napkin. The writing need not have been created at the time

Integrated Agreement
Agreement that is intended to be final and complete

[3]An affirmative defense is part of an answer to a complaint in which the defendant takes the offense and responds to the allegations with his own allegations.

the contract was created; it need not be still in existence at the time of the lawsuit. It need not have been prepared with the intent of formalizing the contract. It need not even be delivered to the other party. The memo or note need only indicate that there is or was an agreement and state, with reasonable certainty, the identities of the parties, the subject matter, and the essential terms. Other terms can be provided by implication, other documents, or other evidence. The **signature** need not be the party's full name, correctly spelled; it can consist of initials, a signature stamp, a mark, or, in some cases, the use of letterhead.

Example

A written denial can satisfy the requirement. Sam Seller and his friend Billie Buyer shook hands on the deal: Billie would buy Sam's house for $250,000, with the closing on May 15, all appliances included, clean title, and no mortgage contingency. They planned to have Sam's lawyer write it up in a few days. After Billie left, however, another person visited Sam's open house and offered Sam $265,000. Sam immediately wrote and mailed a quick note:

> *Billie, I am going to have to back out of our deal to sell you my house for $250,000—Pat came by and offered me $265,000 for basically the same deal, with the closing on May 15 and all the appliances. Since contracts for real estate have to be in writing, we didn't really have a contract, but I am sorry and hope that you aren't too angry. [signed] Sam.*

Upon receiving the note, Billie may have sufficient evidence to support enforcement of the agreement. Furthermore, even if Sam had written a similar note to a mutual friend (rather than to Billie), describing the agreement and expressing his regret, the note could serve as the evidence Billie would need to meet the Statute of Frauds requirement.

D. Contracts in Cyberspace

Contracts formed online present unique issues. They are generally take-it-or-leave-it, so that consumers may feel that it is not even necessary to read the terms. ("Adhesion" contracts, which leave no room for negotiation, are discussed in Chapter 4.)

There is also the issue of the other party's identity and location. Why do we generally feel secure with contracts we enter face-to-face? With face-to-face contracts, we have two clear avenues of enforcement. On an informal level, we know the other party is concerned about her reputation. If I hire a local builder to construct my deck and I am unhappy, word will spread; the builder's business may suffer. On a formal level, I can seek mediation or arbitration with the Better Business Bureau or a similar agency, or I can file a lawsuit.

These options may not exist with online contracts. We often do not know the real identity of the other party or that party's location; the other party may not be subject to the jurisdiction of our courts.

If the matter does reach a court, does the cyber contract have the same value as evidence as a paper contract? A face-to-face contract may have been witnessed or even notarized. It is unlikely that such third-party witnesses exist for an online contract. Passwords, cookies, and IP tracing may provide some security concerning the location and identity of a party but are not perfect security against tampering.

While some Web sites attempt to create a system of enforcement based on reputation, there is nothing to stop an unscrupulous party from creating a new identity as needed. Your local builder cannot easily change his name and appearance to escape your wrath! In fact, there is nothing to stop a party from wrongfully disparaging another party's reputation. Another way of dealing with the problem of disreputable online businesses involves the use of third-party services that can operate like escrow services and not release payment until the buyer acknowledges satisfactory receipt of the product.

Privacy is also an issue, beyond concern about identity theft. The local eccentric "trader" might gather, cleanup, and sell "junk" at a garage sale and stay "under the radar" with respect to the Internal Revenue Service. Doing so on a Web site might catch the attention of tax authorities.

Contracts formed without paper, via the Internet or terminals such as ATMs, also present unique issues with respect to formation and the "writing" requirement. The "signature" for such a contract might be a typed name, use of a personal identification number (PIN), a scan of a person's voice or retina, a signature with an electronic pen on a special tablet, an exchange of e-mails, or other means. ESIGN, discussed in the next paragraph, states: "The term 'electronic signature' means an electronic sound, symbol, or process, attached to or logically associated with a contract or other record and executed or adopted by a person with the intent to sign the record." Electronic contracts can satisfy the statute of frauds." If this seems odd to you, remember that most contracts do not require a writing and that, if a written signature is required, an "X" can suffice. Laws concerning the enforceability of electronic transactions do not address concerns about privacy, trustworthiness of the parties, or whether parties actually read their contracts, but those concerns also exist when contracts are printed on paper.

1. Applicable Law

Every state has a law governing electronic transactions; most have adopted the Uniform Electronic Transactions Act (UETA). Contracts in interstate commerce are governed by the 2000 Electronic Signatures in Global and National Commerce Act, the "e-signature act" or "ESIGN" (15 U.S.C. §7031). The European Union, Canada, and other countries also have laws governing electronic transactions. All of these laws are intended to promote paperless transactions by making those transactions enforceable and electronic evidence admissible and by providing default rules for issues such as when a communication is sent or received.

While Uniform Commercial Code Article 8, covering the ownership and transfer of investment securities, and Article 9, covering security interests in personal property, are excluded from coverage under both UETA and ESIGN, both Articles permit the use of electronic records and signatures for most purposes, according to their own terms. Other exceptions exist, depending on state law or particular agency regulations, for the execution of wills, trusts, and codicils; documents concerning adoption, divorce, and other family law matters; court orders, notices, and pleadings; "consumer" notices, such as termination of utility service, insurance, or foreclosure; and documents concerning hazardous materials.

Keep in mind that while these laws may make an electronic transaction enforceable, they do not require that anyone enter into an electronic contract. For example, many lenders refuse to accept electronic documentation of mortgage or short sale agreements. As discussed below, the parties to the transaction must consent to the electronic format.

Because there are several sources of authority and this is a rapidly evolving area of law, it is more important that you learn to spot issues than that you memorize rules. When you know the questions, you can research the answers. The most common questions concern consent; record retention and access; and the technology used to form an agreement.

Assignment 8-2

- Using your bookmarked site for state law or http://www.uniformlaws.org, determine whether your state has adopted the Uniform Electronic Transactions Act. Determine whether the law permits a notary public to act electronically.
- Determine whether your state permits electronic signatures on court pleadings and on deeds to real property.
- The laws referenced above are "technology neutral" and do not dictate how the "signature" should be authenticated or how the integrity of the data should be protected. Consider when you have either entered a transaction online or simply wanted access to a Web site and have had to click "I AGREE" at the end of a long agreement, disclaimer, or license. Do you feel that simply clicking an icon should form a binding contract? Find a case discussing the issue. You may want to use CALR, but you can find many cases by using the free Internet and searching [**click-wrap agreement**].
- Find and summarize a case from your state involving the Statute of Frauds and report to the class whether the court was willing to strictly apply the writing requirement or found a way to take the agreement out of the requirement.

Click-wrap Agreement Agreement used in connection with software licenses; often found on the Internet as part of the installation process of software packages; usually requires user to manifest assent by clicking an "OK" button on a dialog box or pop-up window

2. Consent

To ensure enforceability of an electronic transaction, the participants generally must agree to use electronic records and signatures in lieu of paper documents and traditional signatures. In many situations, this agreement may be either expressly stated, or implied from the circumstances. As with all things involving contracts, however, a smart legal professional or businessperson will specify that the contents of electronic communications constitute the documents that govern the transaction. ESIGN, certain state UETA enactments, and some agency regulations require more formal consumer consent in some circumstances. For example, electronic records may be used to satisfy any law that requires that records be provided to consumers "in writing" only if the consumer has affirmatively consented to the use of the electronic records, and has not withdrawn the consent. Before obtaining consent, the electronic record provider must deliver a clear and conspicuous statement of certain information, as indicated on Exhibit 8-1.

There should be a clear connection between the consumer's acceptance (signature) and the terms to which she is agreeing. You have probably had the experience of clicking "I agree" without ever having looked at what you are agreeing to. Those terms are, however, on the same Web site and available to you. A consumer who "accepts" a transaction by signing a credit card signature pad, without access to those terms, may not have given consent.

EXHIBIT 8-1
Bank Customer Consent to Electronic Disclosures

The Federal Reserve Bank of Minneapolis has posted the following information for banks with respect to electronic transactions:

Consumers must consent to receiving disclosures electronically. The bank must do the following for customers prior to obtaining their consent:

- Indicate whether customers have a right or option to receive information on paper.
- Identify whether the consent relates to a particular transaction (*e.g.*, account opening discolures [*sic*]) or to ongoing disclosures over the course of the relationship (*e.g.*, monthly statements and change-in-terms notices).
- Explain that the consumer has the right to withdraw consent and provide the procedures to withdraw consent as well as the consequences of withdrawing consent, such as fees, termination of the relationship, loss of preferred pricing or having to switch account types.

EXHIBIT 8-1
(continued)

- Describe the procedures for updating the consumer's contact information.
- Outline the hardware and software requirements for accessing and retaining records.
- Explain how to obtain paper disclosures after consent has been given and describe any associated fees.
- Consumers must also consent electronically, or electronically confirm consent, in a manner that reasonably demonstrates their ability to receive or access the information electronically. Having consumers retrieve a code contained within in a document sent to them is one way to demonstrate accessing of information.

https://www.minneapolisfed.org/publications/banking-in-the-ninth/esign-act-requirements (visited Jan. 11, 2016).

3. Record Retention and Access

If a person is required by law to provide or deliver information in writing to another person, an electronic record only satisfies the requirement if the recipient may print and keep a copy of the record for later reference and review. Being able to establish integrity—that the record has not changed since it was accepted—is essential to confidence in the system. If the law requires that a particular record be retained, an electronic record satisfies that requirement only if it is accurate and remains accessible for later reference. If a particular writing is required by law to be displayed in a particular format or if elements of a document must be placed in a particular physical relationship to each other, UETA does not change that requirement. If a law expressly requires a writing to be delivered by U.S. mail or by hand delivery, UETA does not change those delivery rules.

4. Technology

There are now many vendors providing systems and support for transactions that require, are facilitated by, or are made possible by reliable electronic signatures. Trade groups and other interested parties have developed standards and best practices for electronic signature systems. For example, the U.S. Department of Education has standards for the use of electronic signatures for student loans, https://www.ifap.ed.gov/dpcletters/attachments/gen0106Arevised.pdf, and the HIPAA Journal, http://www.hipaajournal.com/can-e-signatures-be-used-under-hipaa-rules-2345/, has suggestions for the use of electronic signatures in medical offices.

Technology considerations include whether the data can be stored, printed and copied; data integrity and whether the data will endure, unchanged, and be accessible long term; compliance with statutory and regulatory requirements for retention for specified periods; and ensuring that the digital information accurately reflects the underlying information, which may be created by scanning a paper document. Many companies offer, and even warrant, reasonably durable migration of electronic media to ensure durability.

E. The Categories

Contracts that must be evidenced by a written instrument include the following.

1. Promises in Anticipation of Marriage

This category does not cover promises to marry, but other promises that assume that a marriage will take place. The category can even cover promises made by parties other than the husband or wife. Such agreements are often called **prenuptial** or **antenuptial** or marriage settlement contracts, and typically involve a promise to convey property when a marriage occurs or an agreement about the division of property in the event of divorce. Examine the sample in Exhibit 8-1.

Prenuptial
Agreement in anticipation of marriage that typically involves a promise to convey property when marriage occurs or concerns division of property in the event of a divorce; also called antenuptial

Antenuptial
Agreement in anticipation of marriage that typically involves a promise to convey property when marriage occurs or concerns division of property in the event of a divorce; also called prenuptial

"Prenups" are very common among those who have substantial assets before getting married or have been previously married and either have known the pain of property division or want to protect their assets for children from a previous spouse. In recent years, the press has often speculated about the terms of the prenup when a celebrity couple gets engaged or breaks up.

Many states have special requirements for prenups, which may include full disclosure of assets and even representation by separate lawyers. Compliance with these requirements may even have to be stated in the agreement itself. Be sure to check the requirements for your jurisdiction, when assisting with such a contract.

2. Contracts Not to Be Performed Within a Year

The writing requirement applies only if the promise, by its terms, would not permit performance within a year. If performance is possible within a year, even if unlikely and even if the parties do not anticipate performance within a year, the requirement does not apply. Nor does it matter how long performance actually takes, after the contract is made. Promises with an uncertain duration and promises with alternatives, one of which could be performed within a year, are not subject to the requirement.

EXHIBIT 8-2
Sample Premarital Agreement

1. The Parties, Jeanne McCoy ("Jeanne") and Michael C. Kalland ("Michael") *[note use of defined terms]* plan to marry in the near future and wish to establish their respective rights and responsibilities with regard to income and property. *[These paragraphs are* recitals, *giving background.]*
2. Each of the Parties has been previously married and divorced; each has children.
3. The Parties are getting married because of their love for each other and do not wish to change their present financial circumstances.
4. Jeanne has identified all of her financial assets, property, liabilities, and sources of income on Exhibit A, attached hereto and made part of this Agreement.
5. Michael has identified all of his financial assets, property, liabilities, and sources of income on Exhibit B, attached hereto and made part of this Agreement.
6. Each Party has made full disclosure of his or her financial status in the attached Exhibits and has examined the Exhibit prepared by the other.
7. Each Party acknowledges that he or she has separate income and assets sufficient to provide for his or her financial needs.
8. The Parties are in the process of purchasing a residence, which shall be held in tenancy in common; each Party is contributing half of the cost of the purchase of the residence.
9. During the course of the marriage, the Parties shall share in the costs of housing, food, and utilities. Each Party shall be responsible for his or her own personal expenses, including, but not limited to, clothing, grooming, vehicles, travel, gifts, taxes on income, debt payment, and medical care.
10. Each Party waives:
    a. all claim to assets listed on the Exhibit prepared by the other Party and to any property or income resulting from those assets;
    b. all claim to any income, gift, or inheritance received by the other during the course of marriage;
    c. all rights to share in the other Party's estate upon death;
    d. all rights to any pension, profit sharing or retirement income of the other Party;
    e. all rights to support or maintenance in the event of separation or divorce.
11. Each Party has consulted with an independent attorney and is satisfied with his or her representation. *[Note the various waivers and acknowledgments.]*
12. Each Party acknowledges that he or she has been fully advised of the legal claims they might have in the absence of this Agreement and that

EXHIBIT 8-2
(continued)

courts have the authority to disregard this Agreement if necessary to avoid impoverishing a spouse.

13. This Agreement is entered into and shall be construed and enforced under the laws of the state of ________. *[Item 13 is a choice of law clause; item 14 is an integration clause.]*
14. This Agreement constitutes the entire Agreement between the Parties and may only be modified by written agreement, signed by both Parties. In the event that any part of this Agreement is deemed unenforceable, it is the wish of the Parties that the rest of the Agreement be considered valid and enforceable.

Date Signatures
Witness/Notary Seal

Example

- On October 1, 2016, a former U.S. president promises to speak at Yale's graduation in May 2018. This promise must be in writing; the calculation is made from the time when the agreement was made, not from the time when performance begins.
- Following an accident that left Pat Plaintiff with limited use of her right arm, Don Defendant agreed to give Pat $300 per month for the rest of her life in exchange for dropping a lawsuit. This does not have to be in writing because it is possible that Pat will die within a year. Some states disagree and require that lifetime contracts be in writing; see *McInerney v. Charter Golf, Inc.*, 176 Ill. 2d 482 (1997).

3. Contracts Involving Land (Real Property)

A promise to transfer "any interest in land" is generally within the Statute; therefore, real estate sales, leases (in most states only leases for more than a year), mortgages, options on land,[4] and **easements** require a written instrument. The Statute of Frauds does not require a written instrument for an agreement to build or perform some other service on land.

Easement
Limited right to use real property

4. Contracts for Sale of Goods for $500 or More

In most states UCC §2-201 requires a writing for the sale of goods for a price of $500 or more. Remember, the UCC does not cover contracts for services (such as employment) and that the UCC is always subject to amendment. In 2003 the National Conference of Commissioners on Uniform State Laws (now

[4]An option is, essentially, a contract to hold an offer open (see Chapter 3).

called the Uniform Law Commission), together with the American Law Institute, promulgated amendments to Article 2 that include raising the Statute of Frauds amount for sale of goods to $5,000. Whether states will adopt the change remains to be seen. For more information, visit http://www.nccusl.org.

Example

Does the "bright-line" test of price seem arbitrary? Ann is at the mall to buy a gift for her husband. On the clearance table in an electronics store, there is a handheld minicomputer, which would normally sell for $900, but it is marked down to $450 because of a scratch on the case. The line to pay is long, and Ann is in a hurry. She hands the computer to a salesperson, saying, "Hold this for me. I have to run down to Sears and get a gallon of paint. I will be back in 20 minutes to pay." The salesperson says, "Okay, it's yours," but forgets all about it and sets it on a table. Another customer buys it before Ann returns. Could Ann sue for breach of contract? *Yes.* (Of course, she has to prove that it happened, but maybe that's not a problem—maybe she has a friend with her or maybe the salesperson admits to the exchange.)

But if the computer had been marked $600, the oral contract would not be enforceable.

The UCC specifies exceptions, including:

- Contracts for goods to be specially manufactured for the buyer that are not suitable for sale to others in the normal course of business, if the seller has already made a substantial commitment
- Situations in which the party "trying to get out of it" admits in testimony or a pleading that an agreement was made
- Situations in which the goods have been received and actually accepted
- Situations in which payment has been accepted

Collateral Promise
Promise to guarantee the debt of another, made without benefit to the party making the promise

Guarantor
Agrees to be responsible for another's debt or performance under a contract if the other fails to pay or perform; see also Surety

Surety
Liable for the payment of another's debt or the performance of another's obligation; see Guarantor

Default
Fail to meet obligations

Cosigner
One who participates jointly in borrowing

5. Promises to Answer for the Debts of Another

Both the "E" (Estate) and the "S" (**suretyship**) in MYLEGS fall under this category; they are **collateral promises,** not the primary promises of the contract.

Example

The difference between a surety and a cosigner can be very important. Son is buying his first new car; he signs a loan contract, promising to pay $250 per month (Son is primarily liable). Because Son is young and doesn't have a credit history, the lender requires **surety** (also called **guarantor**). Dad signs a promise to pay if Son doesn't pay. Dad's promise is collateral; he is only liable if son **defaults** (fails to pay). If Dad was primarily liable (a **cosigner,** who signed the contract on equal terms with Son) or if Dad promised Son (not lender), "Don't worry, I will pay if you can't," the agreement would not fall within the Statute of Frauds. Some courts have taken this a step further and have taken contracts out of the Statute if the main purpose of the person's agreement was his own benefit. If Dad and Son were to share the car but Son took the loan and Dad acted as a surety, those states would find the Statute inapplicable.

An **executor, personal representative,** or **administrator** is the person who carries on the business of an **estate,** which is essentially the "business" of the finances of a deceased person or a person who has been declared incompetent. The executor is not usually personally liable for the debts of the estate and a promise to assume such responsibility must be in writing.

Executor
One who conducts the business of an estate; also called administrator or personal representative

Administrator
One who conducts the business of an estate; also called executor or personal representative

Personal Representative
One who conducts the business of an estate; also called executor or administrator

Estate
The entity for managing finances of a deceased person or an incompetent

---

Example

People make promises in the heat of emotion, and the Statute of Frauds can protect them. Cody's 25-year-old brother, Ron, died several days after hitting a tree with his motorcycle. Ron had no medical insurance. After being appointed as executor of Ron's estate, Cody discovered that Ron had only about $5,000 in assets, but the outstanding hospital bill was $90,000. Cody tells the hospital staff, "You were so good to my brother, I will pay this even if it takes the rest of my life." Cody had no legal obligation to pay the debt, so this is not enforceable unless in writing. Do you recognize another problem in the example? There is no consideration. Cody's promise was an incomplete gift. If, however, there were consideration, the promise would have to be evidenced by writing.

Exhibit 8-3 contains a sample of a suretyship contract that would most likely be used to guarantee the performance of a contractor working on a big construction project. A **performance bond** surety agreement guarantees that a contract will be performed according to its terms and specifications. If a contractor defaults, these bonds generally obligate the surety to finance the contractor, undertake the completion of the project, obtain a new contractor to the owner, or pay the bond penalty. A **payment bond** surety agreement guarantees that a contractor will make appropriate, prompt, and full payments for labor and material consumed on a project. A **maintenance bond** is intended to assure a project will remain free of defects in workmanship or materials for a specific period of time. This sample is very hard to read. For a future assignment, you will attempt to rewrite it in plain English. For the moment, read it to determine whether you can understand it. What type of bond does it represent?

EXHIBIT 8-3
Sample Suretyship Contract

KNOW ALL MEN BY THESE PRESENTS:

That we, ________________, as Principal, and ____________, as Surety, are hereby held and firmly bound unto ____________ as Obligee in the penal sum of ____________ ($ ____________) for payment whereof the said Principal and Surety bind themselves, their heirs, executors, administrators, and successors, jointly and severally, firmly by these presents.

The conditions of this obligation are such that whereas the Principal entered into a certain contract, hereto attached, and made a part hereof, with the Obligee,

___________, dated ___________, ___________, for ___________ (Project No. ___________).

NOW THEREFORE, the condition of this obligation is such that, if the Principal shall faithfully perform the said Contract in accordance with the Plans and Specifications and Contract Documents, and shall fully indemnify and save harmless the Obligee from all cost and damage which the Obligee may suffer by reason of Principal's default or failure so to do and shall fully reimburse and repay the Obligee all outlay and expense which the Obligee may incur in making good any such default, then this obligation shall be null and void, otherwise it shall remain in full force and effect.

In the event that the Principal is declared in default under the said Contract, the Surety will within fifteen (15) days of the Obligee's declaration of such default take over and assume completion of said contract and become entitled to the payment of the balance of the Contract Price. Conditioned upon the Surety's faithful performance of its obligations, the liability of the Surety for the Principal's default shall not exceed the penalty of this bond.

The Surety agrees to pay to the Obligee upon demand all loss and expense, including attorney's fees, incurred by the Obligee by reason of or on account of any breach of this obligation by the Surety.

Provided further, that if any legal action be filed upon this bond, venue shall lie in the county where the said Contract is to be performed.

Provided further, that the Surety, for value received, hereby stipulates and agrees that no change, extension of time, alteration or addition to the terms of the said Contract, or to the work to be performed thereunder, or the Specifications accompanying the same, shall in anywise affect its obligation on this bond, and it does hereby waive notice of any such change, extension of time, alteration or addition, to the terms of the said Contract or to the work or to the Specifications.

By signature hereon, if the amount of this bond exceeds $100,000, the Surety attests that at the time the bond was executed (Surety shall provide Obligee with evidence of the following):

(1) it was a holder of a certificate of authority from the United States Secretary of the Treasury to qualify as a surety on obligations permitted or required under federal law; or

(2) had reinsured any liability in excess of $100,000 by a reinsurer holding a certificate of authority from the United States Secretary of the Treasury.

IN WITNESS WHEREOF, the above bounden parties have executed this instrument under their several seals this ___________ day of ___________ in the year ___________, the name and corporate seal of each corporate party being hereto affixed, and these presents duly signed by its undersigned representative pursuant to authority of its governing body

SIGNATURES AND WITNESSES.

Assignment 8-3

Even when the agreement is in writing, the parties will sometimes dispute whether a signature was an indication of a guaranty. Read *Yellowbook Sales & Distribution Co. v. Valle* (Conn. App. Ct. 2012), http://caselaw.findlaw.com/ct-court-of-appeals/1591269.html. How might Valle have made his position clearer in the contract and avoided this lawsuit? If Valle had clearly indicated that he was not guaranteeing performance, do you think Yellowbook would have declined to extend credit? Do you think parties to a contract sometimes intentionally avoid directly addressing such issues and just hope for the best?

F. Practical and Ethical Issues

The Statute of Frauds came into existence to prevent fraud and perjury, but might it actually promote perjury in some circumstances? One of the exceptions, recognized by most courts as taking an agreement outside the Statute of Frauds, is an admission, in court or court documents, that an agreement existed.

When a defendant responds to a complaint alleging breach of contract, the defendant can raise the Statute as an **affirmative defense.** An affirmative defense limits or excuses a defendant's liability, even if the plaintiff's allegations are proven, and is based on facts outside those claimed by the plaintiff. If the defendant is able to prove the Statute as an affirmative defense, the case can be dismissed before trial in most jurisdictions.

Affirmative Defense
Part of an answer to a complaint in which defendant attempts to limit or excuse liability, based on facts outside those claimed by plaintiff

Example

Billie Buyer files suit against Sam Seller, alleging breach of a contract for the sale of Sam's house to Billie. Sam responds that no written agreement exists. Assuming that Sam never wrote the note described in the previous example, the lawsuit might be dismissed before trial.

Assignment 8-4

How should a lawyer prepare the client to answer if a case based on an oral contract is not dismissed or if the client is required to testify in another matter and might be asked about the existence of the oral agreement? Identify the relevant ethical rules, some of which have been discussed in previous chapters.

Career Corner

Overview of the FTC's Honors Paralegal Program

Each year, we seek out highly skilled individuals to work in Washington, D.C.,as part of our Honors Paralegal Program. By joining the program, you can takeadvantage of substantive training and challenging legal work offered by theFTC. Honors Paralegals may participate in every step of cases at the FTC, fromconducting interviews and market research to reviewing company documents, preparing exhibits for trial, and assisting attorneys in the courtroom.

Jumpstart your career

Appointments to the Honors Paralegal Program can last from 14 months tofour years. Based on the agency's needs, Honors Paralegals are appointed tothe Bureau of Competition, the Bureau of Consumer Protection, and other-offices throughout the Commission.

Most Honors Paralegals are hired in the winter and spring of each year,with the majority of positions being posted in January and February. However,this is not always the case, and we encourage you to check USAjobs.govthroughout the year for Honors Paralegal vacancies.

Review Questions

1. How should a defendant respond to a lawsuit based on a contract that falls within the Statute of Frauds but that is not evidence by a writing? Why is it essential that the defendant respond in the correct way?
2. Why do courts try to find exceptions to the Statute of Frauds?
3. Why might a court uphold a contract that was not reduced to writing and that would otherwise fall within the Statute of Frauds?
4. What are the characteristics of a writing sufficient to satisfy the Statute of Frauds?
5. What is the difference between primary liability and collateral liability for a debt?
6. What are the major categories of contracts that must be evidenced by a writing?
7. What is a "click-wrap agreement," and why are such arrangements problematic for reasons other than the Statute of Frauds?
8. What special requirements may apply to prenuptial agreements?
9. The ABA Model Rules provide that one type of lawyer-client fee agreement *shall* be in writing. What type of agreement must be written?

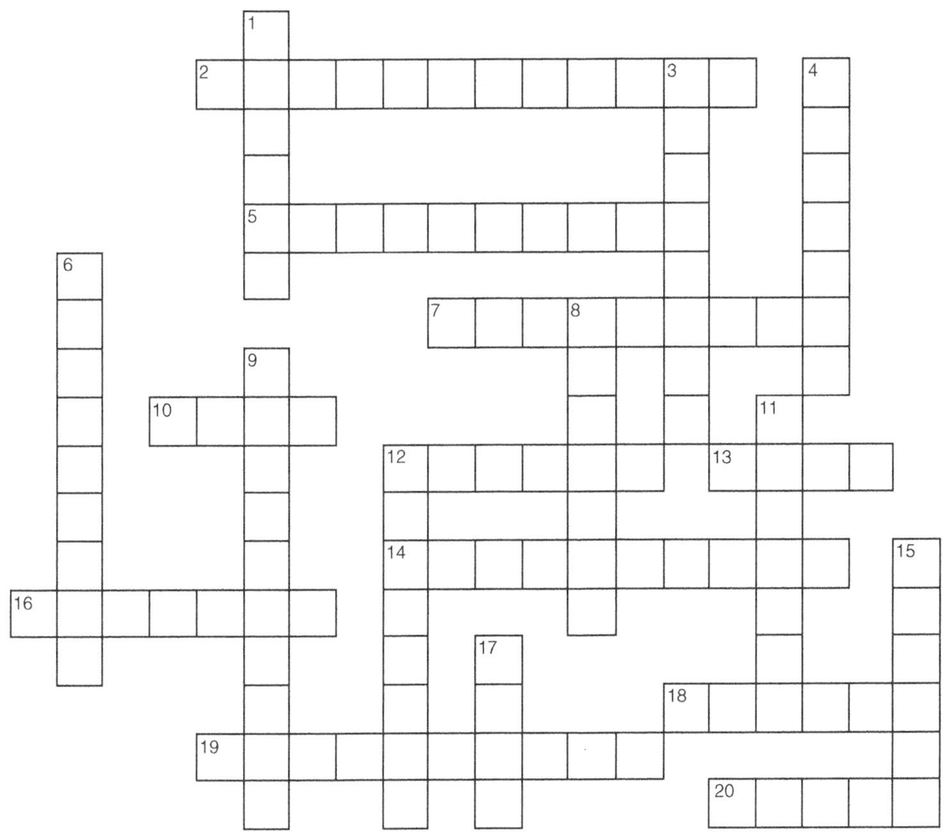

ACROSS

2. UCC has exception for goods specially __________ if seller has made substantial commitment
5. type of signature acceptable for contracts formed online
7. requirement of valid writing; can be satisfied in various ways
10. easement or mortgage must be written because they convey interests in
12. another name for guarantor
13. contract falls within the Statute of Frauds if it cannot be performed within a __________
14. a guarantee of a loan is __________, not primary
16. the Statute of Frauds was intended to prevent this
18. the "business" of handling deceased person's finances
19. check is an example of a __________ instrument
20. contracts for sale of __________ for $500 or more must be in writing

DOWN

1. the Statute of Frauds is ___________ if not raised as an affirmative defense
3. also called administrator; handles financial affairs of deceased person
4. "party to be ___________" is party trying to get out of the contract
6. the Statute of Frauds is inapplicable if the contract has been fully
8. a pre ___________ contract, anticipating marriage, within the Statute of Frauds
9. an agreement intended to be final and complete
11. failure to pay as required by the contract
12. a ___________ interest is an interest in personal property to secure payment of a debt
15. six letters stand for major categories covered by the Statute of Frauds
17. contracts allowing agent to sell ___________ estate or to pay such an agent commission generally must be written

9

Third Parties/ Secured Transactions

In analyzing almost any contract problem, the first question is whether a contract ever formed. That question involves looking at agreement, consideration, legality, capacity, and whether the statute of frauds required a written instrument. If a contract did form, the next question is: What are the rights of the parties? This chapter explores how a contract affects parties who may not have been part of the original agreement or who may have been part of that agreement in a peripheral way.

Skills-based learning objectives	*How you will demonstrate your ability*
Analyze state law concerning power of attorney.	Assignments: Find statute, analyze types of powers of attorney.
Determine the status of property subject to a contract.	Assignments: Research UCC search, recording of mortgages.
Analyze state law concerning rights of third parties.	Assignment: Locate and brief a case.

- A. Parties
- B. Agency
  - 1. Establishing Agency
  - 2. Agency Duties
- C. Contract Beneficiaries

D. Assignment and Delegation
  1. Assignment
  2. Delegation
  3. Novation
  4. Joint and Several Liability and Guarantors
E. Secured Transactions Under the UCC
F. Practical and Ethical Issues

People outside the original contract relationship can have rights with respect to the contract in one of three ways. An outsider might act as an agent for one of the parties. Outsiders might also be beneficiaries. Rights/obligations under the contract might be assigned or delegated to outsiders or an outsider might guarantee performance.

A. Parties

Before the rights of parties outside the original relationship can be analyzed, the parties to the original relationship must be identified. Sometimes the parties to the contract are obvious, but when a contract involves a business, questions can arise about who is liable on the contract. As discussed in Chapter 12, the signature should indicate the capacity in which the party is signing. Am I signing as Laurel, an individual, so that my salary and assets are subject to a judgment for damages if the contract is breached, or am I signing as president of the Laurel Corporation, so that only the business assets are subject to such a judgment? But simply stating that I am acting on behalf of a business does not necessarily make it so; it is often necessary to check the legal status of the parties.

Each state recognizes and regulates various business entities—ways of structuring businesses with different rules governing management, liability, and taxation. A business entity may be seen as an "artificial person" that has legal rights and responsibilities separate from the rights and responsibilities of the actual people who manage that entity and who physically sign contracts for that entity.

To determine whether the party to the contract is the business or the living person who signed the contract (or both), the first step is to determine the type of legal entity involved. The next step is to determine which living human beings have authority to make the entity liable on a contract. The basic types of legal entity are as follows.

Sole Proprietorship A sole proprietorship is a one-owner business. It is not truly an "entity" because the business and its owner are not legally separate. The owner has liability for business debts. A sole proprietorship is not necessarily a small business, however, and it may have many employees. The employees may or may not have authority as agents (discussed in the next section) to enter contracts on behalf of the business.

Example

College students Jan and Dean, unable to find summer jobs, go from store to store in their town's central shopping area, offering to wash windows and "spruce up" the exteriors. At Pat's Pets, they encounter Marty, who identifies herself as the manager and tells them to wash the windows and paint the decorative shutters. When the job is done, Jan and Dean leave a bill for $140. A month later they return to ask why they haven't been paid. Pat, the owner, informs them that Marty was simply an employee and has been fired. Marty had no authority to enter a contract for Pat. While Marty may be personally liable, Marty is now unemployed and unlikely to be willing or able to pay. Can you think of any additional facts that might make Pat liable under an equitable theory, such as quasi-contract?

Partnership A partnership has not traditionally been regarded as an "entity" (a separate legal being) with liability and rights apart from its owners; each partner is normally regarded as an agent for "purposes of the partnership business." As you can imagine, the definition of that phrase has been the subject of many lawsuits.

Example

It is well known in the town of Kaos that Sam Sunny and Fran Share are partners in a successful law firm. It is not well known that the two regularly argue about spending. One day Sam walks into Touch of Elegance and spends hours with the store's owner, a young decorator who recently opened the business and is a bit naïve about business practices. Sam orders furnishings for the firm's reception area, costing $36,000. When Fran finds out, she becomes very upset. The firm does not have sufficient money in its business account to pay the bill, and Fran refuses to use her own savings to pay. Her position is that she would be liable if Sam ordered computers, file cabinets, or other items necessary to the practice of law, but that Sam's preference for high-end decorating is purely personal. Sam claims that he will pay for his half but that he does not have enough money to pay the entire bill. Touch of Elegance only wants the money it is owed.

In some states partnerships can file statements of authority, specifying the contract authority of the individual partners. If a partnership has not filed a statement of authority, those dealing with the partnership in situations involving large or unusual contracts may want to obtain the signatures of all partners. Partnership statements of authority, like information about limited partnerships, corporations, and LLCs (described below), are registered with the secretary of state. To find the Web site for the secretary of state for any state, visit the National Association of Secretaries of State at http://www.nass.org/.

Limited Partnership Limited partnerships consist of limited partners, who are investors without authority to make decisions or bind the business, and a general partner or partners, with authority to bind the business consistent with the terms of the limited partnership agreement. Again, the starting point for obtaining information is the office of the secretary of state. Because the general partner in a limited partnership may be a corporation, be prepared to research two businesses when dealing with a limited partnership.

Many states now recognize other types of partnerships, such as limited liability partnerships, which may have entity characteristics, such as protection from personal liability.

Corporation A corporation is regarded as an entity—a person separate from the many people with whom it has relationships. A corporation has shareholders, who own the business but do not have direct control of the business. The shareholders elect a board of directors; the board directs the "big picture" but does not generally get involved in daily business activities. The corporate officers (president, vice president, treasurer, etc.) are employees who may be authorized to enter into contracts for the corporation. Of course, not all employees are authorized to enter contracts, so it is important to verify that authority.

How do you know who is an officer and who has authority to execute contracts on behalf of a corporation? One way is to obtain a certified copy of the resolution of the board of directors, appointing the officer(s), approving a particular agreement, or authorizing particular officers to sign agreements. Because some corporations are small and run informally, it is always a good idea to check the secretary of state Web site to determine the status of the corporation and who has authority to certify board resolutions. Some state laws include presumptions of authority when certain corporate officers sign documents. State laws differ, and it is important to understand the law of the state in which you are working.

Limited Liability Company A relatively new type of entity called a limited liability company (LLC) has the advantage of providing flexibility as compared to the traditional corporate structure, but that flexibility can present a challenge to those who want to verify authority prior to dealing with the business. An LLC may be managed directly by the members or indirectly, through a board of managers. The office of the secretary of state may be able to verify whether an LLC is in good standing, but in some states you must examine the company's operating agreement to determine who has authority to bind the business.

B. Agency

Agency involves three parties: the principal, the agent, and the outside party. The agent is the mechanism, but the contract forms between the principal and the outsider. An **agent** acts on behalf of another party, the **principal.** For purposes of this book, you will learn about agency as a means of entering into a contract. Many, possibly most, business contracts are created by an agent. Consider when you run into Wal-Mart to buy socks. You don't deal with members of the Walton family or other stockholders of the corporation that owns and sells you the socks; you deal with an agent. Businesses that operate as entities, such as corporations and LLCs, must enter contracts through agents.

Agent
One who acts on behalf of another

Principal
Party for whom an agent acts

1. Establishing Agency

Not everyone who acts on behalf of another is an agent. Agency requires consent of the principal and the agent. Does the consent have to be written? Not necessarily; the agency agreement must be written in cases where the Statute of Frauds applies directly, for example, appointment of an agent for a period of more than one year. In some states, the agency contract must be written because the contracts the agent will deal with must be written, because of the Statute of Frauds. A contract to sell real estate must be in writing, so a contract to employ a real estate agent must be in writing. This requirement is called the **equal dignity rule.** The document that creates an agency relationship is sometimes called a **power of attorney.**

Equal Dignity Rule
Requirement that agency contract be written, if contract to be established by agent must be written

Power of Attorney
Document creating an agency

An agent is not always an employee and agency need not be a compensated relationship. The agent may act as a "gift" to the principal. An agent might not even have contract capacity in some cases. Any teenager who takes Mom's car and money and buys a gallon of milk and a loaf of bread for the family is acting as an agent. The main characteristic of agency is the **control** exercised by the principal over the agent. The principal gives the agent authority to act in one of several ways.

1. **Express authority** is the authority given by words or conduct. Gale engages Andi Agent to sell a house. Andi has express authority to sell the house.
2. **Implied authority** is authority reasonably necessary to accomplish the express purpose. Andi has implied authority to advertise the house.
3. **Operation of law** can create authority in an emergency situation. Rizwana was alone in the store where she is a sales clerk when a car hit and broke out the front window. The manager could not be found; Rizwana did not want to leave the store open to the elements and to thieves and ordered a company to board up the broken window, even though she was never authorized to make purchases for the store.
4. **Ratification** is acceptance of the agent's unauthorized actions after the fact. Ian told his new employee, Jana, that she could not make any purchases without his express permission. Ian was out of town for several days when the fax machine failed. Jana went to the office supply store, where Ian has an account, and bought a new machine. The office supply store clerk was careless and did not check who had authority to order for Ian. When Ian returned, he could have refused to pay, but he did not object to the machine. He started using it and is now obligated to pay. Of course, Jana may be liable to Ian for breach of her obligations as an employee.
5. **Apparent authority** results from the principal's dealings with third parties when the principal has given those third parties reason to believe that an agent has authority. Suppose, in the above example, Jana repeatedly ordered supplies and Ian paid every time, never raising an objection. The tenth time Jana placed an order, Ian decided to put his foot down and refuse to pay. He may be **estopped** from denying liability because he created the impression that Jana had authority to place orders. Similarly, if Jana *did* have authority to place orders but Ian failed

Express Authority
Authority given by words or conduct

Implied Authority
Authority not expressed in writing or spoken words; arises from circumstances

Operation of Law
Rights and obligations are implied by law, for example, in emergency situations

Ratification
Acceptance of acts by agent after they occur

Apparent Authority
Principal's dealings with third parties have given them reason to believe that an agent has authority

Estop
To bar assertion of a claim or right that contradicts what has been said or done before

to notify the office supply store when he fired Jana, Ian might be liable for orders placed by Jana after her termination. For obvious reasons, apparent authority is always based on the principal's conduct; an agent cannot create his or her own authority.

All of the above describe theories under which a principal can be liable on a contract entered by an agent. Normally the agent is not liable on that contract because the third party knows that the contract is really the principal's contract. If the third party does not know that, the agent might be liable.

Example

Disclosure is essential to protecting the agent from liability to the third party. Disney wants to establish a new theme park in the Midwest and contacts Laurel, a noted expert in commercial real estate in the area west of Chicago. Disney hires Laurel to acquire the needed land but tells Laurel that she may not disclose Disney's interest. Such a disclosure would cause a sharp increase in price. Laurel starts immediately and first signs a contract to buy 160 acres from Farmer Brown. Laurel might either say nothing—Disney is an **undisclosed principal**—or might say, "I am working for a corporation but cannot reveal its identity"—Disney is a **partially disclosed principal.** If Disney decides to change plans before the purchase is completed, Farmer Brown *can* sue Laurel. After all, if he is unaware of Disney, who else would he sue? Laurel may be all right, however, because Disney has a duty to indemnify her (discussed below).

Undisclosed Principal
Existence of agency relationship not known to third party

Partially Disclosed Principal
Existence of agency is known, identity of principal is not known

2. Agency Duties

Fiduciary Relationship
Relationship in which one person is under a duty to act for the benefit of the other on matters within the scope of the relationship

Indemnification
Compensation or reimbursement for a loss

Agency is a **fiduciary relationship;** the principal and agent have special obligations to each other unless these obligations are waived.

Principal's Duties to the Agent

- To **cooperate** in performance of agreed duties. For example, Hollis signed a six-month listing to sell her home, and then her job transfer was cancelled. Having spent money advertising the house, the agent refused to cancel the contract. Hollis changed the locks so that the agent could not show the house. Hollis may be liable to the agent.
- To **indemnify** (reimburse) the agent for expenses reasonably incurred in carrying out the agency
- To **communicate** relevant information
- To comply with any contract with the agent

Agent's Duties to the Principal

- To **obey** lawful directions
- To be able to **account** for the principal's money in the agent's care

- To exercise **reasonable care.** While an agent is not expected to have a crystal ball and make only decisions with positive outcomes, the agent is expected to act with reasonable care—to conduct reasonable investigation and use common sense.
- To keep the principal **fully informed.** For example, a real estate agent cannot unilaterally decide that an offer is too low to even discuss with the principal.
- **Loyalty,** which encompasses:
  - Not using or disclosing confidential information obtained from or about the principal
  - Not becoming involved in conflicting relationships without the principal's consent
    - Outside profits: Dana, department head of the paralegal program, has responsibility for choosing and ordering books. A publisher gives Dana a "gift" of $500.
    - Competing with principal: While working as Hal's agent to find an investment property, Ana finds a duplex that is priced substantially below its value. Ana puts in her own bid to buy the property, which would have been an excellent investment for Hal.
    - Working for competing principals: Lyn is a sales rep for Jocko Sports and calls on stores in a four-state area to get those stores to carry the Jocko line of products. Lyn starts to represent a competing line, Team Stuff, and shows both lines when visiting stores.
    - Secret dealing with principal. While working to find Hal an investment property, Ana transfers a building she owns to a trust and then buys the building for Hal, not revealing her ownership.

- Not becoming involved in conflicting relationships without the principal's consent
- Outside profits: Dana, department head of the paralegal program, has responsibility for choosing and ordering books. A publisher gives Dana a "gift" of $500.
- Competing with principal: While working as Hal's agent to find an investment property, Ana finds a duplex that is priced substantially below its value. Ana puts in her own bid to buy the property, which would have been an excellent investment for Hal.
- Working for competing principals: Lyn is a sales rep for Jocko Sports and calls on stores in a four-state area to get those stores to carry the Jocko line of products. Lyn starts to represent a competing line, Team Stuff, and shows both lines when visiting stores.
- Secret dealing with principal. While working to find Hal an investment property, Ana transfers a building she owns to a trust and then buys the building for Hal, not revealing her ownership.

Agency normally ends by agreement of the parties, the passage of an agreed time (*e.g.*, a six-month listing), completion of the purpose (*e.g.*, the house is sold), or the inability of one of the parties to perform (death, incapacity). In some cases termination of agency may be possible, but wrongful. For example, Jocko Sports gave Lyn a two-year contract as a sales representative, but breached the contract by firing Lyn after five months. Jocko is able to end the relationship, but may have liability for doing so.

Agency Coupled with an Interest
Agent has a financial stake in the transaction

On the other hand, a principal may be unable to terminate an **agency coupled with an interest,** in which the agent has a financial "stake" in the transaction. For example, in order to obtain a special price, Lee signed a three-year contract with Onandoff Internet. For convenience, Lee authorized Onandoff to make a monthly charge to her credit card to pay for the service. Unfortunately, Onandoff took on far too many new customers, and for weeks Lee was unable to get online. Frustrated, Lee signed up for a different service and called to cancel the monthly payment to Onandoff. Unfortunately, Lee appointed Onandoff as an agent to make those charges to the credit card, and Onandoff has a financial interest, so Lee may be unable to terminate the arrangement.

Examine this sample agency contract, and look for provisions dealing with cooperation, communication, and outside profits. Would this agreement have to be in writing to be enforceable?

EXHIBIT 9-1
Buyer-Broker Agency Agreement

THIS AGREEMENT is entered into this ___________ day of ___________, 20__, by ("Buyer"), and ___________, ("Broker").

1. Buyer desires to employ Broker to locate and negotiate the purchase of real property on behalf of Buyer and Broker desires to accept such employment and to use best efforts to find a suitable property for Buyer;
2. Broker is duly licensed as a real estate broker in the State of ___________ and maintains an office, properly equipped and staffed to render the services contracted for in this agreement.
3. Buyer desires to purchase property in _____________ County, State of ________, with specifications and intended use set out in Exhibit "A," attached and made a part of this agreement ("Property").
4. Buyer warrants that he has the financial ability to purchase such a Property, at the price and on the terms and conditions set out in Exhibit "B," attached and made a part of this agreement.
5. Broker shall use best efforts to find a suitable Property, shall advertise the desires of the Buyer, and has right to locate and negotiate the purchase of a suitable Property at the price and terms set out in Exhibit "B," or at any different price and terms as may be hereafter accepted by the Buyer
6. The term of this Agreement shall be ___________ months, beginning on the date of signing by both parties, and ending at noon on ___________, 20__,
7. Broker shall inspect prospective properties and obtain complete information before presenting the property to Buyer for consideration.
8. Buyer shall not, during the term of this Agreement, or any extension hereof, contract to buy any property, without providing the Broker with full details of any such action in writing.

EXHIBIT 9-1
(continued)

9. If Broker identifies a suitable Property during the term of this Agreement and Buyer contracts to buy that Property, Buyer shall pay to Broker, at the time of closing of the purchase of the Property, a commission of ________ (________%) percent of the purchase price for the Property.
10. Broker may represent and receive commissions from both Buyer and Seller of the Property.
11. If Buyer locates Property solely through his own efforts, Buyer may enter into a contract for the purchase of the Property without liability to Broker for commission in any amount; however, at the time of closing, Buyer shall reimburse Broker for all documented, reasonable out-of-pocket expenses incurred by Broker during the term of this Agreement. Within twenty-four (24) hours of initial contact with any such prospective seller, Buyer shall provide Broker with the property description, and contact information for the owner of the Property, and the circumstances under which Buyer obtained knowledge of the Property.
12. This Agreement may be terminated by either party, prior to a contract for purchase being executed, upon written notice to the other party. If this Agreement is terminated by Buyer, Buyer agrees to reimburse Broker for all documented, reasonable out-of-pocket expenses incurred by Broker prior to termination.
13. Broker, a cooperating broker, or an authorized escrow agent may accept and hold, money paid by Buyer as a deposit with regard to any Property located pursuant to this Agreement, under the laws of ____________; in the event of forfeiture by a prospective seller, all such sums shall be immediately returned to Buyer.
14. This Agreement in no way guarantees the location or purchase of a Property.
15. Broker (may) (may not) use the name of Buyer in locating and negotiating a purchase.
16. If provisions of this Agreement shall for any reason be held to be invalid, such invalidity shall not affect any other provision of this Agreement.
17. This Agreement contains the entire agreement of the parties and no oral statements or prior agreements shall have any force and effect. This Agreement shall not be modified except by a writing executed by both parties.
18. This agreement, and all transactions contemplated hereby, shall be governed by the laws of ____________. The parties agree to submit to the jurisdiction and venue of a court located in ____________ County, ____________. If litigation arises out of this Agreement the parties agree to reimburse the prevailing party's reasonable attorney's fees,

EXHIBIT 9-1
(continued)

court costs, and other expenses, whether or not taxable by the court as costs, in addition to other relief to which the prevailing party may be entitled. In such event, no action shall be entertained by any court of competent jurisdiction if filed more than one year after the date the cause(s) of action actually accrued regardless of whether damages were then calculable.

19. The agreements contained herein are binding upon the parties and their respective heirs, successors, legal representatives and assigns.
20. This Agreement will not be recorded in the public records of any county.

[Signatures, witnesses, and exhibits omitted.]

C. Contract Beneficiaries

Third-party Beneficiary Not a party to a contract but benefits from contract

As implied by the name, a **third-party beneficiary** benefits from the contract. Whether a beneficiary has enforceable rights under the contract depends on the intent of the original parties. To determine the intent of the parties, courts look at whether they were aware of the third party and whether the relationship makes intent to benefit likely. Courts generally presume that third parties are not intended to benefit from a contract.

Example

A third party does not have the right to enforce a contract if the contract was not intended to benefit that third party. Hugh Homeowner was thrilled to learn that his neighbor, Nils, signed a contract to sell his house to Yuri Yuppie. Nils has never taken care of the property, and as a result, the value of Hugh's property has suffered. Hugh knows Yuri intends to paint the house immediately, have professional landscapers work on the yard, and dispose of the trash on the porch. One day Yuri tells Hugh that Nils is "backing out" of the sale because moving will be so difficult. Yuri does not want to spend the time and money to go to court and plans to simply find another house to rehab. Although Hugh would, in fact, have benefited from performance of the contract, he was not an intended beneficiary and cannot enforce the contract or seek a remedy, based on the breach, in court. Hugh was an **incidental beneficiary.**

Incidental Beneficiary A third-party beneficiary, not intended to benefit from contract, who does not acquire rights under contract

While visiting his insurance agent about his homeowners' insurance, Val buys a life insurance policy on an impulse and names his wife as beneficiary. Val forgets to tell his wife about the policy and she discovers it about a year later, after Val's sudden death in an accident. Val's wife was not even aware of Val's contract with the insurance company, but she can enforce it once she has knowledge. A court will assume that Val had intent to make a gift benefiting his wife, based on the relationship. Val's wife is a **donee beneficiary.**

Donee Beneficiary A third-party beneficiary intended to benefit from contract performance as a gift

Suppose that Val's house was destroyed in a fire and his mortgage lender wanted payment under the homeowner's policy. Mortgage lenders generally require that they be specifically named on such policies as beneficiaries. Even if lender were not named, it could seek to enforce the contract. A court would assume intent to benefit the lender because of Val's legal obligation to the lender. The lender is a **creditor beneficiary.**

In either example, the insurance company could assert defenses that would be valid against the original contract party, such as fraudulent information in the application for insurance or failure to pay premiums.

Creditor Beneficiary
A third-party beneficiary to whom a contract party is indebted and who is intended to benefit from the performance of a contract

EXHIBIT 9-2
Sample Mortgage Clause Requiring That Borrower Make Lender a Creditor Beneficiary

Property Insurance. Borrower shall keep the improvements now existing or hereafter erected on the Property insured against loss by fire, hazards included within the term "extended coverage," and any other hazards including, but not limited to, earthquakes and floods, for which Lender requires insurance. This insurance shall be maintained in the amounts (including deductible levels) and for the periods that Lender requires. What Lender requires pursuant to the preceding sentences can change during the term of the Loan. The insurance carrier providing the insurance shall be chosen by Borrower subject to Lender's right to disapprove Borrower's choice, which right shall not be exercised unreasonably. Lender may require Borrower to pay, in connection with this Loan, either: (a) a one-time charge for flood zone determination, certification and tracking services; or (b) a one-time charge for flood zone determination and certification services and subsequent charges each time remappings or similar changes occur which reasonably might affect such determination or certification. Borrower shall also be responsible for the payment of any fees imposed by the Federal Emergency Management Agency in connection with the review of any flood zone determination resulting from an objection by Borrower. . . .

All insurance policies required by Lender and renewals of such policies shall be subject to Lender's right to disapprove such policies, shall include a standard mortgage clause, and shall name Lender as mortgagee and/or as an additional loss payee. Lender shall have the right to hold the policies and renewal certificates. If Lender requires, Borrower shall promptly give to Lender all receipts of paid premiums and renewal notices. If Borrower obtains any form of insurance coverage, not otherwise required by Lender, for damage to, or destruction of, the Property, such policy shall include a standard mortgage clause and shall name Lender as mortgagee and/or as an additional loss payee.

In the event of loss, Borrower shall give prompt notice to the insurance carrier and Lender. Lender may make proof of loss if not made promptly by Borrower. Unless Lender and Borrower otherwise agree in writing, any insurance proceeds, whether or not the underlying insurance was required by Lender, shall be applied to restoration or repair of the Property, if the restoration or repair is economically feasible and Lender's security is not lessened. During such repair and restoration

EXHIBIT 9-2
(continued)

period, Lender shall have the right to hold such insurance proceeds until Lender has had an opportunity to inspect such Property. . . . If Borrower abandons the Property, Lender may file, negotiate and settle any available insurance claim and related matters. If Borrower does not respond within 30 days to a notice from Lender that the insurance carrier has offered to settle a claim, then Lender may negotiate and settle the claim. The 30-day period will begin when the notice is given. In either event, or if Lender acquires the Property under Section 22 or otherwise, Borrower hereby assigns to Lender (a) Borrower's rights to any insurance proceeds in an amount not to exceed the amounts unpaid under the Note or this Security Instrument, and (b) any other of Borrower's rights (other than the right to any refund of unearned premiums paid by Borrower) under all insurance policies covering the Property, insofar as such rights are applicable to the coverage of the Property. Lender may use the insurance proceeds either to repair or restore the Property or to pay amounts unpaid under the Note or this Security Instrument, whether or not then due.

Privity
Being a party to the contract

Whether an injured party is an intended beneficiary is particularly important with respect to warranties. At common law, lack of **privity** (not being a party to the contract relationship) often prevented injured parties from taking advantage of warranties in a contract. If Dad bought a car, which was subsequently in an accident because of a defect, could family members collect damages from a seller with whom they had no contract relationship? Could Dad sue the manufacturer, or only the dealership with which he had a contract? The common law differs from state to state. While injuries to a person or property are normally addressed by tort law, and privity is not an issue, damages that are purely economic (*e.g.*, lost income) are still addressed by contract law. As you might imagine, the Uniform Commercial Code (UCC) addresses the issue.

Assignment 9-1

- Aunt Liz hired attorney Neil to write her will, leaving her estate in trust to two nieces, Ann and Beth. Unfortunately, Neil established the trust in a way that put the entire burden of taxes on Ann's share. Liz has died and Ann feels Neil breached a contract to create a trust to benefit the two nieces equally. Can Ann sue? Was she a third-party beneficiary under the contract between Liz and Neil? Use computer-assisted legal research (CALR) to find a case discussing whether a non-client can be a beneficiary under a contract to employ a lawyer.
- Search the Internet and find the Uniform Statutory Form Power of Attorney Act. Has your state adopted a form based on the Act?

- Research and report to the class as to whether your state recognizes a **durable power of attorney** or a **springing power of attorney,** which "springs" into effect upon the happening of a stated event—for example, "When my doctor certifies that I am unable to make my own decisions. . . ." For more information about these powers of attorney, visit http://www.nolo.com/legal-encyclopedia/financial-power-of-attorney-in-your-state-31010.html.
- Create a springing, durable power of attorney for yourself.
- Read *Feingold v. John Hancock Insurance* Co. (1st Cir. 2014), http://media.ca1.uscourts.gov/pdf.opinions/13-2151P-01A.pdf. The suit focuses on whether Feingold was a beneficiary under the global resolution agreement (GRA). Why do you think he did not sue as an intended beneficiary of the policy itself; wouldn't his mother have intended to benefit him in these circumstances? Note that Feingold attempts to assert equitable alternatives to contract, such as unjust enrichment. How does the court respond to that?
- In adopting the UCC, each state chose from three alternatives concerning who can be a third-party beneficiary to warranties included in a sale of goods. Find the alternative enacted by your state.

Durable Power of Attorney
Creates an agency relationship that remains in effect during the grantor's incompetency

Springing Power of Attorney
Comes into effect at a later dat

D. Assignment and Delegation

The transfer of a party's rights under a contract is called **assignment;** the transfer of duties is **delegation.** The two often go together.

Assignment
A transfer of property or rights

Delegation
Assignment of obligations

1. Assignment

Assignment is assumed to be allowable unless the contract specifically and validly prohibits assignment, the right being assigned is highly personal, or assignment is prohibited by law. For example, some states prohibit assignment of future wages or of a personal injury claim. An assignment may not substantially change the risks, rights, or duties under the contract. Changing the address to which a payment is made is not substantial, but attempting to change the amount of the payment would be a prohibited substantial change. Courts tend to rule in favor of allowing assignment.

Example

Assignment of contracts for financing is very common. Family Home is a small, independent appliance store. To compete with the "big boys," Family must offer financing to customers who do not have credit cards. When Family sells a freezer and the buyer signs a note to pay $50 per month for the next 24 months, Family cannot afford to "hold the paper." Family's cash flow would not permit it to have several hundred accounts outstanding and be able to buy new inventory. Family therefore "sells the paper" to Acme Acceptance[1]. Acme pays Family $1,800, and

[1]Acceptance companies are "indirect lenders" that work with car dealers and retailers.

Assignor
One who transfers rights to another

Assignee
One to whom rights are transferred by another

Obligor
One who owes an obligation

Gratuitous
Done without compensation; a gift

Family assigns the note promising 24 payments of $50. Acme is happy because it will earn $600 by taking monthly payments. Family is happy because it sold a freezer at a profit and is able to replenish inventory. Customer is not inconvenienced; she is simply given a new address to which the payments should be sent. Family is the **assignor,** Acme is the **assignee,** and customer is the **obligor.**

A valid assignment must provide for notice to the obligor. Whether an assignment is revocable may depend on whether it was **gratuitous** (a gift) or for consideration as well as the degree to which the parties have acted on the assignment. Always check state law in such a situation. Whether the assignment can be cancelled or revoked may also depend on whether the assignment was oral or written. Is an oral assignment valid? Yes, unless the Statute of Frauds applies. For example, assignment of a contract to purchase real estate would have to be in writing.

Normally the assignee has the right to enforce the contract immediately upon valid assignment. The Family-Acme-Customer transaction may be a secured transaction, however, and special concerns arise. What if the freezer does not work and Family Home refuses to fix or replace it? Is Customer limited to suing Family while continuing to make payments to Acme? The answer is generally no.

Mortgage
Security interest in real estate

Real Property
Land and buildings

Collateral
Assets pledged by a borrower to secure a loan or other credit, and subject to seizure in the event of default

Lien
An encumbrance against property, typically to secure payment of a debt

Foreclose
Take property to satisfy debt

Chattel
Moveable items; also called personal property

You are probably familiar with the concept of a **mortgage** against **real property** (land and buildings) to secure a loan; the property serves as **collateral.** The lender has a **lien** and can **foreclose** (take the property) if the borrower fails to pay. Because the lender is generally not also the seller of the property, the issue of defenses based on problems with the property does not come up often. To discover whether real property is subject to a mortgage, check the recorder for the county in which the property is located.

When the seller retains a security interest in personal property, as in the Family-Acme situation, the situation is not the same as a mortgage. Secured interests in personal (**chattel**) property are covered by Article 9 of the UCC.

2. Delegation

You may remember that personal impossibility is not usually an excuse for contract performance. For example, Pat enters a contract to paint Lou's house. A week later Pat is in an accident, has a broken arm, and cannot paint. Performance is not objectively impossible, so what can Pat do? Pat can delegate. Most contract duties are delegable, but delegation does not relieve the delegator (Pat) of liability. As with assignment, delegation may be prohibited by the terms of the contract or may violate the law or public policy. Delegation is also prohibited if the other party has a substantial interest in personal performance. Painting a house is not a service that requires a particular individual, and Lou would probably be unsuccessful in objecting to delegation. If Pat were an artist, under contract to paint Lou's portrait, or a lawyer, under contract to draft Lou's will and trust, the service would be "personal" and Lou could object to delegation.

3. Novation

A **novation** is a new contract. A novation can occur between the original parties to the contract and cancel the original contract, if it is supported by consideration. A novation can also involve a third party, if a new party takes over all of the rights and duties of the original party and the original party is totally discharged from liability under the contract.

Novation
A new contract discharging an earlier contract

A common assignment-delegation situation arises when the original tenant under a lease wants to bring in a new tenant. The most common issue is whether the original tenant is excused by having assigned all of her rights and delegated all of her duties (a novation) or remains responsible on the lease because the sublease did not amount to a new contract. Often the lease will deal with the issue directly by limiting the right to sublease (*e.g.*, requiring landlord's approval) and stating that the original tenant is not excused. Some states have statutes to protect residential tenants in this situation.

EXHIBIT 9-3
Sample Clause Prohibiting Assignment and Disclaiming Agency

ASSIGNMENT/SUBCONTRACTING

The Contractor may not assign this contract or any part thereof, or assign any of the sums to be paid hereunder, nor shall any part of the work done or material furnished under this contract be sublet without the Owner's express written consent.

The Contractor may not enter into subcontracts for any of the work contemplated under this contract unless included in the specific provisions of this contract. Any such subcontract must acknowledge the binding nature of the contract and must incorporate this contract, including any attachments. Contractor is solely responsible for the performance of any subcontractor. Contractor shall not have the authority to contract for or incur obligations on behalf of the Owner.

The following is typical language found in a sublease form:

> Under this sublease agreement, the Principal Tenant (who signed the original rental agreement) remains responsible to the Landlord for all terms and conditions of the lease. For example, if the Subtenant does not pay rent or causes damages, the Principal Tenant remains liable to the Landlord for these damages. For these reasons, many Principal Tenants require a security deposit from their Subtenant, and have the Subtenant pay the rent to them rather than to the Landlord. The Principal Tenant stands in the relationship to the subtenant as a landlord and has the right to terminate the tenancy of the subtenant with proper legal notice. Also note that this form of agreement anticipates that permission to sublet is required by the landlord or his agent and is valid only if signed by the Landlord.

A sample assignment/novation appears in Chapter 10.

Is there a difference between amending an existing contract and using a novation to cancel the earlier contract? Yes. In *Fanucchi & Limi Farms v. United Agri Products* (9th Cir. 2005), http://caselaw.findlaw.com/us-9th-circuit/1008875.html, decided under California law, the Ninth Circuit held that, while the original loan documents specifically prohibited oral modifications, a subsequent oral agreement could constitute a *novation* of the original loan documentation that would displace the earlier detailed and un-amendable written agreement with an amendable oral one.

A novation is also sometimes called accord and satisfaction.

> Black's Law Dictionary defines an "accord and satisfaction" as "[a]n agreement to substitute for an existing debt some alternative form of discharging that debt, coupled with the actual discharge of the debt by the substituted performance." . . . [T]he "doctrine of accord and satisfaction provides that when two parties agree to give and accept something in satisfaction of a right of action which one has against the other, and that agreement is performed, the right of action is subsequently extinguished." . . . A novation, on the other hand, is generally defined as "[t]he act of substituting for an old obligation a new one that either replaces an existing obligation with a new obligation or replaces an original party with a new party." . . . A novation is therefore a "species" of accord and satisfaction. . . . This Court has also characterized a novation as a "substituted contract."

Weaver v. American Power Conversion Corp. (R.I. 2004), http://caselaw.findlaw.com/ri-supreme-court/1420915.html#sthash.bH7d2nLz.dpuf.

4. Joint and Several Liability and Guarantors

In Chapter 8, concerning the Statute of Frauds, you learned about suretyship (the chapter includes a sample of a surety contract), guarantors, and co-obligors, who become part of a contract by "guaranteeing" the performance of a primary party. In some situations the party guaranteeing performance is not liable until the primary obligor has defaulted and, in order to "collect" on the guarantee, the other party has to establish default by the primary obligor. In other situations the party guaranteeing performance is "primarily" liable on the contract along with the "main" party. If parties are both primarily liable, they may be jointly liable or they have **"joint and several liability,"** meaning that each of them could be individually responsible for the entire obligation. A co-obligor or surety under a contract may have rights, in addition to liability under the contract, particularly the right to notice if the primary party is in default.

Joint and Several Liability
Co-obligors can be sued together or any one can be liable for the entire obligation

---

Examples

The difference between primary and secondary liability is key to determining who can be sued and when they can be sued. Jenn cosigns on a lease so that her brother can have his own apartment. After a few months, brother stops paying rent because the landlord has not made needed repairs. Can the landlord immediately bring action against Jenn or must he first take action against brother and establish his default? May landlord sue Jenn without suing brother? The answers depend on whether the language of the contract makes Jenn only secondarily liable and, if she is primarily liable, whether she has joint and several liability.

Tim and Tom rented an apartment together. The landlord checked credit on each of them and had them sign a one-year lease with rent at $600 per month. Tim lost his job and moved back home to live with his parents. Tom has not been able to find another roommate and believes he should not be responsible for Tim's share of the rent because the landlord knew he was renting to two separate adults. What do you think? This clause appeared in the lease:

Example: Sample Miscellaneous Clause in a Lease

In all references to LESSEE herein, the singular shall be deemed to include the plural and the masculine, the feminine. Where this LEASE is signed by more than one person as LESSEE, all such persons shall be jointly and severally liable for the payment of rent and any additional rent and the performance of all covenants and agreements to be kept by LESSEE hereunder.

E. Secured Transactions Under the UCC

When a borrower becomes unable to pay debts, the difference between being a secured **creditor** and being an unsecured creditor is huge. A secured creditor is far more likely to see at least partial payment. A debt incurred to purchase real estate is, for example, secured by a mortgage. If the debtor ceases to have any income or savings, the creditor can foreclose and collect what is owed from the proceeds of a sale of the property. The debtor's unsecured creditors, such as credit card companies, have no claim to that money until the mortgage holder is paid off. The secured creditor has **priority.**

Creditor
One to whom money is owed

Personal property (goods), the subject of the UCC, can also serve a security. For example, debtor borrows $10,000 from a dealership to purchase an automobile, using the automobile as **collateral**; with a security agreement, the dealership retains a right to repossess and resell the automobile if debtor defaults on the loan. This arrangement has priority over the unsecured **note** debtor signed when he borrowed $1,000 from his brother, even if the loan from the brother occurred before the purchase of the car and was part of the down payment.

Priority
Debts paid ahead of other debts, in bankruptcy

Collateral
Security for payment of a loan

Note
A contract promising to pay a debt; may or may not create a security interest in collateral

Some, but not all, states have adopted a revised version of Article 9. Depending on your state, its version of Article 9 may cover security interests in goods, **inventory** (goods held for sale or lease to customers), **instruments** (checks, notes, certificates of deposit), **securities** (investment in a common scheme, such as ownership of stock in a company), and other property (accounts and intangible property, such as patents and copyrights).

Inventory
Goods held for sale or lease

Instruments
Formal written documents

Securities
Evidence of investment in a common scheme

Attachment, or the creation of an enforceable security interest, occurs when the parties make a security agreement, if:

- the lender (the secured party) has given something of value, and
- the debtor has some legal rights in the property serving as collateral, and
- the debtor authenticates a document describing the collateral or the lender takes possession of the property.

Attachment
Creation of an enforceable security interest

The security interest automatically applies to any proceeds if the debtor sells or otherwise disposes of the collateral and can apply to property acquired after the agreement is entered. Once a security interest has attached, the lender can seize the collateral from the debtor if the debtor fails to pay as agreed (*e.g.*, repossess the car). What happens if the collateral is no longer in the possession of the debtor or if the debtor attempts to use the same property as security for additional loans? For example, I signed a note and gave Bank a security interest in my car, but I signed the car over to my brother without paying off Bank. To protect itself from such situations, the lender should **perfect** its security interest.

Perfect
To register or record an instrument so that the public is on notice of its terms

The most common way to perfect a security interest is to file a financing statement with the appropriate state agency. Perfection can also occur when the secured party takes possession of the collateral until the debt is paid. If the collateral consists of **consumer goods**—items used primarily for personal, family, or household purposes—and the loan was a **purchase money security interest** (a loan to buy the collateral items—as in the Family Home/Customer/Acme example), the security interest is automatically perfected without any filing and without possession.

Consumer Goods
Items used primarily for personal, family, or household purposes

Purchase Money Security Interest
Lien against property to secure a loan used to acquire that property

Liens against highway vehicles, all-terrain vehicles and motorboats (these vehicles have certificates of title) are typically *not* UCC filings. To find liens against titled vehicles, search your state division or registry of motor vehicles.

If a security interest is perfected, it follows the collateral even if the collateral is sold or otherwise transferred. So, if I transferred my car to my brother, without paying Bank, Bank would continue to have a security interest in the car (and the right to repossess), even though my brother did not sign the note and had no relationship with Bank. There is an exception for purchases by a **good-faith buyer in the course of ordinary business.** Let's assume that all of the freezers in Family Home's inventory were collateral for financing from Family's supplier. Customer buys a freezer, unaware of the security interest (therefore in good faith) and dealing with a business that routinely sells freezers (course of ordinary business). Customer takes the freezer free from the security interest.

Good-faith Buyer in the Course of Ordinary Business
A buyer who acts honestly, gives value, and has no notice of other claims

On the other hand, if Family's competition, Adams' Appliances, knew that Family Home was in financial trouble and bought all of Family's inventory (a **bulk sale**), the freezers would continue to be collateral even after Adams' bought them. It is, therefore, essential that buyers protect themselves from buying property that might remain subject to a perfected security interest. They protect themselves by doing a UCC search, through the appropriate state agency, to identify security interests recorded against goods not in possession of a consumer.

Bulk Sale
Sale of major part of inventory, not in ordinary course of business

Assignment 9-2

As assigned by your instructor

- Determine whether your state has any statute that limits a landlord who wants to prohibit sublease or assignment of a residential lease.
- Find and report on a case from your state involving one party trying to prevent delegation by the other party.
- Sometimes a third party plays another role with respect to a contract: the third party induces one of the original parties to breach the contract. Find and report on a case from your state involving "interference with a contract relationship."
- Determine how a UCC search is done in your state and write a short report. To get started, search the name of your state and UCC search.
- Report on how you would determine whether real estate in your county is subject to liens. Be specific, give addresses, and so on.
- Report on how liens against vehicles are handled in your state. Does such a lien appear on the title document itself? What is the process for searching the title to a titled vehicle?
- I deal in custom furniture. You want a dining room set priced at $30,000. You don't have the money, but you do have a high-paying job. I propose that, instead of a loan-and-repayment agreement, you rent the furniture from me. After you pay a certain amount of rent, the furniture will be yours. Do some online research and determine advantages and disadvantages to each party from each possible arrangement. Of course, by now you know that what the parties call it and how the law sees it may be two different things! Research the factors a court will look at in determining whether a lease is treated as a secured transaction.

F. Practical and Ethical Issues

Third parties can be a concern in the lawyer-client relationship.

Example

Attorneys must be careful to not let third parties interfere with their obligations to a client. Marie, the owner of a successful restaurant, has been a client of your firm for many years. With her own personal and business matters, as well as her connections in the community, she has been a major source of business for the firm. Marie's son, Freddie, married Joan five years ago, against Marie's wishes. The two are now divorcing. They have never done well financially. Freddie works part-time at the restaurant and Joan has stayed home with their two young children. Marie has provided them with a house and cars, as well as money.

Marie has paid a $5,000 retainer to have the firm represent Freddie. Freddie initially stated that he and Joan had reached agreement that he would have custody of the children with limited visitation for Joan. Joan planned to return to her home state, about 500 miles away, and Freddie said that he would pay all of Joan's living expenses for a couple of years "while she got on her feet." The money would, of course, come from Marie. Freddie said that the firm should work out the details about the payments, visitation, and other matters, and then put the agreement in writing.

About a month later, Freddie came to the office alone, without an appointment, and in an agitated state. He stated that he could never be a good parent because of his drug addiction and that he really wants Joan to take the kids to her family and make a new start. He claimed that the original plan was his mother's idea and that she cannot be told why things have changed. Marie is adamant that the children must stay in this area and that she must have a substantial role in raising them.

Let's take it a step further. Assume that Marie finds out that Freddie is no longer seeking custody and comes into the firm, demanding an explanation. Marie also wants her $5,000 retainer back. The money was initially deposited in a clients' funds escrow account, but only $800 remains. The balance has been transferred to the firm's business account and has been spent on office expenses, such as utility bills. Marie claims that the firm was wrong to cash the check at all, much less take the money before the "work was done" according to her wishes. Freddie is claiming that Marie is not entitled to any of the money, because it constituted a gift to him.

Assignment 9-3

Identify all of the firm's ethical concerns and possible solutions, based on your state's Rules of Professional Conduct. You have dealt with some of the relevant rules in past lessons. In addition to considering those rules, find and analyze rules concerning conflicts of interests with current clients, professional independence, and safekeeping of property.

Career Corner

Misty L. Sheffield is the creator, owner, and lead paralegal of Legal Kick, LLC, a freelance paralegal firm in Atlanta, Georgia specializing in civil litigation. Misty loves both the legal side and the business side of being a virtual paralegal. She also enjoys blogging about the paralegal profession at www.atlantaparalegalservices.com.

Misty began freelancing in 1995 to be able to work from home. She says that market for freelance or virtual paralegals has grown exponentially with the changes we have seen in the legal profession. The combination of technology and the growing number of solo attorneys has created a wonderful environment for paralegals to work virtually on a contract basis.

Misty is a certified paralegal through the National Association of Legal Assistants; a 1992 graduate from the National Center for Paralegal Training, an ABA-approved program in Atlanta, Georgia; and a 1991 graduate of the University of Georgia with a Bachelor of Arts degree in political science.

Misty has more than 13 years of experience working in law firms, the judicial system, and as a freelance paralegal. She volunteers with her local Victim and Witness Assistance Program and as a guest speaker for local paralegal programs. Having worked on contract litigation, Misty says that the key to success, as with any other area of law, is attention to detail.

Review Questions

1. Identify the ways in which an agency relationship can be created. In what types of situations must the agency be created in writing?
2. Identify the duties of an agent to a principal and of a principal to an agent.
3. What is an agency coupled with an interest and how is it different from other agency relationships?
4. How are third-party beneficiaries categorized and which types have the right to enforce the contract?
5. Under what circumstances is assignment prohibited? When is delegation prohibited?
6. What does it mean to "perfect" a security interest?
7. Explain "durable power of attorney."
8. How are bulk sales treated differently with respect to security interests?

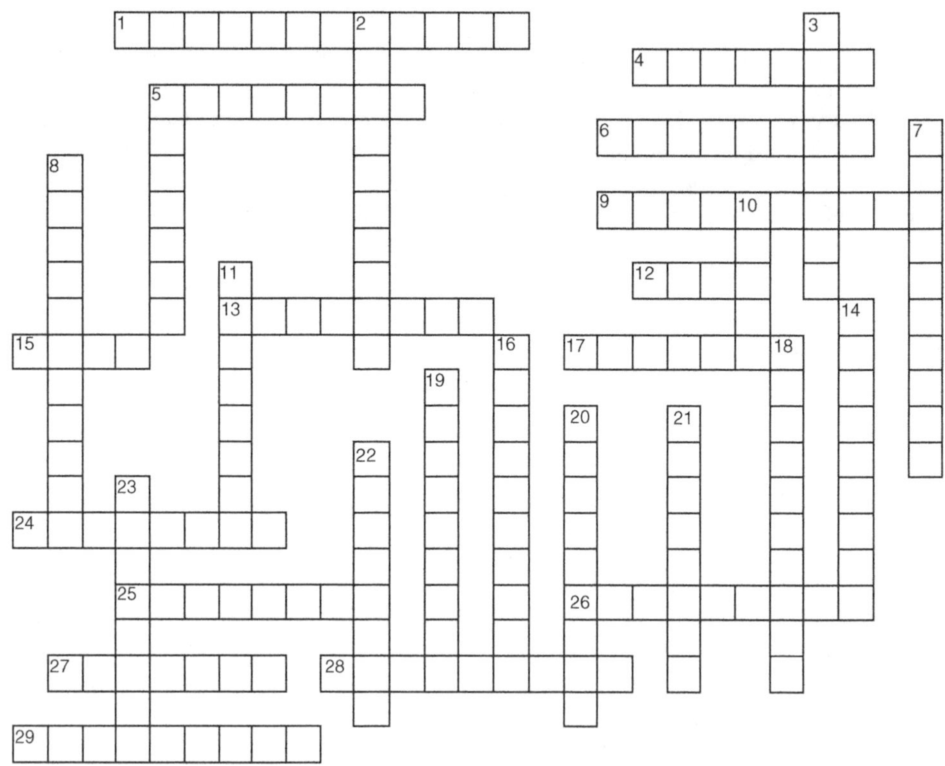

ACROSS

1. acceptance of unauthorized acts after the fact
4. equal ________ rule requires that some agency contracts be in writing
5. ________ money security interest; a loan to buy collateral items
6. third-party beneficiary because of financial interest
9. type of third-party beneficiary with no right to enforce
12. a security interest in property
13. a good-faith purchaser in the course of ________ business is protected from liens
15. ________ sale of all inventory
17. authority reasonably necessary to accomplish express purpose
24. principal is ________ from denying apparent authority
25. party who receives an assignment
26. reimburse
27. being part of contract relationship
28. goods held for sale or lease
29. an agent acts on behalf of a ________

DOWN

2. to pass on contract rights
3. power of ________ creates agency
5. a lender should ________ security interest to protect against third parties
7. property subject to security interest
8. checks, notes, etc.
10. third-party beneficiary as a gift
11. security interest in real property
14. agency by operation of law occurs in
16. creation of a security interest
18. to pass on contract duties
19. to take the collateral
20. agency is this type of relationship
21. agency coupled with an ________ may not be readily terminated
22. authority created by principal's acts/words to third parties
23. original party to contract is discharged, new party takes duties

10

◆ ◆ ◆

Performance: Required or Excused?

Having determined whether a contract formed and, if so, who has rights under that contract, the next step is to determine whether obligations under that contract are still owed or have been discharged. This chapter explores identifying breach, excuses for nonperformance, and related issues.

Skills-based learning objectives	*How you will demonstrate your ability*
Identify and describe UCC and common law assumptions concerning risk of loss and performance issues.	Assignments: Locate and cite UCC sections dealing with risk of loss and performance issues; find and summarize cases concerning performance issues.

A. Discharge Due to Unmet Condition
B. Discharge by Agreement
C. Discharge by Operation of Law
D. Impossibility
E. Breach as Excusing Performance
  1. Common Law
  2. Perfect Tender Under the UCC
F. Other Performance Issues Under the UCC
G. Anticipating Breach
H. Practical and Ethical Issues

If a contract did form, what happens when a party does not meet one or more of the obligations? Chapter 11 discusses the remedies available when a party is in breach of contract. This chapter focuses on whether there was a breach. Failure to perform obligations set forth in a contract is not a breach if performance has been **discharged,** meaning excused.

Discharge
Release

Failure to perform a contract involving a governmental entity can have particularly serious consequences. A "whistleblower" may be able to obtain an award for exposing fraud or misuse of government funds, by initiating a ***qui tam*** *lawsuit.*

Qui Tam
Lawsuit in which a whistleblower can obtain reward for exposing misconduct involving government contracts

A. Discharge Due to Unmet Condition

Some excuses that discharge the obligation to perform have been discussed in previous chapters. For example, there may have been an unmet condition precedent. If a contract states, "I will buy your house if I can obtain a mortgage," and the buyer is unable to obtain a mortgage, the buyer is discharged. Whether a contract provision is a condition precedent or only a promise, not a basis for discharge, can be a complex issue. Suppose Rocha Painting signs a contract to paint the exterior of Joan's house, with "painting to begin on May 1," but painting has not begun as of May 2 because Rocha does not have sufficient staff. Rocha promises to send a crew no later than May 4, but Joan wants to cancel the whole agreement. The issue is whether the May 1 start date was a condition precedent, so that Joan might be excused from the contract, or was only one of Rocha's promises, so that Joan is bound to the contract but may be entitled to damages for the delay. When a contract does not clearly indicate whether a provision is a condition or a promise, courts employ the rules of construction described in Chapter 12. Good legal advice should help the parties clarify their intentions during negotiations and state those intentions in the contract.

Rescission
A mutual agreement to cancel or a unilateral cancellation, based on one of the excuses discussed in this chapter

Novation
New contract; may involve new parties or may involve same parties if cancellation of prior contract is supported by consideration or otherwise legally justified

B. Discharge by Agreement

The parties may have discharged the contract by release or rescission (cancellation), modification of the old agreement, an accord and satisfaction, or a **novation**—a new contract that cancelled the original contract. Novation/accord and satisfaction were discussed in detail in Chapter 9. Remember, new contracts generally must be supported by new consideration.

EXHIBIT 10-1
Sample Condition Precedent

MORTGAGE CONTINGENCY: This Contract is contingent upon Buyer obtaining an unconditional written mortgage commitment (except for matters of title and survey or matters totally within Buyer's control) on or before ________, 20________ for a ________ (type) loan of $ ________ or any lesser amount as Buyer is willing to accept. The initial interest rate shall not exceed ________% per annum, amortized over not less than ________ years. Buyer shall pay any loan origination fee and/or discount points not to exceed ________% of the loan amount. Seller shall pay any loan origination fee and/or discount points not to exceed ________% of the loan amount. Fees or points to be paid by Buyer shall be applied first, with Seller to pay remaining fees or points, if any. Buyer shall pay the cost of application, usual and customary processing fees and Closing costs charged by lender. Buyer shall submit a written loan application within five business days after acceptance of this Contract. Failure to do so shall constitute default under this Contract. If Buyer, having applied as specified above, is unable to obtain a loan commitment and serves written notice to Seller within the time specified, this Contract shall be null and void and earnest money refunded to Buyer upon written direction of the Parties to Escrowee. If written notice is not served as specified, Buyer shall be deemed to have waived this contingency and this Contract shall remain in full force and effect. Any condition in the mortgage commitment requiring sale of Buyer's existing real estate shall not render the commitment conditional. If Seller at Seller's option and expense, within thirty (30) days after Buyer's notice, procures for Buyer a mortgage commitment or notifies Buyer that Seller will accept a purchase money mortgage upon the same terms, this Contract shall remain in full force and effect. In such event, Seller shall notify Buyer within five (5) business days after Buyer's notice of Seller's election to provide or obtain such financing, and Buyer shall furnish to Seller or lender all requested information and shall sign all papers necessary to obtain the mortgage commitment and to close the loan.

C. Discharge by Operation of Law

A party may also be discharged by the death or incapacity of a party under contract to perform personal services or by **insolvency** (**bankruptcy**). Bankruptcy law is federal statutory law that provides for creation of a plan to allow a debtor, who is unable to pay creditors, to resolve debts by division of assets among creditors. A debtor may enter bankruptcy voluntarily or may be "forced" into bankruptcy by creditors. Supervision of bankruptcy proceedings by the United States Bankruptcy Courts and Trustees is a way of ensuring that creditors are treated fairly, while allowing debtors to free themselves of accumulated financial obligations and get a fresh start.

Insolvency
Unable to pay debts

Bankruptcy
Federal system of laws and courts for resolution of debts that exceed the debtor's assets or that the debtor is unable to pay when due

EXHIBIT 10-2
Sample Assignment and Novation Agreement

This "Agreement" is made on __________ by __________. ("Assignor"), having its principal place of business at __________ and __________ ("Assignee"), having its principal place of business at __________ and __________ ("ABC"), having its principal place of business at __________.

1. Assignor and ABC are parties to a Contract for __________, dated __________, which remains in full force and effect, the "Contract");
2. Assignor desires to transfer and assign to Assignee its rights, duties and obligations under the Contract and Assignee desires to acquire the Contract from Assignor for consideration set forth below and on terms and conditions hereinafter set forth;
3. Assignor desires to be discharged from the performance of the obligations enumerated in the Contract and ABC is willing to release Assignor from the obligations of the Contract and to consent to Assignee assuming such obligations;
4. Assignor hereby assigns, transfers, conveys and delivers to Assignee, effective as of __________, 20_______ (the "Effective Date"), all of Assignor's right, title and interest in, to and under the Contract and Assignee hereby accepts such assignment and agrees to assume, from and after the Effective Date, all of Assignor's rights, duties and obligations in, to and under the Contract.
5. Assignee shall reimburse Assignor for and hold Assignor harmless against any obligation to perform any of the assigned duties and obligations included in the Contract.
6. Assignor, Assignee and ABC hereby agree that this Agreement shall constitute a novation of the obligations of Assignor under the Contract. Accordingly, all of the rights, duties and obligations of Assignor under the Contract are hereby extinguished. ABC recognizes Assignee as Assignor's successor in interest in and to all of Assignor's rights, duties and obligations in, to and under the Contract.
7. In consideration of this assignment, Assignee is paying to Assignor an aggregate purchase price of __________ Dollars ($) in cash, and paying to ABC a fee of __________ Dollars ($) in cash, by wire transfers to accounts specified by Assignor and ABC, simultaneous with the execution of this Agreement.
8. This Agreement shall inure to the benefit of and be binding upon the parties hereto and their successors and assigns, and matters herein with respect to the Contract shall inure to the benefit of ABC and its successors and assigns from and after the Effective Date.

IN WITNESS WHEREOF, the undersigned have executed this Agreement as of the date first written above.

There are two basic types of bankruptcy proceedings. The most common type is a filing under Chapter 7 of the Bankruptcy Code; it is called **liquidation,** or **straight bankruptcy,** and involves appointment of a trustee who collects nonexempt property of the debtor, sells it, and distributes proceeds to creditors. Filings under Chapters 11–13 are called **reorganization** bankruptcies and involve rehabilitation of the debtor to allow use of future earnings to pay off creditors.

Liquidation
To convert assets to cash, usually to pay debts in dissolution of a business

Straight Bankruptcy
Generally involves liquidation of assets

Reorganization
Bankruptcy in which debtor continues in operation

After a bankruptcy filing, an "automatic stay" goes into effect. Creditors generally may not seek to collect debts outside the proceeding, and the debtor is not allowed to transfer property. Some transfers of property, secured interests, and liens that occurred before the filing may be delayed or invalidated. Debts are classified as secured (security liens are discussed in Chapter 9) or unsecured and are prioritized while assets available to pay the debts are identified. Understandably, this can create anxiety for parties to an executory contract. Imagine that you are in a lease agreement and either your landlord or your tenant files for bankruptcy.

Bankruptcy rules governing executory contracts are very complex and can depend on the type of contract at issue. The details are beyond the scope of this book, but in general the bankruptcy trustee will decide whether to honor (assume) or reject the executory contract. Until that decision is made, the non-bankrupt party is generally required to continue to perform. The contract may be sold or assigned (discussed in Chapter 9) even if the contract includes a provision prohibiting assignment, so the non-bankrupt party may be required to deal with a new party. In assignment situations, any default must be cured and the new party may be required to show that it can honor the contract. If the trustee rejects a contract, the other party's claim for damages becomes an unsecured claim against the bankruptcy estate, payment of which will depend on whether assets are available to cover such claims.

Example

The intersection of bankruptcy law and contract law has often been in the news in recent years. From http://www.detroitnews.com/story/news/local/wayne-county/2015/02/27/detroit-retirees-pension-cuts-become-reality/24156301/ Detroit: Pension and benefit reductions reached through the city's historic bankruptcy will begin showing up in the monthly checks of Detroit retirees beginning Sunday.

> The cuts affect an estimated 20,000 retirees in the city's two pension funds. They are outlined in a court-approved plan that allows the city to shed $7 billion in debt and invest $1.7 billion into restructuring and service improvements over the next decade. . . . The city used the bankruptcy process to slash its promised retiree health insurance benefits from $4.3 billion to $450 million.

In addition, a court may find that a contract is unenforceable, for example, because it violates public policy or because performance has become illegal (*e.g.*, change in zoning makes construction of gas station illegal). Illegality and public policy are discussed in depth in Chapter 6. Performance may also be excused if one party is preventing the other party's performance; consider whether the party has **tendered** performance—that is, been ready, willing, and able to perform.

Tender Performance
Party indicates that he is ready, willing, and able to perform

---

Example

In *Espinoza v. Arkansas Valley Adventures, LLC,* the Tenth Circuit identified factors for determining whether a release of liability (exculpatory clause) violated Colorado public policy, https://www.ca10.uscourts.gov/opinions/14/14-1444.pdf: "(1) the existence [or nonexistence] of a duty to the public; (2) the nature of the service performed; (3) whether the contract was fairly entered into; and (4) whether the intention of the parties is expressed in clear and unambiguous language."

D. Impossibility

Objective Impossibility
Impossibility in an objective sense; not personal

A court may discharge a contract if performance becomes impossible, in an objective sense. **Objective impossibility** means the impossibility is not personal. For example, if a house is destroyed by a hurricane, a contract to paint that house cannot be performed by anyone. On the other hand, if the painter discovers that he underbid the job and would lose money by painting the house at the contract price, or if the painter overbooked and cannot meet the dates in the contract, the problem is personal or subjective.

Example

A landowner (defendant) granted an easement across its property to the plaintiff, an adjoining landowner, and contracted to build a road on the easement. The defendant failed to perform; the plaintiff sued. The trial court originally granted specific performance but reversed itself upon discovering that the land at issue had been impliedly dedicated to the City of Peekskill for a public park in 1929. The Appellate Division held that the land was "impressed with a trust" the moment it was dedicated to the city, so a road could not be built by a private developer. Finding both impossibility and a mutual mistake, the court held that there was no breach. *Chateau Rive Corp. v. Enclave Dev. Assocs.* (N.Y. App. Div. 2005), http://www.courts.state.ny.us/Reporter/3dseries/2005/2005_07337.htm.

Commercial Impracticability
An event, not anticipated by either party, that makes performance extraordinarily difficult and unfair for one party

Courts rarely discharge a party who entered a contract that turns out to be a bad deal. If the problem arose from bad judgment, the party is almost always bound to the contract. It is possible for a court to discharge a party in cases of **commercial impracticability** if an event that was not anticipated by either party would make performance extraordinarily difficult and unfair for one party. For example, a company under contract to ship material out of New Orleans in November 2005 might have been excused under the doctrine of commercial impracticability because of hardships imposed by hurricane damage.

Frustration of Purpose
Contract has no remaining value for party because of an unanticipated event

An event not anticipated by either party might also result in **frustration of purpose.** Frustration of purpose means that the contract has no remaining value for one party. In either case, the problem must result from an event that was truly unexpected and must go beyond financial difficulty. For example, if a school had chartered buses to take students to New Orleans for an event scheduled for November 2005 and, because of damage from Hurricane Katrina, the event was cancelled, a court might have found that frustration of purpose justified excusing the school from paying for the bus charter contracts.

Because courts do not often discharge parties for impossibility and commercial impracticability, many contracts include **force majeure** provisions.

Force Majeure Clause
Contract provision excusing performance for an event such as an "act of God," fire, labor dispute, accident, or transportation difficulty

Remember, contract law is primarily default law (it applies only if the parties have not stated their intentions to the contrary) and the parties can write the contract they want. A clause permitting cancellation or delay in the event of "act of God, fire, labor disputes, accidents or transportation difficulties" will generally be enforced unless a party is trying to use it in a way that essentially gives him the option to perform or not, depending on whether it is in his best interests.

Sample Force Majeure Clauses

Neither party shall be liable in damages or have the right to terminate this Agreement for any delay or default in performance if the delay or default is caused by conditions beyond control of that party, including, but not limited to Acts of God, Government restrictions (including, but not limited to, denial or cancellation of any export or other necessary license), war, insurrection or any other cause beyond the reasonable control of the party whose performance is affected.

Neither party shall be liable for any failure or delay in performance under this Agreement (other than for delay in the payment of money due and payable hereunder) to the extent said failures or delays are the proximate result of causes beyond that party's reasonable control and occurring without its fault or negligence, including, without limitation, failure of suppliers, subcontractors, and carriers, or party to substantially meet its performance obligations under this Agreement, provided that, as a condition to the claim of nonliability, the party experiencing the difficulty shall give the other prompt written notice, with full details following the occurrence of the cause relied upon. Dates by which performance obligations are scheduled to be met will be extended for a period of time equal to the time lost due to any delay so caused.

Assignment 10-1

- Find the citations to sections in your state's version of the Uniform Commercial Code (UCC) dealing with conditions precedent (nonhappening of presupposed condition) and commercial impracticability.
- Find the appropriate sections and report what happens when goods are destroyed after a sales contract has formed. The answer depends on whether the risk of loss has passed from the seller to the buyer. The UCC contains assumptions about risk of loss, in the absence of agreement. These assumptions depend on whether there has been a breach of contract, who has possession of the goods, and what type of transaction is involved. For this assignment, assume that there is no agreement, that there has been no breach of contract, and that the transaction is a **sale-or-return.** A sale-or-return is similar to a **consignment**—the seller has delivered the goods to a buyer who will resell them or return them to

Sale-or-Return
Seller delivers goods to buyer who resells or returns them to seller; buyer takes title until sale or return

Consignment
An arrangement under which goods are placed for sale but title does not transfer to the seller

the seller. In a sale-or-return situation, the buyer takes **title** (ownership) of the goods until selling or returning them; in a consignment, title remains with the seller.

- ◆ The answer may also depend on whether the goods were **identified** when the contract formed—that is, designated as the particular goods being sold. *Find the UCC provision concerning destruction of goods identified to the contract* before the risk of loss passes. Other goods are **fungible,** meaning interchangeable.

Fungible
Interchangeable

E. Breach as Excusing Performance

1. Common Law

One party's performance can be discharged by the other party's breach of the contract. For example, Norma agreed to sell Travis her house and had the paperwork and the keys ready on the agreed date, but Travis arrived without the money. Norma is obviously not obligated to give him the deed and keys and can likely rescind the contract and sell to another.

Some contracts require **perfect performance,** with no deviations. Perfect performance is also called **strict performance.** In general, a contractual obligation to pay a specified amount of money requires strict performance. If Travis had agreed to pay $600,000 for the house and showed up with cashier's checks for $550,000 and an "IOU" for $50,000, Norma would not be obligated to deliver the deed.

Perfect Performance
No deviations from contract; also called strict performance

Strict Performance
No deviations from contract expectations; also called perfect performance

Title
Ownership

Identified
Goods designated as the particular goods being sold

Substantial Performance
Only minor deviations from contact specification; acceptable in most service contracts

Major or Material Breach
Substantial breach of contract, usually excusing other party from further performance

With respect to other duties, however, the common law generally does not assume that perfect performance is required unless the parties have stated that it is required and the expectation is reasonable. Not every breach merits complete discharge. For example, if Norma had just completed construction of a $500,000 custom house for Travis and Travis discovered that Norma had painted several rooms the wrong colors, Travis would not be entitled to walk away from the contract.

With respect to duties requiring services, **substantial performance** is required. A party who has substantially performed is entitled to the contract price, minus the value of the defects. In the custom house example, Norma would be entitled to $500,000 minus the cost of repainting the rooms incorrectly painted.

If a contract requires substantial performance, the court will discharge the other party only if the performance was so bad as to amount to **material** or **major breach.** If the house Travis expected was to have been a two-story colonial, facing east on a corner lot, but Norma confused the plans for two jobs and built a modern ranch facing north, Travis would be entitled to discharge and, possibly, to an additional remedy (discussed in Chapter 11).

What is substantial performance and to what extent is the breaching party entitled to payment for the imperfect performance? Courts generally look at the following:

- Whether the contract is divisible. For example, Pat agrees to plow Hannah Homeowner's driveway after each snowfall this season for $40 per visit.

Pat visits and plows 12 times, but her truck is destroyed in an accident and she is unable to plow after the last two snowstorms of the season. The 12 visits have independent value for Hannah, even though the contract was not completed. On the other hand, a partially finished basement remodeling job may have no independent value.

- Whether the unfulfilled promise was dependent on some performance by the other party. For example, is an insurance company obligated to pay a claim if the insured party failed to pay the last premium? Is a builder required to complete remodeling if the homeowner has not acquired fixtures as promised?
- Whether the end product can be used for its intended purpose.
- The benefit received by the nonbreaching party.
- Whether the breach was major or minor.
- The degree of hardship to the breaching party.
- Whether money damages can be used to compensate for defects.
- Whether the party whose performance was imperfect acted in good faith. The Restatement defines good faith as remaining faithful to the "agreed common purpose and justified expectations of the other party." Good faith involves consideration of whether the breach was intentional.
- The consequences of any delay. Parties often include a provision stating that "**time is of the essence,**" meaning that any delay constitutes breach. If they do not include such a provision, an injured party may be able to recover damages only if there is proof of damages attributable to the delay. Even if parties do include such a provision, some courts regard it as "boilerplate" and look at whether there has been real harm.

Time Is of the Essence
Any performance delay constitutes breach

EXHIBIT 10-3
Example of a Typical Time-Is-of-the-Essence Provision That Also Includes a Non-Waiver Provision

Time Is of the Essence. Time is of the essence with respect to all provisions of this Agreement that specify a time for performance; any delay with respect to specified times for performance shall constitute a material breach of this contract. The failure of a party to enforce this provision with respect to failure to comply with a specified time for performance shall not affect that party's right to require strict compliance with the specified times for performance at any time thereafter. Waiver of any breach or default shall not constitute a waiver of any subsequent breach or default or waiver of this provision.

Satisfaction Clauses Some contracts require performance to the "satisfaction" of a party. Courts will determine whether to apply an objective test or subjective test based on the type of performance required. A court is likely to apply a subjective standard (was this individual actually satisfied) when performance

Satisfaction Clause
Contract provision requiring performance to the satisfaction of a specified individual

and satisfaction are of a personal nature, for example, painting a portrait. On the other hand, performance may be something that can be judged by common standards of utility or marketability, such as painting office walls. In such cases a court is likely to apply an objective (reasonable) standard. Do you think courts also look at unjust enrichment in these situations? Note that once the office walls are painted, they remain painted whether the customer says he is satisfied or not; the customer who is not satisfied with a portrait does not get the portrait. Such factors may play a role. Some contracts call for satisfaction of an outsider, for example, construction to the satisfaction of the architect. Courts tend to uphold such clauses as written and require the outsider's statement of satisfaction.

Assignment 10-2

As directed by your instructor, find and summarize for class discussion a case from your state involving:

- The meaning of "good faith" in an insurance contract;
- Substantial performance of a contract to construct a building;
- A time-is-of-the-essence clause; or
- A satisfaction clause.

EXHIBIT 10-4
Example Satisfaction Clause

The following language appeared in a construction clause:

"All work shall be done subject to the final approval of the Architect or Owner's authorized agent, and his decision in matters relating to artistic effect shall be final, if within the terms of the Contract Documents. . . . [S]hould any dispute arise as to the quality or fitness of materials or workmanship, the decision as to acceptability shall rest strictly with the Owner, based on the requirement that all work done or materials furnished shall be first class in every respect. What is usual or customary in erecting other buildings shall in no wise enter into any consideration or decision."

After the owner rejected siding installed by a subcontractor because of its appearance, the builder removed and replaced the siding and refused to pay the subcontractor. Although the language appears to allow the owner to reject work for purely subjective reason, the appeals court upheld a jury instruction that the "general rule applying to satisfaction in the case of contracts for the construction of commercial buildings is that the satisfaction clause must be determined by objective criteria. Under this standard, the question is not whether the owner was satisfied in fact, but whether the owner, as a reasonable person, should have been satisfied with the materials and workmanship." The court indicated that it would be possible to contract for subjective approval but that the language in the contract did not achieve that result.[1]

[1] *Morin Bldg. Prods. Co., Inc. v. Baystone Constr. Inc.*, 717 F.2d 413 (7th Cir. 1983).

---

2. Perfect Tender Under the UCC

The UCC differs from the common law in that, under the **perfect tender rule,** a buyer has a reasonable time to reject goods that fail, in any respect, to conform to the contract. The rule seems harsh when compared to the common law doctrine of substantial performance, but the Code does include provisions to lessen the impact.

Perfect Tender Rule
Buyer has reasonable time to reject goods that fail, in any respect, to conform to the contract

Trade Usage
Industry standards for permissible deviations from specifications

Course of Dealing
What has been done by the parties in the past

Cure
Seller delivers conforming goods before contract deadline, after buyer rejects nonconforming goods

- The parties may draft a contract that permits some degree of deviation from the specifications for the goods; this is common in some industries.
- Courts must consider **trade usage;** some industries have standards for the level of permissible "flaws" in products.
- Courts also consider **course of dealing,** what has been acceptable to the buyer in the past.
- If a buyer does reject nonconforming goods, the seller may have the opportunity to **cure** by delivering conforming goods before the contract deadline. The Code even extends the time for cure to a "further reasonable time," in some circumstances.

Example

These rules are part of how the UCC accommodates the "real world" of modern business. Acme Uniforms contracted to provide City Hospital with 1,000 sets of green "scrubs" for personnel, to be delivered on May 1. On April 20, Acme realizes that its inventory is insufficient because of roof damage at a warehouse. Not wanting to leave a big customer empty-handed, Acme ships 500 sets of green scrubs and 500 sets of blue scrubs. On April 25 City Hospital notifies Acme that it does not want the blue scrubs. City Hospital can accept some of the goods and reject others. If Acme can get green scrubs to the hospital by May 1, there is no breach. If Acme had a reasonable belief that City would accept blue scrubs, the time may even be extended beyond May 1. In addition, if City Hospital has accepted mixed colors several times in the past, there may be no breach.

Once the buyer accepts the goods, the perfect tender rule does not apply. The buyer generally has the right to inspect the goods before paying or accepting. Once the buyer has accepted the goods, the buyer may revoke that acceptance if there was a legitimate reason for accepting them in the first place (*e.g.*, the seller had promised to cure or the defects were not visible) and there is a nonconformity that substantially impairs the value of the goods. Acceptance may not be revoked because of minor deviations from conformity.

In some situations the Code implies acceptance. The buyer is viewed as having accepted the goods if, after having a reasonable opportunity to inspect, the buyer indicates that the goods conform to the contract or that the goods are accepted in spite of nonconformity, fails to reject them, or does some act that indicates ownership (*e.g.*, reselling the goods).

The perfect tender rule applies to timing as well as conformity of goods. Under the UCC, time is of the essence except in installment contracts. So, delivery of goods on May 2 would be a total breach if delivery had been promised for May 1.

F. Other Performance Issues Under the UCC

Tender
To make available

For contracts concerning the sale of goods, the UCC describes performance expectations when the parties have not done so in the contract. For example, the Code contains provisions dealing with the time, place, and manner of **tender** (making goods available to the buyer); definitions of shipping terms; assumptions about warranties (mentioned in previous chapters); and other matters.

Assignment 10-3

Use your state's version of the UCC to list the following, as assigned by your instructor, giving citations to sections:

- The section number of the perfect tender rule
- The section number of the provision allowing a party to demand assurances (described below)
- The place of delivery, when none is specified
- The difference between a CIF contract and a C&F contract
- What is meant by ex-ship
- The seller's obligation if the goods are in the possession of a bailee

Bailee
Person, other than owner, who is in possession of goods under an arrangement called a bailment

A **bailee** is a person, other than the owner, who is in possession of goods under an arrangement called a bailment.

G. Anticipating Breach

If one party (A) believes that the other party (B) is going to breach the contract, is A excused from performing A's obligations? A may believe that it would be better to "cut her losses."

Repudiation
A party's words or actions indicating intention not to perform the contract

Repudiation can occur by a statement that a party cannot or will not perform or by a party's voluntary act that makes substantial performance impossible or apparently impossible. For example, Association has a contract to hold a conference at Swank Hotel next month and learns that Swank has just begun a major remodeling project. Guest rooms, conference rooms, and the banquet facility are not expected to be ready for occupancy before the conference dates. A common example of a condition that may make performance appear to be impossible is insolvency. The UCC has specific rules dealing with insolvent buyers and sellers.

Repudiation occurs before the other party has performed, otherwise, it is simply breach. For example, if buyer has fully paid for delivery of a product and seller indicates that delivery is impossible, it is simply breach of contract. On the other hand, if buyer is to pay after delivery and seller states that delivery is impossible, it is repudiation. The situation is also called **anticipatory breach.** The rights of the other party depend on the circumstances.

Anticipatory Breach
Belief that other party will not perform

Example

The 2010 U.K. case *De Beers v. Atos Origin*, http://www.bailii.org/ew/cases/EWHC/TCC/2010/3276.html, involved Atos Origin, a large European IT services company, and De Beers, the famous diamond distributor. Atos argued that De Beers had repudiated by withholding a progress payment and by trying to expand the scope of the project. De Beers argued that Atos had repudiated by refusing to continue to perform unless the contract was renegotiated. The court found that withholding a payment was not repudiation but that refusal to continue was repudiation. Atos's conduct was a "clear and unequivocal" refusal to perform while De Beers's conduct was not.

Anticipatory breach must be clear-cut; it cannot be based on assumption or inference. Under the UCC, if a party has reasonable grounds to believe that the other will not perform, that party may demand **assurances;** failure to give adequate assurances within a reasonable time operates as a repudiation so that the "**insecure party**" may suspend his own performance.

Assurance
A pledge or guarantee that gives confidence or security

Insecure Party
Party having good-faith belief that performance by other party is unlikely

If the contract is not covered by the UCC, the insecure party may have a variety of options, including continuing under the contract, demanding assurances, suspending performance, or canceling the contract. The insecure party's rights depend on state law.

When repudiation occurs, the other party generally has a duty to make reasonable attempts to **mitigate**—limit the damages. For example, Banquet Hall has the Smith-Jones wedding scheduled for next Saturday. Supply House calls on Monday and tells the manager that, because of a fire, it will be unable to provide chicken breasts for the reception. Can Banquet Hall just ignore the situation, hope for the best, and, after the Smith-Jones disaster, sue Supply House? Probably not—Banquet must attempt to mitigate by getting the chicken breasts from another source. To mitigate, the buyer may **cover,** by obtaining substitute goods if reasonably available. Damages are still available and will be discussed in Chapter 11.

Mitigate
Limit or reduce damages

Cover
Buyer obtains substitute goods

Example

The following is mitigation language found in a contract to hold a conference at a hotel:

"If the hotel is able to sell any of the guest rooms canceled, that portion of the damages will be refunded based upon the number of guest rooms resold."

H. Practical and Ethical Issues

When a contract is breached, the nonbreaching party often suffers financial harm and may feel "wronged" in a way that goes beyond financial compensation. This is particularly true when the breach is intentional. Imagine that your wedding reception was to take place at Bella Banquets four weeks from next Saturday. The invitations have been sent, and you expect 180 guests. Last night Bella experienced a fire. The damage could be repaired in time for your reception but only at an expense far greater than the profit expected. In addition, Bella has, for a long time, planned a major renovation. This seems like a good time to do it. Bella notifies you that it will not be hosting your reception. You will not be able to find an equivalent location in the next four weeks and will have to notify all of your guests. While you will be entitled to financial compensation, you will probably not be satisfied by an award of money.

Nonetheless, the law regards breach of contract as a business matter. Sometimes clients decide to breach a contract simply because it makes financial sense to do so. Can a lawyer ethically advise a client to breach a contract? Can a lawyer assist a client in an intentional breach of contract? Read Illinois State Bar Association ethical opinion 728, https://www.isba.org/sites/default/files/ethicsopinions/0728.pdf or search your state's name and [ethics advising client breach contract] for guidance.

Career Corner

Mianne B. is a litigation paralegal for Otten Johnson Robinson Neff + Ragonetti PC, a medium-sized law firm, in Denver, Colorado. Mianne was pursuing a career in purchasing management and found that path to be unfulfilling. She had no legal experience before attending the Denver Paralegal Institute in 1996. Mianne is dedicated to achieving her full potential and credits others for her professional career growth: "I have been fortunate to work with attorneys who encouraged my interest in the law and who shared their knowledge and expertise. These partnerships afforded me the ability to better understand legal principles and practices. In turn, I believe I am more efficient in managing my workload. I fully embrace my role as a paralegal and welcome the opportunity to aid in the education of paralegal students." Asked what she finds particularly fulfilling about her career choice, Mianne said: "I have always found the law intriguing and thought many times growing up that I would become a lawyer. As has been said many times, 'Life is what happens to you while you're busy making other plans,' and my life path took a few turns before I found myself working as a paralegal. My career brings me fulfillment as it creates opportunities for me to be valuable to the litigation practice group in many ways including, but not limited to, project management; budget analyst; document manager; legal and public research; and as an e-discovery specialist. The variety of responsibilities can present challenges, but I work through these things and find personal and professional satisfaction."

Review Questions

1. Identify the ways in which performance can be excused by agreement.
2. Identify the ways in which performance can be excused by operation of law.
3. How does the UCC perfect tender rule differ from common law?
4. Which UCC provisions lessen the impact of the perfect tender rule?
5. Under what circumstances is acceptance of goods implied under the UCC?
6. What options does a contract party have if that party believes that the other party will breach the contract?
7. Under what circumstances would it be unethical for an attorney to assist a client in breaching a contract?

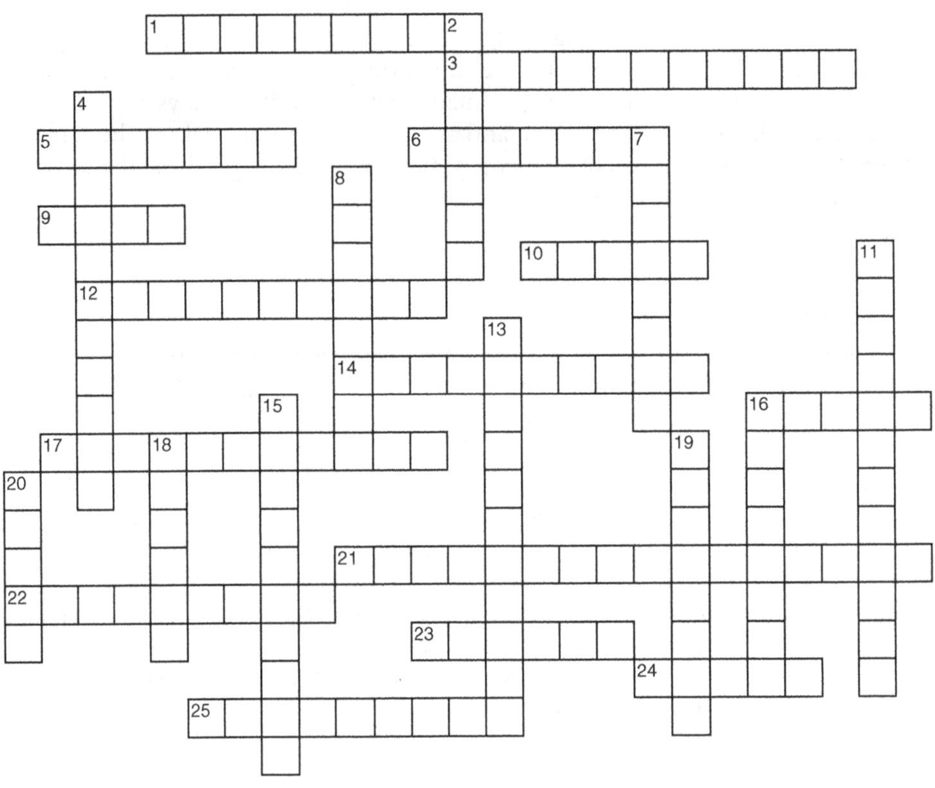

ACROSS

1. released from contract obligations
3. ________ performance; acceptable in most contracts for services
5. courts will look at course of ________ in applying perfect tender rule
6. UCC requires ________ tender in sale of goods
9. seller delivers nonconforming goods, which are rejected, and then delivers conforming goods by required date
10. usage of ________ is considered in applying perfect tender rule
12. if goods have been ________ to the contract and are destroyed before delivery, contract may be discharged
14. party may demand ________ in anticipatory breach situation
16. ________ majeure provision; excuses performance for acts of God, etc.
17. like a sale or return
21. commercial ________; unanticipated event makes performance unreasonably difficult for one party
22. impossibility is judged by ________ standard
23. in possession of goods, not owner
24. to obtain substitute goods
25. an agreement to cancel contract

DOWN

2. time is of the ________; clause requiring strict performance of deadlines
4. an indication that the party does not intend to fulfill the contract
7. a party who is ready, willing; and able to perform has ________ performance
8. ________ damages; limit losses
11. ________ breach; belief that other party will not perform
13. ________ of purpose; unanticipated event leaves party no purpose for contract
15. like bankruptcy
16. goods that are interchangeable
18. ________ performance = perfect
19. new contract, new parties, canceling old contract
20. material breach = ________ breach

11

Remedies

Assuming that performance has not been excused, but that performance is not forthcoming, what are the consequences? This chapter explores alternatives to litigation, handling litigation, and the possible outcomes of litigation.

Skills-based learning objectives	*How you will demonstrate your ability*
Assist in contract litigation.	Assignments: Find local ADR rules, jury instructions, filing rules, and limitations periods; research case management software.
Analyze damage awards appropriate for different types of contract cases.	Assignment: Find and analyze cases concerning awards of damages.

A. Alternative Dispute Resolution
B. Litigation
C. Remedies: Theory
  1. Damages
  2. Equitable Remedies
D. Tort Law Versus Contract Law
E. Practical and Ethical Issues

Most parties enter into a contract with good intentions, seeing the agreement as mutually beneficial and intending to perform as expected. Occasionally something goes wrong; it might be beyond the control of the parties, the result of carelessness, or a decision based on the least damaging of several options. Sometimes the failure to meet expectations or the subsequent breakdown in the relationship is the result of lack of information about options and consequences. Of course the parties should read their contracts to be aware of available remedies, but often they do not. Contracts drafted on behalf of sophisticated businesses generally contain limitations on remedies that those businesses regard as nonnegotiable.

If the contract does not specify remedies, the Uniform Commercial Code (UCC) can be a resource to the parties and help them salvage the situation or avoid litigation by providing a number of self-help remedies. The parties to a sales contract can know what is available to them and expected of them, just by looking at the Code. As discussed in Chapter 10, on performance, some examples of what the UCC has to offer are as follows:

- The Code specifies the measure of damages when a buyer repudiates the contract or does not accept goods and for when the seller repudiates or fails to deliver. The general theory of damages is discussed below; the Code provides methods of calculation.
- The Code sets forth the buyer's duties with respect to rejected goods and the buyer's right to "**cover**" by obtaining other goods (also discussed in Chapter 10).
- A buyer may accept nonconforming goods; the Code sets forth the measure of damages.
- The Code calls for "**substituted performance**" when agreed-upon facilities have become unavailable.
- A seller who discovers that buyer is insolvent has specified rights to reclaim goods, stop delivery, salvage, or resell the goods.

Cover
Good faith, reasonable effort to obtain goods from another source

Substituted Performance
Use of commercially reasonable substitute facility (§2-614)

Alternative Dispute Resolution
To settle a dispute other than by litigation, including arbitration and mediation; called ADR

Arbitration
A neutral hears both positions and imposes a decision

Mediation
Neutral helps parties understand each others' positions and may suggest solutions, but agreement ultimately comes from the parties

Neutral
A third party in ADR, mediator or arbitrator

Court-annexed ADR
Use of the court system's own mediators or arbitrators before going to trial

Sometimes the parties are not able to resolve the matter by reference to the UCC. Sometimes the Code does not apply and negotiations fail. In such cases, the parties may have to resort to more formal means of resolving their dispute.

A. Alternative Dispute Resolution

A recent trend is to participate in **alternative dispute resolution** (**ADR**). There are many types of ADR; mediation and arbitration are commonly used in contract law disputes. In **mediation,** a third party (the **neutral**) helps the parties understand each other's positions and may suggest solutions, but any agreement ultimately comes from the parties. In **arbitration,** the neutral hears both sides and then imposes a decision.

Many courts now require **court-annexed ADR**—going through the court system's own mediators or arbitrators before going to trial before a judge. In contract law, however, it is quite common for the parties to include an ADR requirement in the contract, regardless of whether the court system would require it.

ADR can have many advantages: it generally results in resolution much faster than going to court, is often far less expensive than trial, and keeps the conflict out of court and can salvage the relationship between the parties. Also, the neutral can be an expert in a field that might be a complete mystery to an average judge (*e.g.,* having a structural engineer as an arbitrator in a construction contract dispute). If the parties have a long-term or valuable relationship, such as a landlord and tenant in a 25-year commercial lease, these are extremely important considerations.

ADR can also have disadvantages. In recent years, there have been many cases arguing that ADR requirements that deprive consumers of their "day in court" are unconscionable. A legal professional drafting, reviewing, or negotiating a contract for a client should carefully consider the following:

- Where will ADR take place, and is that location inconvenient to the client?
- What is the timeline for ADR, and is a period of discovery (evidence gathering) allowed?
- How is the neutral to be chosen and paid? Is the neutral truly neutral?
- Under what rules will the hearing be conducted, and do those rules obligate the parties to cooperate in discovery before the hearing?
- Are both parties equally bound to engage in ADR? Is a specific type of notice required to trigger the ADR obligation?
- Does the clause attempt to make the result binding (**binding arbitration**), or do the parties retain the right to go to court to challenge the result?
- If a particular neutral is named—particularly if that neutral is a governmental agency—what is the backlog, and how long would the parties have to wait for a hearing?

Binding Arbitration
Parties give up the right to challenge arbitration result in court

You should be aware of the Federal Arbitration Act (see http://www.law.cornell.edu/uscode/uscode09/usc_sup_01_9_10_1.html) and state arbitration laws. See http://topics.law.cornell.edu/wex/alternative_dispute_resolution and http://topics.law.cornell.edu/wex/table_alternative_dispute_resolution for a summary of the federal law and list of state laws.

Example

Courts generally favor arbitration clauses. In *Jackson v. Rent-A-Center, West, Inc.* (U.S. 2009), http://www.supremecourt.gov/opinions/09pdf/09-497.pdf, summarized below, the Supreme Court refers to the challenged provision as a delegation. It is not the type of delegation described in Chapter 9 because it does not involve the duties of the parties; the Court uses the term "delegation" in its colloquial sense.

Jackson filed an employment-discrimination suit against Rent-A-Center, his former employer. Rent-A-Center filed a motion, under the Federal Arbitration Act (FAA), to dismiss or stay the proceedings, 9 U.S.C. §3, and to compel arbitration, based on the arbitration Agreement Jackson signed as a condition of his employment. Jackson opposed the motion on the ground that the Agreement was unenforceable in that it was unconscionable under Nevada law. The District Court granted Rent-A-Center's motion. The Ninth Circuit reversed in part. The Supreme Court reinstated the District Court holding.

> Under the FAA, where an agreement to arbitrate includes an agreement that the arbitrator will determine the enforceability of the agreement, if a party challenges specifically the enforceability of that particular agreement, the district court considers the challenge, but if a party challenges the enforceability of the agreement as a whole, the challenge is for the arbitrator. Section 2 of the FAA places arbitration agreements on an equal footing with other contracts and requires courts to enforce them according to their terms. Here,

the Agreement included two relevant arbitration provisions: it provided for arbitration of all disputes arising out of Jackson's employment, including discrimination claims, and it gave the "Arbitrator . . . exclusive authority to resolve any dispute relating to the [Agreement's] enforceability . . . including . . . any claim that all or any part of this Agreement is void or voidable." Rent-A-Center seeks enforcement of the second provision, which delegates to the arbitrator the "gateway" question of enforceability. The court must enforce the **delegation** provision under §§3 and 4 unless it is unenforceable under §2.

There are two types of validity challenges under §2: one "challenges specifically the validity of the agreement to arbitrate," and "[t]he other challenges the contract as a whole." Only the first is relevant to a court's determination of an arbitration agreement's enforceability, because under §2 "an arbitration provision is severable from the remainder of the contract." That does not mean that agreements to arbitrate are unassailable. If a party challenges the validity under §2 of the precise agreement to arbitrate at issue, the federal court must consider the challenge before ordering compliance with the agreement under §4. That is no less true when the precise agreement to arbitrate is itself part of a larger arbitration agreement. Because here the agreement to arbitrate enforceability (the **delegation** provision) is severable from the remainder of the Agreement, unless Jackson challenged the **delegation** provision specifically, it must be treated as valid under §2 and enforced under §§3 and 4.

The District Court correctly concluded that Jackson challenged only the validity of the contract as a whole. In his brief to this Court he raised a challenge to the delegation provision for the first time, but that is too late and will not be considered.[Citations omitted]

B. Litigation

Jurisdiction
Area within which judicial authority may be exercised

Choice of Law
Contract language that defines which state's law will apply in case of litigation

Parallel Litigation
Single dispute results in cases in more than one state or in both state and federal courts

If the parties do have the right to go to court, it is common for the contract to include a statement about where the matter will be litigated (**jurisdiction**) and which state's law will apply (**choice of law**). Often one party will try to gain the upper hand by requiring litigation in a state convenient to that party or by requiring application of law more familiar or advantageous to that party, despite the fact that, without such a provision, the matter would be litigated in another place under other law. Constitutional and public policy considerations may prohibit application of a choice of law provision that would cause application of the law of a jurisdiction with no relationship to the parties or the transaction.

Some disputes result in **parallel litigation,** or cases that proceed in more than one state or in both state and federal courts. Such cases require the paralegal to be extremely well organized; law firms engaged in parallel litigation generally use case-management software.

Example

In its 2013 decision *American Express Co. v. Italian Colors Restaurant,* http://www.supremecourt.gov/opinions/12pdf/12-133_19m1.pdf, the Supreme Court discussed the interaction between arbitration and a particular type of litigation, the class action.

An agreement between American Express and merchants who accept American Express cards requires all of their disputes to be resolved by arbitration and provides that there "shall be no right or authority for any Claims to be arbitrated on a class action basis." Merchants nonetheless filed a class action, claiming violation of §1 of the Sherman Act and seeking treble damages for the class under §4 of the Clayton Act. American Express moved to compel individual arbitration under the FAA, but the merchants countered that the cost of expert analysis necessary to prove the antitrust claims would greatly exceed the maximum recovery for an individual plaintiff. The District Court dismissed. The Second Circuit reversed. The Supreme Court reinstated the dismissal.

The FAA does not permit courts to invalidate a contractual waiver of class arbitration on the ground that the plaintiff's cost of individually arbitrating a federal statutory claim exceeds the potential recovery.

The FAA reflects the overarching principle that arbitration is a matter of contract. Courts must "rigorously enforce" arbitration agreements according to their terms, even for claims alleging a violation of a federal statute, unless the FAA's mandate has been overridden by a contrary congressional command.

No contrary congressional command requires rejection of the class-arbitration waiver here. The antitrust laws do not guarantee an affordable procedural path to the vindication of every claim or "evince an intention to preclude a waiver" of class-action procedure. Nor does congressional approval of Federal Rule of Civil Procedure 23 [concerning class actions] establish an entitlement to class proceedings for the vindication of statutory rights. The Rule imposes stringent requirements for certification that exclude most claims, and this Court has rejected the assertion that the class-notice requirement must be dispensed with because the "prohibitively high cost" of compliance would "frustrate [plaintiff's] attempt to vindicate the policies underlying the antitrust" laws. . . . [T]he fact that it is not worth the expense involved in *proving* a statutory remedy does not constitute the elimination of the *right to pursue* that remedy. [Citations omitted]

It is common for a contract to include a **notice of claims provision,** requiring that a party give the other party written notice within a specified time before filing suit. Such a requirement has the effect of shortening the **limitations period** for bringing suit (also called statute of limitations). The impact of a notice requirement is magnified if the particular type of contract is governed by a shorter limitations period in the relevant state. Medical service contracts and construction contracts, for example, may have shorter limitations periods than other contracts. At the very least, the parties should understand the requirements of the notice of claims provision.

Notice of Claims Provision
Contract language requiring one party to give the other party written notice a specified time before filing suit

In drafting pleadings for contract law litigation, you must keep in mind the elements and defenses of contract law learned in this course. You must also understand the court rules for your jurisdiction. Those rules are also important in assisting with **discovery** (pretrial investigation of facts by questioning, inspection, etc.) in contract litigation. **Electronic discovery (e-discovery)** involving recovery of e-mail, drafts of documents, internal memos, and more from computers, servers, and even handheld personal digital assistants (PDAs) has changed the nature of the paralegal's role from clerical to technical.

Discovery
Pretrial investigation of facts by questioning, inspection, and so on

E-discovery
Electronic recovery of e-mail and documents from computers, servers, and handheld PDAs

To see how the federal court rules of procedure deal with some contract litigation issues, visit http://www.law.cornell.edu/rules/frcp/index.html, and look at Pleadings, Rule 9—Pleading Special Matters. For more specific information about filings cases in federal courts, visit http://www.uscourts.gov/rules/distrlocalrules.html, and find the local rules for federal courts in your area.

You have studied contract law for several weeks and, by now, realize that it is complicated. Despite the complexity of the law, juries consisting of people with no legal training are often the decision-makers with respect to the factual issues in contract cases. How do juries know enough about the framework of the law to make those decisions? They are given jury instructions. Paralegals are frequently asked to locate appropriate jury instructions for submission to the judge. A sample of a jury instruction involving the affirmative defense of duress, studied in Chapter 4, appears in Exhibit 11-1.

EXHIBIT 11-1
Sample Jury Instruction Involving Affirmative Defense of Duress[1]

24.08D AFFIRMATIVE DEFENSE—DURESS

The defendant [plaintiff] claims that the agreement upon which the plaintiff [defendant] relies is void because the defendant [plaintiff] was under duress at the time [his][her][its] promise was made.

The defendant [plaintiff] made [his] [her] [its] promise under duress if you decide that the following things have been proved by clear and convincing evidence:

(1) the defendant [plaintiff] involuntarily accepted the plaintiff's [defendant's] terms because the defendant [plaintiff] believed [he] [she] [it] had no reasonable alternative but to accept those terms;

(2) the defendant [plaintiff] had no other reasonable alternative; and

(3) the defendant [plaintiff] had no other reasonable alternative because of coercive words or conduct by the plaintiff [defendant] that was criminal, tortious or morally wrong.

A fact is proved by clear and convincing evidence if the evidence induces belief in your minds that the fact is highly probable. It is not necessary that the fact be certainly true or true beyond a reasonable doubt or conclusively true. However, it is not enough to show that the fact is more likely true than not true.

If you decide that each of these things has been proved by clear and convincing evidence, then the agreement between plaintiff and defendant is void and you must return a verdict for defendant [plaintiff].

Otherwise, the agreement is not void and you must decide some additional things that I will explain to you.

Use Note

The burden is on the party seeking to void the contract to prove these elements by clear and convincing evidence. *Helstrom v. North Slope Borough*, 797 P.2d 1192, 1197 (Alaska 1990). *But cf. Witt v. Watkins*, 579 P.2d 1065, 1070

EXHIBIT 11-1 (continued)

n.16 (Alaska 1978) (Lighter burden may apply where employee executed personal injury release with employer.)

If the allegation is that the plaintiff's conduct was criminal or tortious, consideration should be given to instructing the jury on the elements of the claimed crime or tort.

Comment
In *Helstrom v. North Slope Borough*, 797 P.2d 1192, 1197 (Alaska 1990), the Alaska Supreme Court identified three elements that must be satisfied before a contract can be voided for duress:

(1) one party involuntarily accepted the terms of another;
(2) circumstances permitted no other alternative; and
(3) such circumstances were the result of coercive acts of the other party. (Case discussion omitted)

[1]With permission, from http://www.courts.alaska.gov/juryins.htm.

Not all states have jury instructions online. For more information about jury instructions in general and some links to state jury instructions, visit http://www.llrx.com/columns/reference19.htm.

Your state may have some jury instructions online even if no links are provided on the Law Library Resource Exchange site. For further information, search the Web site for your state court system or the highest court in your state system or the Web site for your state bar association.

Television and movies present a very distorted vision of the litigation process by resolving, in an hour or two, what would actually take years. Examine the docket entries for a contract case at www.justia.com. For example, a contract case filed in July 2010, against Mark Zuckerberg and Facebook, already had almost 670 docket entries as of this writing: https://dockets.justia.com/docket/new-york/nywdce/1:2010cv00569/79861/. Note that the case has involved a jurisdictional dispute, court-ordered mediation, and multiple discovery motions and orders. If the defendant were a small start-up company, rather than Facebook, would it be able to absorb the cost?

Assignment 11-1

As assigned by your instructor:

- Find the Web site for your local state trial court. Does the court have an arbitration or mediation program? If so, get the details: Is it mandatory? What types of cases are covered? Who are the neutrals? What does it cost?
- Find jury instructions, in use in your state, dealing with affirmative defenses to breach of contract.
- Contact the clerk of your local court and find out how you can obtain a sample of a complaint and/or answer filed in a breach of contract case. If possible, obtain the sample and share it with your classmates.
- Using your online state statutes or computer-assisted legal research (CALR), determine the limitations period (statute of limitations) setting the time limit for bringing a case alleging breach of contract. You may find different periods applicable to oral contracts and written contracts. If you have trouble finding the site, visit http://www.law.cornell.edu/topics/state_statutes.html#1commercial.
- Find the statute of limitations for cases involving contracts for sales of goods, under your state's enactment of the UCC.
- Research case management software and write a report on the functions available.
- Find your state code of civil procedure in the online statutes. Then examine your local court rules (probably on the Web site for your local state trial court or the clerk of that court). Are there any particular rules for filing contract cases? For example:
  - Is the plaintiff required to attach a copy of any written contract to the complaint?
  - If the plaintiff is asking for payment, is it necessary to allege that payment has been demanded and denied?
  - Are there any special requirements for pleading a condition precedent?
  - Does a complaint have to state specifically that the parties did have capacity?
  - Are there any particular requirements for pleading fraud or mistake?

C. Remedies: Theory

In awarding a remedy in a case based on breach of contract, the court can look at three concerns: the parties' expectations, what the parties did in reliance on the contract, and what should be restored to the parties. Two of the concerns focus on past conduct and one concerns itself with a theoretical future: what would have happened if the contract had not been breached. With these concerns in mind, a court can fashion a legal remedy or an equitable remedy that is reasonable.

A **legal remedy** is an award of money, also called **damages;** a case requesting damages is called a **case at law.** An **equitable remedy** is nonmonetary; it involves court orders. Equitable remedies are decided by a judge, not by a jury. A case involving equitable remedies is sometimes called a **case in equity** or a **chancery** case. Courts award equitable remedies only under limited circumstances, when a legal remedy would not be adequate. Awards of damages fit into several categories, described below.

The *Madrid v. Marquez* case presented in Assignment 11-2 includes a discussion of the evolution from separate courts for law and equity to a combined system. Historically, the injured party had to choose among available remedies. In the *Madrid* case the injured party had transferred title to his home in exchange for a promise of lifelong care. The other party breached that promise. Under the old view, the injured party would have had to choose between seeking a court order returning title to his home or an award of money damages. The more modern view allows nonbreaching parties to seek remedies in both categories, unless the remedies are inconsistent or would be unjust. The UCC specifically rejects **election of remedies** in cases involving breach of a sales contract.

Legal Remedy
Award of money; also called damages

Damages
Award of money; also called legal remedy

Case at Law
A case requesting damages (money)

Equitable Remedy
Award that is nonmonetary and involves court orders; see also Case in Equity and Chancery

Case in Equity
Courts can issue orders based on fairness; see also Equitable Remedy

Chancery
A chancery court can order acts performed

Election of Remedies
Injured party's choice between remedies available for a single actionable occurrence

1. Damages

Compensatory damages are intended to put the nonbreaching party in the position she would have been in if the contract had been fully performed. Because this is a forward-looking theory, compensatory damages are sometimes called **expectation damages.** Sometimes it is not a difficult calculation. For example, if Banquet Hall ordered 200 stuffed frozen chicken breasts for an awards dinner at $3.00 apiece, learned on the day before the dinner that Supply House would be unable to deliver, and was able to cover by purchasing 200 breasts from another source at $3.50 apiece, direct compensatory damages would be $100. It's rarely that simple, however.

Compensatory Damages
Damages intended to put nonbreaching parties in the position they would have occupied if the contract had been fully performed; also called expectation damages

Expectation Damages
Damages intended to put nonbreaching parties in the position they would have occupied if the contract had been fully performed; also called compensatory damages

---

Example

Banquet Hall may have had **incidental damages.** For example, Banquet Hall had to have an employee come in on her day off to make calls, find another supplier, and place an order. The $50 cost is not directly related to the contract, but it may be part of the award. The court will also look at **costs avoided** because of the breach. For example, assume that Supply House had a $50 delivery charge, in addition to its $600 charge for the goods. If the new source does not charge for delivery, Banquet Hall has avoided that cost. The UCC identifies incidental damages in breach of sales contracts involving goods.

Incidental Damages
Losses reasonably associated with or related to actual damages; indirect damages

Costs Avoided
Expenses nonbreaching party will not incur

Incidental and consequential damages do not flow directly from the contract. When Supply House entered the contract to provide chicken breasts, the contract clearly contemplated the cost of supplying chicken breasts; the contract probably made no mention of the cost of having an employee work to find an alternate source. These types of damages are, therefore, limited to what the breaching party could have reasonably foreseen. The party claiming indirect damages must be able to prove the amount with reasonable certainty; courts will not award damages that are too speculative or unforeseeable.

Consequential Damages
Losses that do not flow directly and immediately from an injurious act

Foreseeable
That which a reasonable person would anticipate

Special Damages
Losses that do not flow directly and immediately from an injurious act but are indirect; also called consequential damages

Consequential damages may include injuries to other property or people that were **foreseeable** at the time of the contract. For example, Pat buys a new washing machine, has it installed, and throws a load of laundry in before leaving for work. The machine had a defect; there was a breach of the contract warranty. Unfortunately, the defect was in the part that told the machine when to stop filling. Pat comes home several hours later and finds extensive water damage. The UCC specifies that consequential damages include injuries to property proximately resulting from breach of warranty.

Consequential damages (sometimes called **special damages**) can also be lost profits. For example, Pat ordered 200 holiday-themed sweaters for his boutique at a cost of $20 per sweater. He planned to sell the sweaters at $40 per sweater. The supplier failed to deliver. Is Pat entitled to the $4,000 profit he anticipated? That depends on the likelihood that he would have made the profit. Courts award only damages that can be proven with reasonable certainty. How long has Pat been in business? What is his history of holiday sales? The certainty of lost profits is a particular problem in cases involving new businesses; some states have statutes or common law doctrines dealing with the issue. As you might imagine, parties often desire to limit liability for consequential damages.

Example

The American Institute of Architects has drafted the following quoted language under which both the contractor and the owner waive claims against each other for consequential damages:

On the part of the owner, a waiver of damages in respect of "rental expenses, for losses of use, income, profit, financing, business and reputation and for loss of management or employee productivity or of the services of such persons" and on the part of the contractor, a waiver of damages in respect of "principal office expenses including the compensation of personnel stationed there, for losses of financing, business and reputation, and for loss of profit except anticipated profit arising directly from the work."

Reliance Damages
Damages awarded for losses incurred by plaintiff in reliance on the contract; puts party in position that would have been occupied if the contract had not been made

Present Worth Doctrine
The value, in "today's money," of payments to be made in the future

If it appears that Pat's anticipated profit was speculative, the court may award **reliance damages** to put him in the position he would have been if the contract had not been made. Perhaps Pat should be awarded the $500 he spent on advertising to sell the sweaters. Reliance damages are usually the only damages awarded in promissory estoppel cases, discussed in an earlier chapter.

Also keep in mind that, under the **present worth doctrine** (also called **present value doctrine**), payments required to be made in the future must be reduced to their present worth. For example, employee has a three-year contract and is to be paid $70,000 in the first year, $75,000 in the second year, and $80,000 in the third year. During the first year of employment, employer fires employee in breach of the contract. Employee has already been paid $50,000. Employee cannot recover the full $175,000 of salary unpaid under the contract right now; a court must reduce the amount to its present value. Money has time value. If the employer must pay the full sum now, he will lose the interest or investment income he might have otherwise earned with the money before paying it as salary to employee.

Example

Because of the uncertainty surrounding calculations of damages, parties frequently limit damages in their contracts. Have you ever taken film to be developed? Think about the print on the envelope in which you deposit the film. That is your contract. What are you entitled to if the developer loses or destroys your film? In all likelihood you are agreeing that your damages will consist of replacement rolls of film. Imagine the possibilities: What if the pictures were the only existing pictures of a historic event? The UCC specifically allows parties to limit remedies unless the limitation would be unconscionable.

Liquidated damages are damages agreed to, in advance of breach, in the contract itself. For example, Owner has agreed to move out of his current home on May 15 and, in the contract with the builder of his new house, inserts a clause that the house must be ready for occupancy by May 15, with a provision that damages for delay will be $200 per day. Of course, both parties have to agree and, in some cases it is to their advantage to agree. It avoids the difficulty of determining actual damages. Courts will enforce liquidated damages clauses that are reasonable and that do not appear to be an attempt to "punish" the breaching party. Sophisticated parties now commonly include incentives, such as "$400,000 if ready for occupancy by May 15; $390,000 if ready by June 1." The UCC specifies that a "reasonable" provision for liquidated damages is enforceable.

Liquidated Damages
Damages agreed to in advance of breach, in the contract itself

---

Examples

The following is a liquidated damages clause in a contract for dormitory housing.

"If, after taking occupancy of a room, the student cancels this housing contract as described in Paragraph 12 above, the student shall pay liquidated damages in the amount of $10.00 (Ten Dollars) per day for the remainder or unexpired portion of the term of the academic agreement, not to exceed $500.00 (Five Hundred Dollars)."

In 2002 a Patriots fan entered into a ten-year contract for season tickets in luxury seats. After a single season, the fan stopped paying for the tickets. The team sued to enforce the contract, and the trial court ordered the fan to pay the full value of the remaining nine years, $75,000. The state's high court modified the amount of the award. Before reading the case, can you identify the type of damages at issue and the issues raised on behalf of the ticket holder? *NPS, LLC v. Minihane,* 451 Mass. 417 (2008).

Craigslist has decided to crack down on companies that use data from its Web sites to generate ads on competing Web sites using software "spiders, "crawlers," and "scrapers." Craigslists' terms of use state that "[b]y accessing our servers, websites, or content therefrom, you agree to these terms of use" and that "[r]obots, spiders, scripts, scrapers, crawlers, etc. are prohibited . . . . You agree not to collect users' personal and/or contact information ('PI')." Further, users are asked to pay Craigslist "for breaching or inducing others to breach the 'USE' section, not as a penalty, but as a reasonable estimate of our damages (actual damages are often hard to calculate): $0.10 per server request, $1 per post, email, flag, or account created, $1 per item of PI collected, and $1000 per software distribution, capped at $25,000 per day." The user's "click-through" acceptance of the terms is required to use the site. Courts broadly uphold liquidated damages clauses as long as they are not punitive in nature. Some of the factors courts consider are whether actual damages would be difficult to calculate after the breach occurs and whether they are unreasonably large. In the *Craigslist* case, an issue may be whether actual damages would be difficult to calculate. Craigslist's statement that its liquidated damages are "not a penalty, but [] a reasonable estimate of our damages" would not be given much weight in court, but liquidated damages present greater judicial efficiencies, which is very relevant. At the time of this writing, there were no reported results. For updates, search Craigslist suit crawlers.

Punitive damages (also discussed in Chapter 4) are not generally available for breach of contract. It does not matter that the breach was intentional. If, however, the breach of contract involved wrongful conduct that would be independently actionable under tort law, punitive damages may be available. Examples include fraud (intentional false statements), duress, and breach of fiduciary duty. The purpose of punitive damages is to punish and deter wrongful behavior that went beyond breach of contract, rather than to compensate the injured party. So, in cases involving wrongful behavior, a court may award punitive damages even though the injured party has been fully compensated for any loss.

Nominal Damages
Minimal amount of damages awarded, even if no financial loss resulted from the breach or if the loss cannot be proven with reasonable certainty

A nonbreaching party is entitled to **nominal damages** even if no financial loss resulted from the breach or if the loss cannot be proven with reasonable certainty. Cases seeking only nominal damages are rare because of the cost of going to court. Parties with the resources to do so sometimes bring a suit to establish their positions for future contract relationships. More commonly, however, nominal damages are awarded to a party who sought compensatory damages because the court decides that the party either suffered no real loss or was unable to prove his loss.

Costs
Examples include filing fees, fees for service of process, and similar charges incurred in litigation

Attorney's Fees
Payment to attorney for services

Fee Recovery or Fee Reversal
An award of attorney's fees

A party might also want to recover **costs** and **attorney's fees** in the event of litigation. Costs include filing fees, fees for service of process, and similar charges incurred in going to court. For some types of contract litigation (*e.g.*, consumer fraud cases) a statute may provide for payment of "prevailing party's" fees and costs by the other party. In other cases the contract itself may call for payment of successful party's fees and costs. Absent such a clause or statute, the parties must pay their own attorneys' fees, regardless of whether they win or lose. Some courts allocate costs among the parties, even without a contract provision. An award of attorney's fees is sometimes called **fee recovery** or **fee reversal.**

Example

The following is an attorney's fees and costs provision:

"In the event of litigation relating to the subject matter of this Agreement, the non-prevailing party shall reimburse the prevailing party for all reasonable attorney fees, costs, and expenses of litigation resulting from such litigation."

Finally, in calculating damages, a court will also consider whether the injured party could have reasonably avoided any of the loss. The UCC specifically addresses **mitigation of damages.** As you may imagine, the parties may not agree on whether mitigation was reasonably possible. The *Edington* case presented in Assignment 11-2 demonstrates how mitigation offsets damages.

Mitigation of Damages
An attempt to reduce the harm

2. Equitable Remedies

Courts have discretion with respect to equitable remedies and will not enter orders mandating specified actions if an award of damages would adequately compensate the injured party. Courts also avoid equitable remedies if parties outside the contract would have to be involved (*e.g.*, property has been resold), if the injured party has delayed in a way that is unfair to the other party (**laches**), if the remedy would cause unreasonable hardship, if the terms of the contract are unclear, or if the contract involves unfairness.

Laches
Injured party delays in seeking remedy in a way that is unfair to the other party

Specific performance is a court order requiring a party to perform her contractual obligations. It is most commonly awarded in cases involving **unique property.** For example, if seller refuses to sign a deed after signing a contract to sell his house, a court will order him to do so. Could Banquet Hall have obtained an order of specific performance for the undelivered chicken breasts? Probably not; chicken breasts are not unique property and are readily available from other sources. Specific performance is not appropriate for contracts involving personal services. Forcing a person to perform work against her will would be similar to slavery and it would be very difficult to ensure the quality of the work.

Specific Performance
Court order requiring a party to perform contract obligations

Unique Property
An item that is not readily available from other sources

An **injunction** is a court order requiring or prohibiting specific actions. For example, Lee has an option to purchase Pat's farm at any time during the next year. Lee learns that Pat is planning to convey the farm to Terry. Lee can obtain an injunction to prevent the transfer. An injunction can be awarded in a personal service contract situation, for example, to prevent an employee under contract to one employer from going to work for another.

Injunction
Court order requiring or prohibiting specific actions

Restitution (also discussed in Chapter 7) is restoration to the position occupied by the injured party before the contract was entered. It usually requires return of consideration and is commonly applied in situations where damages cannot be calculated with the certainty required by the court or situations involving an unenforceable or voidable contract. Restitution is sometimes available to the party in breach of the contract. See the following examples.

Restitution
To return property or its value

Examples

Jan conveyed title to her empty lot to Carl Contractor for construction of a custom house. The contract requires Jan to get a mortgage and pay Carl, who will transfer the lot and house back when construction is complete. Carl fails to begin construction as required by the contract. Jan wants her lot back.

Carl Contractor orally agreed to begin construction on a house for Jill in 15 months and took a deposit of $10,000. The contract is unenforceable under the statute of frauds (not to be performed within one year) and Jill may seek restitution for the return of the deposit. In this type of situation, restitution is used to prevent unjust enrichment; it's a quasi-contract situation.

Jan signed a contract to sell her lot for $75,000 and took a $15,000 deposit from Bill. Bill later tells Jan he cannot complete the purchase. Jan then sells the lot to Connie for $80,000. Bill may be entitled to return of his money, despite his breach.

Replevin
Recovery of property from one who is wrongfully in possession

Reformation
Rewriting contact; also called blue-penciling

The UCC provides for restitution and **replevin** in specified circumstances. Replevin is recovery of goods from one who is wrongfully in possession of those goods.

Reformation (also discussed in Chapter 6) is the "rewriting" of a contract, also called "blue-penciling," and is rare. It is most often employed in cases of mutual mistake, when the court attempts to make the contract reflect the real intentions of the parties, or in cases of unconscionability, where the court wants to give the injured party the benefit of the contract without the burden of the unfair provision.

D. Tort Law Versus Contract Law

Because breach of contract usually does result in some "harm" parties sometimes try to frame their cases as tort actions, rather than (or in addition to) contract actions. This can be an effort to obtain an award of damages not generally available for breach of contract. For example, a party hoping for an award of punitive damages might allege the tort of fraud. Bringing a tort suit might also be necessary if a situation is not covered by contract law. For example, a third party might interfere with the performance of a contract between others and cause a breach; the appropriate action is not for breach of contract, but for tortious interference with contract. In other cases, a party might want to frame his case as contract case or as a tort case because of the statute of limitations applicable to the case or because of particular standards that might be applied to the case. In general, if the lawsuit is based on breach of a duty imposed by society (*e.g.*, the duty to drive in a safe manner) it is a tort case; if it is based on a breach of a duty voluntarily assumed as part of a contract (*e.g.*, an obligation to complete a warehouse by a certain date) it is a contract case.

Example

In 2014, United Airlines sued the 22-year-old creator of a Web site that helps travelers find the cheapest airfare possible between two desired cities. Travelers buy tickets to a cheaper end destination, but get off at a stopover point to which a ticket would have been more expensive. For example, if you want to travel from New York to Chicago, it may be cheaper to buy one-way airfare all the way to San Francisco, not check any luggage, and simply get off in Chicago. The airlines alleged that this was "unfair competition" and "deceptive behavior" and that the Web site promoted "strictly prohibited" travel, a breach of contracts cause of action under the airlines' contract of carriage.

The suit was dismissed for lack of jurisdiction, http://money.cnn.com/2015/05/01/investing/united-airlines-lawsuit-skiplagged/, but there was another potential problem. The Web site was simply a third party with only incidental effects and benefits. A contract claim would likely fail for lack of standing; a tort claim, such as intentional interference with contractual relations, would also likely fail for inability to prove harm. Would United be able to establish that it was injured by not having to transport passengers on the second leg of a flight?

EXHIBIT 11-2
Chart of Remedies

UCC Self-Help Remedies, Seller (depend on the nature of Buyer's breach)	*UCC Self-Help Remedies, Buyer (depend on nature of Seller's breach)*	*Damages: Consider ability to prove with reasonable certainty, foreseeability, mitigation*	*Equitable Remedies: Available only if damages inadequate; consider balance of equities*
Rescission: cancel the contract or accept substituted performance	Rescission: cancel the contract or accept substituted performance	Compensatory: puts nonbreaching party in position would have occupied if contract had been fully performed (loss of value 2 costs avoided 1 incidental 1 consequential)	Injunction: prohibits actions
Withhold or stop delivery	Cover: obtain substitute goods	Liquidated: agreed in advance, must be reasonable	Restitution: restores nonbreaching to position occupied before contract (*e.g.*, return of property)
Resell goods	Replevin: recover goods identified to contract, in possession of another	Nominal: a small amount, available if loss was negligible or not adequately proven	Specific performance: requires party to perform contract
	Security interest: in goods in buyer's possession that do not satisfy contract requirements	Punitive: available only if tort (*e.g.*, fraud) involved in breach	Reformation: court "rewrites" contract, rare
If the above-listed remedies are inadequate, seller may sue for damages; see column 3	If listed remedies inadequate, buyer may seek damages (column 3), or equitable remedy (*e.g.*, specific performance)	Reliance: restores (in a financial sense) nonbreaching party to position occupied if contract not made	

Some situations fit into both areas of law. For example, a seller might breach a contract by delivering a defective product, which causes harm to a person or property. The situation may be covered by the contract warranties (discussed in Chapters 2 and 13). Warranty actions are often inadequate as a remedy in such situations because warranties can be disclaimed, limited, or modified. In addition, depending on the jurisdiction, a warranty action might not provide a remedy because the injured party was, himself, negligent in a way that contributed to the injury; misused the product; or was not in **privity of contract** (not a party to the contract and, perhaps, far removed from the contract relationship).

Privity
The relationship between the parties to the contract

Strict Liability
Liability regardless of fault

The most recent evolution in this area of law is the imposition of **strict liability** (liability regardless of fault) on sellers of products. While the law differs from state to state, a merchant seller (in the business of selling the product) is generally liable for injuries arising from the sale of a product in a defective condition that is unreasonably dangerous. The product must have been in the defective condition when it left the control of the defendant. The injured party is not required to prove that the seller was careless or negligent or how the product came to be defective. The proximate cause of the injury can be a manufacturing defect, a design defect, or failure to warn. The goals of the law are to give consumers (who may not have medical insurance) maximum protection, to put the financial burden on those who profit from selling the product, and to motivate manufacturers to produce safe products. Because of the burden this legal theory imposes on sellers, some states allow consideration of the injured party's negligence or misuse of the product and some states have imposed limits on awards of damages.

E. Practical and Ethical Issues

Attorneys are motivated to hire paralegals not only to get work done efficiently, but also because paralegals are a profit center. In recent years, fee reversal cases (discussed in this chapter) have made well-educated paralegals a particularly valuable part of an efficient law office.

When there is no fee reversal issue, whether the attorney bills the client for paralegal time, as a separate item on the bill is purely a private matter; there is no court involved.

Example

Client consults Lawyer about negotiating and drafting a contract to sell a business. Lawyer estimates that the work will take about ten hours and says, "My hourly rate is $250; my paralegal's hourly rate is $80." "WHAT!" Client exclaims. "You are going to bill me separately for your paralegal?" Lawyer shrugs and says, "Suit yourself. If you'd prefer to not work with a paralegal, I will do all the work myself. Your bill will be about $2,500. If you do work with my paralegal and he does half the work, it will be about $1,650." Suddenly, Client wants to work with the paralegal.

Why is this arrangement beneficial for the lawyer? The lawyer makes a profit on the paralegal. If the paralegal's salary, benefits, office space, and so forth cost the lawyer about $40 an hour, half of the billing rate is profit. In addition, if the lawyer is busy, she can spend the five hours that are "freed up" by the paralegal's work on another client matter. Is there anything unethical about this? No, this is a private contract to which the client has agreed and the lawyer is in business to make a profit, like any other employer.

In a fee reversal case the situation is a little different. The party who ultimately pays the lawyer did not choose the lawyer, did not agree to the hourly rate, and did not have an opportunity to monitor the work as it was done. In order to make sure that the billing is fair, the court making a fee recovery award reviews the bill. This is demonstrated by the *Edington* case you will read in Assignment 11-2. If the court determines that the bill was unfair, it will cut the bill. This motivates lawyers to delegate work to those with lower billing rates.

Imagine that the bill submitted to the court included 40 hours of time for summarizing depositions at $400 an hour. The court might decide that this type of work did not have to be done by a lawyer with a billing rate of $400 and cut the bill to $100 per hour. The firm has learned a valuable lesson: Next time, use a paralegal for deposition summaries! Most courts not only allow separate billing for paralegals in fee reversal cases, they encourage it by scrutinizing the bill. This is not universally true; always check the precedent in the particular court system.

Of course, unscrupulous lawyers might start including billing for photocopying, filing, and other low-level clerical work as "paralegal work." As a result, many courts scrutinize not only the type of work done, but also the credentials of the paralegals who did the work.

Assignment 11-2

a. Read *Madrid v. Marquez* (N.M. Ct. App. 2001), http://caselaw.findlaw.com/nm-court-of-appeals/1427261.html, and *Edington v. Colt's Manufacturing Co.* (Conn. Super. Ct. 2002), https://casetext.com/case/edington-v-colts-manufacturing-co-no-cv-00-0599390-s-nov.

   - Do you think the nature of the defendant's actions in the *Madrid* case influenced the court's decision that both an equitable remedy and an award of damages were appropriate? Might the court have reached a different conclusion if the defendant had not taken advantage of the elderly homeowners in such an extreme way, or is the concept of separating law and equity generally obsolete?
   - In the *Edington* case, the court deducted from plaintiff's award the amount she earned working for Glock after Remington terminated her contract, but did not deduct the amount she earned from a real estate company. Why? The court cut both the hours claimed and the hourly rates in the attorney's fees award. Why?

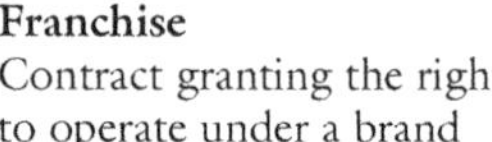

Franchise
Contract granting the right to operate under a brand name

b. Courts employ particular measures for damages in particular cases. As assigned by your instructor, find cases from your state, summarize them, and report to the class how the court measured damages in cases involving:
   - A contractor's delay in completing construction
   - Lost profits in a situation involving a **franchise** (contract granting the right to operate under a brand name, such as McDonald's, Burger King, Taco Bell, Dunkin' Donuts, or AAMCO). Does your state have a rule concerning new businesses?
   - An employer's or employee's breach of an employment contract
   - Mitigation of damages in a situation where the injured party was able to sell the product or service to another customer and claims that the new contract should not offset the damages for breach because it would have been able to fulfill the new contract even if the buyer had not breached
   - A construction defect; if possible, find a case in which correction of the defect would constitute "economic waste"
   - A claim for emotional distress damages
   - Attorney's fees with paralegal fees billed separately in a breach of contract matter

c. Find your state's consumer protection/fraud act. Use your bookmarked state statutes, CALR, or the Web site for the attorney general of your state. Does the statute provide for awards of attorney's fees? Arbitration?

d. Visit http://www.arbitration.com and find an article about an area of law that interests you (*e.g.*, family law arbitration, workplace arbitration, real estate arbitration) and write a report about a recent development.

e. Imagine a client who was a passenger on the Carnival Corporation ship *Costa Concordia*, which ran aground in January 2012. Luckily the client sustained no physical injury, nor was she ever at risk of death or serious injury, but she certainly feels that there was a breach of contract. Her vacation was cut short and she lost her luggage, including some jewelry and an expensive camera. It is highly unlikely that she read the terms of her ticket contract. Examine those at http://www.carnival.com/cms/static_templates/ticket_contract.aspx.
   - Identify all the limits on the client's right to sue: time limits, mandatory ADR, choice of jurisdiction and venue, limits on liability for baggage, and so on.
   - The client's financial loss was comparatively small, so that it may not be practical to pay an attorney unless she can be part of a class action or can seek damages for emotional distress: Can she?

Review Questions

1. What are the two main means of ADR? What is meant by court-annexed ADR?
2. Buyer ordered 200 white lab coats in a variety of sizes. Seller, who lost a substantial amount of inventory as the result of a storm, shipped 200 blue lab coats in various sizes. How does the UCC characterize seller's actions? What essential fact is missing? What options are available to buyer under the Code?
3. Under what circumstances will a court award an equitable remedy? Identify some equitable remedies?
4. Under what circumstances will a court award punitive damages for breach of contract?
5. What type of damages is awarded in promissory estoppel cases? Under what circumstances is this same type of damages awarded in a breach of contract case?
6. Under what circumstances will a court award incidental or consequential damages?
7. Under what circumstances will a court uphold a clause providing for liquidated damages?
8. What "details" should be clarified before a client commits to participation in arbitration?
9. How does an attorney benefit from billing a client for paralegal time, at a rate lower than would be billed for attorney time?
10. Consider your state's consumer fraud statute and the cases presented in Assignment 11-2. What is the purpose of fee award statutes? Do you think courts ever award punitive damages because there is no statute or contract provision to serve as a basis for an award of attorney fees?
11. After reading the *Edington* case cited in Assignment 11-2, identify the factors a court uses, in a fee reversal case, to determine whether attorney's fees are reasonable.

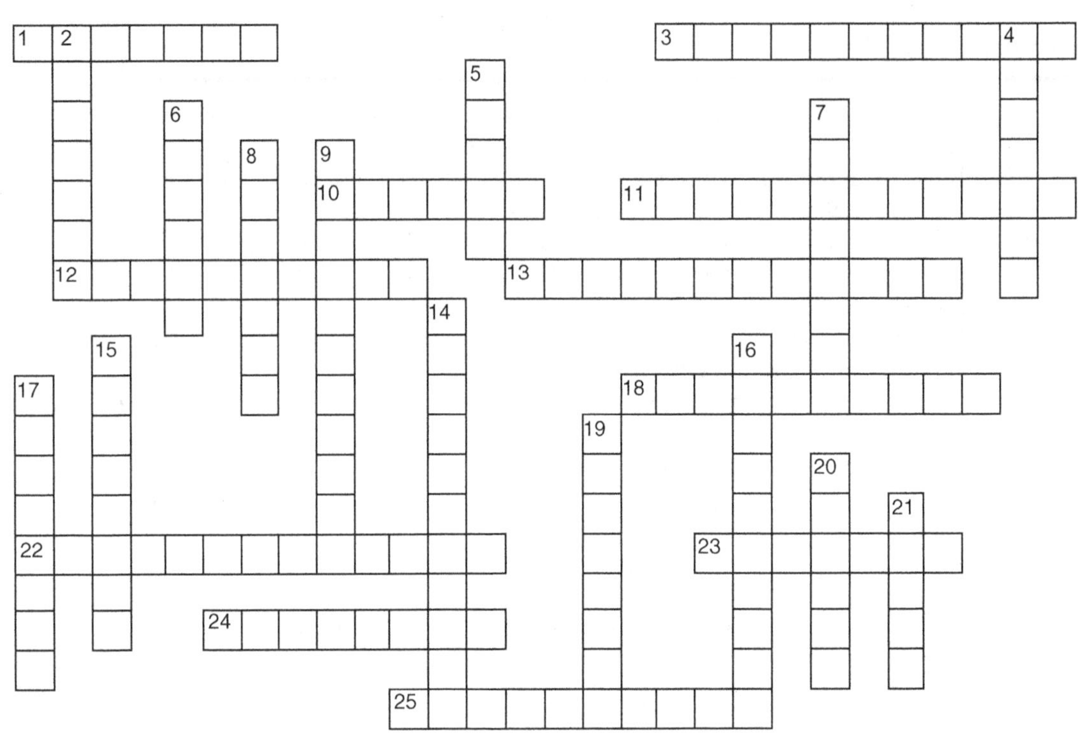

ACROSS

1. court- ________ ADR is increasingly common
3. ________ period; time for bringing suit
10. area of law in which courts issue orders based in fairness
11. ________ damages look to where injured party would be if contract were fully performed
12. damages agreed in advance
13. contracts sometimes dictate the ________ where a case will be litigated
18. ________ damages; *e.g.*, extra transportation costs
22. lost profits are a type of ________ damages
23. another term for a monetary award
24. retrieval of goods from person wrongfully in possession
25. court order prohibiting specified actions

DOWN

2. ________ damages, even if no loss proven
4. another term for a mediator or arbitrator
5. filing fees, etc.
6. specific performance available for contracts involving ________ property
7. damages awarded only if conduct was also intentional tort
8. with ________ arbitration the parties give up the right to challenge the result in court
9. to restore party to previous position
14. rewrites the contract
15. ________ damages put injured party in position occupied before contract formed
16. cutting losses resulting from breach
17. another term for equity
19. ________ performance requires party to fulfill contract obligations
20. ________ provision may require written notice before filing suit
21. ________ remedy; an award of money

12

Contract Interpretation

What happens when the parties disagree about what is required by a contract? In the worst cases, the parties have to resort to alternative dispute resolution (**ADR**, mediation or arbitration, discussed in detail in the previous chapter) or the courts. This chapter first introduces the common component parts of a contract, then focuses on the **rules of construction** that are applied to resolve such disputes. Knowing these rules is critical to drafting a contract that will not result in disputes.

ADR
Alternative dispute resolution (discussed in Chapter 11)

Construction (Rules of)
Rules that are applied to resolve contract disputes and to determine parties' intentions

Skills-based learning objectives	*How you will demonstrate your ability*
Determine formalities required for contract.	Assignments: Perform online research to determine status of business; determine need for notarization.
Draft provisions to meet client needs.	Assignment: Draft a paragraph for a contract.
Interpret the meaning of contract provisions.	Assignment: Research UCC concerning extrinsic evidence and interpretation of contracts.
Implement existing contracts.	Assignments: Identify mistakes and ambiguities in contract; explain contract to client.

A. **Components of a Written Contract**
   1. **Identifications**
   2. **Recitals**
   3. **Consideration**
   4. **Definitions**

5. Body
6. Signatures and Acknowledgments

B. Parol Evidence Rule

C. Rules of Construction

D. Practical and Ethical Issues

Remember, the rules of construction are "default rules" and apply when the parties do not adequately describe the expectations and obligations in the contract. The Uniform Commercial Code (UCC) includes many default provisions, some of which you studied in Chapter 3, concerning offers (the gap-filling or open terms provisions). Good lawyers and paralegals give careful thought to every provision, rather than allowing the default provisions to create the contract.

A. Components of a Written Contract

1. Identifications

This section of a contract, generally at the top of the first page, gives the title, identifies the parties, and states the date of signing. It may indicate how the parties will be identified throughout the rest of the contract. It should never include confusing identifications, such as "party of the first part."

Example

EMPLOYMENT CONTRACT

This employment contract is made on March 15, 2016 ("Contract Date"),[1] between Fox Valley Investors Coop, LLC, an Illinois limited liability company, ("FVIC"), 1012 River Road, St. Charles, IL 60174 and Chris Zehelein, 329 Duncan Ave., Elgin, IL 60120 ("Employee"). *Note the defined terms in parentheses.*

Assignment 12-1

When drafting or implementing a contract involving a business, it is important to determine:

- Is the business a sole proprietorship, a corporation, a limited partnership, a general partnership, or a limited liability company;
- Accurate contact information and address;

[1]Reference to any person, place, thing, or event can be made easier by creating a defined term, essentially a shorthand way of referring to that person, place, thing, or event that might otherwise require a lengthy description.

- Whether the contract gives the correct name; and
- Whether the business is in good standing.

Find the Web site for the agency responsible for registration of business entities in your state. This is usually the office of the secretary of state. Although many online services offer corporate searches for a fee, it is important that you use the official site to get accurate, up-to-date information without paying a fee. Using your state's site, search for corporations in your state that include your last name or given name in their names.

---

2. Recitals

Recitals
Short statements that provide background or explain the reasons for the contract; not technically part of a contract

Short statements that give background or explain the reasons for the contract, recitals are not technically part of the contract. Recitals do not contain essential terms, requiring a party to do or not do anything, but they can play an important role in contract interpretation. In older contracts, recitals often begin with the word "whereas."

Recently, some drafters include a statement that the recitals are accurate, perhaps in an effort to make them part of the contract or set up a defense of frustration of purpose. Other contract authorities advocate eliminating recitals, perhaps to avoid such a possible defense. Regardless of which theory appeals to you, the recitals must be accurate and should not consist of "posturing."

Example

1. FVIC is engaged in the business of providing online training for employees of its clients and requires the services of a Web page designer.
2. Employee is a Web page designer, previously employed by Elgin Community College.
3. Employee terminated his employment at Elgin Community College in order to accept employment by FVIC.

---

3. Consideration

As you know, a contract is not valid without consideration, which means that each party must get something she or he was not legally entitled to before entering the contract and each must give up something to which s/he was legally entitled before the contract. A written contract may contain a "formal" statement of consideration at its beginning, such as "for ten dollars and other valuable consideration, receipt of which is acknowledged, the parties agree. . . ." Remember, however, that stating a dollar amount as a formality is not necessary, because courts do not generally weigh consideration. The mutual agreements and obligations stated in the body of the contract should be sufficient to support the contract.

Incorporation by Reference
A reference to an outside document, making that document part of a contract

Example

4. Employee has left his former employment and agrees to work as a Web designer, as described in the employee handbook ("Handbook"), attached to this contract as Exhibit A and **incorporated by this reference,** for the period beginning April 1, 2016, and ending on April 1, 2018 (the "Term of Employment"), at the salary and with the benefits stated in the Handbook.
5. FVIC agrees to compensate Employee in accordance with terms stated in the Handbook for the Term of Employment.

4. Definitions

If a contract is complex, involving multiple parties, events, locations, or objectives, it is often most efficient to include a list of all defined terms at the beginning, to avoid the distraction of integrating the definitions into the text. It is extremely important that the **defined terms** be used consistently. Even if the contract does not contain a separate section for definitions, adequate definitions are essential. Even common terms may require definition. Consider a standard homeowner's insurance policy that excludes coverage for injuries incurred as the result of conducting business on the premises. Suppose that the homeowner's daughter is babysitting a neighbor's child (anticipating payment) when the child is hurt by a pan of boiling water falling from the stove. Would the policy cover the child's medical care?

Assignment 12-2

- Draft a definition of the term "business" that would exclude coverage for the incident described above; draft another definition that would cover the incident. Keep in mind that babysitting is not the only possibility. The homeowner might, for example, tutor students, do occasional tailoring and clothing repair for a local dry cleaner, or develop and frame pictures for sale at a local gift shop. Keep your definition broad enough to include many possibilities.
- MadCity University has always had a clause in its housing contract that allows school officials to evict a student from the dormitories for various activities involving (among other things) illegal drugs, smoking, open fires, and use of any "hazardous" substance. Last year, two students distributed peanuts in hidden spots throughout the study lounge as a "joke." A third student, severely allergic to peanuts, became violently ill. MCU is convinced that the students knew the likely consequences of their actions, but were unsuccessful in evicting the students on the "hazardous substance" provision. Draft a definition that would cover the situation. Again, keep in mind that you are not drafting for this particular incident, but rather for a variety of possibilities.

- ◆ Professor Vietzen's syllabus includes a statement that late assignments are penalized three points per day. Identify the possible ambiguities and draft a definition to clarify.
- ◆ Your firm's client, Dina Developer, wants to establish a high-end, quiet subdivision. She wants a contract and covenants that will allow homeowners to conduct quiet home occupations, such as an architect who might meet clients in a home office once or twice a week, but wants to prohibit disruptive home businesses that will involve lots of noise or traffic. Draft a definition of home occupation that will meet Dina's needs.

Example

6. "Out of Office Work" means work performed by Employee, for the benefit or at the request of FVIC, at a location other than FVIC's offices or the employee's home, when performed at that location at the request of FVIC. Expenses related to Out of Office Work shall be compensated as described in Exhibit B, attached.
7. "Volunteerism" refers to participation in FVIC's programs for community service, as described on the company Web site, as it may be from time to time amended.

---

5. Body

The body of the contract describes the obligations of the parties and the consequences of failure to meet those obligations. When you receive a contract that has been signed, you do not have control of the contents, but you should look for certain characteristics (described in Chapter 13) to help you understand and implement the agreement. If the contract does not have these characteristics (*e.g.*, good organization and labeling), you may have to create a work copy or an outline to help yourself understand it. When you participate in creating a contract, you can make it user-friendly by remembering these traits. If you use a feature, such as indexing in Word, you can save time and ensure that the contract will have good internal organization and a useful index.[2]

Example

I. FVIC'S PROPERTY RIGHTS

16. Intellectual Property. All material developed by Employee in the course of his employment shall be the property of FVIC. Employee shall sign all necessary assignments and other paperwork, as necessary to secure patent, copyright, or trademark rights in such material for FVIC.

---

[2]https://support.office.com/en-US/article/Create-an-index-and-update-an-index-cc502c71-a605-41fd-9a02-cda9d14bf073?ui=en-US&rs=en-US&ad=US&fromAR=1.

17. Trade Secrets. Employee shall not divulge any information concerning any FVIC product or clients to anyone either during or after termination of his employment with FVIC and shall not use such information for his own benefit.
18. Competition. Employee shall not, during the Term of Employment or for a period of one year after the end of that term, perform work in any capacity for any of the competing companies listed on Exhibit C, attached to this contract and incorporated by this reference.
19. Remedies for Violation of FVIC Property Rights. Employee acknowledges that, in the event of breach of any of the covenants in paragraphs 6-8 above, FVIC shall be entitled to monetary damages as well as injunctive relief.

II. EMPLOYEE'S RIGHTS

20. Transfer. If FVIC notifies Employee that Employee has been transferred to another geographic location, Employee may, by written notice, terminate this contract. Employee shall continue to perform his contractual duties for five working days after the date on which FVIC receives such written notice. In the event of termination because of transfer, FVIC shall compensate Employee for days actually worked plus the sum of Ten Thousand Dollars ($10,000) and shall have no further liability to Employee.
21. Failure to Renew. If, at the end of the Term of Employment, FVIC does not offer to extend Employee's employment on substantially the same terms . . .

6. Signatures and Acknowledgments

To avoid any appearance that pages were switched, signatures should not be on a page separate from the text of the agreement. Some lawyers include a spot to allow the parties to initial each page to avoid claims that pages were switched. Never remove the staples from a signed contract unless your supervising attorney specifically directs you to do so.

Corporate signatures must comply with state law and may require a seal, attestation, or other formalities. Always make sure that the person signing on behalf of a business has authority to do so; this may require review of the documents that created the business (partnership agreement, articles of incorporation/by-laws, organizational agreement).

Example

Date: ______________

______________________	______________________
Frank Transue, CEO Fox Valley Investors Coop, LLC, 1012 River Road	Chris Zehelein 329 Duncan Ave. Elgin, IL 60120
______________________	______________________
Witness	Witness

Date: ______________

Signatures may have to be witnessed by a **notary public,** if the contract will be **recorded.** Contracts concerning the title to real estate are often recorded, so that ownership can be determined by a search of the public records. In addition, contracts that are notarized may be considered **"self-proving,"** meaning that they can serve as testimony in court. Paralegals often witness and notarize documents. When you act as a notary, be sure to comply with the requirements of your state, keep a log, and record information about the form of identification you examined.[3]

Notary Public
Person authorized by state to administer oaths, certify documents, attest to the authenticity of signatures, and perform other official acts

Record
To record a document is to file it with the official charged with keeping documents such as deeds and judgments

Self-proving Document
Complies with formalities and can serve as testimony in court

Assignment 12-3

Find information about becoming a notary in your state (again, probably from the secretary of state) and answer the following:

- What are the functions a notary can serve (Administer oath? Authenticate documents? Witness signature?)
- Is a notary required to keep a log book, with a record of each time s/he performs one of these functions? What is the bond requirement?

B. Parol Evidence Rule

A contract may lack some of the components described above or it may have all of those components and still leave room for disagreement, requiring use of the rules of construction. Before applying those rules, it is necessary to determine what constitutes "the contract" and whether it requires construction. The **parol evidence rule** is employed in making those determinations.

Parol Evidence Rule
A writing, intended by the parties to be a final embodiment of their agreement, cannot be modified by evidence that adds to, varies, or contradicts the writing

As you know, some contracts are comprised of several written instruments, others are evidenced by a single written document, and others involve no writing. Parties often engage in extended oral and written negotiations, with offers and counteroffers being made, accepted or declined, withdrawn, or forgotten. Once the parties agree on terms and reduce that agreement to writing, it is assumed that what went on during negotiations is irrelevant. The written contract is protected from "attack" by the parol evidence rule. The rule concerns evidence. If a contract has been put in writing, evidence of things said before the writing is not admissible to vary, contradict, or add to its terms. Like all legal matters, however, it is not as simple as it appears.

[3]For further information, https://www.nationalnotary.org/.

Example

Sam spent two days looking at models of condominium units and negotiating to buy a unit in a building still under construction. At the end of the second day, exhausted, Sam finally signed a contract to buy a two-bedroom unit for $188,000. Sam was too tired to read the contract, which called for closing and possession in April. During his final inspection in April, Sam was surprised to find that the unit did not have a refrigerator. Sam says that the sales agent orally promised a refrigerator before writing up the contract, but now Sam realizes that it was not listed in the written contract. The sales agent says he remembers talking about a refrigerator, but does not remember promising that the refrigerator would be included at the $188,000 price. Sam's friend Pat, who was with Sam during the negotiations, is willing to testify that it sounded like the refrigerator would be included, but will the testimony be allowed?

Integrated
Final and complete agreement

Merger Clause
Contract provision stating that the document is the complete and final statement of agreement

1. Was this an **integrated** contract, intended to be a final and complete statement of the agreement? If the contract included a phrase, such as "*options as agreed*," or did not list any of the options, Sam might argue that it was not the complete agreement. Many contracts include a **merger clause,** stating that the document is the complete and final statement of agreement. Because a written contract does not have to take any particular form, the status of a document that does not include any reference to outside agreements or a merger clause may be unclear. Might it be simply a proposal or have all parties agreed? Does the document address the disputed term at all? Would such an agreement normally include some provision for dealing with the disputed term?

Sample Merger Clause:

This Agreement and the exhibits and schedules referred to herein constitute the final, complete, and exclusive statement of agreement between the parties with respect to the subject matter of this Agreement. This Agreement supersedes all prior and contemporaneous understandings or agreements between the parties. This Agreement may not be contradicted by evidence of any prior or contemporaneous statements or agreements. No party has been induced to enter into this Agreement by, nor is any party relying on, any representation, understanding, agreement, commitment, or warranty outside those expressly set forth in this Agreement.

2. Is the oral evidence intended to contradict the written contract or simply to **explain an ambiguity or apparent mistake?** If the contract contained a scrawled notation, "*promised buyer R*," or "*option package B*," Sam might argue that he is not trying to change or add to the contract, but only to explain it. Whether the oral evidence is an attempt to change or an attempt to explain is often unclear and some courts look at whether the disputed term is consistent with the rest of the agreement.

3. Is the evidence intended to show fraud, duress, mistake, misrepresentation, unconscionability, illegality, incapacity, or other **facts that would make the agreement void or voidable?** In such a situation, the intent is not to change the written contract, but to show that it might not be enforceable. If Sam had said, "I am too tired to read this and sign it now," and the sales agent had responded, "Don't worry it includes everything you want, even the refrigerator," Sam might be able to argue that the contract was tainted by fraud. *Read the 1992 Illinois case, In re Marriage of*

Johnson, https://casetext.com/case/in-re-marriage-of-johnson-24, for an example of a court allowing parol evidence in a case of mistake.

4. Was there a separate or **subsequent agreement** (novation) that changed or modified the agreement? Of course, a new agreement generally has to be supported by new consideration. Perhaps, after signing the contract for $188,000, which included upgraded kitchen counters, Sam and the salesperson made an agreement under which Sam would give up the upgraded counters in exchange for installation of a refrigerator.

Subsequent Agreement
A separate, later agreement that changes or modifies the original agreement

5. Does the evidence indicate the existence of a **condition precedent,** so that the agreement might never have become effective? Again, this is not an attempt to change the written agreement, but evidence that the agreement did not bind the parties.

The UCC takes a liberal approach to application of the parol evidence rule and specifically allows evidence of the course of dealing, usage of trade, or course of performance to explain or supplement a final written agreement. The Code also allows evidence of consistent additional terms unless the written instrument was intended to be complete and exclusive.

Example

Sam buys four or five new mobile homes (personal property, rather than real property) from the same manufacturer each year for several years. This year, Sam signs an order for five mobile homes and fails to notice that it does not refer to refrigerators. Under the Code, Sam would be allowed to present evidence of the course of dealings between the parties, even without proving that the signed agreement was incomplete or ambiguous. Even if the parties had never done business together, Sam might be able show that inclusion of refrigerators was either customary in the industry or consistent with and not excluded by the signed agreement.

Assignment 12-4

Find the UCC provision concerning parol or extrinsic evidence.

C. Rules of Construction

No one sets out to enter into an ambiguous contract. Everyone thinks their contract is crystal clear. Everyone thinks they've examined the problem from every angle and have exactly what they want. Everyone is often wrong. I include myself in that "everyone." I was thinking of this while flying recently. As usual, the flight was overbooked and the airline was throwing cash around looking for volunteers to take a different flight. I've never done this before, but my travel plans were decently flexible, and when the price got to be high enough, I figured I'd give it a go. I had the following conversation with the airline employee.

> Me: If I give up my seat, when would I get out of here? Her: We can book you on an itinerary that would get you in 30 minutes later than you would have. In fact, I can confirm you for that flight right now. Me: I'm confirmed for that flight?
>
> Her: Yes.

So I gave up my seat and walked down to the gate of the new flight I had been "confirmed" on. And here is where the ambiguity arose: When I heard and repeated back "confirmed," I thought that meant I had a seat on that flight. However, when the airline said the word "confirmed," what it meant was that they had confirmed me on a list of people who desire to take that flight. Basically, I was confirmed on the standby list. This wasn't at all what I wanted. Long story short: I got in 19 hours after I was supposed to, not 30 minutes. The whole time I was kicking myself, because I teach contracts law! I should be alert to the possibility of ambiguity! During that conversation, I should have asked for an actual seat assignment or even used the words "I have a seat on that flight." [Note: example of an oral contract.] But I didn't. I understood "confirmed" to be referring to a completely different concept, and I reused the airline's word, with a completely different understanding in mind. (I like to think we never understood each other and so there was never a meeting of the minds, but that was cold comfort while sitting around O'Hare for many hours.) I decided to use the entire situation as a lesson: The ambiguity entered because I did nothing but repeat their words back to them. I should have, instead, repeated back to them what I understood their words to mean. I tell my students all the time: Say what you mean in your contracts; don't beat around the bush. But it's so easy to flub that in the heat of the contract-making moment. It's so easy to think that, actually, you are saying what you mean. This is why we have contracts cases.[4]

The fact that the parties disagree about the meaning of a contract does not mean that it is legally ambiguous. The party who wants the court to apply the rules discussed in this section may have an uphill battle in convincing the court not to read the contract literally. Once a court identifies what constitutes the agreement and that the agreement is ambiguous it can apply **rules of construction** to try to determine the intent of the parties. Among the rules courts apply in interpreting contracts, in no particular order:

1. In choosing between two reasonable interpretations of a contract term, courts will interpret the contract against the party who drafted it. This is normally the offeror, who had the benefit of the mirror-image rule at common law.

2. When one interpretation will result in a lawful and effective contract and the other will result in no contract or a contract that is not workable, courts generally favor finding an effective contract.

3. Previous dealings between the parties are very important in establishing intent.

---

[4]Thanks to Stacey M. Lantagne, Assistant Professor of Law, The University of Mississippi School of Law, and to Myanna Dellinger, University of South Dakota School of Law and Editor, http://lawprofessors.typepad.com/contractsprof_blog/.

4. Words are given their commonly accepted meanings unless a different intention is clear and courts will not accept evidence of a different meaning when the words of the contract are unambiguous. If I sign a contract agreeing to sell you my 2004 truck, and later try to argue that we were really talking about my 2004 car, the court will probably not accept evidence that I always called my car "the truck." The contract appears unambiguous. Then again, what if I own a 2004 car and a 2002 truck?

5. Courts attempt to ascertain the intentions of the parties by looking at the purposes of the agreement and all of the surrounding circumstances. Let's assume that I own a 2002 car and a 2004 truck. The contract is ambiguous and the court would likely be willing to hear evidence that I knew you needed the truck in order to haul lumber for a construction project.

6. The written document is interpreted as whole and any disputed terms are interpreted so as to make them consistent with the rest of the agreement. If there are several documents that are part of a single transaction, those documents are looked at together. Perhaps you and I signed a contract under which you are building a dock and boathouse at my vacation property. That contract contains a statement that I am willing to sell you a truck for hauling lumber.

7. Specific terms govern over general terms and technical terms are generally given their technical meanings. If the agreement described a 2004 Ford truck with 25,000 miles on the odometer in one paragraph and referred to "the car" in other paragraphs, the specific description of the truck would govern.

8. Terms that were negotiated individually govern over boilerplate. **Boilerplate** refers to standard terms, included in most contracts, often preprinted on a form or taken from a form book, not individually negotiated.

Boilerplate
"Standard" contract language used in many contracts without adaptation to individual circumstances

9. Handwritten terms govern over preprinted terms and "spelled out" figures govern over numbers.

Assignment 12-5

Find the UCC provisions concerning construction of contracts.

- What guidance does the Code provide when there is a conflict with respect to warranties in a contract?
- What does the Code say about situations in which the contract does not say when or how the buyer will pay for goods?

D. Practical and Ethical Issues

Many contracts end up in litigation because of mistakes that should have been caught during careful proofreading. Even lesser mistakes cause the writer to lose credibility. It is especially common for people who use text messaging, instant messenger, or other forms of online or text-based communication to "slip up" and use informal (and incorrect) shortcuts, such as "thru" rather than "through" or "threw."

Common spelling/grammatical errors that may be missed by spell-check:

- *It's* (a contraction meaning it is), when the intention was *its* (the possessive pronoun).
- *Statue,* when the intention was *statute.*
- *Trail,* when the intention was *trial.*
- *Judgement,* rather than *judgment.*
- *Defendent,* rather than *defendant.*
- Homonyms (words that sound alike), such as *to, two, too; there, they're, their; then, than;* or *who's, whose.*

Other common errors relate to numbering. If a contract goes through several drafts, a previously correct reference to "notice as described in paragraph 13 of this Agreement" may have become incorrect. Numbers may be inadvertently skipped or duplicated.

If a contract is adapted from a form previously used for another client, references to the parties and terms of that contract may remain in place unnoticed. Adaptation of a contract may also result in grammatical mistakes. For example, the earlier contract may have involved two buyers, while the current contract involves a single buyer. The result could be subject/verb or noun/pronoun inconsistency, such as "Buyer have paid earnest money" or "Buyer shall be entitled to return of their earnest money if. . . ."

Read *In re Marriage of Johnson,* https://casetext.com/case/in-re-marriage-of-johnson-24, taking particular note of the testimony of the attorneys. Imagine the cost of litigating this problem, which most likely arose from a typographical/proofreading error. Obviously, one attorney has potential malpractice liability. A 2005 article in the American Bar Association publication *Law Practice Today* states that four out of five attorneys will experience at least one malpractice claim in their careers (http://www.abanet.org/lpm/lpt/articles/mgt04052.html).

Lawyers frequently rely on paralegals for proofreading. If possible and permitted by your instructor, exchange papers with a classmate before submitting your next graded assignment. Proofread each other's papers to see how different it is to proof a document written by someone else. Here are some tips to help you avoid the kind of problem that led to this case:

- Avoid proofreading your own work. If you must proofread your own work, allow enough time so that you can set the document aside, ideally for more than 24 hours, before you proof it.
- Proofread from paper, not from your computer screen.
- Proofread at a time of day when you feel alert.
- If possible, read aloud or have someone else read aloud to you.
- To ensure that you look at each word and don't "slide" ahead, keep a piece of paper under each line as you read or touch your finger to each word.
- Proofread in a location that is quiet and free of all distractions.

- For particularly important documents, proofread twice. Read the document once, focusing on meaning and implementation; read it a second time to look for spelling and grammatical errors.
- Some people find that reading backwards, word-by-word, is most effective for finding spelling and grammatical errors.
- Do a final "skim" to check headings, page numbers, and other "structural components" that may have been missed.

Assignment 12-6

1. Read *In re Marriage of Johnson,* http://www.abanet.org/lpm/lpt/articles/mgt04052.html. Explain, in your own words, why the court did not apply the parol evidence rule to bar testimony.

2. Use an online search engine to find the terms of use for Fastcase legal research. Answer the following, citing the contract language on which you base your answer:

- ◆ A paralegal wants to start a legal research business and advertise to the public: "Ask me anything. I will find a case that relates to the situation and e-mail it to you within 24 hours." The business will have a Web site on which the paralegal will simply copy an entire case from the Fastcase site as the "goonie case of the week." Do the terms of use permit these uses? Do you see any ethical problems?
- ◆ The goonie case of the week last week was Vonda Vengeful's divorce. She is upset and humiliated to have private details of her life on a Web site, so she sues both the paralegal and Fastcase. Fastcase wants paralegal to pay its defense costs. Does the agreement contain an indemnification provision or an exculpatory clause?
- ◆ Liam Lawstudent has a job offer with BigLaw (for big bucks), contingent on his graduation no later than next month. Liam is a bit of a procrastinator and put off work on his final paper until the night before it was due. He is using Fastcase for the research, but the site "crashes" just as he signs on. Unable to do his research, he asks for an extension. The professor refuses; Liam fails the course and will not graduate for four months. BigLaw withdraws its offer. Liam sues Fastcase for breach of contract. Liam wants to sue in his home state, Texas, and he wants a jury trial because he knows juries favor the "little guy" over big corporations. What results?

3. A short (and very bad) construction contract appears after this assignment. Identify the mistakes, ambiguities, and other problems with the contract.

EXHIBIT 12-1
Sample Construction Contract

Construction Contract
This contract is entered into on March 13, 2016,
between Jane E. Lehmann, 325 River Bluff Road, Elgin, IL 60120
("Owner") And Robert J. Schell, doing business as Schell Corp.,
P.O. Box 451, Elburn, IL ("Builder")

WHEREAS:

- Lehmann owns property at 776 Diane Ave., Elgin, IL, and wishes to build a house on that property.
- Builder is in the construction business and has agreed to build a house on Lehmann's property.
- The house will be built according to the blueprints and specification list and the final price shall be $475,000.00.

TERMS:

1. Schell shall complete construction on or before September 1, 2015. Construction shall be considered complete when the city issues a certificate of occupancy. The Owner may not occupy the property before the final price is paid.
2. Jane shall pay the purchase price in installments: $50,000 upon signing this contract; an additional $100,000 when the roof is complete; $500,000 when the windows are installed, and the balance upon issuance of a certificate of occupancy.
3. Builder shall comply with all applicable building codes and municipal regulations, but makes no warranty with respect to materials installed in the house, such as roofing, furnace, appliances, windows, and cabinetry. Any warranties must come directly from the seller or manufacturer of the items. It is understood that Schell will not perform all work himself, but will employ subcontractors for work such as plumbing, electrical wiring, and excavation.
4. The price does not include landscaping or a driveway, but only includes those things listed on the blueprints or specifications.
5. During the course of construction, the house shall be kept insured against fire or other casualty.
6. Builder shall pay all subcontractors promptly and shall provide Owner with signed lien waivers.
7. Builder has the right to show the house to prospective customers as a sample of his work.
8. At the time of the third payout, Smith shall make a formal inspection of the property and shall submit to Schell, in writing, a list of deficiencies and defects.

9. Shell shall provide any paperwork required by Owner's lender in order to obtain payouts during the course of construction and shall maintain liability insurance to compensate in the event of any injury to a worker or visitor at the building site.
10. If the Owner makes any changes in the plans or specifications, the Builder shall add the cost to the price and the owner shall pay the amount of the change promptly.

________________________ ________________________

Jane E. Lehmann Robert J. Schell

Career Corner

Stacey Hunt, CLA, CAS, is a litigation paralegal at Duggan Smith & Heath, LLP in San Luis Obispo, California. Her firm prosecutes and defends breach of contract actions, which can take many forms. "We have handled cases involving breach of a lease, a failure to properly survey a property, even breach of a contract to properly store fermenting wine." Whether the firm is representing plaintiff or defendant, the first thing Stacey does is carefully read the contract. "Our client was recently served with a complaint for breach of an operating agreement for a limited liability company. The attorney asked me to prepare an answer to file with the court. Before doing so I read the agreement and saw there was a mandatory arbitration clause that none of the attorneys had even noticed." Opposing counsel agreed to withdraw the complaint and proceed with mediation instead, once the issue was pointed out. "The client was very happy not to have to litigate the matter in court," said Stacey. In a contract dispute, the language in the contract will be looked at under a microscope. "Whoever drafted the contract may have thought it was airtight," says Stacey, "but a clever lawyer can find holes and new interpretations to cast doubt on the intention of the parties. And a clever litigation paralegal can learn to do that as well."

Review Questions

1. What part of a contract often begins with "WHEREAS," and what is the purpose of this section?
2. What is incorporation by reference?
3. What types of contracts require notarization?
4. What is a merger clause?
5. Assuming that the parol evidence rule does apply, for what purposes might evidence of oral agreements made before the written contract still be used?
6. Courts sometimes favor one of the parties in interpreting a contract. Which party is favored?
7. Identify at least five other rules courts use in interpreting contracts.

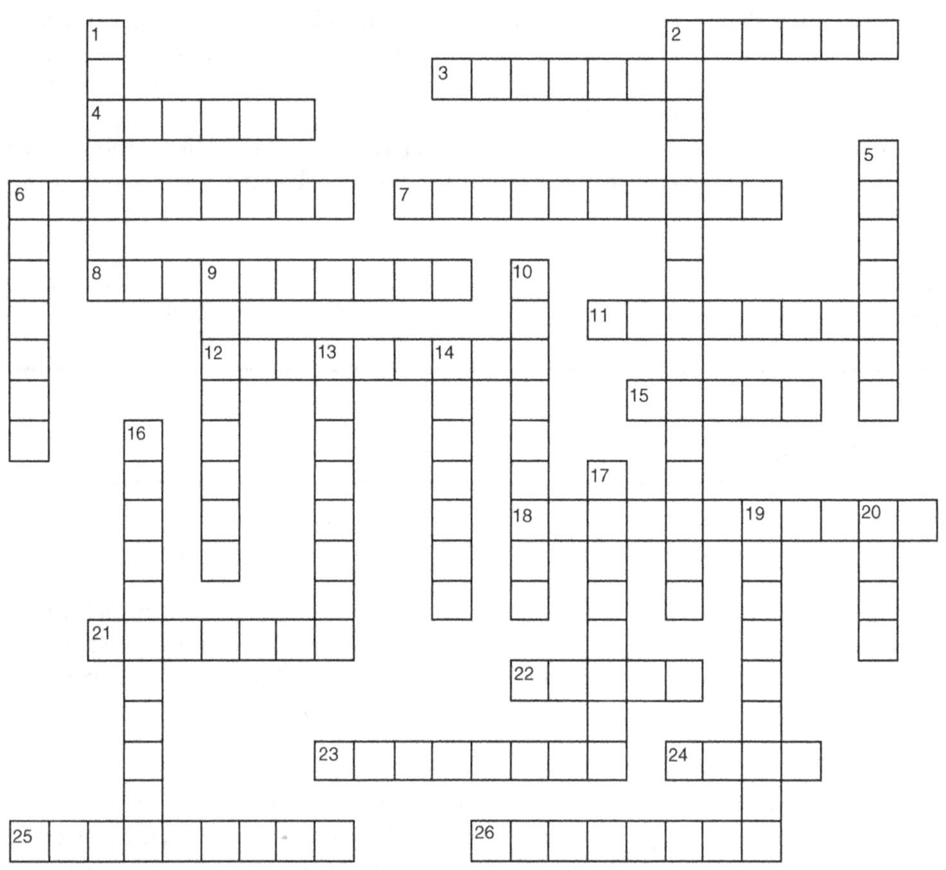

ACROSS

2. courts try to determine __________ of the parties
3. __________ terms; *e.g.*, ("Owner")
4. clause states this is final and complete agreement
6. evidence of a condition __________ not barred by parol evidence rule
7. a contract intended to be entire statement of agreement
8. evidence of __________ agreement not barred by parol evidence rule
11. parol __________ rule protects written contracts from attack
12. another term for parol evidence
15. proofreading is best done from a document on this
18. signatures on behalf of __________ may require a seal or other formalities
21. courts construe contract against party who __________ it
22. in contract interpretation, court looks as document as a
23. give background for contract
24. facts that would indicate contract was __________ or voidable may be admissible
25. courts favor finding an __________ contract
26. courts give words __________ accepted meanings

DOWN

1. spelled-out figures govern over
2. beginning of contract, introduces parties
5. recitals often begin with this word
6. self- __________ documents can serve as testimony
9. terms govern over general terms
10. __________ terms are given their __________ meaning
13. a contract to be __________ may have to be notarized
14. don't remove these from a signed contract
16. individually negotiated terms govern over
17. __________ dealings; important in contract interpretation
19. parol evidence may be allowed to explain
20. a notary can witness a signature or administer an

13

Working with Contracts

In some situations, a law office has not been involved in negotiating or drafting a contract, but is only called upon to implement its provisions. A paralegal's ability to read and understand the contract is essential. Chapter 12 discussed the physical layout of a contract and the usual component parts. This chapter completes the process; students will learn the steps for implementing an executed contract and the process for assisting in the creation of a contract.

Skills-based learning objectives	*How you will demonstrate your ability*
Use forms appropriately.	Assignments: Research sources of forms; choose and organize appropriate provisions for client.
Analyze potential problems in contract arrangements.	Assignments: Prepare interview questions to determine client needs; identify problems and propose solutions for client situation.
Implement client's contract objectives.	Assignments: Prepare a contract outline; negotiate contract terms; draft contract provisions.
Perform contract work without engaging in unauthorized practice of law.	Assignment: Research ethics rules to respond to specific fact situations.

A. Incoming Contracts
   1. Checklist for Incoming Contracts
   2. Understanding Particular Provisions

B. Creating a Contract
  1. Assessing Client Needs and Negotiating
  2. Drafting: Forms and Boilerplate
    a. Characteristics of a Good Contract
    b. Formbooks and Checklists
    c. Legalese
    d. Active Voice and Front-Loading
    e. Parallel Construction
    f. Sexism and the Plural Pronoun
    g. Misplaced Modifiers
    h. Padding
C. Contracts with the Federal Government
D. Practical and Ethical Issues

A. Incoming Contracts

Often, particularly if you work in a corporate law department, you will be called upon to implement or litigate a contract drafted by someone else. That "someone" may be the opposing party or may be out of the picture and not available for consultation about ambiguities. Understanding the contract will require use of the skills and rules learned in Chapter 12 and knowledge of how a contract is negotiated and drafted.

A paralegal working in contract compliance or implementation or even in contract litigation should have a system for dealing with the contract at issue. If you complete every step, every time, you are unlikely to make mistakes. If your position involves compliance and you are responsible for many contracts, uniformity is essential. To the greatest extent possible, try to ensure that the contracts for which you are responsible contain the same terms, are kept in the same place, and are implemented with the same procedures. Keep track of what works and what does not work, for purposes of future negotiations.

1. Checklist for Incoming Contracts

- Make work copies that you, the lawyer, and others can mark up. Do **not** unstaple the original; keep it, in pristine condition, in a safe place.
- Take a moment to think about your client's goals with respect to this contract: best possible price; putting an end to a dispute with workers; most reliable supply of a needed component; tax avoidance; and so forth. Also consider the goals of the other party, whether either party was under pressure in entering the contract, what alternatives were available to each party. Whatever the goal(s) and circumstances, your reading of the contract will be more effective if you keep them in mind.
- Read the contract, making notes as needed, especially concerning ambiguities and issues with regulatory agencies, and discuss those with your

supervisor. For every required action, including required notices, identify who is responsible for that action and the time frame. Enter the dates and actions on your (and your firm's) calendar or docket, giving yourself enough advance warning before each date requiring action. Enter other parties' obligations, too, to monitor compliance. Update as needed. If you are assisting in litigation, make a timeline of required dates as stated in the contract and dates on which the parties acted.

- Pay special attention to automatic renewal provisions, also called "evergreen clauses," and the date by which notice must be given to avoid automatic renewal. At the very least, every contract should be reviewed before it is allowed to renew. Start an assessment file to track problems and modifications during the initial term, so that necessary adjustments can be made upon renewal or renegotiation.
- Consider how to best monitor any indexing provisions and implement a system for doing so. Indexing clauses are also called escalation or de-escalation clauses. Example: Client Company entered into a contract with Top Transport. Because Client's manufacturing operation is far from any rail line and "out of the way" for even trucking, it was important to secure a long-term commitment. Unfortunately, at the time, the cost of gasoline was at an all-time high. Not wanting to be stuck with a price based on that cost for the duration of the contract, Client put in a provision that the cost of transport is XX% of the price of oil as listed on the XXXX Index, to be adjusted at XXX (weekly/monthly) intervals. It is essential that someone have a system of regular reminders to check the index and do the calculation.
- Pay particular attention to warranties and risk-shifting shipping provisions discussed in the next section.
- Obtain documents on the status of the businesses involved (*e.g.*, certified copies of formation documents).
- Note all requirements involving outsiders. If implementing a contract, place or calendar orders; if litigating, verify compliance and obtain copies. For example:
  a. Title search
  b. Certificates of insurance
  c. Copies of business licenses
  d. Survey
  e. Inspections/environmental disclosures
  f. Loan payoff documents
  g. **Uniform Commercial Code (UCC) search**
  h. Any other agency approvals

2. If implementing a contract, list documents you will create (*e.g.*, **escrow** instructions, financial settlement statements, deeds, **assignments**), and begin work. If litigating a contract, obtain copies of those documents if they have been created.
3. Start a "closing binder" or "trial notebook" or an equivalent file so that all of the documentation can be found easily.

UCC Search
Activity conducted to find security interests in personal property that have been recorded under UCC Article 9

Escrow
Account held for the benefit of others, into which parties typically deposit documents, instructions, and funds for a transfer of property

Assignment
Transfer of interest in property or some right (contractual entitlement) to another

In the future, working with contracts may involve "blockchain" technology, the technology that is the basis of bitcoin, to establish self-enforcing "smart contracts." Smart contracts work like automated escrow agreements: Parties get paid upon fulfillment of specified obligations. From http://about.smartcontract.com:

> Because smart contracts are machine readable/executable they can include conditions that allow them to interact with various IT systems eg: data feeds. Taking in data from external data feeds in realtime allows smart contracts to retrieve proof of contractual performance eg: deposit has been released to Y. They can also automatically control various IT systems like payment networks eg: Bitcoin, Stripe, Paypal, Bank APIs, etc . . . to automatically release payment to the correct party once their conditions have been completed. For Example: IF [Advertising Network #564445] sends [1,000,000 clicks] that [convert to purchases at a rate of 15% or more] , THEN release [$.002 for each of those clicks] to User/Account # 899782392.

Will it eliminate the need for lawyers and paralegals in contract implementation? No. Many contract disputes arise because of unforeseen events that are not programmed into the conditions. The same technology could eventually be used for law firm functions, such as time-keeping, billing or client escrows.

2. Understanding Particular Provisions

In working with contracts, admitting what you don't know can be more important than what you do know. It is a terrible "rookie mistake" to see a contract provision that you do not understand and make the assumption that it must be acceptable because it seems to appear in lots of contracts. If you cannot understand a particular clause, it is likely that the client and others won't understand it. When in doubt, ask your supervisor. Often those confusing provisions relate to financing, warranties, or shipment.

a. Financing

To resolve the question of who goes first (Does buyer pay before or after receiving seller's performance?), a contract may call for creation of an escrow. An escrow is an account held by an individual or company (*e.g.*, bank or title company) into which parties deposit documents and funds to complete a transaction. Escrows are very common in sales of real property. The parties deposit money, a mortgage, promissory note, escrow instructions, a financial breakdown, and other documents. When funding is complete and all required documents are in place, the escrow agent records the deed and disburses funds to the seller.

When a transaction involves a sale of goods and is covered by the UCC, particular steps may be required. A UCC search is conducted to find security interests in personal property that have been recorded under UCC Article 9. For example, a bank gives a builder a loan to buy an expensive backhoe. The bank files a **UCC financing statement** (a lien), typically with the secretary of state, listing the builder as debtor and the backhoe as collateral. If the builder tries to sell the backhoe, the UCC filing will show the buyer that the bank has a right to

UCC Financing Statement
Evidence that property is security for debt, typically filed with the secretary of state

collect what it is owed from the proceeds of sale. If the builder tries to borrow more money using that same backhoe as security, the filing shows the new lender that at least part of the value of the backhoe belongs to another lender. When the builder pays off the loan, the bank will file a release and the property will be free and clear. Lenders protect financial interests through UCC filings on consumer goods, commercial and farm equipment and products, fixtures, public-finance transactions, manufactured homes, timber to be cut, and as-extracted minerals. This is discussed further in other chapters.

b. Warranties

Express Warranties
Warranties created by the written or spoken word, demonstration, or depiction of a product

A contract may include **express warranties,** which may be full or limited. Under the federal Magnuson-Moss Warranty Act,[1] every written warranty on a consumer product (the law does not cover services or apply to commercial sales) that costs more than $10 must be designated as full or limited. A full warranty exists if there is no limit to the duration of implied warranties (discussed below); warranty service is provided to anyone who owns the product during the warranty period; warranty service is free of charge, including such costs as returning the product or removing and reinstalling the product when necessary; the consumer may choose express warranties created by written or spoken word or depiction of a product either a replacement or a full refund if, after a reasonable number of tries, the warrantor is unable to repair the product; and consumers are not required to perform any duty as a precondition for receiving service, except notification that service is needed, unless the warrantor can demonstrate that the duty is reasonable. Any written warranty that does not meet all of the criteria is a limited warranty. A warranty can be partially full and partially limited, based on parts of the product or periods of time. Federal regulations, enforced by the FTC, also govern what must be disclosed in a written warranty and when the terms must be disclosed.

The federal laws do not require a warranty, however, but only provide rules for situations in which written warranties are given. The laws do not cover express warranties that are not written. An express warranty can arise from oral statements, demonstrations of the product, or even pictures. A seller who shows a product being used in a way that is not being warranted must be careful to disclaim a warranty.

Implied Warranty of Merchantability
An implied warranty, given by a merchant seller, that goods are fit for usual purpose

Warranty of Fitness for a Particular Purpose
Implied warranty that arises when seller makes a recommendation

The Magnuson-Moss Warranty Act also generally prohibits a seller who offers an express warranty from modifying or disclaiming implied warranties. Those implied warranties are actually created by the states in their adoptions of the UCC. Implied warranties include warranty of merchantability; warranty of fitness for a particular purpose; and good title. The **implied warranty of merchantability** arises when a sale is made by a merchant who normally deals in goods of the type being sold and it is the buyer's right to assume that the goods are reasonably fit for the ordinary purposes for which such goods are used: in other words, that a toaster will toast. The **warranty of fitness for a particular purpose** arises when any seller (merchant or nonmerchant) makes a recommendation knowing the particular purpose for which a buyer will use the goods and

[1] 15 U.S.C. §2301 et seq.

knows that the buyer is relying on the skill and judgment of the seller to select suitable goods. The warranty of good title is an implied promise that the seller has good title without liens or infringements. All of these warranties arise without anything being said or written, but the UCC is very specific about how a seller may avoid making implied warranties

c. *Shipment*

Contracts for sales of goods often use shipping terms defined in the UCC. The shipping term F.O.B. (free on board) may be followed by a place name. If the place of shipment is named, the seller generally must ship the goods and bear the expense and risk of putting them into the possession of the carrier. If the term F.O.B. is followed by the place of destination, the seller generally must, at his own expense and risk, transport the goods to that place. The term F.O.B. may also identify a vessel or vehicle; in that case, the seller must also, at his own expense and risk, load the goods on board.

The term **F.A.S.** (free alongside) generally identifies a vessel and a port, and the seller must, at his own expense and risk, deliver the goods alongside the vessel in the manner usual in that port or on a dock designated and provided by the buyer; and obtain and tender a receipt for the goods in exchange for which the carrier is under a duty to issue a bill of lading.

B. Creating a Contract

1. Assessing Client Needs and Negotiating

As discussed in Chapter 3, a lawyer is in the best position to serve the client when the lawyer is given the opportunity to participate in negotiation and draft the contract. Paralegals are often involved in contract negotiations and must be especially careful to avoid overstepping the invisible line and "practicing law." With that limitation in mind, however, many lawyers would be lost without the assistance of a paralegal to keep the process and the results organized. Organization is particularly important and difficult when several contracts are being negotiated for a single transaction or when a single contract has multiple parties. You may need to keep a chart or spreadsheet to keep track of the details. In Chapter 3, you learned some basics on preparing for negotiations. Once negotiations are under way, prepare for drafting the contract:

- Start getting organized by creating a *checklist of provisions* typically included in a contract of the type you will be working with. You can look at formbooks (discussed later in this chapter) and samples (from your supervisor or your client) to create a checklist. You can also use the formbooks or client interview to start to learn the terminology that may be unique to the particular type of business involved. If your supervising attorney has not done so, you can use the checklist to *interview the client* and gain a thorough understanding of the client's goals and intentions, timeline, and the "chain of approval"[2] for the contract. Be sure to ask clients whether they have had similar contracts in the past: What worked and what did not work? Specifically ask the "what if" questions: What if the work falls behind schedule because of weather? What if your workers go on strike? Think about the parties to the contract. What do they really hope to accomplish? What is the least complicated way of achieving their goals? Use your imagination. How sophisticated are the parties, and what are their attitudes? Will they be able to understand the agreement? Will they want to comply, or are they likely to look for "loopholes"? Do the parties have equal knowledge? Is either party making assumptions about facts? Will this contract have an impact on outsiders, and can outsiders have an impact on the performance of this contract? The answers to these questions will dictate the need for detailed recitals, the tone and level of the language used, and even the obligations imposed.

- Locate and become familiar with statutes and regulations applicable to the parties or transaction and, if the contract involves a governmental entity, with laws such as the Truth in Negotiations Act, 10 U.S.C. §2304, and governmental cost accounting guidelines.
- *Organize* the provisions into an outline of related topics (*e.g.*, Duties and conditions; Breach and remedies; Enforcement). This will be the framework for negotiation and drafting.
- Maintain your own *form file;* keep a copy of every contract you work on to serve as a reference for what works and what does not work.
- Perhaps 95% of all contracts now originate in an electronic format and many of those are never printed. This can lead to sloppiness in keeping track of what is the most current version of the agreement. Even if the contract is printed, it is important to keep *track of its evolution.* Use the **redlining** or *track changes* feature in your word processing software and make sure every new draft is dated.

Redline
Feature in word processing software that enables changes in a document to be tracked

- If the document is being sent back and forth by e-mail, you may want to "lock" the document you send so that *changes cannot escape your attention.* Some word processing programs have a lock feature; some firms send drafts as PDF-format read-only files.
- You can also use the "merge and track changes" feature in word processing software to compare the version of a contract you sent with the version you got back. Being aware of changes and additions is particularly important with contracts governed by the UCC because of the battle-of-the-forms rule.
- Review the language of any letters of intent or "agreements in principle" exchanged during negotiations with the supervising attorney to ensure that the client does not inadvertently create unwanted obligations.

[2]In a business setting, it is common for mid-level employees to negotiate a contract, but people "up the chain of command" may have to approve and/or execute the contract.

2. Drafting: Forms and Boilerplate

In preparing a contract, most lawyers and paralegals start with a form, a sample of a contract prepared by someone else. Forms can be found in formbooks in any law library, can be purchased in office supply stores (landlords frequently buy single-page form leases), and online. The important thing to remember is that a form is just a starting point. There is no such thing as "one size fits all" in law. A form can provide you with a checklist, to help you be sure you haven't overlooked anything, and can suggest particular wording, but if you do nothing but fill in blanks, you are committing malpractice. You need to read every word and ask whether it applies to the situation and whether it is good or bad for your client and make appropriate deletions, additions, and changes. Even with a printed form from an office supply store, you can and must cross out terms you don't like and insert new terms.

Boilerplate
Standard terms included in most contracts

Most forms contain **boilerplate,** or standard terms that are included in every contract. Even boilerplate must be analyzed to determine whether it benefits or hurts the client. Common boilerplate clauses include statements concerning the law that will apply in the event of litigation (Illinois? California?), statements that terms should be read so that a male reference includes females and singular includes plural (would the client want this if the contract is intended to provide a special benefit to a particular person?), or statements that if one part of the contract is found to be invalid, the rest of the contract shall remain in effect (this is called a **severability clause,** or a saving clause, and *may not* be what the client wants).

Severability Clause
Contract provision that in the event that one part of the contract is found to be invalid, the rest of the contract shall remain in effect

---

Example

The following is a severability clause:
If any provision of this Agreement is held unenforceable by any court of competent jurisdiction, then such provision will be severed or modified to reflect the parties' intentions. All remaining provisions of this Agreement shall remain in full force and effect.

The language used in a contract must have the precise level of specificity needed to communicate the intentions of the parties. To achieve that level of specificity, you must become familiar with the rules of contract interpretation, discussed in Chapter 12, and some writing guidelines. As you start to choose or write the individual paragraphs in the contract, remember KISS—keep it short and simple.

a. Characteristics of a Good Contract

A good contract is:

- Well organized and easy to read
    - Related matters should be kept together.

- Sections, and sometimes even paragraphs, should have headings so that people attempting to find specific provisions can do so easily.
- If the contract is long, it should have an index.
- There should be no big blocks of print or extremely long sentences. If necessary, break subjects into subtopics, bullet points, or even charts, to ensure **visual accessibility.**

Example

A picture paints a thousand words. Consider: Prior to the Occupancy Date as defined herein, Tenant shall provide to Landlord proof of insurance with coverage limits of at least One Million Dollars ($1,000,000.00) combined single limit and bodily injury per accident, and Three Hundred Thousand Dollars ($300,000.00) bodily injury per person and property damage.

Before the Occupancy Date [we don't need to keep reminding each other that it was defined], Tenant shall provide to Landlord proof of insurance with the following limits:

Combined Single Limit	One Million Dollars ($1,000,000.00)
Bodily Injury per Accident	One Million Dollars ($1,000,000.00)
Bodily Injury per Person	Three Hundred Thousand Dollars ($300,000.00)
Property Damage	Three Hundred Thousand Dollars ($300,000.00)

- Thorough in identifying actors, consequences, and remedies
  - Every required action should identify the party required to take that action.
  - The contract should address the "who, what, when, where, why, and how" of each obligation of each party. As you know, contract law is "default law." The law will fill in any details not covered in the contract, perhaps to the detriment of your client. If a contract states that a person should do, or not do, something, it should also state what will happen if that person does not comply with the contract. Look at every provision and ask yourself, what if this does not happen?
- Internally consistent
  - A well-written contract never contains contradictory terms. Carefully read the contract as if you were the opposing party, looking for inconsistency and holes.
  - Make sure that the numbering system for paragraphs and sections makes sense, is consistent, and that references remain correct as the contract goes through changes during negotiations.
- Clear
  - Keep in mind that the parties often try to comply with the requirements of the contract without the benefit of legal advice. The contract should be understandable to the average person, who was not present during negotiations and who may not like the agreement.
  - People who are obligated by the terms of a contract may be looking for any possible excuse to avoid that obligation. Again, test the

contract by putting yourself in the position of the opposing party and looking for any ambiguities that might give you a "loophole."

The proper use of formbooks and checklists (such as the ABC checklist that follows) will help you produce contracts that are well organized and thorough. To ensure that your contract is clear and does not include loopholes, avoid legalese and other writing problems described below.

b. Formbooks and Checklists

Formbooks and boilerplate are useful because they make you consider and address matters that the client probably did not consider or mention. Get in the habit of looking for (when reading a contract) or considering (when drafting a contract) all of the following:

Delegation
Pass contractual obligations to another

- Assumptions; do recitals state the purpose and background of the agreement?
- Binding authority; who will sign, title and address of signatory, check status of any business entities and authority to bind the entity. Is notarization required?
- Changes; when and how may the parties modify the agreement?
- Delegation/assignment; may parties **delegate** (pass contractual obligations to another) or assign (pass entitlements to another)?
- Express conditions; conditions precedent, subsequent (see consideration chapter).
- Financing; liens, mortgages; are all payment amounts and terms clearly stated along with information about penalties, taxes, and interest?
- Guarantors, if any.
- Hold harmless/indemnification; is a party agreeing to reimburse for losses suffered as a consequence of specific conduct?
- Integration; is this the entire agreement, or are there outside documents?
- Joint and several liability?
- Kin (okay, it's a stretch); is the agreement binding on heirs, successors?
- Limitations on liability, limitations/standards for performance—*e.g.*, if landlord shall pay tenant's moving expenses in the event of early termination, is there any limit on the expense?
- Mitigation (see remedies chapter); are parties required to "cut losses" in the event of breach?
- Noncompetition/restrictive covenants (see Chapter 6), confidentiality clauses, and trade secrets.
- Ownership and risk of loss; who holds title to subject property at various stages? For example, if a buyer is making installment payments, at what point does buyer become owner?
- Perfect performance; to what extent can performance deviate from specifications? Are all performance terms, such as quantity and descriptions, unambiguously stated?
- Queries and notices; where are inquiries and notices sent? Under what circumstances must a party provide the others with notice of specific events?

- **R**emedies; does every possible breach have a remedy? Liquidated damages? Is ADR required? Is mediation or arbitration in client's best interest; where will it occur; how will arbitrator be chosen; do parties retain right to go to court?
- **S**everability; is this an "all-or-nothing" deal?
- **T**ime; is time "of the essence," or are delays acceptable? Are all dates clearly stated?
- **U**sage of terms; are terms used in ways different than generally understood?
- **V**enue, Jurisdiction; in case of litigation, and choice of governing law.
- **W**arranties; review UCC implied warranties that may arise if not disclaimed and consider express warranties that client may want or give.
- E**X**cuses; on what grounds will the contract terminate (*e.g.*, death, bankruptcy)?
- **Y**ield; if contract involves money that may earn interest, stock that may earn a dividend, or property that may earn rent; does the contract address the issue?

Assignment 13-1

a. Find an online source of legal forms and report to the class the cost of a typical form, whether you were able to determine who prepared the form, and whether the forms appeared to be useful.
b. Assume that the contract in Appendix B came into your office today, having been signed yesterday. Your firm represents the developer. The contract was prepared by the city's attorney. Make a list of tasks, dates to calendar, and any questions, problems, or ambiguities.
c. In Chapter 3 (Assignment 3-6) you met cousins Jane and Barb, who are ready to buy a one-bedroom condo at the beach for vacation use. Based on the interview and negotiation you participated in, draft their contract. If you did not participate in the interview or negotiations, your instructor can give you basic terms about shared expenses, scheduling use of the condo, and so forth.
d. Alternative assignment: Draft only the provisions relating to the furniture in the cousins' condo and/or provisions relating to the schedule of use of the condo and whether the cousins may allow outsiders to use it.
e. Warranty and risk terms are particularly critical in contracts involving sales of goods. Visit your state's enactment of the UCC, and find the provisions concerning warranties.

   - ◆ Find and cite your state UCC's implied warranty of merchantability.
   - ◆ How can a seller exclude the warranty of merchantability?
   - ◆ Find and cite your state's version of the warranty of fitness for a particular purpose?
   - ◆ Find and cite your state UCC's provision relating to express warranties. List the ways that an express warranty may be created.

Now, find the "risk of loss" provisions relating to shipping.

- Find and cite your state UCC descriptions of F.O.B. and F.A.S.
- What does the UCC assume if the parties do not address the risk of loss during shipment? Cite your state's UCC for your answer.
- Use computer-assisted legal research (CALR) to find and summarize, for class discussion, a case from your jurisdiction involving one of the UCC implied warranties. As you probably know, jobs appropriate for people with paralegal credentials do not always have the title "paralegal" or "legal assistant," particularly when those jobs are within corporations. Use a job search site and report to the class about jobs described as contract compliance, contract administration, or contract manager.

Legalese
Overly formal, often archaic language sometimes used in legal documents

c. *Legalese*

While some legal terms have unique meaning, many are simply pompous and confusing. Before you use "legalese," ask yourself whether the term could be replaced with a plain English word without losing unique meaning. Also ask yourself whether you understand the term, and never use a term you do not understand.

Examples

<u>Terms with Unique Meaning</u>
Consideration
Delegate
Assign
Severable
Financing Statement

<u>Pompous Legalese</u>
Party of the First Part
Hereinafter
Aforementioned
Forthwith
Thence
Heretofore
Herewith
Hereby

Active Voice
The subject of the sentence acts

Passive Voice
Subject is acted upon

d. *Active Voice and Front-Loading*

With active voice, the subject of the sentence acts: "The builder shall obtain liability insurance before beginning construction." With **passive voice,** the subject is acted upon: "Liability insurance shall be obtained before construction begins." Active voice usually makes sentences shorter and easier to understand. More importantly, active voice may clarify expectations. If the passive voice example appeared in a contract, isn't it possible that both the builder and the owner would assume that the other party is responsible for obtaining insurance? The result might be catastrophic—no insurance.

Can you understand this? "It is agreed that the use of the Condominium by persons other than the Owners, in compliance with the Association's bylaws, rules, and regulations, shall be subject to prior agreement by the Owners as described herein relating to prior agreement for changes to furnishings or decorating." You probably can understand it, given enough time, but it would be easier to "front-load" the actors or the most important matter and put two ideas into two sentences. "Persons other than the Owners may use the Condominium with the prior agreement of the Owners as described in Paragraph 9. Such use must comply with the Association's bylaws, rules, and regulations." When confronted with a monster sentence, ask yourself: Who/what is the actor and what is the most important clause? If there is more than one important clause, consider breaking it into two sentences, then reorganize the sentence(s).

e. Parallel Construction

Each phrase within a sentence should follow the same grammatical structure. Not parallel: "The employee's responsibilities shall include identification of new potential customers, training support staff, and to minimize loss." Parallel: "The employee's responsibilities include identifying new potential customers, training support staff, and minimizing loss."

f. Sexism and the Plural Pronoun

A good writer consciously avoids sexist language, and, for example, will write "police officer" rather than "policeman," except when referring to a specific male individual. Sometimes, however, that good intention can lead to bad grammar: "Every buyer must pick their own carpet." There are several ways to avoid the singular/plural problem. You could use the plural consistently: "All of the buyers must choose their own carpet" or switch to second person: "As a buyer, you must choose your carpet." Unless it changes the meaning, you could omit the pronoun: "Each buyer must choose carpet." You can also use "his or her" or "he or she" in moderation.

g. Misplaced Modifiers

"The employee must, at all times, keep a complete record of all customer contacts on his desk." Need the record include only those contacts kept on his desk? Sometimes two sentences are better than one: "The employee must keep a complete record of all customer contacts. The record must be available on the employee's desk at all times."

The employee in question undoubtedly understood what was meant in the first example. Consider, however, that the employee might not want to have understood it. The employee is now leaving to start his own business and wants to be able to claim he is not prohibited from having contact with his former employer's customers because they are not in the record.

h. Padding

Many of us learned bad habits in high school when we padded our essays to reach the teacher's requirement for length. In law, despite the tradition of long, impenetrable documents, fewer words make for better writing. Verbosity often makes the contract harder to understand and less accurate.

> Why do we see so many wordy, incomprehensible forms?
>
> In ancient England, few people could read or write and paper was an expensive commodity. On those rare occasions when a person needed to reduce a matter to writing (writing a will or an important contract), a scrivener would prepare the document. The scrivener was paid on a "per word" basis and had a strong interest in writing: "I give, devise, bequeath, and convey to my son Brian, any and all interest I may have in my horse Nell or any other horse I may own at the time of my death," rather than "I give my horse to Brian." From this tradition evolved the forms we see today!

A common example of verbosity at its worst is the use of future tense: "Landlord shall have the right to inspect." If this "shall" be the case, when will it begin? It is simpler and more accurate to say, "Landlord has the right to inspect," or "Landlord may inspect." Similarly, it is simpler and clearer to say, "Tenant shall procure insurance," rather than "The parties agree that tenant shall procure insurance." Similarly, some drafters "over agree," prefacing each obligation with "it is agreed that." It's a contract! The whole thing is an agreement. Instead of "it is agreed that neither Jane nor Barb may rent the condominium," simply say "Neither Jane nor Barb may rent." Always proofread several drafts, trying to eliminate unnecessary words, phrases, and sentences.

Examples

Wordy	***Better***
Due to the fact that	*because*
At that point in time	*then*
In accordance with	*under*
File an action	*sue*
Subsequent to	*after*
Prior to	*before*
Written document	*document*
For the purpose of	*to*
In lieu of	*instead*
In spite of the fact that	*although*
With the exception of	*except*
With reference to	*about*
Afford an opportunity	*allow*
Have a tendency to	*tend*
Have an impact upon	*affect*

Assignment 13-2

Read the interview transcript in Appendix A. Using that transcript, do the following, as assigned by your instructor:

1. Using formbooks in a law library and on the Internet, find forms for contracts involving performers. It is best to use formbooks or sources dedicated to legal forms, but even using a search engine, like Google, will produce results. Outline clauses that should be included in this contract, organized in a logical way, and information that will be needed but was not obtained in the interview.
2. Pick clauses from the forms that meet this client's needs, and put them together, according to your outline, making changes as needed to meet this client's needs.
3. The paralegal in this scenario was not well prepared and allowed the client to steer the interview and, possibly, missed important information. A good way to prepare for an interview is to look at forms in advance. Other great online sources of forms include http://www.ilrg.com/forms and http://www.uslegalforms.com. Look at sample forms, and prepare a list of questions to interview a client for one of the following. You may not find a sample for the exact situation, but looking at contracts for similar situations will help.
   a. A client is going to allow a college student to live in her house in exchange for 15 hours per week of child care.
   b. A client is going to provide hand-painted sweatshirts to a local gift store, which will sell them on behalf of the client. Before starting work on this, be sure you understand the definition of **consignment.**
   c. The client is your former coworker, a paralegal who has decided to work freelance (as an **independent contractor**) and wants a contract to present to the lawyers who will be using his services. Consider the ethical rules in deciding on topics.
4. Rewrite the following so that an average person could understand them.

Consignment
An arrangement under which goods are placed for sale, but title does not transfer to the seller

Independent Contractor
One hired to undertake a specific project using his own methods (not an employee)

The parties hereby agree that use and occupancy of the Condominium and/or common areas, such as the party room and parking deck previously referenced herein, shall be exclusive during each individual Owner's reserved days as previously defined herein; provided that, the Owner using the facilities may agree to share use and occupancy during any specific period, by giving permission in advance of said reserved days. The limitation described herein shall not apply to informal drop-in visits by the Owner during days other than her reserved days; provided, however, that prior to such informal visits shall be preceded in all events by at least one hour's notification by telephone and that said visiting owner shall not use her key to enter. Nor shall either Owner allow any other person, including family members, tradespersons, or deliveries, to enter the Unit during the Other Owner's reserved times without such prior approval.

Promptly after receipt by an indemnified party hereunder of notice of the commencement of any action, such indemnified party, if a claim in respect thereto is to be made against an indemnifying party hereunder, give notice to the indemnifying party of such commencement, but failure to so notify the indemnifying party shall not relieve said party of any liability that it may have to the identified party except to the extent the indemnifying party demonstrates that the defense of such action was prejudiced thereby. If any such action shall be brought against an indemnified party and it shall give notice to the indemnifying party thereof, the indemnifying party shall be entitled to participate therein and, to the extent that it desires, to assume the defense thereof with counsel satisfactory to the indemnified party and, after notice thereof, the indemnifying party shall not be liable to such indemnified party hereunder for any fees of other counsel or any other expenses, in each case subsequently incurred by such indemnified party in the defense thereof, other than reasonable costs of investigation. If an indemnifying party assumes the defense of such action, no compromise or settlement thereof may be effected by said indemnifying party without the indemnified party's express consent (which shall not be unreasonably withheld) and that party shall have no liability with respect to any compromise or settlement thereof effected without said consent.

Notwithstanding any other statement herein contained, if the Tenant shall file a voluntary petition in bankruptcy or shall be adjudicated a bankrupt or insolvent in any court of competent jurisdiction and such adjudication shall not be promptly vacated or if Tenant shall file a bankruptcy petition or answer for reorganization or any involuntary reorganization bankruptcy petition shall be filed and shall be approved or if there shall be any general assignment of tenant's assets for the benefit of creditors or if a receiver shall be appointed for the business or property of Tenant and shall not be promptly vacated or in the event of any assignment or transfer by Tenant in violation of this lease or in the event of the termination or dissolution of tenant as an entity, then, upon the happening of any such event, this lease shall terminate and come to an end and all payments not yet due shall become accelerated and immediately due.

C. Contracts with the Federal Government

Government contracting is a subject so complex that entire books are written about it, the Small Business Administration has an office focused on it, and colleges offer certificates in it. This discussion is intended only to give you an overview.

A government contract is about more than the contract itself. In order to promote other agendas, the government often establishes goals for awarding contracts to particular types of businesses: for example, business that use recycled products; "green businesses," service-disabled veteran–owned, and woman-owned small businesses. These categories change with the government's priorities, and potential contractors may have to register and be qualified for particular programs.

Success in government contracting is all about the process and following the rules. For example, a government contractor is subject to the policy dictates of the governmental entity with which it contracts, including requirements related to affirmative action, drug-free workplace, subcontracting, and minimum employee wages. Compliance with affirmative action requirements is often achieved by subcontracting. Contractors must comply with restrictions on giving a government employee anything of monetary value, including gifts, entertainment, loans, travel, favors, hospitality, lodging, discounts, and meals. The restrictions are found in Office of Government Ethics regulations, 5 C.F.R. §2601 *et seq.* There are also regulations that prohibit contractors from discussing employment with certain federal officers and employees.

Federal contracting is governed primarily by three statutes, which are implemented by the Federal Acquisition Regulation (FAR), Title 48 of the CFR, and many agency-specific regulations that supplement the FAR:

- Armed Services Procurement Act, 10 U.S.C. §§2301-2314 (defense contracts)
- Federal Property and Administrative Services Act, 40 U.S.C. §§471-514 and 41 U.S.C. §§251-260 (contracts with civilian agencies)
- Competition in Contracting Act, scattered sections of 10, 31, 40, and 41 U.S.C. (requires federal agencies to seek and obtain "full and open competition" wherever possible).
  - The "full and open competition" requirement can be met by sealed bidding, subject to rigid requirements, or by way of the more flexible competitive negotiation process.
  - The sealed bidding process is initiated by an agency's contracting officer, who issues an invitation for bids, through display in a public place, announcement in newspapers or trade journals, publication in the federal government's *Commerce Business Daily*, and by mailing to contractors on the agency's solicitation mailing list. Bids must be submitted by the stated deadline and must be "responsive" to the invitation for bids: that is, the bid must contain a definite, unqualified offer to meet the material terms of the invitation. The regulations are very specific on how contract prices may be stated in various types of contracts (*e.g.*,

fixed price, incentives, hourly rates). The FAR also requires a finding of responsibility prior to awarding the contract to the lowest bidder. To be "responsible," a prospective contractor must have adequate financial resources to perform the contract; be able to comply with the delivery or performance schedule; have a satisfactory performance record; have a satisfactory record of integrity and business ethics; have the necessary organization, experience, accounting and operational controls, and technical skills; have necessary production, construction, and technical equipment and facilities.
- If the negotiation process is used, the process begins with issuance of a Request for Proposals (RFP) that states the agency's need, anticipated terms and conditions of the contract, information the contractor must include in the proposal, and factors that the agency will consider in evaluating proposals and awarding the contract. Under the Truth in Negotiations Act, 10 U.S.C. §2306a, 41 U.S.C. §254b, a contractor or subcontractor is required to submit "cost or pricing data" if any negotiated contract, subcontract, or modification is expected to exceed $500,000.

Government contracts often contain 50-75 standard terms and conditions, called "clauses," many of which are nonnegotiable under FAR and will be read into the contract, even if not included. Some are the kinds of clauses often found in private contracts; others are unique:

- A Termination for Convenience clause permits the government to terminate the contract, at any time, without cause, when termination is in the government's best interest. If the government gives notice of intent to terminate, the contractor must immediately consult the FAR and follow the procedures for claiming recovery of costs and losses.
- The Changes clause enables the government to make unilateral changes to the contract during performance, so long as those changes fall within the contract's scope. The contractor is entitled to an "equitable adjustment" if either a formal or informal change results in increased contract costs or time of performance, but the contractor must strictly comply with the FAR to recover those costs.
- The Default clause resembles the "termination for cause" and permits the government to terminate a contract for default when the contractor has breached the contract. Like the "cover" right provided the nondefaulting party under the UCC, the standard Default clause entitles the government to procure the supplies or services required under the terminated contract and charge the excess costs to the terminated contractor

Government contracts distinguish between commercial and noncommercial items and services. Commercial services are items of a type offered and sold competitively in substantial quantities in the commercial marketplace based on established catalog or market prices for specific tasks performed or specific outcomes to be achieved and under standard commercial terms and conditions. Contracting for commercial items and services has been streamlined and is now much simpler than in the past. For noncommercial items or services, contractors who want to recover their costs must comply with very complex cost accounting methods. Under certain circumstances, the government has the right to audit a contractor's price proposal prior to negotiations, as well as to audit pertinent records, books, and other data of the contractor at any time up to three years after final contract payment.

The False Claims Acts impose sanctions for the submission of false or fraudulent claims, 31 U.S.C. §§3729-3733; 18 U.S.C. §287. When the government relies upon a false statement in awarding a contract, and then makes payments under that contract, the invoices may be considered a false claim. Failure to bill strictly in accordance with the contract can also lead to a false claim.

There is a special process for disputes arising under a government contract under the Contract Disputes Act, 41 U.S.C. §601. A contractor that does not strictly follow the process risks losing its right to proceed against the agency. A contractor must continue performance pending resolution of a dispute with the government after initiating the process by presenting a "claim" containing certain specific elements to the agency's contract officer. If the contractor and the government do not negotiate a resolution, the contract officer issues a "final decision," which may be appealed to an agency board of contract appeals. The BCA's decision may be appealed to the U.S. Court of Appeals for the Federal Circuit. If there is no such board with jurisdiction, the contract officer's decision may be appealed to the U.S. Court of Federal Claims.

D. Practical and Ethical Issues

Paralegals and lawyers have unique ethical concerns in contract negotiation. Paralegals and their supervising attorneys must be careful that the paralegal's role does not "cross the line" into unauthorized practice of law. While the line is not clear, some states are making efforts to give lawyers and their assistants more guidance, so that lawyers can make more efficient use of paralegals and keep costs down. For example, the Indiana Rules of Professional Conduct include a special section on Use of Non-Lawyer Assistants (http://www.in.gov/judiciary/rules/prof_conduct).

Assignment 13-3

Read *Cincinnati Bar Ass'n v. Cromwell* (Ohio 1998), http://www.supremecourt.ohio.gov/rod/docs/pdf/0/1998/1998-Ohio-237.pdf. If your state has a good definition of unauthorized practice of law, consult that definition. Otherwise, you may want to visit other state bar association sites, such as http://www.myazbar.org/LawyerRegulation/upl.cfm. With these references in mind, discuss:

- Paul Paralegal is a "contract specialist" for a large corporation. The corporation does not have a legal department or a lawyer on staff. Paul's job includes ordering supplies from various companies. In doing so, Paul negotiates terms, chooses an appropriate contract from several forms in his files, fills in blanks and sometimes writes his own language, and sends the contract to his boss for signature. Is this the unauthorized practice of law?
- Pam Paralegal works for a law firm that specializes in debt collection. She communicates with debtors by phone and mail in an effort to obtain payments. The firm gives her wide discretion. For example, a debtor may owe $10,000; Pam can negotiate with the debtor and can accept a payment of as little as half of the original debt without consulting her supervisor. Pam is motivated to obtain the highest possible payment because she is paid a percentage of what she brings in. Is Pam involved in unauthorized practice of law? Do you see any other ethical problems? Do you think there might be other laws involved?

While prohibitions on unauthorized practice indicate that the lawyer must have ultimate responsibility for the contract, even the lawyer does not have complete authority and must act on the client's decisions.

Career Corner

Jennifer P. is the Global Strategic Project Analyst/Salesforce Administrator at Magnetrol International. Her previous jobs with the company have included Corporate Compliance Administrator and Contract Specialist. After earning her paralegal degree from an ABA-approved community college paralegal program, she worked at private law firms before joining Magnetrol. Jenn, who also has two children, feels that her job is a perfect fit for her personality because she loves projects that require great attention to detail. While she has often been involved in drafting contracts, Jenn finds a greater challenge in dealing with contracts prepared by others. With respect to "incoming contracts," she advises: "Always start by reading the contract in its entirety. Ensure you have all referenced addenda and review all cited regulations. Create a comprehensive summary that includes all deadlines, risks, and requirements for each party."

Assignment 13-4

Use your bookmarked state ethics site. Attorney Al has been negotiating a contract for Chris Client, who is selling a business. The negotiations have not gone well. This morning the opposing party called Al with an offer that was so bad it was insulting. Al does not even want to waste time telling Chris about the offer; Al is concerned that Chris will become upset or angry. May Al simply reject the offer without contacting Chris?

Review Questions

1. What are the four most important characteristics of the body of a contract?
2. How is a UCC search conducted?
3. What is an escrow arrangement?
4. How can a paralegal keep track of changes made to drafts of a contract during the negotiation process? How can a paralegal ensure that the other side does not make changes that go unnoticed?
5. Give examples of typical boilerplate clauses.
6. What is a severability clause?
7. What is the most helpful function of forms and formbooks?
8. Why is it especially important to know the warranty provisions of the UCC when you are working with a contract that is subject to the UCC? Would it be sufficient to simply omit any unwanted warranties from the written contract?

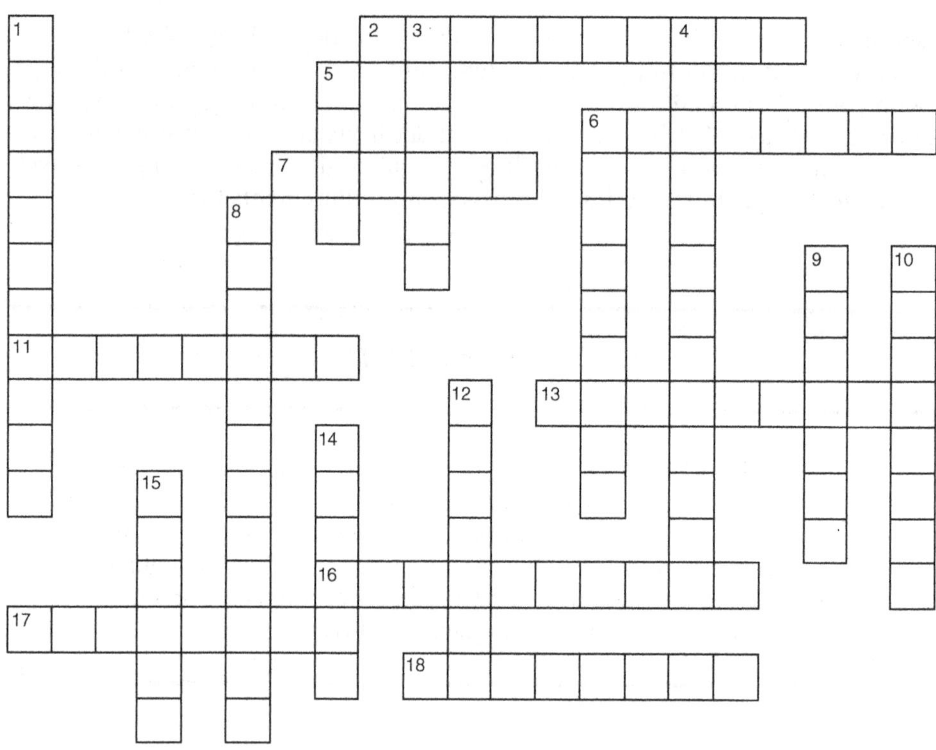

ACROSS

2. passing on contractual obligations
6. a contract that is to be __________ generally must be notarized
7. a UCC __________ is done to determine whether there are liens against personal property
11. pompous and confusing language
13. a UCC __________ statement is filed to make a public record of personal property being used as collateral
16. passing along your contractual entitlements
17. a misplaced __________ can change the meaning of a sentence
18. paragraphs at the beginning, giving background to contract

DOWN

1. standard language common to most contracts
3. an account into which documents and money are deposited to complete a transaction
4. __________ by reference makes an outside document part of the contract
5. another term for a security interest
6. tracking changes as a document is negotiated
8. a __________ clause addresses whether the rest of the contract remains valid if part is found to be invalid
9. __________ term; a shorthand way for reference to a person, place, or event
10. proper spelling; order entered by a judge
12. __________ voice; the subject is acted upon
14. a __________ public may witness a signature, authenticate a document
15. __________ voice is best for legal writing

Appendix A

◆ ◆ ◆

Sample Client Interview for Assignment

◆ ◆ ◆

Marty Gupta has been Attorney Janna Hart's client for many years. Two years ago Marty formed a corporation, M.G., Inc., that bought and remodeled a building in Elgin, Your State, to operate a café. The café, Marty's Place, has been very successful and Marty now wants to offer entertainment on some evenings. Marty made an appointment to discuss creation of a contract form. Ms. Hart had an emergency court call on another matter and asked her paralegal, Guillermo, to handle the interview. This is a transcript; Guillermo is identified as G and Marty is M.

G: Marty Gupta? Hi, I'm Guillermo Ruiz; please call me Bill. I'm going to talk to you about what you need in your contract.

M: Hi. Are you the new lawyer? I expected to see Janna.

G: No, I'm Janna's paralegal. Janna had an emergency and didn't want you to have to wait on this.

M: Paralegal? Are you a law student?

G: No, I graduated from a paralegal program. I assist Janna with research and putting together information and I work on documents. I won't be taking Janna's place as your legal advisor. Today I am just going to get the basic information about what you want, and then I will pull together a few forms and we can start the process. It will be Janna who gives you the finished work and tells you how to use it. Having me today actually saves you money. I know you already have our fee sheet. The hourly rate for talking to me is about half the hourly rate for Janna (grinning) so you might want to see more of me!

M: (laughing) You have a point about that!

G: So, tell me what kind of contract you need.
M: Well, you know my business, Marty's Café? It's just down the street.
G: Yes, I eat lunch there pretty often.
M: Okay, that's where I've seen you before! Well, we are starting to get a pretty good evening crowd, and I was thinking getting some entertainment on a regular basis on Fridays and Saturdays. Maybe sometimes a dance band or a DJ. We have some pretty good folk singers around here. I want to have a contract to use when I hire them. I am kind of worried about advertising, you know, spending the money, then having the act not show up or whatever. I looked into it, and I have to figure it would cost me at least $500 for each date to advertise when I am having entertainment.
G: Okay, so you want to make sure you have a firm commitment. . . .
M: Right, these folks are artists, not businesspeople, and they can be a little difficult. I also want to make sure they know they have to show up on time and can't leave early. Oh, another thing, I want to get the person I want or the band I want. I don't want them sending a friend instead.
G: Let me guess . . . you've already had a couple of acts in and had some problems.
M: You've got that right. One guy was supposed to play guitar, and he got there and decided to do a comedy routine! Well, that fell flat. Then another one, a woman, she spent most of the evening trying to sell a CD she recorded. We've had a couple of them show up drunk or maybe stoned, and one almost started a fight with a customer.
G: That's incredible! You would think they'd want to make a good impression so they would be asked back.
M: Good impression—that is another thing. I don't want any of the guys showing up to do a show not wearing a shirt or shoes . . . and the women too. . . . I did have one show up in a bikini top and a wrap skirt.
G: Wow. Okay, what else concerns you?
M: Believe it or not, safety. That's an old wooden building, you know. We can't have them up there smoking or lighting candles or anything like that.
G: Got that. Okay, now what is the deal with hiring these folks? Will it be long term? Might you have the same band for several weeks?
M: Not at all. I might ask an act back if it's good, but no guarantees. I want it clear that this is not like being hired for a job. One-time deal, they pay their own taxes, whatever. . . .
G: Okay, so they are independent contractors and. . . .
M: What is that?
G: An independent contractor is someone who is self-employed. You hire him to do some work for you, but he isn't your employee.
M: So, if I use that term, I am protected against all liability to these people? I don't want to be paying their hospital bills if they fall off the stage and don't have any insurance.
G: (shaking his head and smiling) Now, you know nothing in law is that simple! There are a number of things we can do to try protect you from liability, and Janna is going to decide what will work best and go over that

with you. I don't want to overstep my bounds here and start giving you legal advice. But don't worry; Janna will give some serious thought to your liability concerns.

M: Well, okay . . . but I am nervous. I do have some employees, and I carry insurance for them, but these performers are different.

G: How does it work with paying them?

M: I don't want to pay them until after the performance. I can give them a check on the night they perform, after they are done. I am always there. Sometimes they want cash, but I can't guarantee that.

G: Do you ever give them a deposit up front?

M: Well, I never have. Not yet. I suppose I might have to if I wanted to get a group that is in demand. You know what? I don't want to do that. Hey, here is a question. What about the music they sing? Could I be sued if they were violating copyright or something?

G: I'll let Janna know you want to talk about that and consider it for the contract.

M: C'mon, just tell me. Could somebody sue me if one of these guys gets up and sings somebody else's music or, I dunno, copies a comedy routine? You know, what about these DJs? What kind of permission do they have to get to play the recordings if they do it as a business?

G: (laughing) Wow, you are a tough one! I'll do some research on that and have Janna get to you with an answer. So, back to the facts. You mentioned something about a stage. Do you have any equipment or lighting you provide?

M: All right, I can see you won't crack under pressure (laughing). There are some can lights above the stage, but some of these folks bring their own. You should see some of the setups they have. Sometimes it takes them an hour to get ready and another to get it taken down.

G: Do you let them in early for that? Does it interfere with your business?

M: They can come early or stay late, but I don't pay for that time if it's hourly. Usually it's not hourly. Usually they just have a price. Some are hourly. Anyway, they can get the stuff in through the alley door. Actually, I have to insist on that. They sometimes don't like it because it involves using some steps. But they can't bring that stuff in through the dining room, where people are eating.

G: Okay, that about covers it. I'll get to work on this, and you can expect to hear from us in about a week.

Appendix B

◆ ◆ ◆

Sample Land Exchange Agreement

◆ ◆ ◆

This Land Exchange Agreement ("Agreement") is made as of this 21st day of March, 201x, by and between Landwer Development Company, a Wisconsin corporation ("Developer"), and the City of Appleton, Wisconsin, a municipal corporation ("City").

WHEREAS, the Developer is the owner of the real property legally described as [legal description] ("Parcel 1"); and

WHEREAS, the City is the owner of the real property legally described as [legal description] ("Parcel 2"); and

WHEREAS, the City and the Developer wish to exchange their properties under the terms and conditions set forth herein.

NOW THEREFORE, in consideration of the mutual covenants and conditions contained herein, the parties agree as follows:

1. EXCHANGE TERMS. Developer and the City acknowledge that Parcel 1 and Parcel 2 are of like kind and equal value. Pursuant to Section 1031 of the Internal Revenue Code, the Developer will convey Parcel 1 to the City and the City will convey Parcel 2 to the Developer at Closing. At Closing, each will execute and deliver a general warranty deed conveying marketable title to the Exchange Property to the other. The Developer shall convey Parcel 1 to the City together with any easements or restrictions of record which do not interfere or prevent the City from utilizing it, but free and clear of all liens, encumbrances, encroachments, and special assessments levied or assessed. The City shall convey Parcel 2 to the Developer together with any easements or restrictions of record, but free and clear of all liens, encumbrances, encroachments, and special

assessments levied or assessed. Developer acknowledges Parcel 2 will be used for development of affordable housing as described in the City's most recently approved Master Plan.

2. DEDICATIONS AND EASEMENTS. After the date of this Agreement, but prior to Closing, neither Party shall dedicate, gift, transfer, mortgage, or convey any interest in either Parcel 1 or Parcel 2.

3. TESTS. The City and the Developer shall each have the right for thirty (30) days after the date of this Agreement, at each party's own expense, to undertake an environmental audit, a professional wetlands delineation, professional floodplain analysis, survey, grading, and soil tests (collectively "Tests") on the property each party is to receive. Each party shall, upon the execution of this Agreement, promptly furnish to the other, any and all documents or reports which each party has in its possession which cover all or any portion of the property to be conveyed with regard to any previous Tests. Each shall allow the other and its representatives and agents reasonable access onto the property to be conveyed to conduct such Tests. Developer agrees to indemnify, defend, and hold the City harmless against all claims for injuries to persons on or damage to the parcel caused by the Tests or by those conducting the Tests requested by Developer; City agrees to indemnify, defend, and hold the Developer harmless against all claims for injuries to persons on or damage to the parcel caused by the Tests or by those conducting the Tests requested by Developer.

4. Each party shall have thirty (30) days after the date of this Agreement to notify the other, in writing, that a licensed professional has reviewed the results of the Tests and has determined and concluded either that the tested parcel may be subject to wetlands protection under federal or state laws or regulations, or that the tested parcel is otherwise not conducive or suitable for its intended uses based upon the Tests. In the event either party notifies the other of the above within such thirty (30) day period, the party giving such notice shall have ten (10) days from the date of notice of the test results to declare this Agreement null and void and if this option is exercised, then the parties shall have no further obligations under this Agreement.

5. TITLE INSURANCE. Within twenty (20) days after the date of this Agreement, or mutual written extension, each party shall, at its own expense, deliver to the other a copy of a title insurance commitment (the "Commitment") bearing an effective date subsequent to the date hereof in favor of the party to take title at closing for an owner's title insurance policy insuring marketability of the title to the property in the amount of the property's appraised value underwritten by a title insurance company acceptable to the party taking title. The copy of the Commitment shall be accompanied by a written statement of any objections to title to the property as disclosed by the Commitment. Any matter not objected to within such twenty (20) day period shall be deemed approved exceptions to title. Prior to Closing, each party shall deliver to the other a written statement of any objections which it could not, upon the exercise of due diligence in good faith, cure prior to or concurrent with the Closing. The party receiving such notice shall have the option of: (i) waiving such objections and proceeding with this Agreement or (ii) terminating this Agreement, and thereupon this Agreement shall be null and void and neither party shall have any further obligations hereunder.

6. TAXES. Real estate taxes on each party prior to the date of Closing shall be paid by the party holding title prior to Closing. Real estate taxes on each parcel after the date of Closing shall be paid by the party holding title after Closing. The taxes for the year of the date of Closing shall be prorated based upon the then most current property valuations and upon the most current tax rate as determined by law.

7. CLOSING. Closing shall occur within forty-five (45) days from the date of this Agreement.

8. RISK OF LOSS. Risk of loss or damage to each parcel shall rest with the party holding title until the time of delivery of possession.

9. CONDITION OF EXCHANGE PROPERTY. Each party acknowledges that its representatives or agents have examined the parcel it is to acquire prior to entering into this Agreement. This Agreement is based upon that inspection and not upon any representation or warranties or conditions by the other party's agents. Each party acknowledges the other is conveying the parcel on an "as is" basis, except for the warranties and representations as provided in this Agreement and the warranties in the general warranty deed.

10. DEFAULT. Time is agreed to be of the essence. In the event either party fails to comply with any of the material terms hereof, then the other party may declare a default and seek any remedy at law or in equity without notice or demand, including specific performance.

11. RIGHT TO EFFECTUATE EXCHANGE. The City acknowledges that the Developer may undertake an additional Internal Revenue Code Section 1031 tax deferred exchange of their interest in all or any portion of the Exchange Property. The Developer's rights and obligations under this Agreement may be assigned to facilitate such exchange. The City agrees to cooperate with the Developer and any assignee of the Developer to enable it to qualify for such exchange; provided that such cooperation shall not require the City to incur any additional costs or liability and the City shall be able to realize all intended benefits of this Agreement.

12. ASSIGNMENT. In the case of the assignment of this Agreement by either of the parties, prompt notice shall be given to the other party, who shall at the time of such notice be furnished with a duplicate of such assignment by such assignors. Any such assignment shall not terminate the liability of the assignor to perform, unless a specific release in writing is given and signed by the other party to this Agreement.

13. SEVERABILITY. If any non-economic mutual term or provision of this Agreement or the application thereof to any person or circumstances shall to any extent be invalid or unenforceable, the remainder of this Agreement or the application of such term or provision to persons or circumstances other than those as to which it is held invalid or unenforceable shall not be affected thereby, and each term and provision of this Agreement shall be valid and enforced to the fullest extent permitted by law.

14. FURTHER ASSURANCES. Each undersigned party will, except as otherwise provided herein, whenever it shall be necessary to do so by the other, promptly execute, acknowledge, and deliver, or cause to be executed, acknowledged, or delivered, documents as may be necessary or proper to effectuate the covenants, contingencies, and agreements herein provided. The Developer and

the City agree to use their best efforts in cooperation to carry out the intent of this Agreement and to provide quality and efficient development sites for both the Developer and the City.

15. INTERPRETATIONS. Any uncertainty or ambiguity existing herein shall not be interpreted against either party because such party prepared any portion of this Agreement, but shall be interpreted according to the application of rules of interpretation of contracts generally.

16. CONSTRUCTION. Whenever used herein including acknowledgments, the singular shall be construed to include the plural, the plural the singular, and the use of any gender shall be construed to include and be applicable to all genders as the context shall warrant.

17. NON-MERGER. All representations and warranties made herein are intended to survive Closing and shall not be merged in the deed unless otherwise stated in this Agreement. This Agreement shall not be cancelled at Closing.

18. ENTIRE AGREEMENT. This Agreement contains the entire agreement of the parties relating to the transaction contemplated hereby, and all prior or contemporaneous agreements, understandings, representations, warranties, and statements, oral or written, are merged herein. This Agreement cannot be modified or altered unless reduced to writing and consented to by all the undersigned parties.

19. NOTICE AND DEMANDS. Notice, demand, or other communication mandated by this Agreement by either party to the other shall be sufficiently given or delivered if it is sent by registered or certified mail, postage prepaid, return receipt requested, or delivered personally at the address stated above.

20. TIME IS OF THE ESSENCE. The parties agree time is of the essence under this Agreement.

Signatures

Appendix C

Self-Tests

Introduction

1. True or False? To avoid over-stepping the authority of the courts, legislative bodies always leave the definition of statutory terms to the courts.
2. True or False? Publishers' enhancements (i.e. synopsis or headnotes) are provided by the judge assigned to writing the opinion and can be cited as precedent.
3. True or False? Because contract law is one of the largest bodies of law, it is primarily federal law.

Identify each of the following as primary or secondary authority. You may have to look up some abbreviations (https://www.law.cornell.edu/citation). If the source is primary law, identify the source and type of law.

4. Mich. Exec. Order No. 2003-4 (Feb. 27, 2003), http://www.michigan.gov/granholm/0,4587,7-168-21975-62542--,00.html
5. Iowa Code § 602.1614
6. Restatement (Second) of Contracts § 30 (1981)
7. 49 C.F.R. § 236.403
8. *Scott v. Harris*, 550 U.S. 372 (2007)
9. Exec. Order No. 12, 89, 59 Fed. Reg. 423 (Jan. 31, 1994)
10. *Sanders v. State*, 947 So. 2d 432 (Ala. Crim. App. 2006)
11. North American Free Trade Agreement, U.S.-Can.-Mex., art. 705(3), Dec. 17, 1992, 32 I.L.M. 289 (1993)
12. Enron Corp., *2000 Annual Report* 30 (2001)
13. Judge Richard Posner (7th Cir.), *Little Book of Plagiarism* (2007)
14. N.Y. Const. art. I, § 9, cl. 2
15. Francis M. Dougherty, Annotation, *Liability for Wrongful Issuance of Life Policy*, 37 A.L.R.4th 972, 974 (1985)

16. Tex. Admin. Code tit. 40, § 705.3101 (2012 effective Sept.1)
17. 42 U.S.C. § 405(c)(2)(C)
18. Cincinnati, Ohio, Municipal Code § 302-3
19. H H 3 Trucking Inc., 345 N.L.R.B. No. 59 (Sept. 15, 2005)
20. Eugene F. Scoles et al., *Conflict of Laws* § 13.20, n. 10 (5th ed. 2010)
21. *Natural Res. Def. Council v. Fox*, 93 F. Supp. 2d 531 (S.D.N.Y. 2000)
22. U.S. Const. art. III, § 2, cl. 2

Chapter 1

1. True or False? In a unilateral contract, each party undertakes a single obligation; in a bilateral contract, each has at least two obligations.
2. True or False? Adam boards a bus and puts a dollar in the slot, saying nothing. This is a quasi-contract.
3. True or False? Either a written contract or an oral contract is an express contract.
4. True or False? A contract can be formed without a word being spoken or written.
5. True or False? In a bilateral contract, acceptance can be by a promise, even if no action has been taken.
6. True or False? Acceptance must be oral or in writing.
7. True or False? Contract law is intended to enable parties to allocate and manage risk.
8. True or False? Quantum meruit is a theory for awarding tort damages when a breach of contract is particularly damaging.
9. True or False? A contract cannot form until both parties have made promises.
10. True or False? Quasi contract is a way of enforcing a contract after the statute of limitations has expired.
11. True or False? Promissory estoppel applies whenever one party has taken unfair advantage of another in a contract situation.

Identify Classifications: Express, Implied, Executory, Executed, Unilateral, Bilateral, Gift, Quasi-Contract, Estoppel, Unenforceable Promise

12. On December 15, Lou promised Jyoti that he would give her diamond earrings on New Years' Eve. Jyoti told all of her friends and is humiliated when Lou does not give her the earrings. She wants to sue.
13. Lou gives Jyoti the earrings, then finds out that Jyoti has been spending time with another guy. Lou wants the earrings back.
14. Jess just bought a cabin on a remote lake and, thinking it was the only way to get television and Internet service, signed up with a satellite provider. The dish will be installed in two weeks. Two days after signing, Jess learns that cable is available and is cheaper. The satellite company has not done any work. Jess wants to cancel.
15. Animal Shelter advertised a vaccination clinic, with shots at $20 per dog. People just get in line with their dogs and volunteers administer shots.

Another volunteer then collects the money and gets the owners' names and addresses, to report the vaccination to animal control. M.J. went through the line, had two dogs vaccinated, and now won't pay, claiming she never agreed to pay.

16. A crew of teenagers wants to make some money. They go through a neighborhood and do a beautiful job of painting the house number of each house on the curb in front of the house. When they finish, they knock on the door, show their work, and ask for payment. Many owners have refused to pay, so the teenagers decide to take them all to small claims court.
17. Homeowner Jules had the same yard service (Vic's) for 12 years. Jules sells to Jan, forgetting to mention Vic's or contact Vic's. As usual, Vic's comes to the house in early May, cuts the lawn and trims the bushes. Must Jan pay? Would it make a difference if Jan let Vic's do the work for several weeks before telling them that Jules had moved?
18. You get a written job offer to work for a large law firm in a city that you love, more than 500 miles from your current home. They want you to start next week! In your rush to pack up and move, you forget to sign and return the contract. You arrive in the city two days before the proposed start date and take the signed contract to the firm. Before you hand it over, they tell you that the firm lost a major client yesterday and that they are revoking the offer.

Chapter 2

1. True or False? The UCC is federal law.
2. True or False? The UCC is identical in all 50 states.
3. True or False? The UCC has been unamended for 50 years.
4. True or False? A consumer is one who enters into a contract for business reasons.
5. True or False? A crop of corn, growing in the field, is covered by the UCC.
6. True or False? The UCC applies only to commercial contracts.
7. True or False? All of contract law can be found in the Constitution, statutes, and judicial decisions.

For each of the following, name the type of property, and if applicable, the source(s) of contract law.

8. Truck
9. Copyright
10. Vacant lot
11. Patents, trademarks
12. Stocks, bonds
13. Furniture
14. Two-year employment contract

Chapter 3

1. True or False? An offer may be valid despite having multiple offerees.
2. True or False? Because of the potential for consumer fraud, most advertising is considered to constitute an offer that can be accepted by a qualified buyer.
3. True or False? During an interview, the candidate says something clever and the interviewer says "you're hired." Although there was no mention of salary, benefits, or start date, the open terms rule can supply those details.
4. True or False? The offeree is the person receiving an offer.
5. True or False? Jay was looking for a classic '67 Mustang. Kay is selling one. The price is right, but the car is black. Jay would prefer red. Jay gives Kay a $100 bill and says "Hold it for me until Saturday while I look around." Kay waits two weeks to hear from Jay, then calls him and learns he bought a different car. Kay turned down offers during the wait. Kay can sue for the lost sales.
6. True or False? On Saturday, having found a red car, Jay returns to Kay and wants his $100 returned. Jay is entitled to the money.
7. True or False? On Saturday, Jay returns to Kay to buy the car only to find that Kay has sold it to somebody who made a higher offer. Kay attempts to hand Jay the $100 bill, but Jay wants more. Kay has breached a contract.
8. True or False? After the agreed period expires (Sunday), Jay calls Kay and says, "If you are still selling it at the same price, bring it over here by 6 and I'll have cash." Kay responds, "We'll see." Jay has made a unilateral offer, which Kay may accept.
9. True or False? Under the firm offer rule, an offer between merchants may be enforceable for a reasonable time, despite the absence of consideration.
10. True or False? Acceptance must be express.
11. True or False? As a UCC rule, the mailbox rule may not be eliminated from a contract's terms.
12. True or False? The battled of the forms rule essentially counteracts the mirror image rule.
13. True or False? Acceptance can be valid even if is not communicated in a single document or statement.
14. True or False? Manifestation of mutual assent depends on determining the actual intentions of the parties.
15. Identify a standard that the UCC might apply to open terms in a contract between merchants.
16. Name two things that will terminate an offer.
17. Dale got two bids for remodeling a bathroom. Each bit stated that Dale could accept by returning a signed copy by Tuesday. On Monday, Joe, who submitted the higher bid, called to follow up because he had an opportunity to accept another job. Dale told Joe she would not be accepting his proposal. Minutes later, Perry, the other contractor, called Dale and stated that he had taken on too many projects and would be

unable to do Dale's work. Furious because starting over on getting bids would mean that the bathroom wouldn't be done in time for a family reunion, Dale called Joe back and accepted Joe's proposal. What is the status of this situation?

Chapter 4

1. True or False? Because it is impossible to prove what another person knew or intended, fraud is implied when a false statement is made to induce a contract.
2. True or False? Unconscionability is primarily used as a defense in commercial contracts.
3. True or False? Punitive damages are intended to compensate for losses incurred when a party negligently breaches a contract.
4. True or False? Because of the intent element, silence cannot constitute fraud.
5. True or False? Unilateral mistake about a basic assumption of fact is a defense to formation of a contract.
6. True or False? Mutual mistake about the legal consequences of a contract constitutes a defense.
7. True or False? Commercial impracticability is a UCC concept.
8. True or False? A threat to sue if the other party does not agree to a proposed settlement amounts to duress.
9. Fill in the blank: The types of fraud are fraud in the inducement and fraud in the ___________.
10. Identify: Another term for "sales talk," does not constitute a material representation of fact.
11. Fill in the blank: The negligent version of fraud is called ___________.
12. Fill in the blank: A contract entered into because of a threat of violence renders a contract void based on ___________.
13. Identify: A term for a "take it or leave it" contract.
14. Fill in the blank: A major factor in determining unconscionability is the respective ___________ of the parties.

In the following situation, give the analysis behind the facts.

15. Buyer asks seller whether car has ever been in an accident. Seller, having owned the car only a few months, does not know and is too lazy to find out. Seller says no. After purchasing the car, buyer discovers that it was in a serious accident.
16. It's been a tough negotiation. The employer previously presented an agreement that the union rejected. Now the parties are meeting to sign the final agreement, but the employer has actually supplied a contract containing many of the terms his previous offer, knowing that the others will not have time to read it thoroughly.
17. The trustee of a family trust has total discretion about how much to spend for the beneficiary's tuition and living expenses. The beneficiary wants to go to Northwestern and live in an upscale lakefront condo. The

trustee requests that the beneficiary sign a release that will enable the trustee to invest trust funds in a new business owned by the trustee's wife.

18. At the very moment that buyer and seller sign the documents transferring ownership of a townhouse, the townhouse is 60 percent destroyed by fire. Neither party wants to deal with insurers and contractors to rebuild.
19. During negotiations, the buyer spoke often of his plans to build a greenhouse addition to the side of the house, for his collection of prize-winning orchids. Seller, having previously investigated the possibility of adding a garage on that location, knows nothing can be build there because of the city's tree protection ordinance. Seller says nothing. Buyer learns of the ordinance after taking title and applying for a permit.

Chapter 5

1. True or False? A statement that the parties agree to "Ten Dollars and other good and valuable consideration" is called nominal consideration.
2. True or False? Consideration must be roughly equal and fair.
3. True or False? Consideration must be "bargained for."
4. True or False? Consideration must be accurately and precisely stated in the contract.
5. True or False? Although performance of a pre-existing obligation does not constitute consideration, the UCC provides for modification of existing contracts.
6. Fill in the blank: Stated consideration that does not really impose any obligation or grant any right is ___________.
7. Fill in the blank: Most contracts to purchase a house contain a mortgage contingency, which is a condition ___________.
8. Fill in the blank: An agreement to accept a payment or performance in exchange for a different payment or performance, required under a contract, is known as ___________.
9. Fill in the blank: A debt that is not in dispute is called ___________.
10. You see your neighbor power-washing his deck and tell him that it looks great and that you wish you could do yours. He says, "You've been a great neighbor, watching the house and feeding the cat when we are gone. Next week, when I wash the front of the house, I will do your deck." Next week, you see him washing the front of his house, but he does not do your deck. Was there consideration?
11. Jack was so glad to finally sell his house! At the closing, Jack gave the buyer a deed and the keys and got a check in return. Leaving the meeting, Jack shakes hands with the buyer and says, in full view of both lawyers and the title agent: "That humidifier is tricky. If it gives you any trouble, let me know and I will fix it." He writes his cell phone number and e-mail address on a card and gives it to the buyer. A few months later, the humidifier is not working and Jack has no interest in fixing it. Is this an enforceable promise?

12. Emily's father, a prominent lawyer, has always told her that if Emily could get into law school he would pay the tuition. Emily worked very hard and her grades are pretty good, but right before she took the LSAT, her father and mother divorced. Dad says he can no longer pay the tuition and is rescinding his offer. Is this an enforceable promise?

Chapter 6

1. What does "in pari delicto" mean?
2. Fill in the blank: A ___________ contract charges an illegal rate of interest.
3. Fill in the blank: An invalid contract provision is often ___ so that the rest of the contract remains valid.
4. True or False? The lack of a license that is not intended to protect the public, but only to raise revenue for the licensing body, generally does not invalidate a contract.

Name the clause that applies to the following situations.

5. In the event that employee shall cease to be employed by the company, for any reason, employee shall not, for two years after leaving the company, accept any form of employment from a number of competitors.
6. Tenant agrees to defend and hold Landlord harmless for any and all claims, liabilities, damages, losses, costs, fees, and expenses arising from or in any way related to the Tenant's use of the party room.
7. The undersigned irrevocably authorizes any licensed attorney to appear in court on the undersigned's behalf, after default in payment hereof and confess a judgment without process in favor of the creditor hereof for such amount as may then appear unpaid hereon.
8. Juan Rufina, as proprietor of Rufina Custom Creations (RCC), agrees to sell all lamps produced by him or by RCC to Beckley Arts.
9. In the event that borrower shall fail to make any monthly payment when due, the entire balance then due under the loan shall immediately become due.
10. The undersigned agrees to release the skating rink from all liability for injury, death, property loss, and damages that result from participation in recreational activities at that facility, including all liability that results from negligence.

Chapter 7

1. True or False? An adult who finds out that he has entered into a contract with a minor can avoid the contract if the adult acts immediately.
2. True or False? Under the UCC an innocent party is free from a minor's power of disaffirmance.
3. True or False? Some states require a minor to make restitution upon avoiding a contract.
4. True or False? Ratification must be express.

5. True or False? A minor who is no longer under the control or care of an adult is said to be emancipated.
6. True or False? An adjudicated incompetent generally has no contract capacity, even for necessities.
7. True or False? Because intoxication is willful, it cannot be a contract defense.
8. True or False? Minors have no liability for their contracts or torts.
9. An adjudicated incompetent generally has an appointed __________.

Identify the issues involved in the following scenarios.

10. Jim, a wounded homeless veteran and non-adjudicated incompetent, cashes his VA benefit check and buys canned food and liquor each month. His brother finds him living under a bridge and wants to become Jim's guardian and recover the money Jim has spent in order to pre-pay rent for a boarding house.
11. A minor, using the password his mother provided, signs into Amazon and downloads books totaling $500. His mother is furious, having believed that he would only download books needed for his literature class.
12. Two weeks before his 18th birthday, Duke bought an iPod, speakers, and downloaded music, spending almost $1000. He used his purchases to provide music at his birthday party, and, three months later, at a graduation party. He then learned about the right to disaffirm and, needing money for college, attempted to disaffirm.
13. Jenna's drink was drugged while she was out with friends. She has no memory of the night. Her friends eventually realized what had happened and prevented her from leaving with the man who likely put the drug in her drink. They took her to an urgent care facility and filed a police report. Weeks later, Jenna discovers that before her friends intervened, she used her credit card to pay for $440 in food and liquor consumed by people she does not know.
14. Ian, while intoxicated, agreed to paint Kay's house before the end of the month for $900. Kay has had other bids of $1,200-$1,500. The contract would be voidable because Kay was aware of Ian's intoxication and was taking advantage of him. After sobering up, however, Ian drives to Kay's house and starts scraping pain.

Chapter 8

1. True or False? In order to encourage people to put their contracts in writing, the statute of frauds is interpreted broadly.
2. True or False? A writing can satisfy the statute of frauds, even if not signed by all parties.
3. True or False? The "writing" for purposes of the statute of frauds, can consist of several documents.
4. True or False? If a defendant does not raise the statute of frauds as a defense, it may be waived.

5. True or False? Most states have adopted the Electronic Transaction Act, which promotes the enforceability of paperless transactions.
6. True or False? ESIGN governs electronic transactions in interstate commerce.
7. Fill in the blank: A _____ is a means of accepting a contract online; usually requires user to manifest assent by clicking an "OK" button on a dialog box.

In the following situations, is a writing required? Why or why not?

8. In November, College Painters agrees to paint a house next summer for $4,000.
9. Paul, a member of the National Guard, was deployed and expects to be gone about 15 months. His employer agrees to hold his job and hires Viggo to fill the position until Paul returns.
10. Jo and Chip are newlyweds. Chip just learned that a novel he wrote is going to be published and may be made into a movie. He wants Jo to agree to take a limited portion of the proceeds in the event of a divorce.
11. Tom has been a tenant, living in Larry's condo for two years. Tom and Larry now agree that at the end of the current term (in two months), Tom will buy the condo for $200,000.
12. Mom agrees to repay daughter's first loan, if daughter fails to pay, in order to help daughter establish credit. The loan has a duration of only six months.
13. Wife agrees to support ex-husband until he remarries.
14. Band agrees to perform at a holiday show in 18 months.
15. Joe agrees to paint all of the apartments in a large building, which will likely take more than a year to complete.
16. Dad and son are going into business together and are taking a two-year, $10,000 loan.

Chapter 9

1. True or False? An agency relationship can be established by the agent's statements to outsiders, indicating that agency exists.
2. True or False? One of an agent's duties to a principal is to secure chattel.
3. True or False? Lou buys a refrigerator for his condo at Big Mart, which allows Lou to make monthly payments; Big Mart has a purchase money security interest.
4. True or False? Because of the duty of reasonable care, an agent who, despite best efforts, does not accomplish the principal's purpose, is liable to the principal.
5. True or False? Lou buys a refrigerator for his condo at Big Mart, which allows Lou to make monthly payments; Big Mart must perfect its security interest by filing.
6. True or False? Objective impossibility can be a defense to breach of contract.
7. True or False? Lou buys a refrigerator for his new home at Big Mart, which allows Lou to make monthly payments Big Mart had not yet paid

for its last shipment of refrigerators and SilentFrig holds a security interest. Big Mart violated the law by selling the refrigerator while it was subject to a security interest.

8. True or False? Lou buys a refrigerator for his condo at Big Mart, which allows Lou to make monthly payments; if Lou takes possession of the refrigerator, the security interest does not attach.
9. True or False? Lou buys a refrigerator for his new home at Big Mart, which allows Lou to make monthly payments Big Mart had not yet paid for its last shipment of refrigerators and SilentFrig holds a security interest. As a good faith purchaser in the course of ordinary business, Lou is free of the SilentFrig interest.
10. True or False? Professor Laurel, having no express authority to purchase for her employer, attends an AAfPE conference, where she orders two books for the college library. When the books arrive, the librarian adds them to the collection. The library has likely ratified Laurel's actions and will have to pay.
11. True or False? My brother and I own a building together and want to sell. Because my brother is a licensed broker, he lists the property. IF my brother did not reveal to potential buyers that I was a co-owner or that there were any other owners, it would be an undisclosed principal situation and my brother could be liable to a buyer for my failure to perform.
12. True or False? My brother and I own a building together and want to sell. Because my brother is a licensed broker, he lists the property. After six months, we've had no offers. I decide that we should just give up trying to sell the building and rent it to a new tenant, and changed the locks so that real estate agents could no longer show the building to prospective buy. I violated my duty to cooperate and could be liable.
13. Fill in the blank: In an anticipatory breach situation, the insecure party may ___________.

Name the interest involved in the following situations.

14. To finance your new car, you obtain a loan through the dealership, which sells the loan to an acceptance company. The acceptance company puts a lien on the car title.
15. You authorize your cell phone provider to automatically bill your credit card for your monthly service.
16. You prepaid for a two-year subscription to a magazine. Finding you no longer have time to read it, you change the delivery address so that it will be delivered to your sister's house.
17. You pay for a beer-of-the-month club subscription for your brother.
18. You enter a contract to build an addition on your house so that your mother-in-law can live with you. Your contractor gets a better offer and tells you he can't get to your job for at least a year. You could sue, but frankly, you are glad. Mother-in-law wants to enforce the contract.
19. You purchase an item and pay for its delivery through Amazon.com. Amazon uses UPS for delivery.

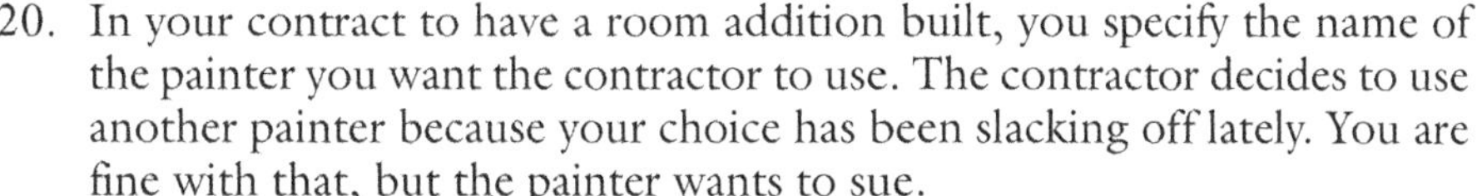

20. In your contract to have a room addition built, you specify the name of the painter you want the contractor to use. The contractor decides to use another painter because your choice has been slacking off lately. You are fine with that, but the painter wants to sue.
21. Kim has a small kiosk at the mall, where she distributes brochures and shows samples for her family's cabinet refinishing business and sells novelty cabinet hardware. When Kim takes a break, Kyle, who has the adjoining kiosk, interacts with Kim's customers, sometimes taking orders and setting appointments Kim returns from lunch and finds that Kyle took an order for 30 cabinet pulls. Kim processes the order and ships the merchandise.
22. Rose Bakery, a sole proprietorship, has an exclusive dealing contract with a local restaurant, providing all of the restaurant's baked goods. Rose is retiring and wants the new owner of the bakery to take over providing the restaurant's needs.
23. The restaurant likes the new bakery owner's products so much, it decides to release Rose from the contract and enter into a new contract with the purchaser.

Chapter 10

1. True or False? Non-occurrence of a condition precedent is generally a basis for discharge from contract obligations.
2. True or False? The Uniform Commercial Code sets a standard for substantial or satisfactory performance.
3. True or False? An obligation to pay money requires substantial performance.
4. True or False? Repudiation is the same as breach of contract.
5. True or False? Coal is a fungible good.
6. True or False? Acme booked its annual employees' retreat in Cozumel. A week before the retreat was to start, a hurricane hit. There is no electricity; the hotel rooms cannot be occupied. Acme had contracted to pay a motivational speaker $5,000 to appear at the meeting. This could constitute a force majeure.
7. Fill in the blank: Under the UCC's ___ rule, buyer has a reasonable time to reject goods that fail, in any respect, to conform to the contract.
8. Fill in the blank: Creditors may not seek to enforce contract rights during the bankruptcy ___________.

Name the legal concept behind the following situations.

9. I'm sorry you can't use the size I sent. I'll get the larger frames to you before the contract date.
10. Ariana leases property, intending to sell exotic endangered animals. Congress passes a law prohibiting the sale of endangered species.
11. Ava agreed to pay $11,000 for the car, but arrives at the agreed time and place with only $10,000.

12. Before seller transfers title to the building to the buyer, the lender forecloses the mortgage and takes title.
13. Ava contracts to open a franchise medical marijuana dispensary at a location where such businesses are prohibited.
14. I will take a crate of the merlot if you can deliver it to my house by Saturday at noon.
15. I know I won't have the shipment ready by the due date, but if you will settle for half an order, I can get it to you a month early.

Chapter 11

1. True or False? An injunction is a legal remedy.
2. True or False? Laches is an equitable concept, referring to waiting too long to act on your rights.
3. True or False? Sue Seller breached a contract to deliver 10 tons of coal to Electric Company. Specific performance would be an appropriate remedy.
4. True or False? If a situation involves a breach of contract it typically also involves tort liability.
5. Fill in the blank: An attempt to reduce the harm resulting from breach is called ___________.
6. Fill in the blank: In ___________, a neutral party hears both sides and imposes a decision.
7. Fill in the blank: It is common for a contract to include a(n) ___________ provision, requiring that a party give the other party written notice within a specified time before filing suit.

Name the remedy to apply in the following scenarios.

8. Not only did Acme fail to complete its work on time, breaching the contract, it had provided falsified invoices and progress reports so that Customer did not realize that the work was not being done. Customer lost $25,000 in actual expenses, but wants more.
9. Contractor's failure to substantially complete the Work within the Contract Time will cause the Owner to incur economic damages and losses of types and in amounts which are impossible to ascertain with certainty. In lieu of actual damages for delay, the Contractor agrees to pay damages to the Owner, without the Owner having to present any evidence of the amount or character of actual damages sustained: One Thousand Dollars ($1,000) for each day that Substantial Completion is delayed beyond the Contract Time.
10. On the contract delivery date, Ava's supplier delivered the wrong size helmets. Ava needs the helmets immediately and orders them from a different company.
11. Fresh Seafood had agreed to ship lobsters to a Chicago restaurant. The chosen airport, Midway, closes due to a security threat on the delivery date. Fresh puts the lobsters on a plane to O'Hare.

12. Antique dealer contracts to purchase necklace that belonged to Mary Lincoln. Seller changes her mind and offers antique dealer cash to cancel the contract. Antique dealer wants that necklace.
13. Seller sent non-conforming goods that buyer cannot use. Buyer spends $5000.00 to place the goods in a secure location, pending Seller's recovery of the goods.
14. Buyer ordered 3,000 U of Iowa t-shirts to sell at the Rose Parade. On the day before the parade, buyer receives t-shirts emblazoned with University of Idaho. Buyer has sold 3,000 t-shirts at each of the last five Rose Parades, always making a 40 percent profit.
15. Contractor spent $15,000 preparing for construction of Lee's house. Lee lost his job and cancelled the contract. Contractor finds another project, he only wants the $15,000 he has spent.
16. Exotic Pets plans to open its first shop and orders expensive cages. Acme fails to deliver the cages and, because Exotic cannot open, it goes out of business. Having no business history, Exotic is unable to prove, with reasonable certainty, what its lost profits would be. The court awards $10.
17. The judge finds a contract ambiguous and rewrites the ambiguity so that the parties can continue in business.

Chapter 12

1. True or False? The term "WHEREAS" generally introduces the defined terms in a contract.
2. True or False? A formal recitation of consideration is essential to the validity of a contract.
3. True or False? The parole evidence rule does not apply if the document has a severability clause.
4. True or False? The parole evidence rule does not apply if the document contains a merger clause.
5. True or False? Under the UCC, evidence of course of dealing, usage of trade or course of performance may be introduced to supplement a final written agreement, even though that evidence might be prohibited by the common law parole evidence rule.
6. True or False? If a court determines that the contract is not an integrated agreement, it may allow parole evidence.
7. True or False? In order to remain objective, courts look only at contract language when there is an ambiguity, and will not look at "outside" information, such as the purpose of the agreement.
8. True or False? The parole evidence rule does not prohibit evidence of a condition precedent or of facts that would make the agreement void or voidable.
9. True or False? The parole evidence rule prohibits evidence of a subsequent agreement.
10. Fill in the blank: "In construing this contract, the use of masculine terms, such as 'he, him, or his,' shall be interpreted as including female actors." This is an example of ______________________ language.

What is the problem with the following terms in a contract?

11. Temporary and part-time workers may be terminated at any time.
12. Reimbursable expenses shall include court reporting services, expert witness fees, reasonable travel expenses, and the cost to create trial exhibits.
13. The monthly payment of Two Hundred Dollars ($2200.00) shall be mailed to . . .
14. Peters, Inc., of Seattle WA, shall pay to Tremblay Properties, of Vancouver, Canada, the sum of Two Thousand Dollars on the first day of each month . . .
15. Employees must report any absence prior to the beginning of their shift.
16. The company may, upon 30 days notice, cease operations at the Springfield plant and the Elgin plant.

Chapter 13

1. True or False? When an incoming contract arrives, it is essential to first unstaple it and make good copies for everyone.
2. True or False? The Magnuson-Moss Act is federal law concerning warranties.
3. True or False? The warranty of fitness for a particular purpose can be implied.
4. True or False? FOB and FAS are both UCC terms by which the seller disclaims all responsibility for shipment and delivery.
5. True or False? An example of passive voice, poor writing for a contract: the building shall at all times be insured.
6. True or False? The False Claims Acts impose sanctions for the submission of false or fraudulent contract claims or bids.
7. Fill in the blank: Activity conducted to find security interests in personal property that have been recorded is a(n) ___________.
8. Fill in the blank: One hired to undertake a specific project using his own methods (not an employee) is a(n) ___________.

Appendix D

◆ ◆ ◆

Self-Tests Answer Key

◆ ◆ ◆

Introduction

Answer	Section Where Material Is Covered
1. F	B.4., D.1
2. F	D.2.b.
3. F	A.; B.1.
4. primary, executive order, state	
5. primary, legislation, state	
6. secondary	
7. primary, administrative, fed.	
8. primary, judicial, fed.	
9. primary, executive, fed.	
10. primary, judicial, state	
11. primary, treaty, fed.	
12. secondary	
13. secondary	
14. primary, constitution, state	
15. secondary	
16. primary, administrative, state	

Answer	Section Where Material Is Covered
17. primary, legislative, fed.	
18. primary, legislative, local	
19. primary, administrative, fed.	
20. secondary	
21. primary, judicial, state	
22. primary, constitution, fed.	

Chapter 1

Answer	Section Where Material Is Covered
1. F	A.2.
2. F	B.3.
3. T	A.1.
4. T	A.1
5. T	A.2.
6. F	A.2.
7. T	A.
8. F	B.3
9. F	A.2.
10. F	B.3.
11. F	B.2.
12. unenforceable promise	B.1.
13. completed gift	B.1.
14. bilateral contract	A.2.
15. implied contract	A.1.
16. gift	B.1.
17. gift (Vic may have a claim against Jules), but once Jan is aware, quasi contract	B.1.; B.3.
18. possible promissory estoppel	B.2.

Chapter 2

Answer	Section Where Material Is Covered
1. F	B.1.
2. F	B.1.
3. F	B.1.
4. F	B.1.
5. T	B.1.
6. F	B.1.
7. F	E.
8. goods, UCC	B.
9. intellectual prop., common law, statutes other than UCC	A.
10. real prop. common law, statutes other than UCC	A.
11. intellectual prop., common law, statutes other than UCC	A.
12. intangible property	A.
13. goods, UCC	B.
14. services, common law, statutes other than UCC	A.

Chapter 3

Answer	Section Where Material Is Covered
1. T	A.3.
2. F	A.1.
3. F	A.1.
4. T	A.
5. F	A.4.a.
6. F	A.4.a.
7. T	A.4.a.
8. T	A.4.a.
9. T	A.4.a.

Answer	Section Where Material Is Covered
10. F	B.
11. F	B.2.
12. T	B.2
13. T	B.
14. F	4.
15. course of dealings (performance) or industry standards	A.2.
16. revocation, rejection, counter-offer, operation of law, illegality, passage of time	A.4.
17. Dale rejected Joe's offer; Perry revoked his offer. Dale made Joe a new offer.	A.; B.

Chapter 4

Answer	Section Where Material Is Covered
1. F	A.
2. F	F.
3. F	Chapter Intro.
4. F	A.
5. F	C.
6. F	C.
7. T	C.
8. F	D.
9. execution	A.
10. puffing	A.
11. misrepresentation	B.
12. duress	D.
13. adhesion	F.
14. bargaining power	F.
15. misrepresentation?	B.
16. fraud	A.
17. duress	D.

Answer	Section Where Material Is Covered
18. mutual mistake of material fact	C.
19. fraud by silence	A.

Chapter 5

Answer	Section Where Material Is Covered
1. T	B.
2. F	B.
3. T	D.
4. F	B.
5. T	E.
6. illusory or sham	B.
7. precedent	C.
8. accord and satisfaction	E.
9. liquidated	F.
10. No, past consideration	D.
11. No, not bargained-for	D.
12. Probably not; estoppel a remote possibility	A.

Chapter 6

Answer	Section Where Material Is Covered
1. the parties are equally at fault	Chapter Intro.
2. usurious	A.
3. severable	Chapter Intro.
4. T	A.1.
5. non-compete	C.
6. indemnification	B.
7. confession of judgment	Example 6-1
8. exclusive dealing/ output	C.
9. acceleration	Assignment 6-4
10. exculpatory	B

Chapter 7

Answer	Section Where Material Is Covered
1. F	A.
2. T	A.4.
3. T	A.2.
4. F	A.4.
5. T	A.
6. T	B.1.
7. F	B.2.
8. F	A.
9. guardian	B.1.
10. necessities? incompetent at time of transactions? ratification by failure to timely disaffirm?	
11. minor acting as agent	
12. implied ratification during three months of continued use	
13. involuntary intoxication; ratification by failure to timely disaffirm?	
14. ratification	

Chapter 8

Answer	Section Where Material Is Covered
1. F	B.
2. T	C.
3. T	C.
4. T	B.
5. T	D.1.
6. T	D.1.
7. click-wrap agreement	Assignment 8-2; E.
8. No, not goods, not one year	E.2.; E.4.
9. No (both), Paul could return in less than a year	E.2.

Answer	Section Where Material Is Covered
10. No, after marriage	E.2.; E.3
11. Yes, real estate	E.3.
12. No, sounds like primary liability	E.5
13. No, could be less than a year	E.2.
14. Yes	E.2.
15. No, could be less than a year	E.2.
16. No, the parties both have primary liability	E.5.

Chapter 9

Answer	Section Where Material Is Covered
1. F	B.
2. F	B.
3. T	E.
4. F	E.
5. F	E.
6. T	C.
7. F	E.
8. F	E.
9. T	E.
10. T	B.
11. T	B.
12. T	B.
13. demand assurances	G.
14. assignment; if you were aware that the dealership would assign, creditor beneficiary	C.
15. agent, couple with an interest	B.
16. assignment	D.1.
17. intended beneficiary	C.
18. incidental beneficiary	C.
19. delegation	D.2.

Answer	Section Where Material Is Covered
20. incidental beneficiary	C.
21. Kim is an agent for family business; she might delegate to him or he may have an implied subagency. Kim ratifies his actions.	B.
22. Rose wants to delegate	D.2.
23. novation	D.3

Chapter 10

Answer	Section Where Material Is Covered
1. T	A.
2. F	E.2.
3. F	E.
4. F	G.
5. T	E.
6. T	D.
7. perfect tender	E.2.
8. automatic stay	C.
9. cure	E.2.
10. frustration of purpose	D.
11. material breach	E.
12. impossibility	D.
13. illegality	C.
14. condition precedent	A.
15. offer of accord and satisfaction/novation	B.

Chapter 11

Answer	Section Where Material Is Covered
1. F	C.
2. T	C.
3. F	C.2.

Answer	Section Where Material Is Covered
4. F	D.
5. mitigation	B.1.
6. arbitration	A.
7. notice of claims	B.
8. punitive damages	C.1.
9. liquidated damages	C.1.
10. cover UCC	C.
11. substituted performance UCC	C.
12. specific performance	C.2.
13. incidental or consequential indirect damages	C.1.
14. expectation damages	C.1.
15. reliance damages	C.1.
16. nominal damages	C.1.
17. reformation	C.2.

Chapter 12

Answer	Section Where Material Is Covered
1. F	A.2.
2. F	A.3.
3. F	B.
4. F	B.
5. T	B.
6. T	B.
7. F	B.
8. T	B.
9. F	B.
10. boilerplate	A.5.
The problem . . .	
11. Do they have to be both temporary and part-time, or can they be either?	C.

Answer	Section Where Material Is Covered
12. Are these just examples? Could there be more?	C.
13. Which is it: two hundred dollars or ($2200.00)?	C.
14. U.S. or Canadian dollars?	C.
15. Each day if multi-day absence?	C.
16. Must the company close both plants?	C.

Chapter 13

Answer	Section Where Material Is Covered
1. F	A.1.
2. T	A.2.b.
3. T	A.2.b.
4. F	A.2.c.
5. T	B.2.d.
6. T	C.
7. UCC search	A.1.
8. independent contractor	B.2.h.

Glossary

Acceleration Clause: Causes payments to become immediately due upon the happening of stated event

Acceptance: Compliance or agreement by one party with the terms of another's offer so that a contract forms

Accord and Satisfaction: Agreement to accept and give payment or performance, different from that originally required by contract

Active Voice: The subject of the sentence acts

Adhesion Contract: A take-it-or-leave-it contract in which one party has all of the bargaining power

Adjudicated Incompetent: Court has declared person incompetent

Administrative Agencies: One of five sources of legal authority; administers a particular law or program

Administrator: One who carries on the business of an estate; also called executor

Adversarial: Argues a position

Affirm: Appellate or higher court's decision to support or uphold the decision of the lower court

Affirmative Defense: Part of an answer to a complaint in which defendant attempts to limit or excuse liability, based on facts outside those claimed by plaintiff

Agency Coupled with an Interest: Agent has a financial stake in the transaction

Agent: One who is authorized to act for or in place of another; representative

Agreement: "Meeting of the minds"

Allowances: Contract total price includes "estimates" for components; if actual price of components differs from allowances, total contract price changes

Alternative Dispute Resolution (ADR): To settle a dispute other than by litigation, including arbitration and mediation

Analogize: To compare cases and find them similar

Annotated Statute: Statute with references to articles, cases, and other materials that explain and interpret the law
Antenuptial: Agreement in anticipation of marriage that typically involves a promise to convey property when marriage occurs or concerns division of property in the event of a divorce; also called prenuptial
Anticipatory Breach: Belief that other party will not perform
Apparent Authority: Principal's dealings with third parties have given third parties reason to believe that an agent has authority
Appellant: Party bringing an appeal; lost in the lower court
Appellee: The party that won in the lower court
Arbitration: A neutral hears both positions and imposes a decision
Arm's-length Transaction: Relationship where parties have equal power to negotiate terms
Assignee: One to whom rights are transferred by another
Assignment: Transfer of interest in property or some right (contractual entitlement) to another
Assignor: One who transfers rights to another
Assurance: A pledge or guarantee that gives confidence or security
Attachment: Creation of an enforceable security interest
Attorney for the Child: Attorney whose role is to advocate the child's position
Attorney's Fees: Payment to attorney for services
Auction Without Reserve: A seller agrees to sell to the highest bidder and cannot revoke the offer to sell, even if bids are disappointingly low
Avoid: Make a contract void; see also Disaffirm
Bailee: Person, other than owner, who is in possession of goods under an arrangement called a bailment
Bankruptcy: Federal system of laws and courts for resolution of debts that exceed the debtor's assets or that the debtor is unable to pay when due
Bargained-for: Each party is induced to enter contract by consideration offered by other party
Bargaining Power: Ability to influence
Basic Assumption of Fact: An assumption essential to the value of a transaction
Battle-of-the-Forms Rule: UCC rule, overrides mirror image rule when merchants use forms
Bilateral: Contract in which both parties make promises
Bill of Lading: Documentation of the receipt of goods for shipment, issued by a party in the business of transporting goods
Binding Arbitration: Parties give up the right to challenge arbitration result in court
Blue Law: Prohibits certain transactions on Sundays; also called a Sunday statute
Blue-penciling: Court edits parts of a contract
Boilerplate: Standard terms included in most contracts
Brief: Short case summary
Bulk Sale: Sale of major part of inventory, not in ordinary course of business
CALR: Computer-assisted legal research system

Capacity: Ability, as determined by age and mental competence, to enter into a contract
Case at Hand: The case under consideration
Case at Law: A case requesting damages (money)
Case Brief: Short summary of facts, issues, holding, and reasoning of a judicial decision
Case in Equity: Courts can issue orders based on fairness; see also Equitable Remedy
Case Law: Judicial decisions
Chancery: A chancery court can order acts performed
Chattel: Moveable items; also called personal property
Choice of Law: Contract language that defines which state's law will apply in case of litigation
Citation: Address at which authority is found in law books or online
Cite: Verb form of citation (i.e., to cite)
Civil Law: Type of law pursued by an individual or group of people, a business, or a governmental body acting in a private capacity; result may be damages or court order
Click-wrap Agreement: Agreement used in connection with software licenses; often found on the Internet as part of the installation process of software packages; usually requires user to manifest assent by clicking an "OK" button on a dialog box or pop-up window
Code: Legislation; also called statute
Codify: To enter a statute into a topical system
Cognitive Test: Mental incompetence determined by inability to understand the nature and consequences of a transaction
Collateral: Assets pledged by a borrower to secure a loan or other credit, and subject to seizure in the event of default
Collateral Promise: Promise to guarantee the debt of another, made without benefit to the party making the promise
Commercial: Between or pertaining to businesses
Commercial Contract: A contract between businesses
Commercial Impracticability: A party may be excused from contract obligations if an unforeseen circumstance makes performance impracticable
Common Law: Law from judicial decisions; governs contract disputes involving real property, intangible property, and services; also called precedent
Compensatory Damages: Damages intended to put nonbreaching parties in the position they would have occupied if the contract had been fully performed; also called expectation damages
Concurring Opinion: Written by a judge who agrees with majority decision but for different reasons
Condition Precedent: Event that must occur before the contemplated transaction is completed
Condition Subsequent: Event that may "undo" an executed contract
Confession of Judgment: A clause that permits immediate entry of judgment without notice or an opportunity to present defenses

Conflict of Interest: Ethical issue: legal professional's loyalties divided
Connector: Symbol describing relationship between CALR search terms
Consequential Damages: Losses that do not flow directly and immediately from an injurious act
Consideration: Something promised, given, refrained from, or done that has the effect of making an agreement a legally enforceable contract
Consignment: An arrangement under which goods are placed for sale, but title does not transfer to the seller
Constitution: One of five sources of legal authority
Construction (Rules of): Rules that are applied to resolve contract disputes and to determine parties' intentions
Consumer: Party to the contract who is not engaged in business, but has entered the contract for personal or family reasons
Consumer Goods: Items used primarily for personal, family, or household purposes
Consumer Loan: Loan for personal or family purposes
Contract: Set of legally enforceable promises
Contracts Under Seal: Formal contracts
Contrary to Public Policy: Not good for society
Corporation: Organization formed under state law to conduct business as an "artificial person"
Cosigner: One who participates jointly in borrowing
Cost-plus Contract: A way of sharing risk
Costs: Examples include filing fees, fees for service of process and similar charges incurred in litigation
Costs Avoided: Expenses nonbreaching party will not incur
Counteroffer: Offeree responds to an offer with an offer
Course of Dealing: What has been done by the parties in the past
Court-annexed ADR: Use of the court system's own mediators or arbitrators before going to trial
Covenant Not to Compete: Provision under which party agrees to refrain from engaging in specified business activities ("noncompete")
Cover: Buyer obtains substitute goods
Creditor: One to whom money is owed
Creditor Beneficiary: A third-party beneficiary to whom a contract party is indebted and who is intended to benefit from the performance of a contract
Criminal Law: Category of law prosecuted by a governmental body involving a matter of concern to society as a whole
Criminal Plea Agreement: An agreement in which a prosecutor and a defendant arrange to settle a criminal case against the defendant
Cure: Seller delivers conforming goods before contract deadline, after buyer rejects nonconforming goods
Damages: Award of money; also called legal remedy
Decision of the Court: Majority decision, governs outcome of the case
Default: Fail to meet obligations
Defined Term: Shorthand way of referring to a person, place, thing, or event that might otherwise require a lengthy description
Delegation: Pass contractual obligations to another

Disaffirm: Make a contract void; see also Avoid
Discharge: Release
Discovery: Pretrial investigation of facts by questioning, inspection, and so on
Dissenting Opinion: Opinion written by a judge who disagrees with the majority; not law but provides interesting facts and opinions about case
Distinguish: To compare cases and find them to be different
Donee: Person receiving a gift
Donee Beneficiary: A third-party beneficiary intended to benefit from contract performance as a gift
Donor: Person making a gift
Durable Power of Attorney: Creates an agency relationship that remains in effect during the grantor's incompetency
Duress: A wrongful threat, intended to induce action by the other party
Easement: Limited right to use real property
E-discovery: Electronic recovery of e-mail, and documents from computers, servers, and handheld PDAs
Election of Remedies: Injured party's choice between remedies available for a single actionable occurrence
Emancipation: Minor is no longer under care/control of an adult
Equal Dignity Rule: Requirement that agency contract be written, if contract to be established by agent must be written
Equitable: Based on fairness and individual circumstances
Equitable Remedy: Award that is nonmonetary and involves court orders; see also Case in Equity and Chancery
Err: To make an error
Escrow: Account held for the benefit of others, into which parties typically deposit documents, instructions, and funds for a transfer of property
Estate: The entity for managing finances of a deceased person, or an incompetent
Estop: To bar assertion of a claim or right that contradicts what has been said or done before
Exclusive Dealing: Contract under which parties agree to deal only with each other with respect to particular needs
Exculpatory Clause: Provision that attempts to excuse a party from liability for that party's torts
Executed: Contract in which all obligations have been fulfilled
Executive Action: One of five sources of legal authority; including orders signed by the president or governor
Executor: One who carries on the business of an estate; also called Administrator
Executory: Contract in which obligations have not been fulfilled
Expectation Damages: Damages intended to put nonbreaching parties in the position they would have occupied if the contract had been fully performed; also called compensatory damages
Express: Contract with significant terms stated orally or in writing
Express Authority: Authority given by words or conduct
Express Ratification: To state or write intent to honor a contract or, if the contract has been executed, to acknowledge the contract

Express Warranties: Warranties created by the written or spoken word, demonstration, or depiction of a product
F.A.S: A shipping term, Free Along Side
F.O.B.: A shipping term, Free On Board
Factual Issues: Trial courts use testimony and evidence to decide facts, (*i.e.,* what happened)
Fee Recovery: An award of attorney's fees; also called fee reversal
Fee Reversal: An award of attorney's fees; also called fee recovery
Fiduciary Relationship: Relationship in which one person is under a duty to act for the benefit of the other on matters within the scope of the relationship
Firm Offer: UCC rule; no consideration required to hold offer open between merchants
Force Majeure: Contract provision excusing performance for an event such as "act of God," fire, labor dispute, accident, or transportation difficulty
Foreclose: Take property to satisfy debt
Foreseeable: That which a reasonable person would anticipate
Formal: A contract required to be in a particular form
Franchise: Contract granting the right to operate under a brand name
Fraud: False statement of material fact, made with intent to deceive, on which another reasonably relies, to his detriment
Fraud in the Execution: Fraud relates to the nature of the agreement
Fraud in the Inducement: Fraud relates to the party's motivation in entering the contract
Frustration of Purpose: Contract has no remaining value for party because of an unanticipated event
Fungible: Interchangeable
Gift: Completed transfer of property without consideration
Good Faith: UCC definition: as applied to a merchant, means honesty in fact and the observance of reasonable commercial standards of fair dealing in the trade
Good-faith Buyer in the Course of Ordinary Business: A buyer who acts honestly, gives value, and has no notice of other claims
Goods: Also called personal property or chattel; moveable, tangible items
Gratuitous: Done without compensation; a gift
Guarantor: Agrees to be responsible for another's debt or performance under a contract if the other fails to pay or perform; see also Surety
Guardian: Individual with legal responsibility for the minor
Guardian ad Litem: Court-appointed person to advocate best interests of a child or incompetent during litigation
Headnotes: Summaries of individual points made in the case
Hold Harmless Clause: One party agrees to compensate the other for losses arising from the contract; also called indemnification clause
Holding: Answer to the legal issue in a judicial decision
Identified: Goods designated as the particular goods being sold
Illusory: An illusion; stated consideration does not really obligate the party
Implied: Contract formed without express statement of terms, by words and actions

Implied Authority: Authority not expressed in writing or spoken words; arises from circumstances
Implied Ratification: Intent to honor contract or acknowledgment of contract can be inferred from behavior or words
Incentive Consideration: Consideration changes to motivate faster or better performance
Incidental Beneficiary: A third-party beneficiary, not intended to benefit from contract, does not acquire rights under contract
Incidental Damages: Losses reasonably associated with or related to actual damages; indirect damages
Incorporation by Reference: A reference to an outside document, making that document part of a contract
Independent Contractor: One hired to undertake a specific project using his own methods (not an employee)
Indemnification: Compensation or reimbursement for a loss
Indemnification Clause: One party agrees to compensate the other for losses arising from the contract; also called hold harmless clause
Infant: A minor
Informal: Contract for which no particular form is required
Injunction: Court order requiring or prohibiting specific actions
In Pari Delicto: The parties are equally at fault
Insecure Party: Party has good-faith belief that performance by other party is unlikely
Insolvency: Unable to pay debts
Instruments: Formal written documents
Insurable Interest: Legitimate financial interest in a person
Intangible Property: Has no physical existence, such as debt
Integrated Agreement: Agreement that is intended to be final and complete
Intellectual Property: Includes patents, trademarks, copyrights, trade secrets
Intent to Deceive: Knowledge of falsity
Interoffice Memo: Also called objective memo, analyzes fact situation with citations to sources of law
Intoxicated: Under the influence of alcohol or drugs
Inventory: Goods held for sale or lease
Issues of Fact: Trial courts use testimony and evidence to decide facts (*i.e.*, what happened)
Joint and Several Liability: Co-obligors can be sued together or any one can be liable for the entire obligation
Judicial Decisions: One of five sources of legal authority; also called common law or precedent
Jump Cite: The exact page number on which a fact or quote appears in a case
Jurisdiction: Area within which judicial authority may be exercised
Justifiable Reliance: Reliance on assertion is reasonable
Laches: Injured party delays in seeking remedy in a way that is unfair to the other party
LAPs: Lawyers assistance programs
Legalese: Overly formal, often archaic language sometimes used in legal documents

Legal Issues: Determining appropriate consequences of the facts or whether a trial court handled a case properly
Legality: An element of an enforceable contract
Legal Remedy: Award of money; also called damages
Legislation: One of five sources of legal authority; also called code or statute; enacted by an elected body (*e.g.*, Congress)
Letter of Credit: An irrevocable promise by a buyer's bank to pay the seller when conditions are met
Liable: To be found responsible
Lien: An encumbrance against property, typically to secure payment of a debt
Limitations Period: Time limit on bringing lawsuit, based on statute of limitations
Limited Partnership: A business form in which some owners do not have a voice in management and do not have personal liability
Liquidated Damages: Damages agreed to in advance of breach, in the contract itself
Liquidated Debt: Debt that is not in dispute
Liquidation: To convert assets to cash, usually to pay debts in dissolution of a business
LLC: Limited liability company; a business entity
Mailbox Rule: Common law rule, acceptance occurs when dispatched by appropriate means
Major Breach: Substantial breach of contract usually excusing other party from further performance; also called material breach
Majority: The age of adult status (typically 18)
Majority Decision: That which governs the outcome of cases; also called decision of the court
Malum Per Se: Inherently bad
Malum Prohibitum: Not inherently bad; less serious
Manifestation of Mutual Assent: Appearance that an agreement has been reached
Material Breach: Substantial breach of contract usually excusing other party from further performance; also called major breach
Mediation: Neutral helps parties understand each others' positions and may suggest solutions, but agreement ultimately comes from the parties
Merchants: Deal in goods of the kind involved in transaction or, by their occupations, hold themselves out as having knowledge or skills relating to the goods or practice
Merger Clause: Contract provision stating that the document is the complete and final statement of agreement
Minor: A person who has not reached adult status, typically the day before his/her eighteenth birthday
Mirror Image Rule: Acceptance must be identical to offer
Misrepresentation: False statement made without intent to deceive, upon which a party justifiably relies to his detriment
Mitigate: Limit or reduce damages
Mitigation of Damages: An attempt to reduce the harm

Modify: Appellate or higher court's decision to change the decision of the lower court
Mortgage: Security interest in real estate
Municipal Law: Local law (as opposed to federal or state law)
Mutual Mistakes: All parties are mistaken about a basic assumption
Necessities: Things indispensable to life; reasonably needed for subsistence, health, comfort, and education, considering the person's age, station in life, and medical condition
Needs Contract: Contract under which buyer agrees to purchase all of buyer's needs from seller (see exclusive dealing); court may impose requirement of reasonable performance
Negotiable Instruments: A promise or order to pay, such as a check; can be passed along like cash
Neutral: A third party in ADR, mediator or arbitrator
Nominal: Minimal
Nominal Damages: Minimal amount of damages awarded, even if no financial loss resulted from the breach or if the loss cannot be proven with reasonable certainty
Non-adjudicated Incompetent: Incompetence has not been determined by court
Notary Public: Person authorized by state to administer oaths, certify documents, attest to the authenticity of signatures, and perform other official acts
Note: A contract promising to pay a debt; may or may not create a security interest in collateral
Notice of Claims Provision: Contract language requiring one party to give the other party written notice a specified time before filing suit
Novation: New contract involving new parties; cancels earlier contract
Objective Impossibility: Impossibility in an objective sense; not personal
Objective Memo: Also called interoffice memo, analyzes fact situation with citations to legal authority
Objective Standard: Used to determine whether parties had "meeting of the minds," looks to what a reasonable person would believe, based on circumstances
Obligor: One who owes an obligation
Offer: An indication of current willingness to enter into a contract, communicated by the person making the offer
Offeree: Party receiving an offer
Offeror: Party making an offer
Open Terms: Also called "gap-filling" provisions; under the UCC a contract may form despite failure to specify certain terms
Operation of Law: Events, including death, insanity, destruction of subject matter, and illegality, may terminate an offer
Option: An offer, supported by consideration, may not be revoked at will
Output Contract: Contract under which buyer agrees to purchase all that seller produces; court may impose requirement of reasonable performance
Parallel Litigation: Single dispute results in cases in more than one state or in both state and federal courts

Parol Evidence Rule: A writing, intended by the parties to be a final embodiment of their agreement, cannot be modified by evidence that adds to, varies, or contradicts the writing

Partially Disclosed Principal: Existence of agency is known, identity of principal is not known

Partnership: A business owned and controlled by two or more owners

Party to Be Charged: Party attempting to avoid contract liability

Passive Voice: Subject is acted upon

Perfect: To register or record an instrument so that the public is on notice of its terms

Perfect Performance: No deviations from contract; also called strict performance

Perfect Tender Rule: Buyer has reasonable time to reject goods that fail, in any respect, to conform to the contract

Personal Property: Also called chattel or goods; tangible, moveable items

Personal Representative One who conducts the business of an estate; also called executor or administrator

Power of Attorney: Document creating an agency

Precedent: Judicial decisions; also called common law; past decisions used to justify current decisions

Prenuptial: Agreement in anticipation of marriage that typically involves a promise to convey property when marriage occurs or concerns division of property in the event of a divorce; also called antenuptial

Present Worth Doctrine: The value, in "today's money," of payments to be made in the future

Primary Authority: One of the five sources of law

Principal: Party for whom an agent acts

Priority Debts paid ahead of other debts, in bankruptcy

Privity: Being a party to the contract

Procedural History: The history of the court decisions that have moved the case to its current position

Promissory Estoppel: Theory under which a promise can be enforced, despite lack of consideration, because of reliance on that promise and knowledge of that reliance

Puffing: "Sales talk"

Punitive Damages: Damages unrelated to loss, intended to punish

Purchase Money Security Interest: Lien against property to secure a loan used to acquire that property

Pyramid Scheme: Multilevel arrangement in which money is made by recruiting new people

Quantum Meruit: Theory for determining award in absence of contract; "as much as is deserved"

Quasi-contract: Theory for avoiding unjust enrichment in situations in which a contract did not actually form

Qui Tam: Lawsuit in which a whistleblower can obtain reward for exposing misconduct involving government contracts

Ratification: Acceptance of acts by agent after they occur

Ratify: To acknowledge or validate a contract after its execution

Real Estate: Also called real property or realty, consists of land and buildings
Real Property: Land and buildings
Reasoning: Summary of the court's explanation of its decision
Recision: Mutual agreement to cancel
Recitals: Short statements that provide background or explain the reasons for the contract; not technically part of a contract
Record: To record a document is to file it with the official charged with keeping documents such as deeds and judgments
Redline: Feature in word processing software that enables changes in a document to be tracked
Reformation: Rewriting contact; also called blue-penciling
Regulations: Established by administrative agencies
Rejection: Offeree terminates offer
Reliance Damages: Damages awarded for losses incurred by plaintiff in reliance on the contract; puts party in position that would have been occupied if the contract had not been made
Remand: Appellate or higher court's decision to send the case back to the lower court
Reorganization: Bankruptcy in which debtor continues in operation
Replevin: Recovery of property from one who is wrongfully in possession
Reporters: Print volumes that contain judicial decisions
Repudiation: A party's words or actions indicating intention not to perform the contract
Rescind: To terminate a contract before all of its terms are completely performed
Restatement of Contracts: Summary of judicial doctrines on contract law
Restitution: Return of, restoration of, or compensation for
Reverse: Appellate or higher court's decision to invalidate the decision of the lower court
Revocation: Offeror terminates offer
Root Expander: Symbol used to pick up word variations in a CALR search
Sale-or-Return: Seller delivers goods to buyer who resells or returns them to seller; buyer takes title until sale or return
Satisfaction Clause: Contract provision requiring performance to the satisfaction of a specified individual
Search Query: Terms and connectors or natural language used in CALR search
Secondary Authority: Material such as text books and articles that help locate (finding tools) and understand primary law; form books, handbooks, encyclopedias, digests, etc.; not actual law
Securities: Evidence of investment in a common scheme
Security Interests: Interest in personal property to secure performance of an obligation; evidence of indebtedness
Self-proving Document: Complies with formalities and can serve as testimony in court
Services: Actions, not items
Severability Clause: Contract provision that in the event that one part of the contract is found to be invalid, the rest of the contract shall remain in effect

Severable: Remainder of agreement can be enforced without unenforceable provision contained in the agreement
Sham Consideration: Stated consideration did not really occur
Silence as Fraud: A party has a duty to disclose and knowingly conceals the truth
Slander: False statements that hurt the reputation of another
Sole Proprietorship: Business with a single owner
Special Damages: Losses that do not flow directly and immediately from an injurious act, but are indirect; also called consequential damages
Specific Performance: Court order requiring a party to perform contract obligations
Springing Power of Attorney: Comes into effect at a later date
Statute: Legislation; also called code
Statute of Frauds: Dictates types of contracts that must be written
Statutory Construction: See Statutory Interpretation
Statutory Interpretation: Interpretation of statute's terms; also called statutory construction
Straight Bankruptcy: Generally involves liquidation of assets
Strict Liability: Liability regardless of fault
Strict Performance: No deviations from contract expectations; also called perfect performance
Subjective Standard: Imposed or influenced by individual position or bias
Subsequent Agreement: A separate, later agreement that changes or modifies the original agreement
Substantial Performance: Only minor deviations from contact specification; acceptable in most service contracts
Substituted Performance: Use of commercially reasonable substitute facility (§2-614)
Sunday Statute: Prohibits certain transactions on Sundays; also called a blue law
Surety: Liable for the payment of another's debt or the performance of another's obligation; see also Guarantor
Synopsis: Summary of case, often provided in publishers' enhancements
Tender: To make available
Tender Performance: Party's indication that he is ready, willing, and able to perform
Third-party Beneficiary: Not a party to a contract, but benefits from contract
Time Is of the Essence: Any performance delay constitutes breach
Timeline: A schedule of the times at which certain events took place
Title: Ownership
Topic: Generally, statutes are organized by topic; breaking the code into Titles, Acts, Chapters, or Sections
Tortious: Constituting a tort
Torts: Law applicable to injuries to people or property
Trade Usage: Industry standards for permissible deviations from specifications
Trial Court: Court in which most cases start, generally concerned with deciding issues of fact

UCC Financing Statement: Evidence that property is security for debt, typically filed with the secretary of state
UCC Search: Activity conducted to find security interests in personal property that have been recorded under UCC Article 9
Unconscionable: A contract that is so unreasonable that it is "shocking"
Undisclosed Principal: Existence of agency relationship not known to third party
Undue Influence: A dominant party takes advantage of that position in entering a contract with party under domination
Unenforceable: A contract, otherwise valid, that cannot be enforced in court
Uniform Commercial Code (UCC): A uniform law, enacted as statutory law in all 50 states, in an attempt to harmonize the law of sales and other commercial transactions Code
Unilateral: Contract formed when one party acts in response to other party's promise
Unilateral Mistake: Where only one party is mistaken about a basic assumption
Unique Property: An item that is not readily available from other sources
Unliquidated Debt: Debt, the amount of which is in dispute; settlement of an unliquidated debt can constitute consideration
Usurious Contract: Charges an illegal rate of interest on a loan
Variant: Word form that differs from other forms of same word
Void: An agreement with no legal effect
Voidable: One party has power to invalidate contract
Volitional Test: Mental incompetence shown by inability to act reasonably with respect to a transaction
Waived: Claims have been abandoned
Waiver: Intentional relinquishment of right, claim, or privilege
Warranty of Fitness for Particular Purpose: Implied warranty that arises when seller makes a recommendation
Warranty of Merchantability: An implied warranty, given by a merchant seller, that goods are fit for usual purpose
Wildcard: Symbol used to pick up word variations in a CALR search

Index

3-day rule, 31

ABA, 220
ABA Model Rules, 14, 32, 50, 86, 101, 121
Acceleration clause, 101
Acceptance, 47-49
Accord and satisfaction, 83, 160, 170
Accounting, duty of, 150
Acknowledgements, signature, 214
Act, *See* Statutory Law
Act for the Prevention of Fraud and Perjuries, 11, 128
Act of God, 175
Active voice, 238
Additional terms, 50
Adequacy of consideration, 77-79
Adhesion, 66, 79, 131
Adjudicated incompetents, 119
Administrative law, xxxiv-xxxv, 29
Administrator, 112, 139
ADR, 188, 209
Adversarial, xxxv
Advocacy, 14
Advertising, 43
Affirm, xl
Affirmative defenses, 129, 141, 192
Agencies, xxxiv-xxxv
Agency relationship, 112, 120, 146-148
Agency coupled with an interest, 151
Agents, 112, 120, 146-148
Agreement
  integrated, 216
  subsequent, 216-217
  marriage, 200
Alaska, 192-193
Airlines, 87, 200
Alderman case, 67-68
ALI, 22, 137
Allocation of risk, 82
Allowances, 82
Alternative Dispute Resolution, *See* ADR
Ambiguity, 216-217
American Contract Compliance Association, 22
American Express v. Italian Colors, 190
American Institute of Architects, 195
American Law Institute, *See* ALI
Analogize, xl
Annotations, xxxix
Antenuptial agreement, 135
Anticipatory breach, 179-181
Antitrust laws, 29
AOL, 96
Apparent authority, 149
Appellant-appellee, xli
Appellate courts, xli
Arbitration, 67-68, 188

Archaic language, 238-241
Arm's-length transactions, 97
Armed Services Procurement Act, 243
Article 9, 24, 158, 161, 230
Artificial persons, 146
Assignment, 157-158, 172-173, 229
Assignor, assignee, 157-158
Assurance, 181
ATM, 131
Attachment, 161
Attestation, 214
Attorney for child, 121
Attorney, power of, *See* Power of Attorney
Attorney's fees, 86, 198, 202-203
Attorney-client relationship, 14, 50, 67, 86, 121, 163-164
Auctions, 45, 47
Authority, contractual, 149
Automatic renewal, 229
Automatic stay, 173
Avoid, 112
Avoided costs, *See* Costs
Award of attorney fees, *See* Attorney's Fees

Baby M case, 98, 106
Bailee, 179
Bailment, 179
Banking, 23-24.133
Bankruptcy, 171-174
Bargained-for, 77
Bargaining power, 66, 80
Battle of the forms rule, 49-50
BCA, 245
Beneficiaries, 154
Benefits, employee, 87, 173
Bidding, 243
Bilateral contracts, 4
Bill of lading, 9
Binding arbitration, 189
Bitcoin, 230
Blockchain technology, 230
Blood signature, 76
Blue Law, 95
Blue-penciling, 92, 200
Board of contract appeals, 243
Body of contract, 213
Boilerplate, 176, 219, 234
Bonds, 139
Brainstorming, xxxv-xxxvi
Breach, 176
  Anticipatory, 179-181
Brewer v. Missouri Title Loans, 67
Brief, case, xli-xlii
Brokerage agreement, 152
Bulk sales, 23, 162
Business entities, 146
Business status, 146
Business, sale of, 98

C & F, 180
California court, 76
California statutes, 113-114
CALR, xxxv-xxxvii
Care, duty of, 151
Carnival ship Costa Concordia, 204
Case at hand, xli
Case brief, xli-xlii,12
Case law, xxxiv
Chancery, 194
Changes Clause, 244
Changes, tracking, 233
Chapter 7, 11-13 (bankruptcy), *See* Bankruptcy
Charities, 11, 76
Chattel, 23, 158
Chateau Rive Corp. v. Enclave, 174
Checklist, 228, 232
Checks, 24, 84
Choice of law, 34, 137, 190
CIF, 180
Cincinnati Bar Assoc. v. Cromwell, 246
Citadel Group, Ltd. v. Washington Regional Medical Center, 50
Citation, xxxv
Civil law, xxxiv
Claims court, 245
Claims, notice of, 191
Class actions, 190-191
Click-wrap, 132
Code, *See* Statutory Law
Codes, state, xxxiv
Codification, xxxix
Cognitive test, 118
Cognovits, 94
Cohen v. Lord, Day, 98, 101
Collateral, 158, 161
Collateral promises, 138
Colorado, 14, 68, 174
Commerce Business Daily, 243

Commercial, 26, 66, 78
Commercial impracticability, 63, 174
Common law, xxxiv, 22, 26
Communication of offer, 42
Communication, duty of, 150
Compensatory damages, 194
Competition, 28, 98, 151
Competition in Contracting Act, 243
Competition, in agency, 151
Compliance, monitoring, 228
Computer-assisted legal research, *See* CALR
Concurring, xl
Conditions, precedent and subsequent, 79, 171, 217
Conduct, professional, *See* ABA Model Rules
Confession of Judgment, 93-94
Confidentiality, 50
Conflict of interest, 14, 151
Connectors, xxxvii
Consequential damages, 194
Consent to e-transaction, 133-134
Consideration, past, 81
Consignment, 5, 175, 241
Consistency, 235
Constitution, xxxiv
Construction contract, 2, 82, 222
Construction, rules of, 209, 218
Consumers, 26, 93, 96, 162
Contests, 76
Contingency, 171
Contract Dispute Act, 245
Contracts
- exclusive, 98-99
- executory or executed, 4
- express or implied, 4,12
- formal or informal, 8, 76, 81
- government, 28, 243
- incoming, 228
- needs, 80
- option, 5
- output, 80
- quasi, 12
- sharing risk in, 2
- signatures, *See* Signatures
- smart, 230
- unconscionable, 66
- under seal, 81
- unenforceable, 8
- void or voidable, 8

Cooperation, 150
Copyright, 16, 22, 28
Cornell website, 25, 33, 93, 192
Corporate search, 147-148
Corporations, 147-148
Co-signing, 76, 138, 160
Costa Concordia, 204
Cost-plus, 82
Costs, 188
Costs avoided, 194
Council of the European Communities Directive on Unfair Terms in Consumer Contract, 96
Counteroffer, 45
Course of dealing, 179, 217
Course of performance, 179, 217
Court-annexed ADR, 188
Courts, Xl-xli, 192
Courts, federal, 192, 245
Covenant, restrictive, 98
Cover, 181,188
Credit Practices Act, 93
Creditor beneficiary, 155
Creditors, 161
Criminal law, xxxiv, 64
Crops, 24
Cruz v. Stapleton, 15, 19, 128
Cure, 179
Cyber Contracts, 130-131

Dahl, Mali, 122
Damages, 60, 194
Dealing, course of, 179. 217
Death, 46
DeBeers Case, 181
Debt, 22, 85, 171
Deception, 61
Default, 138, 244
Defense Acquisition Workforce Improvement Act, 22
Defenses, affirmative, *See* Statute of Frauds
Defined terms, 5-6, 136, 210, 212
Definitions, 212
Delay, *See* Time
Delegation, 157-158, 189-190, 236
Dellinger, M, 218
Department of Education, 134-135
Department of Justice, 29, 65
Department of the Treasury, 29
Department of Health & Human Services, 30

Detroit, 173
Disability, 119
Disaffirm, 112, 116-117
Discharge, 170
Disclosure of agency, 150
Disclosure, duty of, 62
Disclosures, 50, 62
Discovery, 191
Dispatch of acceptance, 47-48
Dispute resolution, *See* ADR
Dissent, xl
Distinguish, xl
Divisible contracts, 176
Donee, 10, 76
Donee beneficiary, 154
Donor, 10
Draft, 23
Durable power, 120, 156
Duress, 63-64
Duties, agency, 150

Easements, 137, 174
Economic duress, 83
Edington v. Colt's Manufacturing Co., Inc., 203
E-discovery, 191
Elderly, 120-121
Election of remedies, 194
Electricity, 26
Electronic discovery, 191
Electronic Signatures in Global and National Commerce Act, 131
Emancipation, 114
Employment contract, 28-29,
Endorsement, *See* Checks
Entities, 146-148
Environmental Protection Agency, 29
Epinoza v. Arkansas Valley, 174
Equal Credit Opportunity Act, 28
Equal dignity rule, 149
Equitable, 9-11, 194, 199
Equity, 9-11, 194, 199
Escrow, 229
ESIGN, 131
Essential terms, 41-42
Estate, 139
Estoppel, 10, 76, 81, 129, 149
Ethical issues, *See* ABA Model Rules
European Union, 28-29, 96
Evergreen, 229
Evidence, *See* Discovery
Exclusive dealing, 80,99
Exculpatory clause, 96-97, 117, 174
Executed contracts, 4
Executive actions, xxxiv
Executor, 139
Executory contracts, 4, 17
Expanders, xxxvii
Expectation damages, 194
Exports, 28
Express authority, 149
Express contracts, 4
Express ratification, 116
Express warranties, 231
Ex-ship, 232
Extrinsic evidence, *See* Parole Evidence

F.A.S., 232
F.O.B., 232
Facebook, 15, 193
Fact issues, 61
Fair Credit & Charge Card Disclosure Act, 28
Fair Credit Billing Act, 28
Fair Credit Reporting Act, 28
Fair Debt Collection Practices Act, 28
Fair Housing Act, 27
False Claims Act, 245
Fanucchi & Limi Farms v. United Prods., 160
FAR, 243
FBI, 121
Federal Acquisition Regulation, 242
Federal Arbitration Act, 242
Federal Consumer Credit Protection Act, 189
Federal Trade Commission, 28, 69
Fee reversal or recovery, 198
Fees, attorney, 86, 92, 198, 202-203
Fiduciary relationships, 64, 68, 150
Financing, 230
Fire Insurance Exchange v. Bell, 50, 60
Firm offer, 44, 78
Fitness for particular purpose, 231
Florida Bar Association, 92
Florida State University Law Review, 32
Florida Statutes, 96
FOIA, 30
Food and Drug Administration, 29-30
Force Majeure, 175

Foreclosure, 158
Foreseeable, 195
Forest Park Pictures v. USA Network, Inc., 16
Formal contracts, 8, 76, 81
Formalities, 214
Forms, 49-50, 236
Franchise, 204
Freedom of Information Act, 30
Fraud, 28, 50, 60, 116, 121
Free alongside or onboard, *See* FAS or FOB
Frequent flyer miles, 87
Frustration of purpose, 174
FTC, 28, 31, 69, 93, 95
Fungible, 176

GAL, *See* Guardians
Gambling, 94
Gap-filling, 78, 209
Garvin, Larry 32
Gift, 10
Golden Ocean Group Ltd v. Salgaocar Mining Industries, 46
Good faith, 27, 78, 176
Good-faith buyer in the course of ordinary business, 162
Goods, 137, 161
Goods over $500, 137
Government contracts, 28, 243
Grammar, 238-240
Gratuitous, 76, 158
Guarantees, 138, 160
Guarantor, 138, 160
Guardian, 112, 119, 121

H & S HOMES, L.L.C. v. McDonald, 114, 116, 118
Headnotes, xli
History, procedural, xli
Hold harmless, 97
Holding, xlii
Huffman, N., 34
Hunt, Stacy, 223
Hurd v. Wildman, 86, 101
Hurricane Katrina, 2, 174

Identification to contract, *See* Fungible
Identifications, 5-6, 176, 210
Illegality, 46, 92
Illinois, 40, 182
Illusory, 77
Implied acceptance, 47
Implied authority, 149
Implied contracts, 4, 12
Implied ratification, 116
Implied warranties, 231
Impossibility, 174
Impracticability, 63, 174
In pari delicto, 92
In re Marriage of Johnson, 220
In re Moran, xliii
Incidental beneficiary, 82
Incidental damages, 154
Incoming contracts, 194
Incompetence, 118
Incorporation by reference, 212
Indemnification, 97, 117, 150
Independent contractor, 241
Index provisions, 213
Indiana Rules of Professional Conduct, 245
Infant, 112
Informal contracts, 8
Initials, 214
Injunction, 199
Innocent parties, 117
Insanity, 46
Insecure party, 181
Insolvency, 171, 188
Instruments, 128, 161
Instruments, negotiable, 128
Insurable interest, 95
Insurance, 22, 95, 155
Intangible property, 22
Integrated agreement, 129, 137, 216
Intellectual property, 22, 28
Intended beneficiary, 154
International Association for
Contract & Commercial Management, 22
International Chamber of Commerce, 8, 28
International law, 28
Internet, 130-131
Interoffice memo, xxxv
Interpretation of statutes, xxxv
Interstate Land Full Disclosure Act, 27
Interviewing, 232
Intoxication, 120
Inventory, 161
Investments, 23

Irwin, Bindi, 114
Issues, fact and law, xliii

Jackson v. Rent-a-Center, 189
Joint and several liability, 160
Judicial decisions, xxxiv
Juries, 192
Jurisdiction, 190
Jussino, Channet, 87-88
Justia, 193
Justifiable reliance, 61

Laches, 199
Lagen v. United, 87
Land, 22, 137
Lantagne, S., 218
LAP, 122, *See also* ABA Model Rules
Law Library Resource Exchange, 193
Law
  case at, *See* Equity
  sources of, xxxiv
  types, xxxiv
Lawyer's Assistance Programs, 122
Lawyers, 32, 50, 122, *See also* ABA Model Rules
Leases, 24, 161
Lectric Law Library, 93
Legal issues, *See* Equity
Legalese, 238
Legality, 4
Legislation, *See* Statutory Law
Lemon law, 31
Lending, 28
Letter of credit, 8, 23
Letters of intent, *See* Negotiation
Lexis and Lexisone, *See* CALR
Liability
  joint and several, 160
  strict, 202
Licensing, 28, 83
Lien, 24, 158, 162, 173, 230
Limitations period, 8
Limited liability company, 148
Limited partnership, 147
Limited warranty, 31
Linkedin, 22
Liquidated damages, 197
Liquidated debt, 85
Liquidation, 173
Litigation, 190
LLC, 148
Loans, 93
Loyalty, 151

M&G Polymers v. Tackett, 87
Madrid v. Marquez, 194, 203
Magnuson-Moss Act, 31, 231
Mailbox rule, 47-48
Maintenance bond, 139
Major breach, 176
Majority, 112
Malum per se, 93
Malum prohibitum, 93
Managers, 148
Manifestation of mutual assent, 4, 40
Marriage, 135
Marriage of Johnson, 220
McInerney v. Charter Golf, Inc., 137
Mediation, 188
Meeting of the minds, 4, 40
Members, 148
Memo, xxxv
Mental competence, 118
Merchantability, *See* Warranties
Merchants, 26, 41
Merger, 216
Mileage Plus Program, 87
Minor breach, 176
Minors, 112
Mirror image rule, 49
Misrepresentation, 50, 60-61
Mistake, 63, 216
Mitigation, 181, 198
Modifiers, 239
Monitoring compliance, 229
Moral obligations, 81
Mortgage, 155, 158, 171
Motivations, 2
Multijurisdictional practice, 101
Municipal law, xxxiv
Mutual assent, 4
MYLEGS, 128

NALA, 164
National Alliance on Mental Illness, 119
National Association of Legal Assistants, 164
National Association of Secretaries of State, 147

National Conference of Commissioners on Uniform State Laws, 33, 138
National Contract Management Association, 22
NCSL, 23
Necessities, 114
Needs, 80
Negligence, 2, 96, 200
Negotiable instruments, 24, 128
Negotiations, 45-46, 53, 215, 232
Neutral, 188
New Orleans Saints, 95
New York Arts and Cultural Affairs Law, 114
NFPA, 34
Nominal consideration, 78
Nominal damages, 198
Non-adjudicated incompetents, 119
Notary, 215
Notes, 129, 161
Notice of claims, 191
Novation, 159-160, 170-172
Numbering, 219

Obey, duty to, 150
Objective Impossibility, 174
Objective memo, xxxv
Objective standard, 40, 78, 177
Obligation, preexisting, 82
Obligor, 158
Offer, 40-41, 43
  communication of, 42
  firm, 44
Offeree, offeror, 40-41
Office of Government Ethics regulations, 243
Officers, 148
Open terms, 42, 209
Operation of law, 46, 149, 171
Opinion of the court, xl
Option, 5, 44, 137
Oral agreements, 11
OSHA, 29
Output, 80
Outside profits, 151

Padding, 240
Paperless transactions, 131
Paralegals
  billing for, 202-203
  compensation, 92
  employment, 92, 228
  job description, 30, 191
  unauthorized practice by, 232, 245
Parallel construction, 239
Parallel litigation, 190
Parole evidence rule, 215
Partnership, 147
Party to be charged, 129
Party, disadvantaged, 79
Party, insecure, 181
Passive voice, 238
Patent, 22, 28
Patterson v. Law Office of Lauri J. Goldstein, 92
Payday loans, 93
Payment bond, 139
Payton, Sean, 95
PDF, 233
Pensions, 173
Perfect performance, 176-177
Perfect tender, 177
Perfecting security interest, 162
Performance, 129
  bond, 139
  specific, 199
  substituted, 188
  tender of, 173
Personal property, 23, 158, 161
Personal representative, 139
Persons, artificial, 146
Plea agreements, 2, 64-65
Pleadings, 192
Power of Attorney, 112, 120, 149, 156
Practice of law, 232, 245
Precedent, xxxiv-xxxv
Precedent, conditions, 79, 217
Preexisting obligation, 81
Premarital agreement, 135
Present worth, 195
Primary authority, xxxv
Principal, 148-149
Priority, 161
Privity, 156, 202
Procedural history, xli
Product liability, 202
Professional organizations, 22
Profits, lost, 195
Profits, secret or outside, 151
Promissory estoppel, 10, 76

Pronouns, 239
Proofreading, 220
Property
  classifications of, 22, 23
  unique, 199
Protection, consumer, *See* Consumers
Public Policy, 92, 95, 117, 174
Puffing, 60
Punitive damages, 60, 198
Purchase money security interest, 162
Pyramid scheme, 95

Quantum meruit, 14, 114
Quasi-contract, 12, 114, 129
Queries, xxxvii
Qui tam, 170

Ratification, 116, 149
Real estate, 22, 27, 137, 158, 171
Real Estate Settlement Procedures Act, 27
Real property, *See* Real estate
Reasonable care, 151
Reasoning, xlii
Recission, 84, 170
Recitals, 5-6, 78, 136, 211
Record retention, 134
Recording, 215, 230
Redlining, 233
Reference, incorporation by, 211
Reformation, 200
Regulations, xxxiv
Rejection, 45
Relationships, special, 62, 64, 150
Reliance, 61
Reliance damages, 195
Remand, xl
Remedies, 194
Renewal, 229
Reorganization, 173
Replevin, 200
Repudiation, 179, 188
Request for Proposal, 244
Rescind, 84, 170
Rescue, 81
Research, checklist, xxxv
Resolution of disputes, *See* ADR
Restatement of Contracts, 22, 176
Restitution, 115-116, 199
Restraint of trade, 28, 98
Restrictive covenant, 98
Retainer agreement, 68
Reversal, xl
Revocation, 43
Rewriting, 200
RFP, 244
Root expanders, xxxvii
Royal Pains television show, 16
Rules of construction, 209, 217
Rules of professional conduct, *See* ABA Model Rules

Sale of business, 98
Sale or return, 175
Sales, bulk, 162
Salita, S., 40
Satisfaction clauses, 176-177
SBA, 243
Scriveners, 240
Seal, 76, 81, 214
Search terms, xxxvii
Search, UCC, 229
Searches, 229
Secondary authority, xxxv
Secret dealings, profits, 151
Secretary of State, 147
Secured transactions, 24, 173
Securities, 23-24, 161
Security interests, 24, 128, 158, 161, 173
Self-proving, 215
Senior citizen, 120-121
Services, 22, 26
Severability, 92, 233
Sexism, 239
Shall vs. may, 240
Sham consideration, 78
Sheffield, Misty, 164
Shipping, 232
Shoplifting, 59
Signatures, 76, 130, 214
Signed in blood, 76
Silence, 47, 60
Slander, 95
Small Business Administration, 243
Smoking Everywhere case, 52

Social Security, 29-30, 119
Software, 26
Sole proprietorship, 146
Sources of law, xxxiv
Spear case, 14-15
Special damages, 195
Special relationships, 62, 150
Specially manufactured goods, 138
Specific performance, 199
Spelling, 220
Springing power, 156
SSDI, 119
Standard terms, *See* Boilerplate
Staples, 214, 228
Statute of frauds, 11, 128
Statutory interpretation or construction, xxxv
Statutory law, xxxiv, xxxviii, 93
Stay, automatic, 173
Strict compliance, 176
Strict liability, 202
Strict performance, 176
Subjective standard, 77
Sublease, 159
Subsequent agreements, 217
Substantial performance, 176
Substituted performance, 188
Sunday law, 95
Surety, 138
Synonyms, xxxv
Synopsis, xl

Tariff, 28
Technology, e-transactions, 134
Tender, 173, 179
Tender, perfect, 177-179
Terminating representation, 151
Termination for Convenience clause, 244
Terms
  additional, 50
  defined, 5-6
  essential, 41-42
  open, 42
  standard, *See* Boilerplate
Tests, mental competence, 118
Third parties, 154
Threats, 50
Time, 23, 176
Timeline, xlii
Title, xxxviii, 93
Title loans, 93
Topic, xxxviii
Torts, 2, 96, 200
Tracking changes, 233
Trade secret, 28
Trade usage, 179, 217
Trade, restraint, 28
Trademark, 22
Trial courts, xl
Truth in Lending Act, 93
Truth in Negotiations Act, 233, 244
Typographical errors, *See* Proofreading

UCC Financing Statement, 230
UCC
  departures from common law, 26-27, 78-80, 83, 117, 131, 137, 179, 217
  gap-filling provisions, 79
  presumptions under, 27
  search, 229
Unconscionability, 27, 66, 79, 189
Undisclosed agent, 150
Undue influence, 64
Unenforceable contracts, 8, 199
Uniform Customs & Practices for Documentary Credits, 8
Uniform Electronic Transaction Act, 131
Uniform Statutory Form Power of Attorney Act, *See* Power of Attorney
Uniform Transfers to Minors Act, 117
Unilateral contracts, 4-5, 44
Unilateral mistake, 63, 216
Unique property, 199
United Airlines, 200
United Nations Convention on Contracts for the International Sales of Goods, 28
University of Illinois, 40
Unjust enrichment, 12, 14, 177
Unliquidated debt, 65
UPL, 245, *See also* Practice of Law
Usage of trade, 179, 217
Usury, 93

Vehicles, 28
Verbosity, 240

Vermont Law, 115
Visual accessibility, 235
Voice, 238
Void, 8, 112, 119, 199
Volitional test, 118
Waiver, 84, 129
Warranties, 31, 202, 231
Washington, statutes of, 61
Weaver v. Am. Power, 160
Webb v. McGowin, 81
Whistleblowers, 170
Wildcards, xxxvii
World Trade Organization, 28

Yang v. Voyagaire, 97
Year, contracts extending beyond, 135
Yellow Book Sales & Distribution Co. v. Valle, 141
Young v. Weaver, 118

Zuckerberg, Mark, 193